Their Right to Speak

Their Right to Speak

*Women's Activism
in the Indian and Slave Debates*

Alisse Portnoy

Harvard University Press
Cambridge, Massachusetts
London, England
2005

Library of Congress Cataloging-in-Publication Data

Portnoy, Alisse, 1969–
    Their right to speak : women's activism in the Indian and slave debates / Alisse Portnoy.
      p. cm.
    Includes bibliographical references and index.
    ISBN 0-674-01922-9
     1. Women political activists—United States—History—19th century. 2. Political participation—United States—History—19th century. 3. Women abolitionists—United States—History—19th century. 4. Antislavery movements—United States—History—19th century. 5. Indians of North America—Relocation. 6. Indians, Treatment of—United States—Public opinion—History—19th century. 7. Petitions—United States—History—19th century. I. Title.

HQ1236.5.U6P67 2005
305.43'3268'0973—dc22
                                                   2005046071

For my loving grandparents
Lillian and Jack Rothstein,
who always encourage their granddaughters
to speak up and speak out

Contents

Acknowledgments

Luckily, I get to do what I love for a living. Even taking care of business is fun. Parts of the first and second chapters of *Their Right to Speak* originally were published in two essays. "'A Right to Speak on the Subject': The U.S. Women's Antiremoval Petition Campaign, 1829–1831," appeared in *Rhetoric and Public Affairs* 5, no. 4 (2002), published by Michigan State University Press. "'Female Petitioners Can Lawfully be Heard': Negotiating Female Decorum, United States Politics, and Political Agency, 1829–1831," appeared in *Journal of the Early Republic* 23, no. 4 (2003), is copyrighted by the Society of Historians of the Early American Republic, and is reprinted here by permission of the University of Pennsylvania Press. I am grateful to the American Antiquarian Society and the Arthur and Elizabeth Schlesinger Library on the History of Women in America at Harvard University's Radcliffe Institute for Advanced Study for permission to quote from, and to the Sterling Memorial Library at Yale University for access to, their collections.

The University of Michigan's Department of English Language and Literature funded research assistance and travel for this book, as did the University of Michigan's Center for the Education of Women through its Jean Campbell Faculty Research Fund and its Margaret Reicker Undergraduate Research Fund, and the University of Michigan's Horace H. Rackham School of Graduate Studies through its Faculty Grants and Fellowships programs. Rackham and the Department of English also contributed a subvention for this book's publication. I appreciate the Summer Stipend Award I received from the National Endowment for the Humanities in 2003. The views, findings, and conclusions expressed in this book do not necessarily reflect those of the NEH.

Many people helped with the views, findings, and conclusions of this book, and thanking them truly is a pleasure. Alysha Black, Richard Hunt, and other members of the staff at the Center for Legislative Archives at the U.S. National Archives and Records Administration provided wonderful assistance. Much credit, too, goes to the University of Michigan's Inter-library Loan and FAST Services office. Sumner Webber shared with me his knowledge of early nineteenth-century Hallowell families and scouted the *American Advocate* for relevant information. S. J. Wolfe reported on the American Antiquarian Society's collection of Cheever family papers. My undergraduate and graduate students at the Universities of Maryland and Michigan helped me work through ideas in this book, as did the rhetoric group in the English Department at Pennsylvania State University; partici-pants in the Prospects of Public Address Studies/Criticism in the New Cen-tury Seminar of the Department of Communication Studies at Northwestern University; and the audience for talks given at Rhetoric Society of America, National Communication Association, Modern Language Association, and American Studies Association conferences.

Kathleen McDermott at Harvard University Press has been enthusiastic, supportive, and responsive. She also secured careful, thoughtful readings of my manuscript from two anonymous reviewers. Thanks to Kathi Drummy at HUP for her kind assistance, to Tonnya Norwood at NK Graphics for cheerfully shepherding the manuscript through production, and to Martha Carlson-Bradley for her attentive copyediting. Lewander Davis, Donna Johnston, and Carol Meszaros always make getting the job done easier. I have had some terrific research assistants while working on this project: Anne-Marie Sinay, Lauren LaFauci, and especially Kavita Padiyar. Kavita's patience, hard work, sense of humor, and intelligence contributed immea-surably to this book.

Michigan colleagues Paul Anderson, Judy Avery, Seema Bhatnagar, George Bornstein, Anne Curzan, Geoff Eley, Lincoln Faller, Sandra Gunning, Carol Hollenshead, Arlene Keizer, Mary Kelley, John Kucich, Marjorie Levinson, Anita Norich, David Porter, Tobin Siebers, Sid Smith, Jean Waltman, and Patsy Yaeger supported this project in myriad ways. Thanks especially to Sara Blair, Julie Ellison, Jonathan Freedman, Anne Gere, June Howard, Carroll Smith-Rosenberg, and Martha Vicinus for reading sections over the years and to Jay Cook, Gina Morantz-Sanchez, and Alan Wald for their helpful last-minute tutorials. Diane Blair, Linda Coleman, Kate Dobson, Kevin Dukes, Jim Greenberg, Lisa Gring-Pemble, Shirley Wilson Logan, Mary Montgomery, and Mark Turner contributed while I was at the Uni-versity of Maryland. I am grateful for conversations about things rhetorical with Fred Antczak, Barbara Biesecker, Stephen Browne, James Darsey, Anne Demo, Rosa Eberly, Greg Clark, Jerry Hauser, Jim Jasinski, Michael Leff, Andrea Lunsford, Marty Medhurst, Jackie Jones Royster, Jack Selzer, Susan Wells, and David Zarefsky.

The generosity of Nancy Hewitt, Priscilla Wald, and Steven Mailloux continues to amaze me. Each illustrates the possibility of simultaneously being very smart, very successful, and very kind. I have known Nancy Hewitt for only a short time, but she reminds me what a difference one person can make. Conversations with Priscilla Wald inevitably inspire and energize me. It is no wonder that Priscilla's focused readings of this manuscript prompted important changes to its structure and helped me clarify several of its arguments. Steve Mailloux has read and commented on essays, written letters, responded to talks, answered questions, played out theoretical approaches, and shared many a meal with me. He is a wonderful teacher, mentor, teammate, and friend.

Although the dissertation that Jeanne Fahnestock and Martha Solomon Watson codirected looks almost nothing like this book, their influence is everywhere. From them I learned much about rhetorical history and criticism, the importance of primary research, and ways to write more clearly and more persuasively. Martha has been teacher, reader, landlord, roommate, career counselor, and cheerleader. Jeanne embodies for me the teacher, scholar, advisor, and mentor I aim to be every day. It truly is a privilege to have worked with them and to continue to learn from them.

Teachers Sheila Spicer and Dan Bentley-Baker inspire me each time I walk into a classroom. Because Glen Altschuler took me seriously as a student, I started taking my studies more seriously. It was my good luck to move next door to Jim, Claudia, and Sabrina Hartwell. I'm grateful for their good cheer and friendship (with special thanks to Sabrina for helping me harvest tomatoes). Peggy and Dennis Carroll remind me that I have family in Ann Arbor. Colin Theodore's love and friendship contributed in ways I continue to appreciate. Anne Carroll has been a good friend since the first day of graduate school, and I treasure that she understands.

My writing group helped me with this book at crucial times in its—and my own—development. Although the group remains unnamed, I'm thrilled to name its members: Viv Soni, Cathy Sanok, and Joshua Miller. I learned so much from reading their work, hearing them talk about one another's texts, and talking with them about my own manuscript. The writing group emerged, as so many good things have, from a conversation I had with

Cathy. Our friendship easily moves between work and family, academics and entertainment, collegiality and companionship, and it is one of my favorite things about life in Ann Arbor. Joshua read almost every page of this manuscript at least once. He listened and read and asked and talked and listened, read, asked, and talked some more. He shared his work and he shared himself; he bought us a tape recorder and engaged me in the kinds of conversations that made one necessary. He believed in this project, and in me, when I simply was unable.

The peace of mind that comes with knowing that Nat Leventhal will move mountains if Danielle or I need a mountain moved is something for which I always will be grateful. My grandparents, Lillian and Jack Rothstein, taught my family the importance of staying close. With a family this great—Dianne and Alan Collins, Albie, Ryan, and Hale Rothstein, and Todd Greene—it's easy. My father, Richard Portnoy, takes an interest in my work that makes it more fun. My mother, Shelley Portnoy, and my sister, Danielle Greene, make it easier for me to see, to experience, and sometimes even to conjure the magical in any given moment of every single day. I appreciate their gifts and the gifts that they are in the world.

A Note on Terminology

There are four sets of terms used in this book for which I frequently choose more recent rather than conventional nineteenth-century descriptors. One set includes "African American," "person of color" (for the nineteenth-century European Americans featured in this book that phrase always meant African Americans, never Native Americans), "black," "colored," and "descendant of Africans." When it matters to my argument (especially in the fourth chapter, in which I discuss competing categories), I use the nineteenth-century term or phrase. Otherwise, typically I use "African American" even though the term rarely was used by the discourse communities featured in the book. Another instance in which I choose contemporary rather than historical usage concerns "Native American" and "Indian." I use "Indian" when I want to emphasize nineteenth-century constructions of Native Americans. Otherwise, I use "Native American." I follow a similar pattern for "European American" and "white."

More frequently I use "nation" rather than "tribe" to refer to Native American communities, including the Cherokees, Creeks, and Choctaws. This choice, as are the others, clearly is political. In *The Pioneers* James Fenimore Cooper makes this point: "they consisted of the tribes, or, as their allies were fond of asserting, in order to raise their consequence, of the several nations, of the Mohawks, the Oneidas, the Onondagas, Cayugas, and Senecas." I am persuaded by those "allies," including Jeremiah Evarts, who argued that Native American communities were and are nations and that the United States treated those communities as nations until it became inconvenient to honor their sovereignty. Occasionally, though, I use "tribe" to emphasize the powerfully political force of the term in early nineteenth-century discourse.

Their Right to Speak

Introduction

Resolved, That we view, with unfeigned astonishment, the anti-
[C]hristian and inconsistent conduct of those who so strenuously
advocate our removal from this our native country to the burning
shores of Liberia, and who with the same breath contend against
the cruelty and injustice of Georgia in her attempt to remove the
Cherokee Indians west of the Mississippi.

— "A RESPECTABLE MEETING OF THE COLORED PEOPLE OF
PROVIDENCE, R.I." (NOVEMBER 1831)

They called it their "right to speak on the subject." When Charlotte Cheever,
her daughter Elizabeth, their friends Hannah Dole, Hannah's sister-in-law
Nancy and Hannah's niece Mary, their minister's wife Mary Gillet, their neighbors Abigail, Lydia, Julia, Harriet, Martha, Sarah, and Adelaide Page, and
forty-eight other women from Hallowell, Maine, asked the United States
Congress in January 1830 to permit Cherokee, Choctaw, and Creek Indians
"to abide by the graves of their Fathers, and enjoy the sweets and endearments of *home*," these women declared in their petition that they had "a
right to speak on the subject."[1] A few weeks earlier, a little less imperatively
but no less inspired, Catharine Beecher publicly announced, "It may be, that
female petitioners can lawfully be heard, even by the highest rulers of our
land."[2] In her anonymously published and widely distributed "Circular Addressed to Benevolent Ladies of the U. States," Beecher reasoned that women
offered a unique perspective on this extraordinary national crisis. She urged
women to intervene on behalf of Native Americans by petitioning the federal government. Within two years, almost fifteen hundred women from
seven northern states submitted to Congress antiremoval petitions protesting the forced removal of Native Americans who lived on their nations'
lands within United States borders. Together these women conducted the
first national women's petition campaign in United States history.

1

A few years later, Angelina Grimké and her sister Sarah urged women to petition the United States federal government for the immediate abolition of slavery. In November 1836 the Grimké sisters completed their training as agents for the American Anti-Slavery Society (AAS). Just as they commenced a multistate AAS lecture tour the following spring, Catharine Beecher's *Essay on Slavery and Abolitionism, with Reference to the Duty of American Females* was published. In this essay, Beecher—an old friend of Angelina's—aimed to render ineffective the Grimkés' efforts to enroll northern women in the abolition movement and its antislavery petition campaign. Despite her abhorrence of slavery, Beecher insisted that women forgo direct appeals to United States senators and representatives. In 1837, Beecher told Angelina Grimké and her readers, "In this country, petitions to congress, in reference to the official duties of legislators, seem, IN ALL CASES, to fall entirely without the sphere of female duty."[3] Grimké wrote back, declaring Beecher's articulation of separate spheres of duty for men and women anathema. "Whatever it is morally right for man to do," Grimké explained in her public response to Beecher, "it is morally right for woman to do."[4] Beecher seemed to agree with that principle when she initiated and orchestrated the women's antiremoval petition campaign in 1829. Why did she argue against women's antislavery petitions so adamantly in 1837?

Reconciling the apparent paradox of Beecher's positions on women's antiremoval and antislavery activism motivated this study, and it suggested a lens through which to conduct it: gender. Like many people interested in United States history, I celebrate Angelina and Sarah Grimké's protofeminist principles and practices. I assumed that the Grimké sisters moved too far out of women's sphere for Beecher when they took up their antislavery activism and that Beecher's denial of woman's right to petition the national legislature aimed to reinscribe conventional gender norms. Beecher valued and also used those norms as a leader in the female education and domestic economy movements. Besides, Beecher published her 1829 "Circular" and orchestrated the antiremoval campaign anonymously. She and her close friends managed the secret very well, so although her 1829 and 1837 texts circulated publicly, her apparent contradiction did not.[5]

But most antiremovalists actively embraced African colonization at the same time that they denounced Indian removal. Simultaneously, they called the forced removal of Native Americans oppressive and the voluntary removal of African Americans benevolent, "a subject of almost romantic interest."[6] Yet most African Americans living in the northern states reacted with disgust to the colonization program which, under the auspices of the largely southern-led American Colonization Society (ACS), hardly was voluntary: slave owners refused to emancipate their slaves unless slaves "volunteered" immediately to colonize Africa. One resolution against colonization at a meeting of African Americans in 1831 particularly inspired William Lloyd Garrison to convert from colonization to abolition: "Resolved, That we view, with unfeigned astonishment, the anti-[C]hristian and inconsistent conduct of those who so strenuously advocate our removal from this our native country to the burning shores of Liberia, and who with the same breath contend against the cruelty and injustice of Georgia in her attempt to remove the Cherokee Indians west of the Mississippi."[7] Garrison recognized his own conduct as inconsistent and began criticizing the federal government for trampling the rights of both Native Americans and African Americans. Garrison converted from gradual to immediate abolition in 1829 and renounced the ACS and its colonization program in 1832. A small but growing group joined Garrison in the early 1830s. Theodore Weld abandoned colonization for immediate abolition in 1832. Lydia Maria Child did the same in 1833. Arthur Tappan shifted allegiances in 1832, as did his brother Lewis in 1833. Gerrit Smith was convinced in 1835. Two of the few prominent early abolitionists who did not begin their antislavery activism by advocating colonization were Sarah and Angelina Grimké. That almost every other early second-wave abolitionist leader relinquished colonization in favor of immediate abolition had an effect that cannot be underestimated: most early abolitionist rhetoric attacked the institution of slavery and, to underscore its dramatic differences with the dominant antislavery program of the era, also attacked the colonization movement.[8]

Most antiremovalists, however, even those decidedly against slavery, rejected abolition as an antislavery option through at least the 1830s (and often for far longer). Senator Henry Clay, who loudly protested President Andrew Jackson's plans to remove forcibly Native Americans in 1830 and 1831, became president of the ACS in 1836. Senator Theodore Frelinghuysen, renowned for his defense of Native Americans on the Senate floor until he left the Senate in 1835, remained a national and local auxiliary officer of the ACS after he returned to his home state of New Jersey. Joseph Gales Jr. and William Winston Seaton, editors of the nationally influential newspaper the *National Intelligencer* and recorders of the daily business of the United States Congress through the Jackson administration, simultaneously defended Native Americans and the American Colonization Society on the pages of their widely circulated daily newspaper. And the Reverend Doctor Lyman Beecher, nationally known as a Christian leader and reformer and as head of Lane Theological Seminary, encouraged his daughter Catharine to advocate on behalf of Native Americans in 1829 but publicly chose colonization over abolition in 1834 when Theodore Weld, a student at Lane and the future husband of Angelina Grimké, forced Reverend Beecher's hand by staging an abolitionist rebellion at the seminary.

Catharine Beecher was an antislavery activist of the colonizationist persuasion. She believed abolition to be dangerous and illegal and she thought little better of abolitionists themselves. When she challenged Angelina Grimké in 1837, she argued that neither men nor women should join the AAS. Beecher could not condone women's abolitionist petitioning at the same time that she adamantly condemned abolition. Without a detailed understanding of the antiremoval and antislavery movements, we easily could interpret Beecher's denying women the right to petition the federal government as a result of her thinking too conservatively about gender norms. But her denial in 1837 of women's right to petition followed her embrace of that right in 1829, and both Beecher and Grimké actively were engaged in heated debates about Indian removal, colonization, abolition, and complicated questions about cultural, religious, and national identities. In the context of these debates the women's antiremoval and antislavery petition campaigns emerged. A study of women's political activism in this period structured dominantly by gender, or even gender and the politics of just one of these movements, simply is insufficient for understanding the dynamics of women's emergent national rhetorical activism in the United States.[9]

The most fundamental argument I make in these pages, then, is that a study of United States women's earliest, collective, national political activism must occur inside broader studies of the Indian removal, African colonization, and second-wave abolition movements. That argument compels two more: we should not continue to segregate the nation's Indian removal and antislavery debates in our scholarship of United States history, nor should we continue to marginalize or to forget the nation's debates about colonization, given the ways that debates about colonization, abolition, and removal all captivated the nation in the 1820s and 1830s.[10] When Henry Clay addressed the Colonization Society of Kentucky in 1829, instead of limiting his focus to African Americans he began by acknowledging the coexistence of "three separate and distinct races of men" in the United States and its territories. In 1826, James Madison wrote, "Next to the case of the black race within our bosom, that of the red on our borders is the problem most baffling to the policy of our country." In 1833, the *National Intelligencer* published a letter arguing that the federal government had to support Georgia in the Georgia-Cherokee disputes to ease sectional tensions caused by slavery debates. In the 1830s, secular and nonsecular newspapers were filled with stories about removal and slavery debates as well as stories and advertisements about Indians, slaves, and free blacks—frequently on the same day, sometimes even adjacent to one another.[11]

National Indian removal debates commanded less attention after the Indian removal bill was signed into law, and they ended when the United States federal government forced remaining Cherokees to move west in the 1838 Trail of Tears. Colonization, too, faded in the late 1830s as second-wave abolitionism increasingly dominated slavery debates.[12] In the public imagination abolitionists' "radical" and "aggressive" tactics overshadowed the "peaceful" and "patient" methods toward gradual emancipation that colonizationists preferred. Abolitionists demanded immediate emancipation no matter the cost, and they quickly became the most visible and controversial opponents to slavery in the decades preceding the Civil War. Perhaps that is why we think of "antislavery" and "abolition" as synonymous despite the dramatically different ways antebellum United States Americans understood the terms. Or perhaps colonization remains an afterthought for us because the radical methods and just principles of the abolitionists are so much more attractive now than the conservative methods and prejudiced principles of the colonizationists.[13] But in the first two decades after its founding in 1817, the ACS advocated the most dominant and widely supported program to end slavery in the United States. While abolitionists were tarred and feathered, colonizationists raised thousands of dollars annually and had as their leaders clergymen, congressmen, Supreme Court justices, and former presidents of the United States. Most antislavery advocates during Jackson's presidency believed colonization to be a more viable—and legal—solution to slavery than immediate emancipation. In 1832 even Theodore Weld called colonization the only alternative to slavery.[14] But when second-wave abolitionism emerged, abolitionists defined their new movement by leveling aggressive critiques against colonization. Colonizationists fought back, and, prompted in part by waves of backlash against abolitionists, their movement enjoyed several years of growth in the northern states. Through most of the 1830s, the decade to which we typically assign the starting point of the active antislavery movement in the United States, colonization claimed more northern antislavery advocates than abolition.

The 1830s were remarkable in that the decade included three interdependent debates about rights and power: United States women's early negotiations for their collective "right to speak" occurred in the context of heated and concomitant national debates about what European Americans believed the United States should do about Native American and African American populations living within its borders.[15] *Their Right to Speak* recognizes that complexity and multiplicity by revitalizing the study of African colonization and reweaving the rhetorics of Indian removal, African colonization, and second-wave abolitionism as they occurred in the 1820s and 1830s. In this way the book helps us to understand more fully the ways that women legitimated their "right to speak" on issues of national policy in a nation that collectively denied them that right.

The recovery of the women's antiremoval petition campaign compels a revision of our narrative of women's emergent political participation and our history of women's right to speak on issues of national policy.[16] The antiremoval campaign replaces the women's antislavery petition campaign as the first known instance of women's national, collective political activism in United States history. The knowledge of the two campaigns—and Catharine Beecher's role in both—presents us with an extraordinary opportunity to compare the ways a group (here, women) acquires the authority to speak about a topic for which they usually have no authority (national policy) in a community from which they typically are excluded (the national legislature).[17] How do the debates about Indian removal and slavery legitimize, delegitimize, and legitimize again some United States women to speak and to be heard more than a decade before the first woman's rights convention in 1848?

To answer that question, I apply the methods of a rhetorical critic. So, for example, if one hundred and six "colored emigrants" departed for Liberia on March 22, 1833 and one hundred were emancipated for the journey, I note the facts of the departure but am interested especially in the ways those facts were interpreted and used.[18] Colonizationists celebrated the departure as another step toward the Christianization of Africa, and they used the emancipations as proof that the ACS was an effective antislavery program. Abolitionists anguished over the millions who remained enslaved without hope of release, and these activists saw numbers in these proportions as proof that free people of color refused to emigrate. In the contradictory ways that facts like these were interpreted and deployed as arguments, conflicting calls to action emerged.

So, too, with issues and situations. In 1829, Andrew Jackson articulated Indian removal as a question of law and politics: laws directed the federal government to support state sovereignty; politically, removal best served the United States. Jeremiah Evarts, a leader of many Christian reforms and a lobbyist to the federal government on behalf of Native Americans, articulated the same question as one of law, morality, and piety: decades of treaties rendered Jackson's policies illegal; the policies surely would stain the nation's character and invoke God's wrath on the United States. Catharine Beecher articulated the same question as one of piety and benevolence: the Bible authorized women to intervene because forced removal threatened the survival of fellow Christians unable to help themselves. Which construction most closely reflected the actual situation? That question seems neither interesting nor valid to me (even the dispute over the legality of removal rested on interpretation, not fact—both men used the same laws and treaties to arrive at their conclusions). All of these constructions were powerful because people believed them to be true and acted according to those beliefs. Each construction served different actors, different acts, different goals, and each imposed and affirmed different ideologies. What kind of work gets done in the competition among and negotiation of these differences? In this case, women got to speak. As a lobbyist and prominent Christian reformer, Evarts had the authority to reconstruct or pose a competing construction of Jackson's removal policies. Evarts destroyed the sanctity of the presidential construction, making other iterations possible. He also moved the issue into domains other than politics, such as morality and religion, which opened the door for claims like those Beecher made on the issue and, subsequently, Beecher's claims that women could petition the federal government on behalf of Native Americans without violating the gender norms she and many others held so dear.

These two examples—three articulations of the same issue, two interpretations of the same facts—underscore a basic premise of contemporary rhetorical theory: discourse is powerfully constitutive.[19] Texts create exigencies and identities; they generate and call forth new, sometimes transcendent or transformational, ways of being in and relating to the world; sometimes they foreclose possibilities and sustain extant power dynamics. A uniquely compelling kind of power occurs in the telling of experience, in the interpretations of facts, the constructions of situations, the articulations of issues by auditors and rhetors alike. In this study, I read petitions from the Indian removal and antislavery movements, presidential and congressional speeches debating the fate of Native and African Americans, more than a decade of the nation's most prominent daily newspaper, several years of religious and reformist newspapers, best-selling novels, and other documents to track discourses about the Indian removal, abolition, and colonization movements in Jacksonian America. I treat these texts as constitutive rhetorics with an eye to three particular constructs: rhetorical situations, first personae, and objects of advocacy.

First, with Richard Vatz and Barbara Biesecker, I treat rhetorical situations—situations that seem to demand or to invite a discursive response— as created, not given or discovered in "actual" events.[20] Power inheres in the act of naming or defining situations. When we assign meaning to an act or event, when we declare its urgency, when we assert causes or effects, we subtly but necessarily prescribe appropriate responses to that act or event.[21] When we dispute the nature of an event or an act, we often provoke constitutive contradictions, contradictions that allow new possibilities for agency to emerge. In Chapters 1 and 5 of this book, I attend particularly to competing articulations of the crises of Indian removal and slavery and trace the deployments of power manifested in and between these articulations.

Second, I explore what it means to understand a rhetor—the speaker or writer of a text—as a construct rather than as the individual who is speaking or writing. The rhetor of a text is as distinct from the individual speaker as a novel's narrator is from its writer, even though the generic constraints of nonfiction (especially political address) make the constructed nature of the rhetor more difficult to expose. Who, for example, does an individual woman appear to be when she acts as an antiremoval petition's rhetor or an antislavery petition's rhetor?[22] The same woman appears differently in the two texts. What about when we study texts "authored" by dozens, sometimes hundreds, of women, like antiremoval and antislavery petitions? Which individuals do the text's rhetors—the text's "first personae"—truly or accurately represent?[23] The "we" of the Hallowell petition submitted to Congress in 1829 is a composite of individuals who demand their "right to speak" based on the ways they appear in the petition: as respectful, deferential, pious, virtuous, philanthropic, sympathetic, and benevolent females who "unite their prayers with those of ten thousand in our land."[24] Women including Charlotte Cheever, Mary Gillet, and Hannah Dole acquired agency and power in the positions they occupied discursively. Attending to those positions enables us more fully to understand how women such as Cheever, Gillet, and Dole obtained the power they needed to demand—and to receive—a right to speak.

Third, I compare the ways European Americans constructed the objects of their advocacy—the people they imagined Native and African Americans to be. Most European Americans who opposed removal and slavery in the 1830s had little if any actual contact with African and Native Americans, and even the little contact they had was mediated through stories that other European Americans told and wrote.[25] Based on these stories, on reports, novels, advertisements, treaties, and laws, whites imagined blacks and Indians. Their imaginings, of course, were untrue—which is not to say that they were unreal. As constructions, they had tremendous power. People behave toward others according to the ways they imagine those others to be; the ways European Americans imagined African and Native Americans fundamentally influenced the nature of European American advocacy. What imaginings of blacks and Indians did white antiremovalists, colonizationists, and abolitionists bring to their 1830s rhetorical advocacy?[26] It is impossible to answer that question without comparing the imaginings of African and Native Americans by European Americans, not only because people construct identities through their relationships with others, but also because images and representations of Native and African Americans appeared at the same time and often in the same place.[27] Whites constructed their own identities in relation to blacks and Indians, and whites also constructed blacks and Indians in relation to each other. Abolitionist Lydia Maria Child could not understand how someone could declare that "*Indians certainly have* their rights" but deny those same rights to blacks, and yet it frequently happened in the northern states in the 1830s.[28] These often conflicting constructions authorized particular (and particularly competitive) modes and arguments of European American advocacy on behalf of Native Americans and African Americans, and these constructions powerfully and even constitutively contributed to the emergence of women's rhetorical activism in the early nineteenth century.

In fact, the ways European Americans imagined African and Native Americans more significantly influenced women's early national, collective political activism than conventional gender constraints of the period. Catharine

Beecher and most of the women who petitioned in 1830 and 1831 rejected political power for women, but they made an exception for the "unique" and "extraordinary" case of removal. Why did Beecher and other northern white women of privilege refuse the exception for slavery? Based on analyses of popular and political rhetorics of the Indian removal, African colonization, and second-wave abolition movements, I argue that, while constructions of gender crucially affected these debates, gender was not the main nor even the dominant explanation for the rejection of immediate emancipation as an appropriate topic for women's political activity.

Two other factors restricted women's advocacy: the inability of most European Americans to imagine African Americans as neighbors and equals, and the ongoing debates about the safest means by which the nation could end the peculiar institution of slavery. These factors led most antislavery advocates, including those opposed to Indian removal, to embrace colonization—a more popular answer to the evils of slavery—rather than abolition. Colonizationists did not and could not sanction many forms of political intervention on behalf of African Americans, whether those methods of political advocacy came from men or from women. And although conservative reformers accepted articulations of Indian removal that invited women's political intervention on behalf of Native Americans, conservatives dismissed abolition as fanatical. Thus, to interpret women's participation in the antislavery petition campaign as a litmus test for protofeminist beliefs is to ignore that, for many people, ideologies of race and nation more than ideologies of gender precluded petitioning the federal government to end slavery.

In this significantly expanded context, the question remains. How did United States women transgress prohibitions to engage discourses of power in the early nineteenth century? This book is organized around four issues that reflect the complexity and urgency of the 1830s, a decade whose technological advances enabled debates about Indians, slaves, and ladies on a national scale unimaginable even a few years earlier: the emergence of Indian removal as a national crisis, the transformation of gender as a source of authority in women's national antiremoval and antislavery petitions, the simultaneous and comparative imaginings by European Americans of African and Native Americans as objects of advocacy, and the fiery rivalry between the colonization and abolition movements. Each of these sites of rhetorical negotiation provides fertile ground upon which to study the ways women—and men—constituted and constrained their own and others' "right to speak."

In Chapter 1, I introduce Indian removal, one of the most discussed and most controversial issues of the 1820s and 1830s, and I ask why this particular topic became the first issue of federal policy on which women demanded their "right to speak." A history of the facts of the case cannot adequately answer the question. Working from the same facts, for example, Andrew Jackson, Jeremiah Evarts, and Catharine Beecher came to very different conclusions about appropriate responses to the national crisis. In his 1829 presidential address to Congress, Jackson explained that he had "informed the Indians inhabiting parts of Georgia and Alabama, that their attempt to establish an independent government would not be countenanced by the Executive of the United States; and advised them to emigrate beyond the Mississippi, or submit to the laws of those States." In the same year in a series of popular essays on removal, Evarts interpreted the issue as one of unconscionable United States land usurpation. At the end of 1829, Beecher offered yet another interpretation of removal: the crisis was a series of "calamities . . . causes of alarm to our whole country." In her widely distributed "Circular Addressed to Benevolent Ladies of the U. States," Beecher made it clear that "our" meant men and women and that "whole" included the domains of politics, the church, and the home. Beecher's interpretation, even more than Evarts's, not only invited but required women's political intervention on behalf of "the oppressed." By attending to the competing rhetorics of the Indian removal debates, I discern the means by which women's intervention in this particular piece of federal policy was legitimized as within women's lawful province, according to Christian and natural laws.[29]

Within weeks after Beecher completed her circular, women began sending petitions to the federal government protesting the forced removal of Native Americans from their nations' southern lands. The first petition that the United States national legislature received from a group of women on an issue of national policy was the antiremoval petition from Hallowell, Maine, submitted in January 1830. When Hallowell women submitted their petition, they advocated for two causes: Native Americans' right to their property and what these women called their own "right to speak on the subject." Within two years nearly fifteen hundred women joined the campaign initiated by Catharine Beecher. In 1832, the year after the antiremoval petition campaign ceased, women began petitioning the federal government against slavery. Initially, female antislavery petitioners relied on the same rhetorical strategies that female antiremovalists used. They declared the occasion unique and women's political intrusion extraordinary, identified topics of debate beyond the merely political, and employed gendered arguments. But within five years, when thousands of women annually petitioned Congress against slavery, these arguments had become less viable. By 1837, in their petitions female activists supplemented and occasionally even replaced arguments that featured their gender with arguments that named their status as citizens.

In Chapter 2, I introduce the antiremoval petition campaign in the context of the public debates as well as the completion of the United States postal system, advances in print technology, increases in literacy, a growing sense of nationalism, and ongoing religious and benevolent reform. Through a rhetorical analysis of women's antiremoval petitions and a comparison of their petitions with those submitted by the men of their towns, churches, and even households, I argue that although they did not create a revolution in women's political consciousness, the antiremoval petitions did extraordinary work. Because the petitions effectively combined essentializing ideologies about womanhood with strategically selected topics of debate, the political intrusion of female antiremoval petitioners appeared to be a natural extension of women's roles and responsibilities. These petitions articulated a viable political persona for northern white women of privilege, one that effectively negotiated the Jacksonian-era tension between politics and decorum.

But antislavery activism posed a different sort of challenge to the nation, and most of the men and women petitioning against slavery subscribed to much more radical politics. Rhetorical exigencies, opportunities, and identities had dramatically shifted by 1837, and female antislavery petitioners could not use only the gender-specific arguments espoused a few years earlier by community leaders wishing to conserve the status quo. Instead, these female petitioners claimed a right to speak as citizens. They still used gendered arguments—arguments that relied on traditional notions of Jacksonian womanhood—but they looked to petitioning as a right, rather than an exception granted for a unique situation. By comparing discourses of and about the women's antiremoval and antislavery petition campaigns, I conclude Chapter 2 by generalizing from specific historical cases innovative means by which members of an excluded group can argue for their right to speak.

To understand why women such as Catharine Beecher argued against women's antislavery activism, though, we need to move beyond questions of woman's rights and woman's sphere, as I do in Chapters 3 and 4. Beecher categorically denied women's right to petition during the latter half of an incredibly turbulent decade. She and her interlocutors debated in the midst of fierce local and national debates about Indian removal and Indian wars, African American slavery, "black codes" and other racist restrictions on the movement and rights of free blacks in the northern states, colonization of free people of color to Liberia, and immediate emancipation.

Most northern whites had no way to imagine African Americans in ways that could fuel or sustain abolitionist rhetoric—rhetoric that advocated both immediate emancipation and the integration of African Americans into what European Americans believed to be their nation—during the 1830s, a point that becomes especially clear when we compare the discursive imaginings of African and Native Americans circulating at the time. Most European Americans, especially moderate reformers, imagined Native and African Americans in strikingly divergent fashion, and so the logics of antiremoval and of procolonization arguments were consistent even though one argument concluded with appeals to leave the group where they were and the other concluded with appeals to send them away.

Colonization—typically defined by European American colonizationists as the gradual emancipation and subsequent emigration to Africa of free Africans and their descendants living in the United States—emerged as a viable alternative to slavery, immediate emancipation, and the troubled relationships between European Americans and "free people of color" (an expression that at this time always meant African Americans, never Native Americans). Since colonizationists believed that slavery was wrong (even "evil") but also that it was constitutional and less dangerous than immediate emancipation, they did not and could not sanction abolitionist intervention—whether the political advocacy came from men or from women. Neither men nor women had "a right to speak on the subject" of immediate emancipation, which, of course, precluded petitioning the national legislature to emancipate the nation's two million slaves. Women who demanded a right to speak against Indian removal in 1829 to 1831 likely avoided the women's antislavery petition campaign not primarily because they were conservative in their gender politics but rather because the ways that they imagined African Americans, especially compared to Native Americans, led them to embrace removal of African Americans as a benevolent solution to the challenges they believed free and enslaved people of color posed to the nation.

Catharine Beecher adhered to that position. Angelina Grimké found it highly objectionable, even hateful. Although Catharine Beecher and Angelina

Grimké's friendship dated back to the summer of 1831, there was nothing remotely friendly about their public exchange in 1837. In the preface of her *Essay on Slavery and Abolitionism, with Reference to the Duty of American Females,* Beecher explained that she aimed to strip the abolition movement, for which Grimké was a paid agent, of any credibility. Grimké deemed Beecher's challenge so urgent that she published her response, *Letters to Cath[a]rine E. Beecher, in Reply to an Essay on Slavery and Abolitionism, Addressed to A. E. Grimké,* serially as each letter to Beecher was completed. Both women wanted to rid the United States of slavery, but they embraced dramatically different antislavery programs.

Their public debate emerged within intensely competitive, antagonistic, and rival organizations, the American Colonization Society and the American Anti-Slavery Society, organizations whose rivalry I detail in Chapter 5. Yet this exchange between Beecher and Grimké has received almost no contemporary attention as representative of that aggressive rivalry. Instead, scholars typically read the confrontation as an early debate about feminist principles. Both women had a vested interest in woman's rights and responsibilities, but for none of the central participants—Angelina and Sarah Grimké, Theodore Weld, James Birney, Catharine Beecher, and many other antislavery advocates—was the exchange between these two women predominantly about woman's rights. Nor was it marginalized because its interlocutors were women. As I explain in Chapter 6, in 1837, people treated this exchange between Catharine Beecher and Angelina Grimké as a high-stakes confrontation between compelling rhetorical advocates seeking to persuade their readers that their organization, their methods, and their principles would rid the nation of its most dangerous and despicable evil, and that their organization, methods, and principles would do this great deed most effectively.

Ironically, only by returning to this perspective can we fully understand the role of this exchange in the United States woman's rights movement and Jacksonian-era judgments about women's right to speak. Once we situate the exchange amid the rivalry of the ACS and the AAS and the interwoven rhetorics of the Indian and slave debates, we see why conservative reformers permitted women's exceptional political intervention on behalf of Native Americans in 1829 but not African Americans in 1837. Colonizationists sought an end to slavery but remained loyal to their "southern brethren." They defended the Union and accepted a gradual end to slavery. They also championed the Christianization of Africa, which colonization but not abolition made possible. Although we now dismiss these arguments as without merit, Beecher's *Essay* reminds us that during the Jackson presidency most Americans believed colonization to be a much more viable and acceptable solution to slavery than abolition. The logics of colonization contradicted the logics of immediate emancipation and precluded any sort of interference by the federal government on the rights of states—and, by extension, slave owners—to choose gradually when and how to end slavery. Quite simply, colonizationist principles precluded petitioning for federal interference in slavery for its male advocates as well as its female advocates.

Beecher and Grimké argued specifically about women's roles and rights in their public exchange. Beecher categorically denied women the right to petition in what she imagined to be the Christian democracy of the United States, whereas Grimké urged petitioning as one of women's primary antislavery activities within an ideology of democratic Christianity. Their positions on women's participation existed inside larger concerns about how to end slavery, concerns informed by national debates about Indian removal, and I conclude my last chapter by reiterating a central claim of this book: it is only inside the rhetorics of the Indian removal, African colonization, and abolition movements that we can understand the emergence of United States women's "right to speak" on issues of national concern.

— 1 —

"Causes of Alarm to Our Whole Country"

Articulating the Crisis of Indian Removal

The present crisis in the affairs of the Indian nations in the United
States demands the immediate and interested attention of all who
make any claims to benevolence or humanity. The calamities now
hanging over them threaten not only these relics of an interesting
race, but, if there is a Being who avenges the wrongs of the oppressed, are causes of alarm to our whole country.

—CATHARINE BEECHER, "CIRCULAR ADDRESSED TO
BENEVOLENT LADIES OF THE U. STATES" (DECEMBER 1829)

During his first annual message to the United States Congress in 1829,
President Andrew Jackson assured the nation's senators and representatives
that he would not permit any Indian tribe "to erect an independent government, within" the states belonging to the Union. A year earlier, Andrew
Jackson—renowned for his remarkable acquisitions of Native American
lands in the 1810s and 1820s—defeated John Quincy Adams to become the
seventh president of the United States. In 1827, the year before Jackson defeated Adams, the Cherokee nation adopted its own constitution and declared
its sovereignty, infuriating the Union's southern states. In response, Georgia
passed a law announcing it formally would subordinate Native Americans
to its state laws beginning in June 1830. The Cherokees turned to the United
States government, with which they had signed many treaties, for help.
President Jackson gave them this advice: "emigrate beyond the Mississippi,
or submit to the laws" of Georgia and its neighboring state, Alabama.
Jackson insisted in his address to United States congressmen that "this emigration should be voluntary." But he also reiterated that "the aborigines . . .
should be distinctly informed that, if they remain within the limits of the
States, they must be subject to their laws." Those laws included the exclusion

of Native Americans from the redistribution of Cherokee lands usurped by the Georgia legislature and the prohibition of Cherokee testimony in any legal case that involved European Americans. Jackson knew acquiescence to the laws of the southern states portended disaster for Native Americans. He himself recalled that northern Indians were "doom[ed] to weakness and decay" once they were "surrounded by the whites" and predicted of the southern tribes "that this fate surely awaits them, if they remain within the limits of the States."[1]

The politics of the case were clear to the president. Jackson reminded the national legislature that the United States Constitution forbade the federal government from allowing "the erection of a confederate state" inside the borders of a member state. The Cherokees initiated the troubles facing their tribe by "establishing an independent, substantive government, within the territorial limits of the State of Georgia," explained Jackson's secretary of war, John H. Eaton, and the Cherokees, along with any other tribe competing for sovereignty within what the Union recognized as the territories of its member states, could expect no help from the United States unless these tribes wanted to move west—an alternative the United States promised to facilitate, Jackson explained, "to preserve this much-injured race."[2]

Jeremiah Evarts agreed with Andrew Jackson that Native Americans were a "much-injured race" and that living under Georgia's proposed laws might destroy them. But the two men profoundly disagreed about what that assessment meant or even how to characterize the controversy. Should Native Americans leave to protect themselves from the legal expansion of a more civilized nation? Should the United States protect Native Americans from Georgia's nefarious and avaricious plans? Evarts believed that the Cherokee nation legitimately owned the lands it occupied; that the United States government had for years affirmed the status of Indian tribes as foreign nations by signing treaties with them; that greed motivated recent usurpations and subordinations of Native peoples, nations, lands, and cultures by Union states; that removal would devastate the inroads Christian missions had made in "civilizing" Native Americans, especially members of the Five Civilized Tribes (Cherokee, Chickasaw, Choctaw, Creek, and Seminole) that lived within or adjacent to six southern states (Alabama, Florida, Georgia, Mississippi, North Carolina, and Tennessee); and that these aggressive acts offended God and man. Although Evarts was not a politician, his and Jackson's competitive articulations of the issue had important implications. Indian removal was one of the most popular and controversial debates to engage the nation during Jackson's presidency, and with institutional support from the American Board of Commissions for Foreign Missions (ABCFM), Evarts led an organized, widely supported movement against Jackson and his administration's Indian removal policies. From almost the moment he arrived in Washington, D.C., to lobby against removal in 1829 until he died of exhaustion in 1831, Jeremiah Evarts was one of the most troubling opponents with whom the Jackson administration had to do battle.

Jackson won that battle and so our histories of the Indian removal debates say little about Evarts's role in the tragic expulsion of Native Americans from their homelands. But Evarts orchestrated one of the largest petition campaigns the nation had yet seen, dramatically increasing individual participation in national affairs. In a series of widely circulated essays he posed the most prominent European American counternarrative to the one that Jackson used to justify the series of southern removals that climaxed with the 1838 Trail of Tears. Evarts's narrative also was patronizing, based largely on "Christianizing" and "civilizing" Native Americans. His popular petition campaign for the most part was conducted by northern, privileged European Americans on behalf of what Catharine Beecher called "a singular and peculiar race," who were primarily (often only) known to their advocates through other people's stories.[3]

It is easy, then, to dismiss Evarts's antiremoval movement and its petition campaign because the movement failed and because it employed arguments and espoused motives that to us are problematic and often deeply troubling. But the antiremoval movement played a pivotal role in the trajectory of benevolent and Christian antebellum reform in the United States, largely because of the ways Jeremiah Evarts and other movement leaders articulated what they identified as the issues of the case. For many benevolent Christian reformers including Lyman Beecher, Theodore Frelinghuysen, Arthur and Lewis Tappan, William Lloyd Garrison, and Theodore Weld, the antiremoval movement bridged the national Sabbatarian movement and the nation's African colonization movement: this close-knit circle of reformers went from advocating a Christian cause to advocating in the name of Christianity on behalf of people it considered oppressed, from advocating about locally relevant causes to advocating at the level of national policy. Also, the antiremoval movement provided these Christian reformers a chance to work with political leaders who would become key players in the Whig Party, including Henry Clay, and to involve individuals rather than churches in matters of national policy.

Evarts's articulation of the Indian removal controversy also provided another critical bridge. On what we might call a continuum of possible articulations of the debate, Evarts's version bridged Jackson's strictly political, legal, secular interpretation of the crisis and Catharine Beecher's social, religious, and domestic interpretation of the crisis. Because of Evarts's interpretation, Beecher could imagine and articulate the debate in ways that not only allowed but actually compelled extraordinary political intervention from women who subscribed to conservative ideologies, who celebrated separate spheres for men and women, and who accepted what they believed to be divinely ordered hierarchies between the sexes. This chapter begins with a basic United States history of the Indian removal crisis and then examines three disparate, influential articulations of the controversy.

A Provisional History of Indian Removal

In the presidential election of 1828 Andrew Jackson defeated John Quincy Adams, with heavy support from the southern states. The south gave Jackson a clear mandate: establish state sovereignty throughout the south, including in territories owned and occupied by the Cherokee, Choctaw, Creek, Chickasaw, and Seminole nations. Adams concluded before leaving office that the best solution for the southern tribes was to move west, so in that belief he was not far from Jackson. But Adams was not prepared to forcibly remove Native Americans from their lands. In his last message to Congress in December 1828, Adams reminded members of Congress that, in its documents and in its actions, from its founding the United States treated Native Americans "as foreign and independent Powers, and also as proprietors of lands. They were, moreover, considered as savages, whom it was our policy and our duty to use our influence in converting to Christianity, and in bringing within the pale of civilization." Adams concluded that "the acquisition of their lands" through treaties and negotiated land purchases had been more successful than facilitating assimilation. True, land acquisition had stalled in the southern states. Yet Adams denounced forced removal. He proposed "a remedy" that he believed would "do justice to those unfortunate children of nature" while "secur[ing] to the members of our Confederation their rights of sovereignty and soil." He hoped for a solution so advantageous to Native Americans that they willingly would move west.[4] But such a solution proved untenable, and in 1829 President Jackson was unwilling to wait.

For most European Americans (and probably many Native Americans), Andrew Jackson was at the center of the removal debates.[5] One historian argues that Jackson almost single-handedly constructed the United States' Indian removal policies: he "dominated the treaty proceedings" that governed land purchases and exchanges in the southern states between 1814 and 1820, was instrumental in their enforcement during the Monroe and Adams presidencies, and, after his own election as president, continued the path he had established. As early as 1814 General Jackson refused to return land (approximately twenty-three million acres) and belongings seized from Indians in the previous three years. The Treaty of Ghent, signed to end the War of 1812, mandated the return of land and other property to Native Americans. But as Robert V. Remini notes, "nobody stopped him, nobody dared—not even the administration, which feared western reaction to such a move and feared rebuking a national hero (which Jackson had become on account of his victory at New Orleans) to please the British or the Indians."[6] Jackson then used his influence to be named one of three commissioners charged with United States–Indian negotiations in the south. "By the end of 1820," according to Anthony Wallace, "Jackson had personally forced the Southern Indians to cede . . . about half the territory that had been held by the Southern Indians at the beginning of the war [of 1812] and it opened on the order of 50 million acres to white settlers and speculators."[7] Although Jackson conducted this acquisition through treaties, he argued that treaties were "absurd" tools with which to conduct United States–Indian business: "is it not absurd for the sovereign to negotiate by treaty with the subject?" In a letter to newly elected President James Monroe in 1817, Jackson presented his interpretation of United States–Indian relations as "fact": "all Indians within the Territorial limits of the United States, are considered subject to its sovereignty, and have only a possessory right to the soil, for the purposes of hunting and not the right of domain." Jackson reasoned that the United States treated with Indians for years because the United States "was not sufficiently strong to enforce its regulations amongst them, [and] it was difficult to keep them at peace." He tried to convince Monroe in 1817 that the United States now could "prescribe their bounds at pleasure."[8] But this assertion of sovereignty was far less settled than Jackson's reasoning suggested, even when Jackson finally had the power as president to advocate a congressional Indian removal act.

When Jackson became president in 1829, however, he did make official the tactics, principles, and "facts" he embraced during the 1810s and 1820s. States including Georgia anticipated and perhaps precipitated Jackson's presidential policies. In 1802, Georgia gave land to the United States in exchange for a promise that the United States would facilitate the emigration of Native Americans from within their state borders as soon as such movement was feasible. By the late 1820s, Georgia grew impatient. The United States advocated "civilization" and even assimilation as a means to improve relations between Native and European Americans, spending thousands of dollars to support missions and other educational efforts. But the more "civilized" the Cherokees became, the more threatening they became to whites in Georgia. In 1817, the Cherokees adopted a government that, like its United States model, comprised judicial, legislative, and executive branches. In 1827, they adopted a constitution; written in English and based on the United States Constitution, it declared the Cherokee nation's sovereignty. In 1828, they passed legislation making it illegal for Cherokees to sell land to the United States. The Cherokees were no closer to leaving their lands in 1828 than they had been in 1802. Arguably, they were further than they had been twenty-six years earlier. Then gold was discovered on tribal lands in 1829, and whites throughout the south claimed that tribal lands were being used as havens for escaped or stolen slaves. Subsequent white encroachment into Indian territory virtually was unstoppable, prompting two different readings of the situation at the national level. Out of the dominant reading emerged the conclusion that Native Americans had to vacate southern lands for their own safety and survival. The other prominent European American reading resulted in the argument that the United States government had to step in to protect Native Americans from Georgia's white citizens.

Georgia counted on—or forced—Jackson's hand when state legislators passed a law shortly after his election to the presidency. In December 1828 Georgia decreed that all lands within what it called its borders would become state lands and that all people living inside its borders would be subject to state laws beginning on June 1, 1830. Georgians argued that the state had a right to its lands, that the federal government affirmed that right when it signed the treaty in 1802, and that the state was justified in taking action because the federal government failed to facilitate removal in a timely manner. Georgians wanted the land for its gold, for its agricultural value, and for its location on a natural route between the Atlantic Ocean and the Tennessee River. Georgians also worried that federal policies that supported one minority group might support another, and the threat to the southern slave system felt real to them.[9] Jackson's decision to remain neutral signified tacit approval of Georgia's claims and rights. It also led to his arguments in his inaugural and first congressional addresses that removal—

under just and liberal terms—was the best solution for all parties, especially for what he perceived to be the dying race of Native Americans.

In significant ways, Jackson's policies aligned with the policies of previous presidents, including John Quincy Adams. George Washington predicted the extinction of Indians as white settlements expanded. Thomas Jefferson hoped that Native Americans would move from the southern states to the newly purchased Louisiana Territory in 1803, and James Madison imagined Indian emigration as a salve after the War of 1812. James Monroe recommended that Congress authorize generous terms that would encourage Indians to move west. John Quincy Adams admitted more than once his belief that removal was the only solution for all participants, although he, like his predecessors, advocated voluntary removal. Jackson also advocated voluntary removal but, as he told Monroe in 1817, he accepted forced removal as a means to American sovereignty.[10] Indian removal was codified as law during Jackson's first term, and the Indian Removal Act was one of the most important pieces of legislation of Jackson's two terms as president. It was also one of the most controversial. Two distinct but overlapping European American groups emerged and worked together in opposition to Andrew Jackson and Indian removal: National Republicans or Whigs, and Evangelical reformers in the northern states.

Early in Jackson's first term, Whigs (not yet organized as a fully formed political party) argued against removal, basing their arguments on politics and principle. Henry Clay watched the ways Jackson, the first man elected president from a state other than Massachusetts or Virginia, worried the former National Republicans (who would become Whigs), and he predicted the party could capitalize on this distress to send a Whig candidate—Clay himself, in fact—to the White House in 1832. As one of the most polarizing issues of Jackson's first term, Indian removal looked to Clay like a political wedge that seriously could hurt Jackson's reelection bid.

Removal worked well as a political tool because many people believed Jackson's removal plans got in the way of a primary Whig aim: the "collective redemption of society," as Daniel Walker Howe calls it, attainable if the federal government provided a "centralized direction to social policy."[11] Contrary to Democrats who put a premium on individual autonomy, a strict separation of church and state, and control from the nation's periphery rather than its center, Whigs advocated individual restraint and what Ronald Formisano calls the "use [of] state power to foster economic growth and moral improvement, as well as to protect the weak and disabled."[12] The Whig party reached its peak as the effects of the Second Great Awakening reached theirs, and Evangelical leaders and their congregants in the northern states not only influenced but also to a large degree composed the Whig political base.[13] Protestants envisioned the United States as God's chosen nation. That status meant privilege as well as responsibility. What would it look like—and what sorts of commitments would it take—to live up to that covenant? The amazing proliferation of benevolent societies during the 1810s and 1820s gives some indication. Organizations worked on myriad causes, from increasing the number of Bibles in a community to decreasing the number of drunks, and, Ronald Walters writes, "by 1830 Protestant voluntary associations constituted a loosely interconnected 'benevolent empire.'" Although they were distinct, these associations had in common donors, leaders, and even convention sites: "these linkages permitted a measure of coordinated action," and they also helped establish the critical mass necessary to influence national politics.[14] The leaders of these associations and the theocrats who led church services on Sundays (often the same men) believed that the Christian principles that inspired and sustained benevolent societies should inspire and sustain the nation.[15] Whig political leaders encouraged this coupling of Christianity and government. Throughout the emergence and existence of the Whig party, Clay, Daniel Webster, and others, Howe notes, "cultivated good public and private relations with clerical opinion-shapers."[16]

Lyman Beecher was one theocrat whose influence reached beyond his congregation and into the political sphere, especially through his duties as an officer of various national benevolent societies. Theodore Freylinghuysen illustrated, even embodied, the cooperation between Protestants and Whigs during the Jacksonian era. When New Jersey citizens elected Frelinghuysen to the Senate, they elected a benevolent reformer as well as a politician. In addition to serving six years in the Senate, Frelinghuysen served as an officer of many benevolent societies, acting for sixteen years as president of the ABCFM (founded by Congregationalists, including Lyman Beecher, in 1810), six years as president of the American Tract Society, and fifty years as vice president of the American Sunday School Union. Senator Frelinghuysen's role in the Indian removal debates earned him some fame and the moniker "Christian statesman." At one point during those debates, Frelinghuysen held the Senate floor for a six-hour speech that spanned three consecutive days. That speech owed a great deal to the writings of Jeremiah Evarts, a Protestant whose political work was predicated on the articulation of the United States as a Christian nation.

Evarts, like many Whigs, viewed benevolence as a function of government and advocated an influential role for the federal government in the daily lives of its people. This role of government, especially at the federal level, fundamentally contradicted the role advocated by Jacksonians, who wanted minimal federal government and maximal state and local autonomy. But Whigs believed a Christian government would secure the survival and prosperity of their Christian nation, and partnerships between Protestant and Whig leaders reflected that commitment. Evarts, a New England theocrat but also a lawyer, lobbied for just such a partnership in response to Andrew Jackson's Indian removal policies.

When Jackson was elected as the nation's seventh president, organizations founded and funded by Evangelicals realized their missionary work with North American Indians was in jeopardy. Evangelicals had formed groups including the American Board of Commissioners for Foreign Missions (1810) and the Missionary Society of the Methodist Episcopal Church (1819) in the early part of the century, and these groups worked throughout the United States, its territories, and Canada to "civilize" and "Christianize" Native Americans. Although most missionary societies worked internationally, they concentrated their efforts on North American Indians during the 1820s.[17] Mission reports were published regularly in newspapers such as the *Christian Advocate and Journal and Zion's Herald (CAJZH)*. The Methodist *CAJZH* had a circulation of approximately twenty thousand when most of the mainstream periodicals printed not more than sixteen hundred copies, and *CAJZH* news both reflected and generated interest in communities throughout the United States.[18] Because the *CAJZH* often reprinted letters and reports published in newspapers such as the *Boston Recorder* (a Congregationalist paper), the *New York Observer* (a Presbyterian paper), and the *Western Luminary*, seemingly local news took on a national feel. Typical reports printed in these newspapers announced the conversion of a number of Native Americans, described a moment of conversion for one or two individual Native Americans, reported on the increasing desire to learn about the gospel from members of various tribes, or congratulated a group of Native Americans for its "civilizing" advancements. One annual report concluded that, in eight years of missions sponsored by the Methodist Episcopal Church, more than seven thousand Native Americans were Christianized, not including children, and "at most of the Indian missions, houses are builded [*sic*], farms improved, and the former desolations now present the appearance of neatness, clothed in the smile of comfort; while the savage war whoop is exchanged for the mild halo of friendly greeting; and among the Cherokees, the science of civil government is rapidly advancing."[19] Thousands of northerners felt connected to these missionary successes. Many of the connections were forged by more than the act of reading missionary reports. Subscribers to the religious newspapers that popularized missionary efforts wrote letters to editors advocating missions, and some supported the work financially. In 1829, many issues of the *CAJZH* included lists of contributors to the missionary cause.

These reports and affirmations of Indian missions became more frequent and more zealous as forced removal became more likely. So too did the warnings about this forced removal. One letter about a Choctaw mission published in 1829 concluded with this appeal: "What account will our people render to God, if, through their neglect, this people, now ripe for the gospel, should be forced into the boundless wilds beyond the Mississippi, in their present state of ignorance? We have no time to lose. They are now accessible by us; they are now hungry for the gospel. That precious nation, which must in a few generations be exterminated if thrown together in the western wilderness may now be turned."[20] Particularly typical about this appeal is its motivation. There is no evidence to suspect that Evangelicals cared only about themselves; there is ample evidence to suggest that their concern for Native Americans was genuine, if patronizing and condescending. But one cannot ignore the culpability many of these privileged white Christians expressed when they considered whether they were doing enough of God's work to avoid his wrath. This line of argument—are we doing enough to save our own souls, to prepare this nation for its hallowed status?—found expression not only in these news reports and letters but also in extended arguments and petitions to the federal government. Could the young nation expect God's blessings if its people treated others oppressively? That question was an important one in antiremoval discourse, especially as Evangelicals embraced the United States' status as a chosen land, and it became more urgent as Andrew Jackson's new administration revealed its plans.

In late 1828, the ABCFM mobilized. They sent Evarts, corresponding secretary of the organization, to Washington, D.C., to lobby against removal. In addition to serving on the board of the ABCFM, Evarts was a long-standing editor of a Christian newspaper and an active member of the American Bible Society. He also had experience in the politics of evangelical reform. He, Lyman Beecher, Theodore Frelinghuysen, William Lloyd Garrison, Arthur and Lewis Tappan, and other prominent reformers worked together to increase the sanctity of the Sabbath in the face of growing economic pressures, work that included organized protests of Sunday mails as part of the Sabbatarian movement. That movement mobilized citizens in novel ways. For instance, individuals—rather than local governments or churches— petitioned the federal government to prohibit Sunday mail service. Most of this Sabbatarian activism failed (Sunday mail service continued until 1912). But it gave Evangelical leaders like Evarts experience with public mobilization on behalf of national reform tied to religious commitments. Antiremoval- ism fell into that category, and Evarts worked so hard to oppose Jackson's policies that his relentless efforts left him exhausted. Yet he protested until his dying day, January 10, 1831, just over two years after he began the anti- removal campaign. When he died, the battle was to reverse the Indian Re- moval Act that Jackson signed into law in May 1830; by January 1831, the war was all but lost. For all intents and purposes, when Evarts died the fight on behalf of what people called the Five Civilized Tribes died as well.

In the two years of his zealous activism, though, Evarts led the biggest charge against Jackson's removal efforts. The volatility of the Indian removal debates peaked virtually at the same time as the Christian benevolence movement, and Evarts directed benevolent efforts against removal. He ef- fectively recruited people to the cause, mentoring young men like George Cheever. Cheever, a young man from Hallowell, Maine, wrote a response to a proremoval essay written by Lewis Cass, the governor of Michigan. Evarts encouraged Cheever, instructing the young man to publish and circulate his response and also to initiate and circulate petitions where possible.[21] Cheever, whose mother Charlotte and sister Elizabeth signed the first national women's antiremoval petition before Evarts and Cheever began corresponding, be- came a popular minister, social reformer, and abolitionist. But his activism started with his work against removal. Evarts also spent time in Washington talking with congressmen whenever possible. He wrote to friends throughout the northern states, men like his good friend Lyman Beecher, and encour- aged them to petition as well as to stir the passions of their neighbors, rela- tives, and, when he wrote to members of the clergy, their congregants. Evarts authored a series of twenty-four essays, the "William Penn" essays, formally titled "The Present Crisis in the Condition of the American Indians," which originally were published between August and December 1829 in the *Na- tional Intelligencer* under the name "William Penn" and which ardently ar- gued against Indian removal.[22] Although circulation figures vary, the Penn essays apparently were reprinted in at least forty newspapers and also were circulated as pamphlets.[23] The essays were enough a part of the national conversation that several congressmen complained about them during floor debates. Georgia's Wilson Lumpkin, for example, bemoaned the meddling "William Penns of the whole land" during a debate in January 1830.[24] The *National Intelligencer* reported that "the Letters of WILLIAM PENN have had a more general circulation in the public prints than any other series of Letters that have ever been published during our time."[25] Evarts's interpretation of the issue had far-reaching influence on United States policy and also on women's emergent rhetorical activism in the young nation.

One Case, Three Different Situations

In the twenty-four William Penn essays, Jeremiah Evarts unequivocally argued that Native Americans possessed permanent title to their lands. More than making that argument, though, his essays argued for a particular characterization of the debate and a particular justification for European Americans to intervene. Evarts imagined the Indian removal debates as a referendum on the nation's Christian morality and virtue, and he entered into the heated controversy to save the United States from national policies that would incite God's wrath. So inspired, Evarts willingly and emphatically jumped into the political fray. He used as his immediate exigence for the Penn essays a public letter that John H. Eaton, President Jackson's secretary of war, wrote to leaders of a Cherokee delegation on April 18, 1829. (It is telling that conventionally in the United States the secretary of war handled these matters.) Eaton's letter, a response to a letter from the Cherokees, laid out the administration's position on Native Americans in the southern states. The letter's popularity and its status as representative of Jackson's position made it a useful starting point for Evarts's arguments, and Evarts referred to Eaton several times in his essays. When the Penn essays were reprinted in pamphlet form the Eaton letter was appended to them, a representation of the opposition's stance.

The Case Is "Plain and Obvious"

Eaton's letter began by characterizing Jackson's position as "plain and obvious," adjectives of judgment that attempted to make the position much more obvious than the volatile debates suggest it was. Eaton claimed that Great Britain's eighteenth-century sovereignty included all of the thirteen states, and after the Revolutionary War ownership of these lands trans-ferred to the states that composed the Union. Native Americans possessed but did not own these lands; moreover, they remained occupants of these lands because of Georgia's "mildness and forbearance," an interpretation of the situation that echoed Andrew Jackson's 1817 analysis. Georgia antici-pated a time when the land "could peaceably be obtained, and on reasonable terms." Jackson's secretary of war blamed Native Americans for bringing on the current controversy themselves. He told the Cherokee delegates, "The course you have pursued of establishing an independent, substantive gov-ernment, within the territorial limits of the State of Georgia, adverse to her will and contrary to her consent, has been the immediate cause, which has induced her to depart from the forbearance she has so long practised." For Secretary Eaton and President Jackson, the expectation that the federal gov-ernment would deny Georgia its sovereignty was foolish. Eaton considered that possibility briefly, "merely for the purpose of awakening your better judgment." Eaton concluded his discussion about sovereignty and the fed-eral government's responsibility in the matter by telling delegates that the president would protect the right of Native Americans to live on the land in Georgia—which "is demanded of the justice of this country"—but not to establish a separate government ruling that land.[26]

Although that pronouncement concluded the discussion regarding sov-ereignty, it did not conclude the letter. Given the circumstances, Eaton deemed it "proper to remark that no remedy can be perceived, except that which frequently heretofore has been submitted for your consideration—a removal beyond the Mississippi, where alone can be assured to you protec-tion and peace." The secretary of war suggested removal as the only guar-antee of protection, despite having committed the federal government to the protection of Native Americans. Next came a veiled threat, delivered in the friendliest terms by Eaton from the president: "to continue where you are, within the territorial limits of an independent State, can promise you nothing but interruption and disquietude." Remarkably, in the sentences which followed that warning, Eaton used forms of "justice" and "friend" four times to characterize the United States' and the president's relations with Native Americans.[27] But these sentiments were diplomatic formalities. The Jackson administration, like southern congressmen and state legisla-tors, construed the situation as strictly political, the solution dictated by claims of national sovereignty.

"We Shall Be Guilty of Manifest Injustice"

Evarts found the president's articulation of the United States–Indian conflict immoral, indefensible, and basically incomprehensible. Like Eaton, Evarts declared the question a simple one. But he articulated the case very differently. Based on his readings of United States–Indian treaties and other legal precedents, Evarts claimed that Native American "tribes" were sovereign nations with guaranteed rights to their lands. Based on his Christian ideologies, Evarts also claimed that the United States had to act justly and piously with these less powerful but increasingly civilized nations. The lawyer, leader of the Sabbatarian movement, manager of the American Bible Society, and secretary and lobbyist for the ABCFM articulated this case as political and moral: first, Native Americans not only possessed but owned their remaining lands, and second, the United States had to honor the agreements that established this fact. It was as if Evarts worried that even if he won the first point, he still might lose the second. And, especially for this Protestant theocrat, that second point made all the difference.[28]

Near the end of his first essay, Evarts explained, "The simple question is: *Have the Indian Tribes, residing as separate communities in the neighborhood of the whites, a permanent title to the territory, which they inherited from their fathers, which they have neither forfeited nor sold, and which they now occupy?*" In two paragraphs, he summarized the case for the Cherokees as he saw it and the case as articulated by John H. Eaton. But most of the essay Evarts spent establishing the significance of the case. First he reported that the question was to come before Congress in its next session, that most people were unaware of the facts of the case, and that there were between three hundred thousand and five hundred thousand Indians in the United States, more than sixty thousand of whom lived on lands contained by or adjacent to the southern states. Then Evarts got to the main point of this first essay:

> The character of our Government, and of our country may be deeply involved. Most certainly an indelible stigma will be fixed upon us, if, in the plentitude of our power, and in the pride of our superiority, we shall be guilty of manifest injustice to our weak and defenceless neighbors. There are persons among us, not ignorant, nor prejudiced, nor under the bias of private interest, who seriously apprehend, that there is danger of our National character being most unhappily affected, before the subject shall be fairly at rest.

Evarts developed this point, arguing "that the character which a nation sustains, in its intercourse with the great community of nations, is of more value than any other of its public possessions." But the respect of other nations was not the top step of the moral hierarchy Evarts delineated. At the top was God's sanction—or wrath. Evarts called God "The Great Arbiter of Nations" and suggested that Indian removal was not just a political wrong but a "national delinquency." Because the United States government represented the people of the country, "systematic legislation" by the federal government leading to forced removal would implicate all Americans in moral dishonesty, setting up the nation to "incur the displeasure of the Most High." Evarts constituted the issue as moral and then called upon his audience to respond to it morally. Speaking especially to those readers who feared God's wrath upon the nation for its lapse in moral character, Evarts drove home his point with a threat about as veiled as Eaton's threat to the Cherokee delegates. Heaven's judgment "is more important, and should be more heeded, than all other considerations relating to the subject; and the people of the United States will find it so, if they should unhappily think themselves above the obligation to *do justly, love mercy, and walk humbly with their God.*"[29] Although this construction of the case did not work for all European Americans (or even most European Americans, since the Indian Removal Act passed and was not reversed despite political changes in the 1840s), it appeared to thousands of pious people of the United States to entail not simply an option but an obligation to influence the nation's behavior toward Native Americans.

Following the design of the first essay, the rest of the Penn essays argued on two fronts, the legal and the moral. Although the moral and legal arguments went hand in hand throughout the series of twenty-four letters, Evarts initially focused more of his attention on the legal arguments and then inverted the ratio as he felt the legal case had been made. The Penn essays suggested that, like many Evangelists from the Second Great Awakening, Evarts believed he had to convince his countrymen not only what was right but also that they should do right. Evarts made his legal case by reading treaties, precedents, and federal and state laws. He made his moral case primarily by empowering his readers to evaluate the facts of the case, by suggesting points of identification with Native Americans, by using Christianity as a valid standard for judgment in the case, by holding the national character of the United States and its founders in the balance, and by demanding the importation of private morality into the public domain.

The legal case was easier to make. For instance, in the fourth, fifth, sixth, and seventh essays Evarts closely read the Treaty of Holston, a treaty between the Cherokees and the United States ratified by President George Washington and the U.S. Senate in 1791. Establishing the status of the Cherokees, Evarts reported that "the word nation, as applicable to the Cherokees, occurs no less than twenty-seven times, and always in its large and proper sense," a point he supported by quoting treaty passages.[30] Included in the Treaty of Holston was an agreement about the transfer of lands from the Cherokees to the United States: the Cherokees "ceded" portions of their land, and in return the United States agreed to pay the nation for those lands. In his close reading of the treaty, Evarts declared, "The word 'cede' is the most common and operative word, in all transfers of territory from one nation to another. Unless explained and limited, it conveys the right of sovereignty . . . [N]o party can convey what it does not possess; and it would have been absurd for the United States to ask and accept a cession, without admitting that the Cherokees had power to make one."[31] For Evarts, treaties including the Treaty of Holston undeniably demonstrated the nationhood of Indian tribes, and the United States' acceptance of that status could be traced to documents written and signed by the founding fathers.

Evarts responded to Eaton's claim that Georgia acquired sovereignty of Cherokee lands when the United States won the Revolutionary War. In the sixteenth essay, he read the charters between England and Spain regarding lands that eventually became Georgia. Those English-Spanish charters distinctly excluded land belonging to Indians, so Evarts reasoned that Georgia could not exercise ownership of these lands based on United States wars with England because the lands in question never belonged to England.[32] Evarts also dismissed the notion that the federal government was unable to interfere in the dispute between Georgia and the Cherokees. Not only could the federal government interfere, but states relied on federal government mediation in their dealings with Native Americans—until, according to Evarts, the Cherokees refused to sell the United States any more land. In the ninth Penn essay, Evarts used as a precedent a deal the United States made on behalf of South Carolina. In 1816, the South Carolina legislature decided it wanted to acquire Cherokee land adjacent to its borders, and the state asked the U.S. government to broker a deal. The federal government complied. Evarts summarized the transaction for his readers:

The State wished to obtain possession of this little fraction of mountainous territory. In a manner perfectly fair and honorable, she applied to the

General Government, requesting that the territory might be purchased of the rightful owners. She does not say, that the land belongs to her; but simply that North Carolina has agreed with South Carolina, as to the boundary between them, when the land shall have been obtained of the Cherokees. She does not pretend that the Cherokees are bound, or that their rights are in any degree affected, by agreements between third parties. This is a correct view of the subject; and quite as applicable to Georgia, as to South Carolina, or any other State.[33]

Trained as a lawyer, making arguments based on careful readings of treaties, precedents, and laws, Evarts used the Cherokees as a case through which he decried forced removal of any Native Americans from their lands by the United States government. For Evarts, the legality of Native American sovereignty was undeniable. Usually, Evarts told readers, one treaty between two nations "would bind the parties." He reminded readers of this fact as he examined "the fifteenth Treaty with the Cherokees, every one of which is perfectly consistent with every other; and they all unite in leading to the same conclusion."[34] In what must have been a moment of tremendous frustration, Evarts wrote, "It is humiliating to be obliged to prove, that parties to a treaty are bound by it. To pretend the contrary is an utter perversion of reason and common sense."[35] Legally, as evidenced in treaty after treaty and precedent after precedent, the land belonged to its Native American occupants.

On the other hand, or, more accurately, with the same hand, Evarts laid out a multifaceted moral argument against removal. He began by enrolling his readers as participants in the crisis. "Let each intelligent reader consider himself a juryman in the case," Evarts told his readers in the fourteenth Penn essay. Just as Evarts and other Sabbatarians turned to individuals in their communities, rather than to churches or other organizations, to protest against mail delivery on Sundays, Evarts sought to enroll individuals as arbiters of this case. "Let it be remembered," he urged, "that the honest, fair minded, intelligent members of the American community are to decide this question; or at least that they *may* decide it justly and properly, if they will take the trouble to understand it, and will distinctly and loudly express their opinion upon it. And here let me humbly intreat [sic] the good People of the United States to take this trouble upon themselves, and not to think it an unreasonable task."[36] Evarts's encouragement occurred within a new nationalist tradition that emerged as print technologies sharply improved, literacy rates dramatically increased, and local postal routes were completed. It became easier for people to imagine themselves as part of a national community, and Evarts's turn to individual power and responsibility made use of that nationalist ideology. In fact, Evarts used individual responsibility regarding the issue as exigence for his essays. In the ninth essay, in which Evarts increasingly introduced the moral dimensions of the issue, he finished by reminding readers, "This is a serious matter to the Indians and to the People of the United States. It is a matter which must be decided by the great body of the People, through their Representatives in Congress. The People must therefore have the means of understanding the subject."[37] It would be impossible to ignore the ways in which Evarts invited public, individual participation in the national debate. The invitation framed his arguments, which should be of no surprise given his training as a lawyer. At the end of his eighteenth essay, one imagines Evarts in a court of law, resting his case: "and, in conclusion, having considered the demands of justice, I shall briefly inquire, whether a benevolent and upright man, with a full knowledge of the case, would advise the Cherokees to sell their country, and remove beyond the Mississippi?"[38] Any good lawyer knows that erotema—the use of rhetorical questions—increases audience participation by asking readers to collaborate on the construction of the argument. Evarts presented evidence, imagined his readers as members of a jury, and asked them to make a decision. In that process, he positioned his readers as capable participants in the national debate.

But Evarts also described that participation as an obligation, a move consistent with his theocratic belief that men must not only know what is right but also do what is right. Using another strategically placed rhetorical question, Evarts asked, "And shall we now—(I speak to the People of the United States at large)—shall we now hesitate to acknowledge the full force of the obligations by which we bound ourselves?"[39] The question was one of public morality, and it was one to which the people of the United States had to respond to prevent the federal government from acting immorally. As early as the first of the twenty-four essays, Evarts made clear his interpretation of the issue as one not solely the responsibility of the federal government: "the people of the United States are not altogether guiltless, in regard to their treatment of the aborigines of this continent; but they cannot as yet be charged with any *systematic legislation* on this subject, inconsistent with the plainest principles of moral honesty."[40] Evarts emphasized two things: first, the most damaging sort of culpability could not be charged—*yet;* second, not only the federal government but "the people" would be held culpable.

Having positioned his readers as viable and responsible actors in the debate, Evarts worked to ensure a moral outcome. To that end, Evarts encouraged identification between his readers and the victims of Jacksonian removal policies. In contrast to writings that portrayed Native Americans as curiosities, exotics, or children, Evarts frequently showcased what he imagined to be the humanity of Native Americans. As early as his second essay, he remarked that "the Cherokees are human beings, endowed by their Creator with the same natural rights as other men."[41] Of course, none of Evarts's readers would have missed the allusion to the Declaration of Independence. But the argument for the humanity of the Cherokees was at least as important as Evarts's insistence on natural rights. Evarts echoed the idea in the eleventh essay, in his analysis of an 1816 treaty between the Cherokees and the U.S. government: "On this treaty I would observe, that there are several things in it worthy of special commendation . . . [Cherokees] were to be dealt with as intelligent and moral beings, having rights of their own, and capable of judging in regard to the preservation of those rights."[42] In that moment, Evarts called attention to U.S. policy that presumed Native Americans to be intelligent, moral, capable human beings. At other moments, Evarts simply chose words that signified a common humanity. Rather than exclusively referring to Native Americans as Indians or Cherokees or calling attention to the ways they had been civilized, for example, sometimes Evarts employed seemingly neutral nouns in his discussion of the objects of his advocacy:

> Sixty thousand men, women, and children, in one part of the United States, are now in constant expectation of being driven away from their country in such a manner as they apprehend will result in their present misery and speedy extermination. Sixty thousand human beings, to whom the faith of the United States has been pledged in the most solemn manner, *to be driven away*—and yet the People of the United States unwilling to hear their story, or even to require silence till their story can be heard![43]

Although words such as "men" and "women" appear neutral, when contrasted with other terms used to talk about Native Americans during this time—"savages," "barbarians," and "children," whether one referred to adults or minors—his "neutral" words marked Evarts as significantly more sympathetic toward Native Americans than many of his contemporaries. And immediately to repeat the number of Native Americans affected in a clause whose subject is "human beings" ("sixty thousand human beings") was to emphasize subtly through antonomasia the status accorded to Native Americans by Evarts and by the treaties he analyzed.

Evarts also encouraged his readers to identify with Cherokees by drawing parallels between Native Americans and his imagined audience. It was so important for Evarts to establish Cherokees as farmers, for instance, that one of the subheadings in the pamphlet reprint of his second essay read "They are not hunters." In that essay, Evarts assured readers, "From about the commencement of the present century, they have applied themselves more and more to agriculture, till they now derive their support from the soil, as truly and entirely as do the inhabitants of Pennsylvania or Virginia. For many years they have had their herds, and their large cultivated fields. They now have, in addition, their schools, a regular civil government, and places of regular Christian worship."[44] In later essays, Evarts dramatically shifted his style of argument to highlight potential points of identification between Cherokees and his readers. In two essays in particular, the twelfth and fifteenth essays, Evarts drew extended comparisons between Cherokees and citizens of the United States. Evarts positioned his readers as witnesses to plausible but ultimately hypothetical situations created by "William Penn."

For instance, in the twenty-second essay, Evarts assigned to a foreigner the role of judge:

> How would an intelligent foreigner, a German, a Frenchman, or an Englishman, be astonished to learn, that the Cherokees are neither savages nor criminals; that they have never encroached upon the lands of others; that their only offence consists in the possessions of lands which their neighbors covet; that they are peaceful agriculturalists, better clothed, fed, and housed, than many of the peasantry, in most civilized countries; . . . that they have a regularly organized government of their own, consisting of legislative, judicial, and executive departments, formed by the advice of the third President of the United States, and now in easy and natural operation; . . . that a considerable number of the young, and some of the older, can read and write the English language; . . . and, to crown the whole, that they are bound to us by the ties of [C]hristianity which they profess, and which many of them exemplify as members of regular Christian churches.

These are the men, whose country is to be wrested from them, and who are to be brought under the laws of Georgia without their own consent.

These civilized and educated men; these orderly members of a society . . .
these laborious farmers, and practical republicans; . . . these fellow [C]hris-
tians regular members of Moravian, Presbyterian, Baptist, and Methodist
churches, are to be suddenly brought under the laws of Georgia, according
to which they can be neither witnesses nor parties, in a court of justice.[45]

Evarts's tone and his extensive list of descriptors and parallels between
Cherokees and citizens of the United States and other civilized countries—
a list that continued for paragraphs although it comprised a mere three sentences, one of which consisted of twenty long, separate clauses that followed
from the opening phrase, "How would an intelligent foreigner, a German, a
Frenchman, or an Englishman, be astonished to learn"—conveyed the
magnitude of the injustice. But Evarts did not ask his readers whether they
were astonished to learn these twenty things about Cherokees; instead, he
asked them to imagine what others would think about what was happening
in the southern states. Evarts's readers were not cast as judges. They were
hailed as witnesses or reporters, roles less burdensome, roles easier to don.
As witnesses to the foreign judge, Evarts's readers were charged to imagine
the judge's response; it was the judge, not the witness to the judge, who had
to evaluate the veracity of the claims Evarts laid out. Relieved of at least
some of the burden of skepticism, Evarts's readers were more likely to identify with Evarts's Cherokees than to judge them.

In the fifteenth essay, Evarts fabricated a verbal exchange between Georgians and Cherokees that also positioned his readers a step away from
judges in the case. The turn to dialogue, which Evarts explained "fairly
state[d] all the reasons" Georgia legislators and citizens gave for the seizure
of Indian lands, enabled Evarts to use Indians to make his argument.[46] The
irony must not be lost: many antiremovalists, including Evarts, patronized
Native Americans and believed they were better represented in the removal
debates by whites than by members of their own tribes. Nonetheless, this
act of prosopopoeia lasted long enough for readers to begin to imagine it
was a Cherokee, rather than Evarts, describing his tribe, and the shift to
dialogue between Georgians and Cherokees enabled northerners to sympa-
thize more easily with Native Americans rather than to imagine themselves
as skeptics about the Cherokee position.

Evarts positioned Georgians as the aggressors in the dialogue. The essay
opened, "The Georgians say to the Cherokees: 'We are a civilized people;
you are a vagrant, hunting and savage people. By virtue of this distinction

the lands which you occupy, and which your fathers called their hunting grounds, belong in reality to us; and we must take possession.'" Since Evarts saw and presented this dissociative argument as the primary justification for the land confiscation, he had to persuade his readers that they had things in common with the Cherokees. So in response to Evarts's Georgians, Evarts's Cherokees implied, demonstrated, and described many associations between the two groups. First, they defended their "peaceable possession" of their lands by turning to the Bible: "We do not profess to be learned in the law of nations," they said, "but we read the Bible, and have learned there some plain principles of right and wrong," including the idea that "*to oppress a stranger wrongfully*' is a mark of great national wickedness." First, then, Evarts's Cherokees used the Judeo-Christian Bible as a standard for judgment, a move with which Evarts's readers would have concurred. Second, Evarts's fictional Cherokees defined themselves, and "their" remarks bear repeating in full:

> But we are not the sort of people that you take us to be. We are not vagrants, like some tribes of which we have heard; nor were our fathers. They always had a fixed place of residence. And as to our wandering about, we have not the time. We are busy with our crops; and many of us do not go so far as our nearest county court once a year, unless called out as jurymen. We do not hunt. Not a family within our bounds derives its subsistence from the chase. As to our being savages, we appeal to the white men, who travel on our turnpike roads, whether they receive any ill treatment. We have a legislature and a judiciary, and the judges of our supreme court are very rigid in punishing immorality. We have herds of cattle, farms and houses, mills and looms, clothing and furniture. We are not rich; but we contrive, by our industry, to provide against hunger and nakedness; and to lay up something comfortable for winter. Besides these things, we have schools and places of public worship. Judge ye, whether we are such a sort of people, as the writers on the laws of nations had in their minds, when they talked of vagrants, hunters, and savages.[47]

Evarts's Cherokees, like the readers of the Penn essays, had heard of uncivilized tribes but did not identify with them, and apparently for good reasons. Cherokees inherited lands and agricultural traditions from their fathers (an ironic assertion of European American patriarchy, given that Cherokee women farmed Cherokee lands).[48] Tending their lands, Evarts's Indians explained, kept them so busy that few left home—except when called for a very "American" duty, serving as a member of a jury. Evarts's Indians asserted that "not a family within [their] bounds" hunted as a means of survival; "family," rather than individual, clan, or tribe, marked the unit of division within the Indian nation, as it did for Evarts's readers. After affirming an agricultural tradition as central to their lives, Evarts's Cherokees transitioned into a protest of the label "savage" with a phrase that perhaps most vividly illustrated the poignancy of Evarts's generic choice of dialogue for this extended argument: "As to our being savages . . ." Evarts's use of the first-person pronoun "our" rather than the third-person "their" dramatically pointed to the "humanity" of Cherokees and thus heightened the pathos of what was, really, Evarts's own description of this foreign people. Then came a list: a legislature, a judiciary, cattle, farms, houses, mills, looms, clothing, furniture, "schools and places of public worship." This list suggested to Evarts's intended audience a stable "American" lifestyle, a democratic system of government, and a respect for religion as practiced throughout the United States.

By the end of the paragraph, the absolute artifice of the dialogue between the Cherokees and the Georgians appeared both transparent and efficacious. At a time when northerners—including most if not all of Evarts's target audience—were preparing for winter, the "Cherokees"—who resided within the borders of the southern and more temperate state of Georgia—made a point of annual preparations "by our industry" for the winter ahead. Not only did this announcement reinforce the rootedness of the Cherokee nation, but it also provided Evarts's readers with two opportunities for identification: an ideological advocacy of hard work and the active preparation for the winter months to come.

The paragraph concluded with an imperative that might as well have been directed to Evarts's readers, except that the fabrication of its direction toward Georgians facilitated a sympathetic acquiescence from northerners: they were positioned as outside the debate, watching a dramatic sequence unfold. The Cherokees said, "Judge ye, whether we are such a sort of people, as the writers on the laws of nations had in their minds, when they talked of vagrants, hunters, and savages." But it was Georgians, not Evarts's readers, who were being addressed by Evarts through his strategic if patronizing assumption of a Cherokee voice. Evarts's readers simply were witnesses to the debate. As judges, Evarts's readers would have had to question; as witnesses, they were free to identify. By turning to a fictitious dialogue that cast Georgians as antagonists, Evarts skillfully increased the likelihood of identification between his readers and his Cherokees, increasingly the likelihood of sympathy and what Evarts would have called a moral response to the debates.

Evarts also increased the chances of a moral response to the Indian removal debates by using Christianity as a valid standard of judgment for the case. Evarts imposed Christianity as a standard in the first of his twenty-four William Penn essays. In the first essay Evarts placed God at the top of his moral hierarchy, he established God's wrath as a serious threat to the young nation, and he affirmed the relevance of God's judgment to many members of his audience. Additionally, several times during his five months of writing under the pseudonym "William Penn," Evarts told his readers that United States national and state laws were based on Christian principles, as when he reported that "another learned judge has recently declared, on a public and solemn occasion, that Christianity is a part of the common law."[49] Evarts also argued, "If Christianity is the basis of the law of Nations and of the common law of the United States, it surely is not out of place, though it should be unnecessary to remind our lawgivers and judges, that one of the great maxims of Christianity, for the regulation of intercourse among men, is, that *we should do to others whatever we would desire that they, in like circumstances, should do to us.*"[50] Evarts counted on his audience's familiarity with the scriptures throughout his William Penn essays. In this passage, he italicized but in no other way identified the biblical expression of the Golden Rule. At other times he dropped in biblical allusions without citations or explanations (a reference to the "court of Ahab and Ojezebel," for example, or an analogy to Samson and his ability to break through ties that bound him).[51] By using without calling attention to a shared belief system, Evarts circumscribed a community that felt comfortably familiar for his readers. He also offered his readers a point of entry into the debates: they knew the Golden Rule, they knew the Christian allusions and analogies Evarts used to construct his arguments, they brought a particular expertise to the debates that Evarts found useful. They knew how to respond, then, to the issue that Evarts characterized as a godly trial: "May it not be said, then, that the case of the Cherokees has been prepared by Providence, that we may show to ourselves and to the world, whether *engagements can bind us;* or whether the imagined present interest of a small portion of the American people will transform itself into a Samson, and break national treaties by dozens, and by scores, '*as a thread of tow is broken when it toucheth the fire?*'"[52] Evarts counted on his readers to bring those Christian standards to the issue. He concluded his last essay, the twenty-fourth, published in December 1829, with the same fear of God's wrath he articulated in his first essay, published in August of that year:

> In one of the sublimest portions of Divine Revelation, the following words are written:
>
> *Cursed be he, that removeth his neighbor's landmark: and all the people shall say, Amen.*
>
> *Cursed be he, that maketh the blind to wander out of the way: and all the people shall say, Amen.*
>
> *Cursed be he that perverteth the judgment of the stranger, fatherless, and widow: and all the people shall say, Amen.*
>
> Is it possible that our national rulers shall be willing to expose themselves and their country to these curses of Almighty God? Curses uttered to a people, in circumstances not altogether unlike our own? Curses reduced to writing by the inspired lawgiver, for the terror and warning of all nations, and receiving the united and hearty *Amen* of all people, to whom they have been made known?[53]

Even members of Evarts's audience who knew or understood little of the legal dimensions of the Indian removal debates would have felt obligated to participate in them, given the ways Evarts wrote their central question as fundamentally Christian.

Another way Evarts encouraged his readers to cast the question of removal ultimately in moral ways was by staking the reputation of the nation on the outcome of the debates. Removal would defile the nation's honor, especially given the United States' history of treaties with the Cherokees. If the United States forced Native Americans to vacate their own lands, wrote Evarts, "it must be expected that shouts and hisses of shame and opprobrium will be heard in every part of the civilized world."[54] Because a nation's character "is of more value than any other of its public possessions," international condemnation of U.S. relations with the southern Indian nations would damage the United States for generations to come. The argument was predicated not only on national status for Indian tribes but also on a respect for honor rather than force in United States foreign policy. Evarts told his readers,

> If this case should unhappily be dicided [*sic*] against the Cherokees, (which may Heaven avert!) it will be necessary that foreign nations should be well aware, that the People of the United States are ready to take the ground of fulfilling their contracts so long only, as they can be overawed

by physical force; that we, as a nation, are ready to avow, that we can be restrained from injustice *by fear alone;* not the fear of God, which is a most ennobling and purifying principle; not the fear of sacrificing national character, in the estimation of good and wise men in every country, and through all future time; not the fear of the present shame and public scorn; but simply, and only, the fear of bayonets and cannon.[55]

Evarts treated United States–Indian relations within the domain of foreign policy and argued that, in foreign policy, might did not make right. This line of argument would not have convinced southerners and Jacksonian Democrats. Jackson embraced might as absolutely relevant to United States–Indian policy decisions. His refusal to return Indian property and land despite stipulations in the 1812 Treaty of Ghent and his advice to President Monroe in 1817 stand as early examples. But Evarts's link between Indian removal and national honor counted for those Evarts imagined he could move to action: northern Christians with proto-Whig leanings.

Evarts made a broader patriotic appeal that played on this burgeoning partisan divide between Democrats and Whigs. To side with Jackson was to side against, even "to dishonor Washington, the Father of his country."[56] Evarts considered the possibility that the treaties signed during the first six presidents' terms were bad for the United States. But his sarcasm was palpable: "if Washington and Knox, Hamilton and Jefferson, compromitted the interest of this country, by indiscreet and thoughtless negotiations, we must gain wisdom by experience, and appoint more faithful and more considerate public agents hereafter." Another alternative Evarts considered was that Washington and his successors meant to commit fraud in their treaties or to swindle another nation of its lands. "But such an interpretation, so insulting to the Cherokees and to the common sense of mankind, and so cruel in its operation, cannot be admitted," Evarts reasoned. "Washington was neither a usurper of unconstitutional power, nor an intriguing oppressor."[57] According to Evarts's careful reading of the history of United States– Cherokee relations, negating the treaties by seizing southern tribal lands desecrated the legacy of the founding fathers. And the theocrat aiming to defeat Jackson's plans pinpointed the weak link: "The five first Presidents of the United States made treaties with the Cherokees, all resting on the same acknowledged principles," Evarts began. On President Monroe's behalf Jackson negotiated a treaty with the Cherokees that included a letter written by President Jefferson that represented President Washington's policies. When Jackson violated that treaty as president, concluded Evarts, he violated the "political consistency of [the nation's] most prominent statesmen" through five presidential administrations.[58] The argument was a strategic one, given the political commitments—and emerging fears—of Evarts's Whiggish target audience.

In his William Penn essays, then, Evarts invited and enabled individual intervention in the national crisis, created several opportunities for his audience to identify with the objects of his advocacy, characterized the question as fundamentally Christian, and implicated the nation's character in the settling of the controversy. But the rhetorical move most important to the bridge Evarts constructed between Andrew Jackson's and Catharine Beecher's interpretations of the issue was Evarts's importation of a private code of morality into the public domain. Sometimes Evarts used familial or personal examples to make his point, as when he asked whether a father might oppress his children (an analogy that clearly illustrated the paternalistic attitudes even Native American sympathizers maintained), or whether a husband might abuse his wife, or when he asked in his final essay,

> What should we say, in private life, to a man, who refused to pay his bond, under hand and seal,—a bond, which he did not dispute, and which he had acknowledged before witnesses a hundred times over,—and yet should ostentatiously profess himself disposed to make a great many handsome presents to the obligee, if the obligee would only be so discreet as to deliver up the bond? Would it not be pertinent to say, "Sir, *be just before you are generous;* first pay your bond, and talk of presents afterwards."[59]

At other times, Evarts expressed an expectation that people be held to the same standards regardless of the public and private divide: "I expect honest men, whether public or private, willingly to execute their bargains; and, as to dishonest men, I shall do all in my power to *hold them to their bargains,* whether they are willing or not."[60] In his most explicit discussion of the public and private divide, and in what surely would have been read as a criticism of the Jackson administration given the attention paid to Andrew and Rachel Jackson's marriage during the campaign and the Eaton affair's political effects in 1829, Evarts declared,

> It is one of the most encouraging signs of the present times, that public men are made to feel their accountability to the public, and their obligation to bring their measures of state within the rules of private morality.

I speak on a large scale, and not with reference to a single country; much less, in regard to a single administration. This demand of accountability will ultimately be made by the people of every country; and if rulers, whether Kings or Presidents, Parliaments or Congresses, perpetrate acts in their public character, which would be perfidious in a private man, they will be pronounced *guilty.*

To emphasize the propriety of importing private standards into the public domain, Evarts quoted the legal theory of Chancellor James Kent: "states, or bodies politic, are to be considered as moral persons, having a public will, capable and free to do right and wrong, inasmuch as they are collections of individuals, each of whom carries with him, into the service of the community, the same binding law of morality and religion, which ought to control his conduct in private life."[61] For Jackson, many southerners, and many Democrats, the matter was an affair of state. Relevant topics included national security, strength, and sovereignty. For Evarts, many theocrats, and many Whigs, the topics of debate were private morality, national character, and Christianity. Evarts articulated the Indian removal crisis in a way that compelled intervention by Christian reformers and that set the stage for the entry of women into matters of United States national policy.

A "Course Alike of Policy and Benevolence"

While Evarts was writing his Penn essays, lobbying Congress, asking people in every northern state to petition, and generally doing his best to protest the oppression of the southern nations, he stopped in Boston to visit his good friend Lyman Beecher. Evarts and Beecher shared many beliefs and commitments. They worked together for years promoting Sabbatarianism, and Beecher included Evarts in his circle of confidants and advisors. Evarts's visit coincided with a trip home for Catharine Beecher, Lyman's eldest daughter. Catharine was taking a break from the Hartford Female Seminary, a school for girls that she had founded and for which she served as principal. Years later in her autobiography, Catharine remembered Evarts telling her about the removal crisis and that "American women might save these poor, oppressed natives." Inspired by Evarts's personal request that she "devise some method of securing such intervention" and encouraged by her father to do what she could, Catharine Beecher returned to the Hartford Female Seminary and to a community that respected her and treated her if not as a member of then certainly as an advisor to the town's upper-class community.[62] She enjoyed friendships with leading women who conspired with her to initiate and orchestrate the first national women's petition campaign in United States history.

Beecher was very proud of the method devised, proud of the women's antiremoval petition campaign and her role as initiator and organizer. Beecher recalled the campaign in her autobiography, writing with enthusiasm of her plan to involve women in the crisis facing Native Americans and the United States. Beecher proposed that women "were to secure public meetings in behalf of the Cherokees and then to circulate petitions and gain as many signatures as possible, to be sent to Congress, praying for the intervention of the National Government to protect the Indians."[63] Beecher and some of her friends, "the most judicious and influential ladies of Hartford," contributed names of female friends and relations throughout the northern, middle, and western United States. Each woman received a letter of encouragement with "a large number of the circulars" that Beecher had written. Beecher and her cohort requested that each woman in turn send a circular to "the most influential and benevolent ladies of her acquaintance." She reported that "a simultaneous movement occurred, public meetings were held in all the cities to which our circulars went, and many other towns and cities followed the example," and she reprinted a letter from her sister, Harriet Beecher [Stowe], written from Hartford while Catharine was traveling:

> Last night we teachers all sat up till eleven o'clock finishing our Cherokee letters. We sent some to the principal ladies of New Haven by Martha Sherman, to put in the Post-office there. Margaret Brown says the circular is making a great excitement in New York. The Hartford ladies have received theirs from several cities, we among the rest. There is a great wonderment as to whom composed the circular. The girls [at the school] come and tell us such marvelous stories about a circular for the Cherokees around in Hartford. They say public meetings and petitions are getting up in New York and other places, and here they are moving for the same. The excitement, I hope, is but just begun. So "great effects come from little causes."

Catharine Beecher continued by relating brief anecdotes in which she and her Hartford friends received the circular in the mail from women unaware of the circular's authorship or town of origin. She also described times when she and her group had "narrow escapes from falsehood in efforts to preserve our secret" or encountered women who complimented the efforts while wondering "who wrote the circular and how the plan was so well managed." In December 1829 the circular even was reprinted as "Circular Addressed to Benevolent Ladies of the U. States" on the front page of the widely subscribed *Christian Advocate and Journal and Zion's Herald.* According to Catharine Beecher, "The result exceeded our most sanguine expectations."[64]

The circular, which took up two full columns on the *Christian Advocate and Journal and Zion's Herald*'s front page and continued on the second page, began by declaring that "the present crisis in the affairs of the Indian nations in the United States demands the immediate and interested attention of all who make any claims to benevolence or humanity."[65] That a crisis existed was not a matter of dispute. Three questions were at issue: What kind of a crisis is this? What should be done about it? Who should respond?

First, the crisis was one of "calamities . . . [that] threaten not only these relics of an interesting race, but, if there is a Being who avenges the wrongs of the oppressed, are causes of alarm to our whole country." A culture was at stake in this crisis. So was the wrath of God. From the beginning, Beecher wrote the crisis of Indian removal as moral and religious as well as political. After all, the United States government's relations with Native Americans had been simultaneously political and benevolent to date. Beecher told her readers, "Ever since the existence of this nation, our general government, pursuing the course alike of policy and benevolence, have [sic] acknowledged these people as free and independent nations, and has protected them in the quiet possession of their lands." Whether the federal government's agenda had in fact been grounded both in policy and benevolence, Beecher's reading of the agenda in that way opened the door for women's participation. "Policy" pertained to the treaties and other dealings with Indian nations, and Beecher did not ignore politics in her circular. But Beecher advocated conserving—not altering—national policy. Additionally, she spent little time on treaties and other legal details. For that information, Beecher pointed readers to the William Penn essays and other statements recently printed in public media. In her circular, Beecher detailed not the legal issues but rather the tragic consequences of proposed policies: "It appears, then, that measures are fast ripening, which, if put in execution, are to exterminate the Indians." So Beecher was most interested in benevolence as a way to prevent the "deed of infamy and shame." According to Beecher, "benevolence" guided what she called the United States's "parental" relations with Native Americans—as when the federal government supported missionary efforts to bring literacy and Christianity to southern tribes.[66] Beecher distinguished in the crisis policy and benevolence, not benevolent policies or even political benevolence. That duality—policy and benevolence—enabled Beecher to engage the issue of removal, aligning her cause with a conservation of the status quo without focusing on the politics of removal.

In addition to featuring the benevolent dimensions of the question in the circular, Beecher labeled the crisis as religious. Like Evarts, Beecher affirmed that more and more Cherokee Indians enacted the same religious practices and subscribed to the same religious beliefs that her readers did. For years and with success, "the charities of Christians and the labours of missionaries have sent them the blessings of the gospel to purify and enlighten." Why should the United States or Georgia governments oppress—to the point of extermination—those "becoming a free and Christian people"? Especially since the United States professed to be a Christian nation? Beecher counted on that line of argument as a defense of southern tribes. She also counted on her audience's fear of God as a means of persuasion. The crime of extinction would "be perpetrated . . . in the face of high Heaven," and in the implementation of "this wicked project, the 'voice of our brothers' blood' would cry unto God from this guilty land."[67] These religious arguments—Native Americans practice Christianity and God protects those whom others oppress—brought into relief the dimensions of removal that marked the crisis as more than merely political.

What then should be done about this religious, moral, and political crisis? "Final annihilation" might be stopped, Beecher predicted, if "the feelings of a humane and Christian nation shall be aroused to prevent the unhallowed sacrifice." Later in the essay Beecher repeated this hope: "But humiliating as is the reflection, *the Indians must perish,* unless their destruction can be averted by a most decided and energetic expression of the wishes and feelings of a Christian nation, addressed to the congress now assembling, and which is soon to decide their doom." As Christians, people of the United States needed to express their "wishes and feelings" to Congress. And they needed to act quickly: "*a few weeks* must decide this interesting and important question, and after that time sympathy and regret will all be in vain."[68] Called forth in this manner, with wishes, feelings, and sympathy as well as religious commitments, the intervention Beecher proposed looked like a religious, benevolent sentiment rather than a secular political protest.

If the nature of the crisis and what should be done about it could be imagined as religious and moral as well as political, then those involved in resolving the crisis could situate themselves inside the national debate without claiming political rights. Beecher asked her readers, "Have not then the females of this country some duties devolving upon them in relation to this helpless race?"[69] Beecher believed they did. Significantly, "duties" suggested obligations rather than rights, and Beecher argued not for women as citizens of the United States who therefore possessed the right to petition Congress, but rather for women as moral, religious beings best suited and therefore obligated to intervene on behalf of the pitiable Native Americans.

First, Beecher declared women apolitical. She said that women "are protected from the binding influence of party spirit, and the asperities of political violence. They have nothing to do with any struggle for power, nor any right to dictate the decisions of those that rule over them."[70] Beecher gave up a tremendous amount of political power in this brief statement about women. But their apolitical status made women immune to political pressure. This immunity increased the service to which women could be put by men with proto-Whig leanings as these men attempted to link morality and benevolence to the political sphere. The apolitical and therefore more "pure" position of women in fact protected and even warranted women's influence in this case. Second, Beecher confirmed the exclusion of women from politics, going so far as to affirm submission to the men who governed the nation. Women had no "right to dictate the decisions of those that rule over them," which meant that national legislators were not their representatives in government but rather their rulers, despite legislators' status as representatives of their male relations and neighbors.[71]

But the classification of women as apolitical hardly meant that women had no political influence. The distinction between political influence and political rights was crucial for Beecher, and she explained it in greater detail in *Suggestions Respecting Improvements in Education,* an essay written and published a few months before the antiremoval circular. In that essay, an extended argument for improvements to female education, Beecher affirmed that woman "is bound to 'honour and obey' those on whom she depends for protection and support" and that the "truly feminine mind" does not "desire to exceed this limitation of Heaven." However, women influenced others through affection and reason, and as physical force daily declined as a prime motivator "in the political world," women's influence increasingly needed to play a role: "where the dictates of authority may never controul, the voice of reason and affection, may ever convince and persuade; and while others govern by motives that mankind are ashamed to own, the dominion of woman may be based on influence that the heart is proud to acknowledge." This influence based on affection and reason mattered, and in fact "*affection* can govern the human mind with a sway more powerful than the authority of reason, or the voice of conscience." So when Beecher declared in *Suggestions,* "Here then is the only lawful field for the ambition of our sex," she designated what she called at various times a noble, useful, and honorable field, and one from which women could impact national and international affairs.[72] Beecher asserted a platform and even a methodology for women that honored gendered spheres and roles and that permitted women, as she advised in her circular, to "sway the empire of affection" and "interest the feelings of her friends, relatives, and acquaintances, in behalf of these people."[73]

In her "Circular Addressed to Benevolent Ladies of the U. States," Beecher also claimed issue-specific reasons for women's participation in the national debate over removal. For example, the influence Beecher urged for woman in the debate "falls within her lawful province" because Native Americans stood to lose their homes, and women particularly could empathize: "You who gather the youthful group around your fireside, and rejoice in their future hopes and joys, will you forget that the poor Indian loves his children too, and would as bitterly mourn over all their blasted hopes?" Although both men and women had "hearts [that] thrill at the magic sound of home," by using the trope of "home," Beecher, the nineteenth-century leader of the expressly female domestic economy movement, here offered her female readers a particularly appropriate means by which they could identify with the objects of national concern. Beecher also linked women sentimentally to Native Americans, explaining that women "may *feel* for the distressed; they may stretch out the supplicating hand for them, and by their prayers strive to avert the calamities that are impending over them."[74] "Feel" easily could be interpreted as a signal for female intervention by women like Beecher who advocated gendered spheres and roles in the early nineteenth century.

In *Suggestions,* Beecher wrote that women should not "thunder from the forum," excluding that occupation from the "lawful field for the ambition of our sex."[75] Although Beecher spent no time distinguishing "thundering from the forum" from signing one's name on a petition in either *Suggestions* or her circular, the difference in performance was critical in Beecher's petition campaign. Petitioning meant women approaching legislatures and supplicating, in a form that looked disarmingly like prayer ("we pray that," "we humbly beseech you")—not women becoming legislators or initiating policy. In her circular she asked, "Why may we not approach and supplicate that we and our dearest friends may be saved from the awful curses denounced on all who oppress the poor and needy, by Him whose anger is to be dreaded more than the wrath of man; who can 'blast us with the breath of his nostrils,' and scatter our hopes like chaff before the storm." "Our dearest friends" in this passage did not refer to Native Americans. Native Americans were "the distressed" facing impending calamities. "Our dearest friends" were white neighbors and relations, those people who composed the United States citizenry. They and female antiremovalists stood to receive God's ire because they were the United States, guilty by association if their nation pursued policies of oppression against the Indians. Thus protection against God's wrath by preventing crimes against "the poor and needy" (an accurate description of Native Americans from Beecher's pa ternalistic point of view) justified women's intervention, whereas political concerns about treaty negotiations did not. Beecher built a case for women's national political advocacy without demanding political rights for women. Decorously, then, she declared in her circular, "It may be, that female petitioners can lawfully be heard, even by the highest rulers of our land."[76]

In her most deliberate and adamant call for women's petitions, Beecher predictably turned to the Bible. She wrote, "It may be this will be *forbidden;* yet still we remember the Jewish princess who, being sent to supplicate for a nation's life, was thus reproved for hesitating even when *death* stared her in the way: 'If thou altogether hold thy peace at this time, then shall deliverance arise from another place; but thou and thy father's house shall be destroyed. And who knoweth whether thou art come to the kingdom for such a cause as this?'"[77] Invoking the story of Esther, Beecher put God's word above the United States' conventions regarding women's participation in this federal debate. She established in the contemporary crisis a role that mimicked Esther's role in the crisis facing the Jews during the rule of King Ahasuerus. When Esther told Mordecai that she could not approach the king to plead on behalf of her people, Mordecai urged her to consider whether she had come to be the queen for just this reason, as part of God's plan. Esther yielded to this argument, petitioned the king, and successfully saved the Jewish people from annihilation. For Beecher, the role of supplicant in this case achieved a legitimacy authorized in the Bible: like Esther, these women had the support of male relatives and neighbors to petition against the annihilation of people who shared their religious beliefs. For Beecher's religious audience, that authority legitimized their own actions as supplicants for an oppressed, increasingly Christian people: the "civilized" tribes of the south.

Beecher concluded this section of the circular with a brief, sentence-long paragraph that summarized her arguments for women's participation. The biblical authorization of women's performance as supplicant carried so much weight that Beecher repeated the legitimizing quote. She also reminded readers of the "natural" division between the genders, attributing to women benevolence and affection: "To woman it is given to administer the sweet charities of life, and to *sway the empire of affection;* and to her it may also be said, 'Who knoweth whether thou art come to the kingdom for such a cause as this?' "[78] Beecher constructed a position of petitioner of the federal government for her readers. By casting this role in biblical terms and characterizing it as deriving from women's natural concerns and talents, Beecher legitimized petitioning the federal government in this particular crisis as within women's lawful province, according to Christian and natural laws.

Beecher could not have made the arguments she made for women's intervention—the cause was religious, moral, and domestic as well as political; the cause was susceptible to intervention from Christians uninterested in political power; and Esther was a suitable model for women given the urgency of the case and the fear of God's wrath—using John Eaton's and Andrew Jackson's interpretation of United States–Indian policies. But Jeremiah Evarts posited an interpretation that moved the issue beyond the domain of politics. His interpretation opened a door into the debate for groups including the women led by Catharine Beecher. Another group used the same point of entry: the ABCFM. In October 1830, when Evarts asked the ABCFM's annual meeting to submit a petition to Congress signaling the group's condemnation of removal, the group agreed, with an interesting qualification. The ABCFM sent Evarts to Washington to lobby the Jackson administration and Congress against Indian removal. But they had very specific ideas about the nature of appropriate intervention for their organization:

> Because of the argument of a large number present that as a missionary the American Board should not interfere in politics, the resolution [to petition Congress] was passed with the understanding that the petition should not insist upon the treaty rights of the Indians but should dwell on the injurious consequences of removal to the Indians and not upon the obligations

of the United States to protect them where they were. It would be proper for individuals to present the later case, but not for a religious body.[79]

The ABCFM clearly delineated the topic—the only topic—that rendered appropriate its advocacy on behalf of the southern nations: injuries to an oppressed group. Like the ABCFM, Beecher used Evarts's construction of the situation as a starting point. Then she built a bridge between women's concerns and national policy, rendering women's intervention in this particular case not only appropriate but obligatory.

Beecher's interpretation of the issue was no less true than Jackson's or Evarts's. Telling, though, are the points of divergence and even irreconcilability. In those conflicts and gaps, in the spaces between the tellings of Indian removal and United States–Indian relations, new possibilities for rhetorical invention emerged. In those spaces, Christian reformers imagined avenues of access into the debate. In those spaces, too, Christian women imagined arguments that obliged their participation in what Andrew Jackson imagined to be strictly a matter of politics: the forced removal of Native Americans from their nations' southern lands.

— 2 —

"A Right to Speak on the Subject"

Petitioning the Federal Government

There is one consideration, connected with this subject, which adds much interest, and gives us, as we think a right to speak on the subject.

—LADIES OF HALLOWELL, MAINE, PETITIONING AGAINST
INDIAN REMOVAL (1830)

In a letter dated September 3, 1829, one of Elizabeth Cheever's older cousins asked eighteen-year-old Elizabeth about her progress in school. The letter reveals a sympathetic and also patronizing imagining of Indians by this northern European American family. "I hope the dear children in N. England who have such great and precious privileges," J. Arnold wrote, "will not suffer themselves to be outdone by the children of the savages and heathen, of whom we hear such interesting accounts—their readiness to learn is certainly surprising."[1] Talk of Native Americans, especially members of the Cherokee, Chickasaw, Choctaw, Creek, and Seminole nations located within and adjacent to the borders of southern Union states, peppered the letters between the Cheevers and their friends between 1829 and 1831. After reading an essay written by her son George Cheever that demanded federal protection of southern tribes, Charlotte, Elizabeth's mother, wrote proudly to him in January 1830: "I am so delighted with . . . your piece upon the Indians that I cannot refrain from saying so, tho I did not intend writing you so soon again, but gratitude as well as affection obliges me to acknowledge the rich treat."[2] Less than two weeks later, George, who received active encouragement from Jeremiah Evarts to distribute his essay widely, wrote to his sister Elizabeth about the urgency of the antiremoval cause. On February 10, he complained that his illness "delays the appearance of the Indian pamphlet full a fortnight longer than if I could have been

52

in Boston only two days at the time I expected. Verily I hope the poor Indians wont [*sic*] suffer from my influenza; but the time to do them good is *now*."[3] These letters illustrate the ways the Cheevers—a family active in the nation's campaign to stop the United States' plans to forcibly remove southern Native American nations from their homelands—imagined Native Americans and also white patronage. Indians were heathens becoming civilized or groups needing to be saved from extinction. Either way, positive outcomes required white intervention. George Cheever gave significant credence to white intervention, especially his own, when he assumed a causal relationship between the extermination of whole nations of Indians and his flu. Other European Americans intervened financially, and these contributions were noted publicly. In her letter to Elizabeth Cheever, J. Arnold asked her cousin whether Elizabeth had read newspaper accounts of people donating money to the cause. Of a group of young boys who contributed fourteen dollars to the Indian missions, Arnold wondered whether Elizabeth were "not charmed with their self-denial?" One could not and would not want to ignore the patronizing sensibility of the Cheevers and their friends. But that sensibility carried with it a critical correlative: the Cheevers and hundreds of other northern families believed they could make a difference in the fate of what they imagined to be a dying race. That belief in individual as well as collective agency drew in the whole family, children as well as adults, women as well as men.

Interventionist participation occurred in different ways. In a February 17, 1830, letter to his mother, George asked Charlotte to distribute some of his pamphlets on Indian removal in their hometown of Hallowell, Maine. On April 4, 1830, George and Elizabeth's brother Henry wrote to Elizabeth (who was visiting George at the time) that the town's lyceums "have become very interesting on account of the admission of ladies." An upcoming lyceum was to feature Indian removal, and the newspaper advertisement mentioned that "ladies are invited to attend."[4] But even before these instances of female participation in the affairs of Native Americans, Charlotte Cheever, her daughter Elizabeth, and fifty-nine other women from Hallowell signed and submitted to the United States Senate a petition protesting the forced removal of Native Americans from their southern lands. Although the Hallowell women probably did not realize that their petition would be the first of the women's antiremoval campaign to arrive in Washington, D.C., their January 1830 appeal happens to mark the first time in United States history that a group of women petitioned the national legislature regarding an issue of national consequence, the first time women demanded from the federal government what ladies from Hallowell called their "right to speak on the subject."[5]

Before 1830, women petitioned local, city, and state governments, and they often used a "discourse of domesticity" to do that work. Those petitions dealt with issues such as city services, orphanages, and female education, however—not issues of federal policy. Anne M. Boylan notes that these women "did not view petitioning as political because it involved private efforts to influence powerful men." Catharine Allgor, too, details early nineteenth-century women's "profound political work [that] took place in spaces entirely female and private."[6] Before 1830 women influenced policy, but women's antiremoval petitions were the first announced instance of women's federal activism in a space declared national and political. These petitions marked and transgressed a boundary that, though symbolic, had material consequences.[7]

Yet despite the national, political nature of the antiremoval petition campaign, scrutiny of the petitions reveals that these "actions took on conservative meanings" in 1830 and 1831 and that they did not appear dissonant to Beecher nor to her prominent family.[8] In fact, the campaign served as an early example of the strategic use of "Whig womanhood," an ideology based on what Elizabeth E. Varon defines as "the notion that women could—and should—make vital contributions to party politics by serving as both partisans and mediators in the public sphere" but which, Varon explains, required women's embodiment of "true womanhood" to validate their contributions.[9] By the 1840 presidential campaign, Whigs actively and openly solicited women's political involvement. As early as 1830, though—four years before the official formation of the Whig party—future Whig leaders were courting women in proto-Whig efforts to oppose Jackson. Aiming to defeat the president's Indian removal policies, for example, Henry Clay encouraged Jeremiah Evarts to take advantage of women's sympathy toward and support for Native Americans residing within the United States–drawn boundaries of the southern states by enrolling women in the antiremoval campaign.[10] Evarts was a step ahead of Clay: he already had inspired Catharine Beecher to organize women to protest the Jacksonian initiative.

How did women negotiate the tension between their political activism and decorous female behavior as conceived by women such as Beecher? The petitions that composed the women's antiremoval campaign and the circular Beecher wrote to instigate the campaign provide remarkable examples of that negotiation as women argued not only against removal but also for their own "right to speak." Sometimes women's petitions echoed men's arguments against Indian removal. More frequently, however, the petitions used women's piety, benevolence, and morality to purify national character in what the petitioners identified as a uniquely troubling issue. These topics of argument aligned with what Norma Basch calls early Whig "ties between household and polity," which increasingly came into focus during the marital controversy that plagued Andrew Jackson's 1828 presidential campaign.[11] In their petitions, women adopted a political persona that, in the context of proto-Whig ideologies, enabled women's collective participation in a national political debate to appear conservative, appropriate, and even natural despite its novelty.

In its historical context, the accomplishment is worthy of recovery and celebration. This instance of early national political intervention also illustrates more broadly the ways people transcend what Michel Foucault calls rules of discourse: who can speak on what topics under which circumstances.[12] What can this historical event—a group of United States women in 1829 to 1831 effectively negotiating the tension between the constraint of decorous female behavior and the desire to intervene in a national political debate—tell us about transgressions of symbolic or discursive power? These petitions and the personae female antiremovalists created and adopted functioned not only persuasively but also constitutively, and it is as constitutive rhetorics that women's antiremoval petitions enabled petition signers to transcend multiple constraints and to achieve agency on a question of national policy.

Women who participated in the women's abolitionist petition campaign, which almost immediately followed the antiremoval campaign, initially employed the same rhetorical strategies as the women who petitioned on behalf of Native Americans. But in the late 1830s female abolitionists faced distinct rhetorical challenges in the United States Congress. Attending to the shifting strategies of the women's abolition petition campaign underscores an important lesson to be gained from a study of women's nascent national rhetorical activism in the United States: one of discourse's most powerful functions is the constitution of political agency.

The Emergence of the Women's Antiremoval Petition Campaign

The "Circular Addressed to Benevolent Ladies of the U. States" announced its authorship and distribution as "solely by the female hand." Yet when the

Christian Advocate and Journal and Zion's Herald (CAJZH) "oblige[d] a *Female Friend of Humanity*" by reprinting the exhortation, the Methodist weekly placed the circular not in its regular ladies' column but rather on the front page of its December 25, 1829, issue.[13] Despite its unusual placement, the inclusion of the circular was not without precedent. The *CAJZH* featured Evarts's William Penn essays and regularly printed letters from and stories about Native American missions. It also publicized women who, in groups and individually, raised awareness of and contributed money to the missionary cause before and during the national removal debates. As Boylan notes, such publicity played an important role for the emergence of women's activism in the early nineteenth century.[14] In the specific domain of United States–Indian relations, reports like these not only advertised but also provided instructions and models for European American women's active participation in the "Christianizing" and "civilizing" of Native Americans.

Occasionally, individual contributors to the missionary cause were noted in the *CAJZH*. In a typical announcement, printed in a March 1830 issue, of twelve people listed four were women.[15] At other times, women celebrated a group's collective work. In January 1829 the *CAJZH* published a letter from Eliza Anna Mercein that announced the collaborative efforts of Philadelphia and New York Female Missionary Societies to raise one hundred dollars to support the Cherokee Mission.[16] Mercein's letter credited women for taking the initiative to raise funds after reading a missionary report published in the *CAJZH,* and her letter illustrated for others how to increase contributions to missions by partnering with "sister societies," even those in other towns. Announcements like this one implied that supporting missionary activities, which included organizing into active groups, was appropriate behavior for women.

Sometimes the idea that these reports provided models of women's participation was explicit, as when Susan Harris, the secretary of a female missionary society in New York, wrote to *CAJZH* editors:

A few females of Queensbury and places adjacent, have been waked, and moved to action by reason of the cry from the wilderness, (heard through the Christian Advocate,) "Help! O, sisters, help!" We therefore have organized ourselves into a society denominated, "The Queensbury Female Missionary Society, auxiliary to the Missionary Society of the Methodist E. Church:" the form of our constitution not varying materially from that which we saw in the Advocate.

We were disposed, knowing our own weakness and comparative in-
significance, to do what we could, and not let our right hand know what
our left hand was doing; but we were advised by our beloved brother, Rev.
R. Kelly, preacher in charge of the Washington circuit, to submit it to you
for publication, as an example to others.[17]

Harris provided additional helpful information, including the group's meeting schedule and the amount of its first donation. Her letter confirmed the
importance of the *CAJZH* in the Queensbury Missionary Society's formation, given that these women adopted a "constitution not varying materially
from that which we saw in the Advocate." Another woman who viewed her
group's activism as a model, Sarah E. Hendley, the secretary of the Union
Female Missionary Society (UFMS), wrote to the editors of the *CAJZH*:
"believing that every communication of this kind is calculated to prompt
other communities to a more hearty co-operation in the spread of the
gospel, we think proper to solicit you to devote a corner of your paper in
giving publicity to our infant society."[18] As did so many of her peers, Hendley
focused on religious exigencies—here "the spread of the gospel"—for white
intervention in Native American issues. Relying on a deeply felt commitment to Christian missions, the UFMS asked neither for assistance nor approval but rather for publicity. Hendley presumed propriety, and the
CAJZH affirmed that propriety by printing the report as well as the solici-
tation. The presumption and affirmation demonstrated for *CAJZH* readers
and for us that women's involvement appeared simultaneously novel and
yet recognizable within contemporary cultural codes.

On December 4, 1829, three weeks before the *CAJZH* published Beecher's
circular, editors printed a short essay called "The Cause of Missions" and
identified its writer only as "Emma." Emma aimed to convince readers of
the religious virtue of Indian missions:

Much as missionary societies are doing for the advancement of Christ's
kingdom upon the earth, and great as the good *is* which they are accomplishing, there are those who would seem willing to raise their frivolous
objections . . . Have their suspicions ever told them that in heaven there
would not be enough room for all, and therefore they must not be anxious
to crowd its hallowed seats with the tawny sons of yonder western forest? . . . It would not appear so strange, if those who have never been re-
newed by the Spirit of grace, or blest with the perusal of your excellent

paper, were the only ones who should oppose the efforts for evangelizing the world; but they are to be found among the warm advocates of what they call Methodism.[19]

Editors chose not to relegate this essay to the regular "Ladies' Department," despite its female authorship. Emma questioned the piety and judgment of Methodists—all Methodists, not just female Methodists—who were apathetic about or resistant to Christian missions in Indian territories. The *CAJZH* legitimized her authority to correct both sexes by positioning Emma's essay in the nonfemale section of the weekly newspaper. Benevolence as well as piety made this intervention agreeable within a culture of true womanhood. Two weeks after Emma's essay appeared, another essay defined the missionary cause as both benevolent and pious: "The missionary cause appeals not merely to your benevolence, but to your allegiance to the Prince of peace. Its claims are founded not only on good will to man, but on submission and loyalty to the Lord Jesus."[20] It probably was to Catharine Beecher's benefit that this description of missionary work appeared in the *CAJZH* the week before its editors published her "Circular Addressed to Benevolent Ladies of the U. States."

Reports and essays like the ones printed in the *Christian Advocate and Journal and Zion's Herald* very specifically described European American women's activities undertaken in sympathy with Native Americans, and they offered explanations for their activities that suited local and regional ideologies governing ladies' appropriate, decorous behavior. Novels published in the decade preceding the campaign, including the remarkably popular historical romances by Lydia Maria Child and Catherine Sedgwick, *Hobomok, A Tale of Early Times* (1824) and *Hope Leslie; Or, Early Times in the Massachusetts* (1827), played similar roles. They, too, provided European American women with narratives that romanticized Native Americans, questioned the integrity of European American or English relations with Native Americans, and admired European American women who intervened on behalf of Native Americans. Novels also encouraged imaginings about and identifications with people and events relevant to contemporary issues, including the Indian removal debates.

Novels and religious reports were influential. They offered women heroic models of intervention as well as points of identification with oppressed individuals and groups. But to confine a history of the women's antiremoval petition campaign to these kinds of textual trajectories would be to oversimplify greatly the conditions of the campaign's emergence. This approach also would celebrate too emphatically the women who first petitioned rather than affirming sociopolitical trends that significantly increased the probability of—or, more likely, contributed to—the campaign's inception. Material circumstances mattered, and two major turns in material conditions mattered most directly: the leap in print technology and the completion of the United States postal system. Other cultural events that played important roles in the emergence of the woman's antiremoval petition campaign included the Second Great Awakening, with its concepts of civic participation and higher-law democracy; the Sabbatarian movement, especially the Sunday mail campaigns; and the election of Andrew Jackson, along with the organization of an oppositional party, the Whigs. Any student of United States history would recognize these events as significant to the time period. My point is not to rehearse them here but rather to make several overlapping arguments about women's earliest national political activism in the United States. At a most basic level, it would be problematic to recover or interpret this activism solely in the context of women's history or women's political participation.

That perspective is tempting, given its proclivity for celebrating the creativity and courage of women leaders. Yet it would lead to erroneous understandings of the campaign. For example, because the antiremoval campaign was the first performative and declarative act of national political participation by a group of women in the United States, it is easy to label it radical. But it was not radical. It was novel, but not radical. As a second example, consider the stories we tell about male support of woman's rights in the 1830s and 1840s. We glorify Elizur Wright and Theodore Weld for hiring and training the Grimké sisters as abolitionist agents in 1836 and William Lloyd Garrison for joining Lucretia Mott, Elizabeth Cady Stanton, and other female abolitionists in the galleries to which they had been exiled during the 1840 World Antislavery Convention for the crime of being female. We glorify Frederick Douglass for publicly insisting at Seneca Falls in 1848 that women demand their right to vote. While these moments of empathy and courage are worthy of celebration, they inaccurately suggest that only radical men supported women's political participation in the nation's antebellum years. Gender solidarity around women's activism was not the norm during the Jacksonian period. But some groups of women acted within recognized social structures and communities, and they benefited from the active support, even direction, of men in their churches, neighborhoods, and families. These groups included female antiremoval petitioners. The campaign was supported rather than attacked by most members of the communities to which female participants belonged. Furthermore, the campaign shaped—it was not just shaped by—concurrent sociopolitical trends.

The idea here, then, is actively to resist reading female antiremovalist petitioners as somehow exceptional or protofeminist. As supported members of their communities, female antiremovalists employed previously unused channels of communication to craft and express arguments grounded in ideas emanating from their communities. I am interested in the patterns and trends present in that moment, in logics of articulation swirling about at that time, rather than an imposition of causality onto a series of events.[21] Given the confluence of transformative events that occurred in the late 1820s and early 1830s, it would be irresponsible to suggest a hierarchy of causality anyway. How could one privilege, for example, the completion of the United States postal network in 1828 above—or below—the remarkable advances in print technology or the saturation of newspapers into communities throughout the young nation?[22] Instead, I begin with an increasingly pervasive logic of the day: nationalism.

In his groundbreaking work on nationalism, Benedict Anderson uses the United States to think about nationhood. "By the second decade of the nineteenth century, if not earlier," Anderson says, "a 'model' of 'the' independent national state was available for pirating." One important model (in concept if not in practice) was the United States: "out of the American welter came these imagined realities: nation-states, republican institutions, common citizenships, popular sovereignty, national flags and anthems, etc." Newspapers, and even more basically a reading public, contributed significantly to the propagation of these imagined realities. In a highly evocative passage, Anderson describes the enabling seduction of the newspaper, a medium that exploits "calendrical coincidence" (we connect through sharing an experience in a particular moment, and also time and "the world" march on regardless of our attention to them) and mass production (we hold in our hands an exact replica of the text thousands of others hold in their hands). On the routine of reading the paper, Anderson writes, "Each communicant is well aware that the ceremony he performs is being replicated simultaneously by thousands (or millions) of others of whose existence he is confident, yet of whose identity he has not the slightest notion.

Furthermore, this ceremony is incessantly repeated at daily or half-daily intervals throughout the calendar. What more vivid figure for the secular, historically clocked, imagined community can be envisioned?"[23] Anderson identifies simultaneous, shared consumption of newspapers—reading weeklies and dailies—as a context for the emergence of the imagined political communities he calls nations. Michael Warner argues that republican readers actually transformed the meaning of print culture in the United States. Readers newly understood print to be "normally impersonal," which means that readers recognized that authors were not talking directly to them but rather to "the potentially limitless others who may also be reading."[24] Printed texts (pamphlets, newspapers, and other genres) delivered more than a message to their readers; they brought an awareness of other readers who could be imagined as companions, even coconstitutors of a national community.

Print and nationbuilding function correlatively throughout United States history, but there are synergistic periods particularly worthy of attention. For example, Warner notes that when "public print discourse" emerged during the early eighteenth century, "in every instance the emergent mode of publication entailed a reconceptualization of the public sphere."[25] The Revolutionary period, with its pamphlets, newspapers, and of course state and federal constitutions, is another example. A third example is the period during which Indian removal debates were at their most heated. By the time the federal government completed the United States postal network in 1828, tremendous transformations had occurred, and congressmen knew it. The numbers are telling: by 1820, congressmen used their official speaking time at least as much to communicate with constituents back home as with fellow lawmakers, and by 1830 government or government-related publications, as Richard R. John notes, "made up fully 30 percent of all the imprints in the United States . . . [and] a large percentage of the total volume of the mail consisted of newspapers, magazines, and public documents that described the proceedings of Congress and the routine workings of the central government."[26] These shifting patterns of communication coincided with the circulation among United States residents throughout the land of what John calls "two key ideas" early in Jackson's first term: "that the boundaries of the community in which they lived extended well beyond the confines of their individual locality, state, or region, and coincided more or less with the territorial limits of the United States; and that the central government might come to shape the pattern of everyday life."[27] It is important to remember, though, that at the moment when print culture changed the nature of the public sphere in the United States, texts flowed both ways.

We spend a lot of time thinking about the ways reading and reading culture, print and print culture facilitated and also illustrated the increasingly national perspective of many people in the United States. Although reading need not be a passive act—Warner talks, for example, of the ways readers transform the meanings of print—it is substantively different than writing. Reading, after all, implies a unidirectional transmission of ideas even as it allows for multiple interpretations of a text. It is worth noting that, as a genre, petitions provide to people who are normally positioned as receivers of the message—readers of the government imprints so popular in the 1820s and early 1830s, for example—with a way to talk back. Anderson persuasively argues for the importance of reading in building nations. But individuals need ways to imagine themselves not only as part of a community but also as participants in that community. Because in the early nineteenth century petitions functioned creatively in that way, petitions should be read as an important complement to newspapers in the process of United States nation building. Although their numbers fell far below the numbers of newspapers circulated daily, the right to submit petitions was paramount. The right to petition originally meant more than, and probably inspired, the other First Amendment rights of free press, religion, assembly, and even speech. Next to Anderson's examples of people reading their ways into nationhood, petitions illustrate people writing their ways into imagined communities. The Sabbatarian movement serves as an early and transitional example.

Sunday mails ceased across the United States in 1912, more than one hundred years after Christian reformers began organized campaigns to protect the Sabbath from what they imagined to be the corrupting influence of commerce. Evangelical leaders initiated two waves of Sabbatarian protests focusing on Sunday mails, one from 1810 to 1817 and the other from 1826 to 1831. Both times the protests failed to stop Sunday mails. But the campaigns were valuable on other levels. Some businesses ceased on Sundays, for example. More to my point, the second campaign, led by men including Jeremiah Evarts, Lyman Beecher, and William Lloyd Garrison, took advantage of and contributed to an increasing sense of nationalism in the United States in the late 1820s and early 1830s. Both campaigns used petitions to appeal to federal legislators. But in the first campaign and the early part of the second campaign, church leaders and officers of other organized groups—for example, a benevolent society's corresponding secretary—signed petitions as representatives of the membership, or individuals who signed as a rite of membership in an organized group. During most of the first three decades of the nineteenth century, people petitioning as part of this Protestant movement felt it inappropriate to petition Congress directly, to take issue with legislative affairs as individuals. But that position changed by 1828. As part of the increasingly pervasive logic of nationalism (simultaneously evidence for and constitutive of the emerging imagined community), individuals expressed themselves via petitions. Interestingly, Jeremiah Evarts, soon to be the primary white leader of the anti-removal movement, recognized and took advantage of this trend. Within a logic of nationalism, the debate over Sunday mails signified a much more important debate, as Richard John points out: "whether the central government had acquired the capacity to shape the pattern of everyday life. By 1828, it was plain to Sabbatarians that it had."[28] In response, the Sabbatarian campaign to avoid Sunday mails was articulated and operated inside proto-Whig ideologies. A centralized government needed to channel morality and higher law as it conducted the nation's business, especially as the federal government's penetration into the lives of individuals throughout the large and growing nation increased. The petition campaign amounted to a structural as well as an argumentative response, then, to a commercially prudent policy as it advocated and literally provided a form for individual penetration into the affairs of state.

Petitions suited this sort of intervention well. Most of their generic constraints befitted the needs of the campaign; others were malleable enough to be transformed by the process. The petition entered into United States politics by way of English law. Colonists routinely used petitions to communicate with King George and his representatives in England and North America. After repeated dissatisfaction with those communications, colonists' Declaration of Independence took the form of a petition to the king. And when the newly independent people wrote their state constitutions, they repeatedly protected the right to petition.[29] Petitions played an important role in the cultural fictions of republican government, and they were a key component of representative democracy. Initially, Congress designated the first Monday of each month during congressional sessions for the presentation of petitions. People petitioned their representatives for "redress of grievances," using the generic form to improve their lives in some way. Petitions ranged from the individual (military pensions and land grants, for instance) to the communal (postal routes, lighthouses, import and export taxes). That petitions almost always were submitted to the House of Representatives and that memorials, used by states and corporations to protest policy, were submitted to the Senate, underscores both the roles of each house (the House represented the people and the Senate represented the states) and the generic role of petitions as instruments of personal (whether individual or collective) redress.

Despite its history as a form of political intervention, the petition as a genre particularly suited women's early rhetorical activism. Formally, the petition represented a prayer and conventionally began or ended with signers affirming their prayer or commitment to continue praying on the subject. Petitions could be signed in the home or, for instance, at sewing or reading circles. Because of its written form, petitions gave to their signers a degree of anonymity. And yet women refrained from petitioning collectively on a national, political issue until the crisis of Indian removal emerged. Why? Sabbath observation was a benevolent, Christian issue. But there were no oppressed peoples in that reform movement, and the nation hardly faced terminal threats over the issue from either God or man. Sabbatarianism was not the sort of exceptional crisis that led Queen Esther, Beecher's biblical inspiration, to supplicate. Indian removal was exactly that sort of crisis—one that not only permitted but that obligated Christian women to demand their right to intervene.

Petitioning the Federal Government against Removal

Not all of the women who organized or joined female missionary societies participated in the antiremoval petition campaign that Beecher advocated. For example, southern women occasionally reported their societal efforts in the *CAJZH,* but there is no evidence that southern women petitioned. It does appear, however, that the women who petitioned the federal government on behalf of southern Indian nations were the kinds of women Beecher and her friends hoped would petition: pious white women who belonged to prominent families in their communities. The first two women's antiremoval petitions to reach Congress came from Hallowell, Maine, and Steubenville, Ohio, and histories of these towns provide information about many of the first 124 petition signers. Two things warrant particular mention: these women often modeled appropriate womanly behavior in their communities, and they petitioned in protest of removal with the support of their communities.

On January 8, 1830, sixty-one women from Hallowell signed what would become the first petition from a group of women submitted to the United

States Congress concerning an issue of national policy. More than two-thirds of the women who signed this petition or their relatives are mentioned in town histories as important members of the community. Signers married lawyers, captains, clergymen, goldsmiths, bakers, heads of educational academies, and lumber mill owners, and these men included women in their conversations about Indian removal, as evidenced in the lyceum advertisement in the *American Advocate*. More than half of the signers and their families belonged to the Old South Congregational Church of Hallowell. The first minister of that church served for thirty-two years, and upon his retirement in 1827 he became secretary of the Maine Missionary Society—suggesting that a beloved member of the religious community provided an important link between piety and the paternal protection of Native Americans. That many women from this congregation—including the minister's wife—signed the Hallowell petition illustrates the degree to which members of the community considered the petition an appropriate means of female intervention.[30]

The same appears true for the community in Steubenville, Ohio, which submitted the second women's federal petition protesting removal. Steubenville's first lots had been purchased and settled in 1797, and at least a dozen of the sixty-three petition signers represented founding families. Signers were the sisters, daughters, wives, and mothers of clergymen, judges, postmasters, bank presidents, and even a few temperance activists. Six petition signers are listed in a town history as early members or officers of the Steubenville Female Bible Society, an auxiliary to the American Bible Society, of which Jeremiah Evarts was a national officer. Almost half of the women shared a surname with at least one other female signer of the petition. Others are mentioned as attending the same church, being married by the same clergy, or belonging to a common organization in town records.[31] That many of the signers traveled in the same social, religious, and economic circles is clear. All indications suggest that these women, prominent members of their community, voiced their position on this controversial political issue with the support of prestigious family, social, and religious networks, not as rebels but as benevolent Christian women.

Over a two-year span, nearly fifteen hundred women joined the women from Hallowell and Steubenville to petition the federal government against its removal policies in 1830 and 1831. These women came from seven states: Connecticut, Maine, Massachusetts, New Jersey, New York, Ohio, and Pennsylvania. An analysis of their petitions now housed at the National

Archives in Washington, D.C., reveals that women participated in the anti-removal petition campaign in one of two ways. The least common form of participation, accounting for 237 women's signatures on four petitions, consisted of women and men signing the same petitions (on three of the petitions, men and women signed in different columns or all of the men signed before any of the women affixed their signatures).[32] Congressional petitions including men's and women's signatures were exceedingly rare through the middle of the decade and were not common practice until 1837, so these petitions neither initiated nor were part of a trend integrating men's and women's positions on political matters.

Much more common in the archives are the kind of petitions that contain the other twelve hundred women's signatures. They are petitions signed exclusively by men or women—and such explicit segregation occurred even when family members signed antiremoval petitions at the same time. The material or physical separation of signatures reflects the different methods men and women employed in their advocacy of Native American rights, despite the similarities of their convictions.[33] For four women's petitions (accounting for 238 women signers) for which men's petitions from the same town are available, the pairings are telling. Two of the pairs displayed minor but important gender differences. Men and women from Huntsburgh, Ohio, signed antiremoval petitions on January 31, 1831, and 70 percent of the surnames on the women's petition are shared by men on the other petition.[34] Even though family members protested the same issue on the same day, they were compelled to segregate by gender. Despite comparable arguments, women appealed as "Ladies of the Town of Huntsburgh" whereas men were "citizens of the town of Huntsburgh." Men "do heartily and earnestly pray" while women "with a modesty and reverence becoming our Sex and with all the ardour of female tenderness do heartily and earnestly pray." Similar differences occurred on petitions signed in Virgil, New York, on March 25 and 29, 1830.[35] Based on legible signatures, thirty-nine of the fifty-nine surnames, accounting for 66 percent of the female petitioners, also occurred on the men's petition. And yet family members segregated themselves by gender. Two other pairs of petitions exhibit more variation across gender lines: although more than half of the female petitioners from Farmington, Maine, and more than half from Hallowell, Maine, had relatives who signed men-only petitions, arguments submitted by these men and women illustrate dramatic rhetorical differences based on gender.[36] The rest of the twelve hundred women who signed petitions separately from men also employed gendered appeals, appeals which we can conclude were unique to women despite there being no extant petitions from the same towns for comparison. For example, the sixty-three women from Steubenville, Ohio, signed a petition that read in part, "Even in private life we may not presume to direct the general conduct, or control the acts of those who stand in the near and guardian relations of husbands and brothers, yet all admit that *there are times* when duty and affection call on us to *advise* and *persuade,* as well as to cheer or to console."[37] Three hundred and fifty-five women from Burlington, New Jersey, agreed that they were "endowed with a capacity to discern good from evil, and right from wrong, as reflecting and accountable Beings, [and so] they deem it no departure from the reserve and decorum befitting their Sex, briefly and unpresumingly, to make known their opinion of Measures fraught as they believe, with injustice and oppression."[38] This Burlington petition was one of nine petitions— a grouping that represented 840 women, more than half of the female antiremoval petitioners—that explicitly argued for the propriety of women's voice in the national political debate. This subset of petitions most completely demonstrates the strategies by which these texts constituted political agency for the signers.

The petitions that marked the beginning of the campaign, the Hallowell and Steubenville petitions, typify this grouping, and so I read most closely those two petitions as illustrative of the rhetorical strategies that enabled women's earliest national political activism in the United States: the petitions recast the debate by calling it unique or extraordinary, invoked particularly feminine readings of ideologically salient republican terms, and invested the issue with more than basic political significance—as they employed different topics of debate than petitions submitted by their male relatives and neighbors. These strategies worked together to constitute a platform for women that conformed to decorous, proper female behavior while standing inside the arena of national politics.

The most consistent and most basic gesture in women's antiremoval petitions was the articulation of the Indian question as an isolated case, a move probably intended to assure congressmen that women's "interference" was not the beginning of a widespread challenge by women to the ideology of separate spheres for men and women. In almost all of the antiremoval petitions, women interpreted the debate as extraordinary, as unusual or unique to public policy. Hallowell women explained that "we would not ordinarily interfere in the affairs of government," and Steubenville women went so far as to remind their audience that "your memorialists would sincerely deprecate any presumptuous interference on the part of their own sex, with the ordinary political affairs of the country, as wholly unbecoming the character of American females." Women marked Indian removal as a special issue, as the women from Farmington, Maine, explained, different than "any ordinary occasion" that would require attention from the national legislature. In a particularly interesting qualification, women from Burlington, New Jersey, "hop[ed] that circumstances may seldom occur requiring or authorizing the expression of their sentiments to the Representatives of the People." The 355 women who affixed their signatures to that petition emphasized Beecher's argument that women were doing their duty, what was required of them, by intruding into the business of the federal government.[39]

Female antiremovalists also reconceived the issue of United States–Indian policy by using concepts integral to and yet ambiguous in contemporary republican ideology. For example, both the Hallowell and Steubenville petitions relied on virtue as a topic of argument. Hallowell women began their petition:

> To the Honourable Senate and House of Representatives in Congress assembled, we the undersigned, feeling deeply interested in the honour, integrity, and virtue of our Country, and considering the question soon to be presented before you in relation to several tribes of Indians in the western [sic] States, as affecting all these, we do most humbly and ardently unite our prayers with those of ten thousand in our land, that your determination may be favourable to these devoted, persecuted, and interesting people.

The opening address to the legislative body was a standard opening for petitions in the first half of the nineteenth century. But most petitioners before and through 1830 did not write that they were "deeply interested in the honour, integrity, and virtue" of the United States. Since most petitions requested specific redress of grievance or legislative action (for instance, an increase in import taxes on lace or an establishment of a local postal route), most petitioners did not explicitly concern themselves with virtue. But these women used virtue as a bridge into the political sphere. As Philip Gould notes, in the early nineteenth century virtue still conveyed the "masculine legacy . . . of classical republicanism and liberal individualism," which perpetuated virtue as a central tenet of republican ideology into the Jacksonian era. Yet virtue also began to signify "the precepts of affect, benevolence, and pious, universal love . . . traits [that] became increasingly associated in early national America with women themselves." Civic virtue as a republican construct, according to Carroll Smith-Rosenberg, became "fused . . . with more private and moral understandings" of the term, one associated with women. Catharine Beecher's writings illustrate this movement. Two years after writing and distributing her "Circular Addressed to Benevolent Ladies of the U. States," Beecher published *The Elements of Mental and Moral Philosophy, Founded Upon Experience, Reason, and the Bible*, a book she intended for the instruction of girls who attended schools such as the Hartford Female Seminary. In one of the chapters, "On Right and Wrong, Virtue and Vice," Beecher distinguished between "common usage" and "true virtue":

> According to the world, the virtuous man is he who ordinarily conforms his conduct to the rules of rectitude, from education, circumstance, and natural conscience. The *truly* virtuous man, is one who habitually conforms his actions to the rules of rectitude, from a principle of love and obedience to his Creator . . . The virtuous mind is one that is habitually regulated by the principle of love and obedience to the Creator, in promoting general happiness, according to the rules of the Bible. Virtuous actions are those which are in agreement with the will of God, and also those which are *believed* to be in agreement with his will by the acting mind.

Beecher taught girls that they could be virtuous if they acted in accordance with God's will, that they could know that will through Bible study, and even that their own beliefs could serve as an adequate standard of judgment for virtuous action if they based their beliefs thoughtfully on Christian principles. So when women noted that the question of Indian removal concerned topics of honor, integrity, and especially virtue, they engaged the overdetermined Jacksonian-era concept of virtue to recast the issue as one which women could judge. Since, as Gould explains, virtue "began to signify new, modern republican adhesives of sociability and Christian benevolence," women's use of the topic altered the nature of the debate.[40]

Steubenville women also used virtue in their petition. In its final paragraph, they wrote, "When, therefore, injury and oppression threaten to crush a hapless people within our borders, we, the feeblest of the feeble, appeal with confidence to those who should be the representatives of national virtues as they are the depositories of national powers, and implore them to succor the weak and unfortunate." In this sentence women acknowledged the masculine understanding of virtue, especially with regard to republican virtue of the young nation: congressmen "should be the representatives of national virtues." The use of the conditional verb phrase "should be" rather than the simple verb "are" in this phrase suggests a causal relationship between republican men and national virtue: because men had national power, they should enact national virtue. But it was women making this causal argument, enabled by the multiple understandings of virtue. They invoked a particular authority linked to virtue's feminine connotations of benevolence, Christianity, and love. Furthermore, as James Jasinski argues in his study of virtue, liberty, and power in the early republic, when virtue was domesticated in the postrevolutionary United States, public virtue came to imply deference. People enacted virtue by ascertaining and then supporting "those who displayed the most virtue." This implication of virtue meant that women (and men) acted virtuously when they supported people who committed virtuous deeds, so women acted virtuously, rather than inappropriately, by supporting men who could enact national virtue in the political arena. This philosophy aligned with proto-Whig principles that urged the application of private standards of morality to conflicts in the public sphere.[41]

The Steubenville and Hallowell petitions offer another example of women recasting the issue of Indian removal by using productively ambiguous concepts. Hallowell women closed their petition with a short final paragraph: "We do therefore repeat our prayer, that they may be permitted to abide by the graves of their Fathers, and enjoy the sweets and endearments of *home*." The last word of the last paragraph of the first petition regarding a national issue submitted to the United States federal government by a group of women was "home." The emphatic "home" resembled "virtue" here and elsewhere in women's antiremoval petitions, as it signified both domestic and national spaces. In the Hallowell petition, "home" represented the domestic space in which one's family resided, a space clearly gendered as feminine during this period in United States history. In this final paragraph of the petition, though, the petitioners also linked "home" to nationhood, one's civic genealogy: women privileged the patriarchal concept of fathers serving as critical links between generations. Women from Steubenville invoked both meanings of home as well, when they lamented that, "in despite of the *undoubted natural right,* which the Indians have, to the land of their forefathers, and in the face of solemn treaties, pledging the faith of the nation for their secure possession of those lands, it is intended, we are told, to force them from their native soil, and to compel them to seek new homes in a distant and dreary wilderness." Defining or maintaining a nation's or a people's home was a masculine, political act. But defining or maintaining a family's home was a feminine, domestic act. The ambiguity of "home" rendered the boundary of the removal debate itself ambiguous.[42]

In addition to reinterpreting the removal debate by using multivalenced concepts or marking the case as extraordinary, female antiremovalists instilled the debate with a significance beyond the strictly political. For example, women from Lewis, New York, assured congressmen that "they would disclaim any intention or even wish to interfere with the political ritations [sic] of the General Government," but they "consider the subject of this petition as involving the principles of national faith and honor."[43] The Farmington petition spoke "of the miseries which [Indians] would experience if driven from their native lands and homes" and of "all that is [C]hristian, that is humane, that is noble." Steubenville women called the issue "a cause of mercy and humanity" and emphasized its effects on "the prosperity and happiness of more than fifty thousand of our fellow [C]hristians." These women asked congressmen, by protecting Native Americans, to "shield our country from the curses denounced on the cruel and ungrateful, and . . . shelter the American character from lasting dishonor." Hallowell women explained that they "are anxious that others,—that the wandering Choctaw, Creek, and Cherokee should participate in these privileges" of Christianity and they "refer to exertions made by the pious and benevolent, to enlighten and [C]hristianize this long neglected people." In their petition they claimed to be "unwilling that the church, the school and the domestic altar should be thrown down before the avaricious god of power."[44]

Most petitions submitted to Congress between 1789 and 1830 dealt with issues like alien and immigration acts, import and export duties, the financing of lighthouses, and the establishment of new postal routes. Those issues primarily were political or economic. Indian removal, however, became much more expansive in the texts of women's petitions. Some female petitioners acknowledged political elements like treaties, but according to these petitions the treatment of Native Americans required pious, benevolent, merciful, and humane decisions. The issue necessarily involved religion: missionaries daily converted Native Americans to Christianity, many with funds raised by female missionary societies, and God's wrath—"curses denounced on the cruel and ungrateful"—would be forthcoming if the federal government decided the issue strictly on political grounds. Because women interpreted the issue as multifaceted and included in their interpretation topics of argument with which they had familiarity and even authority, they opened doors to their active participation in the debate.[45]

The sixty-one female petitioners from Hallowell, for example, began their petition by aligning treatment of Native Americans with "the honour, integrity, and virtue of our Country." In the second paragraph of their petition, they repeated the sentiment with a minor but critical modification: "We have said this question affects our honour, our virtue, and our faith." In the first paragraph, petitioners invoked national honor, integrity, and virtue and inscribed themselves into the issue by marking their national belonging: they referred to the United States as "our Country." But in the next paragraph, they emphasized their national participation: they referred to "our honour, our virtue, and our faith." The shift from the general article ("the") to a possessive pronoun ("our"), a pronoun that petitioners repeated preceding each topic—"our honour, our virtue, our faith"—established a claim for women on the question besides the political or economic.[46]

Charlotte Cheever and her neighbors grounded their most explicit claim to participate in the Indian removal debate on its religious aspects. "There is one consideration, connected with this subject which adds much interest, and gives us," they explained, "a right to speak on the subject." That consideration was the Christian missions, which women often financed: "We say it without any desire of vain glory, that these efforts have been sustained chiefly by the charity of our own sex." But these women also reassured congressmen that "we would not ordinarily interfere in the affairs of government; but we must speak on this subject. We are aware what we owe to Christianity—all that is sacred to virtue." Again, interference was unusual and specifically not to be read as precedent-setting. But women interpreted the question as involving Christianity, both as a standard of judgment and also as a basis for advocacy, so they could stake a claim in this particular conversation about national policy.[47]

The Hallowell petition illustrates an extended interpretation of the question as religious. The Steubenville petition focused its attention primarily on the inhumane treatment that would result—that in fact did result—from a federal policy of forced removal. Steubenville women introduced topics including mercy and humanity, and then they participated in the debate by asserting their authority as women regarding these topics. They told congressmen that "the present crisis in the affairs of the Indian nations, calls loudly on *all* who can feel for the woes of humanity." First, petitioners wrote the debate as more than political; it spoke to the woes of humanity. Second, women claimed their right to speak. The emphasis on "all" marked this (no longer entirely) political issue as inclusive, rather than exclusive. The word "feel" unmistakably implied the appropriateness of women's political participation. Although both men and women expressed feelings in their anti-removal petitions and sentimentality had a role in masculinist politics, this use of "feel" activated an ideological binary between feeling and thinking common during this period—especially for men and women likely to advocate Whig policies. Women wrote themselves into the debate by characterizing their presence as essential and their authority as natural, despite its novelty.[48]

Later in the Steubenville petition, women invoked their particularly gendered authority when they

> acknowledged, that the wise and venerated founders of our country's free institutions, have committed the powers of government to those whom nature and reason declare the best fitted to exercise them . . . Even in private life we may not presume to direct the general conduct, or control the acts of those who stand in the near and guardian relations of husbands and brothers, yet all admit that *there are times* when duty and affection call on us to *advise* and *persuade,* as well as to cheer or to console. And if we approach the public representatives of our husbands and brothers, only in the humble character of suppli[c]ants in the cause of mercy and humanity, may we not hope that even the small voice of *female* sympathy will be heard?[49]

Petitioners hardly could have made more clear their acceptance of what they identified as the natural, reasonable, and gendered division of labor. In language echoing Catharine Beecher's "Circular Addressed to Benevolent Ladies of the U. States," these women from Steubenville gave up all claims to political rights. Men governed the country. Women advised and persuaded. With this division of labor, petitioners applied the principles Beecher laid out in her 1829 *Suggestions Respecting Improvements in Education,* when she wrote that women's "voice of reason and affection, may ever convince and persuade" men as they made decisions in "the political world."[50] But these women, like Catharine Beecher in her circular, discovered a way to blur the typical political-domestic division by "approaching the public representatives of [their] husbands and brothers." They enabled this move into the political domain of national legislators by characterizing the question as merciful and humane and by claiming a right to speak on familiar topics as suppliants and advisors, rather than as citizens of the United States. Their participation looked conventional and decorous, yet it altered the rules of discourse in dramatic ways.

Hundreds of other women used the same strategy in their petitions. For example, women from Monson, Massachusetts, described the emotional responses they had to the oppression of Native Americans:

> That the melting cries of the oppressed have broken in on the stillness of our retirement,—that various appeals have been made to our sympathy and benevolence, in behalf of the helpless, hunted and persecuted Indian tribes inhabiting the wilds of our free and happy country,—that our interest and commiseration have been excited in view of their sufferings and their wrongs,—that seventy thousand men, women, and children, who have no power to defend themselves, and no earthly protector from robbery and oppression and injustice;—have made a deep impression on our hearts.

Sympathy, benevolence, and heartfelt impressions were expressions appropriate for European American women of this socioeconomic class in the early 1830s. These reactions constituted a viable relationship between the speakers and the issue, positioning women inside the discourse community debating the issue. These women concluded their petition by "trust[ing] that they may enroll their names as suppli[c]ants for the poor Indians without overstepping the bounds of female propriety" because they "make their fervent request in behalf of suffering humanity, for the sake of justice, mercy and the honor of our beloved country." The request had nothing overtly to do with politics or treaties. Although Monson women gestured toward national honor, a seemingly masculinist element of republicanism, women frequently dissociated the nation's character with politics in their petitions. Women from Lewis, New York, for instance, affirmed their "depart[ure] from the usual sphere which they occupy in society. They would disclaim any intention or even wish to interfere with the political ritations [sic] of the General Government. Your memorialists consider the subject of this petition as involving the principles of national faith and honor which they in common with every other member of society are interested to prescribe inviolate." The distinction between "political ritations" and "national faith and honor" may in fact have been an artificial one, but in important ways that was the point of these petitions: they interpreted the question in particular ways, and these interpretations supported the bridges that petitions built between women's "usual sphere" and the domain of national politics. This distinction certainly was plausible. It could be read as a transition between the Revolutionary-era ideology of "republican motherhood" and proto-Whig tendencies to align public policy with private values. Women could speak to national faith and honor without denying its conventionally masculinist connotations in republicanism. Rather, the topic became another example of conceptual change at work in these petitions.[51]

In fact, men used the topic of national character differently in their petitions. In March 1830, women from Pennsylvania submitted a petition containing the same text as the women's petition from Steubenville, Ohio. At around the same time, Congress also received a petition from male inhabitants of Pennsylvania. The hundreds of men from towns throughout Pennsylvania invoked national character:

> Our national character will be looked for, not in times anterior to our existence as a nation, but in the period which has succeeded in the formation of our General Government. Your memorialists trust that the Senate and the House of Representatives of the United States will not consider the *crimes* of our provincial times, as worthy of imitation; but will rather to endeavor to wipe off any stain which may thence arise, by a rigid performance of national obligations, and scrupulous adherence to the path of justice and humanity.

Compare this approach to that of the Pennsylvania and Steubenville women who simply prayed that Congress would save Native Americans "to shelter the American character from lasting dishonor." Although both men and women invoked the nation's reputation, the details of their appeals reflected different approaches. Men worried about repeating crimes of previous generations—and words such as "crimes" and "scrupulous" probably hinted at early Whig complaints of Jacksonian corruption in government—implying the partisan commitments of these men petitioning against Jackson's Indian removal policies. The national character of which these men spoke was more politically framed than the honorable and virtuous American character that women prayed would be sheltered. When women spoke of national character they spoke not of crimes but of "sin" (as did the women from Burlington) or "injustice" (as did the women from Hadley)—misdeeds, but imagined as moral violations of a higher law rather than crimes committed within the human laws prescribed by the national legislature.[52]

The petitions submitted by men and women differed in other ways, and these differences bring into sharp relief the gendered strategies that contributed to women's abilities to negotiate the tension between feminine decorum and national politics. The Pennsylvania petition submitted by hundreds of men began:

> Independently of the acts of those whom they may justly consider as foreigners and invaders of their country, would not the Cherokees be an independent sovereign people, and the rightful inheritors of the lands on which they reside?
>
> Have not the lands which they now hold been solemnly guarant[e]ed to them by treaties with our National Government, more especially the treaty of Holston?
>
> Are not treaties made by the National Government with a sovereign and independent people the supreme law of the United States, agreeably to the Constitution?

The petition continued in this manner for two pages, visiting topics such as ownership of lands, congressional acts, and comments made by the U.S. secretary of war. Men from Pennsylvania compared the United States' treatment of Indians to "the worst of all tyranny—that of one nation over another." They questioned Congress's handling of the treaty it made with Native Americans in 1802, given constitutional law and decisions of the Supreme Court. All of these topics of debate were absent from the women's petitions submitted at the same time.[53]

Another set of petitions illustrates the disparate paths of political protest. Several weeks after women from Farmington submitted a petition to Congress regarding Indian removal, Congress received a petition from their townsmen regarding the same issue. At least half of the female petitioners shared surnames with men who signed the second petition. And yet the petitions of family members and neighbors differ in striking ways. Women from Farmington, for example, conceded that "the delicacy of feeling and modesty of deportment which should ever characterize the *female* sex, might forbid the propriety of obtruding ourselves upon the notice of the Legislative Council of a Nation, on any ordinary occasion." Women identified themselves as intruders and marked the situation as extraordinary, whereas their male relatives and neighbors simply "come before the National Legislature with an earnest request." Furthermore, women made a religious argument, one not echoed in the other petition. They quoted the Bible when they asked the government to protect Native Americans because of "the moral obligation we are under to 'do unto others' . . . by the venge[a]nce of Heaven which we would not incur, [and] by all that is [C]hristian." Farmington men, on the other hand, quoted the Supreme Court chief justice's pronouncement that Native Americans had "a *legal and just claim*" to their lands, a topic of argument absent from the women's petition. In addition, Farmington women sympathized with those who might be dispossessed, pitying the "miseries which they would experience if driven from their native lands and homes." Although Farmington men requested "that these dependent allies, some of whom have been models of good faith and good neighborhood, may be treated with kindness and generosity, as well as with justice," they expressed none of their own emotion regarding the relationship between their government and those whom they called their nation's allies.[54]

Both groups of petitioners mentioned treaties between Native Americans and the United States government, but their references to the treaties were notably distinct. When we remind ourselves that these petitions were circulated nearly simultaneously among families and friends, the distinctions take on heightened significance. Farmington men asked "that the public faith may be preserved inviolate, in all the transactions of the Government with the Indians . . . [and] that no encroachment may be made upon their right of territory, or the right of self-government, as guaranteed by numerous treaties." Farmington women "regret that an attempt is made to wrest from [Indians] those privileges and rights which they have so long enjoyed, and which hitherto have been secured to them by our Government."[55] If both groups of petitioners concerned themselves with treaties, why not use the same language in their petitions? Why did men speak of "transactions of the Government," "encroachments" on the rights of territory and self-government, and even "numerous treaties" whereas women invoked more vague "privileges and rights" and avoided legal terms when they spoke about the government's securing of such rights?

Each of these topics was available to men and women in Jeremiah Evarts's William Penn essays, Beecher's circular (in abridged forms), newspaper articles, and probably even church sermons. But, appropriately, women selected topics consistent with popular, conventional ideologies about or easily available to women. Because women's petitions effectively combined essentializing ideologies about womanhood with strategically selected topics of debate, the political intrusion of female antiremoval petitioners seemed a natural extension of their female roles and responsibilities. The result, though, was a rhetorically constructed, distinctly gendered political authority that enabled women's collective participation in national debates for the first time in United States history.

Antiremoval Petitions as Constitutive Rhetorics

How was that political authority constructed in these texts? In Beecher's circular and in women's antiremoval petitions, a popular question of United States–Indian policy was interpreted as an extraordinary event, a complex, impending crisis that invited not only legal and political responses but also pious, moral, benevolent, and sympathetic appeals. The texts also declared women of a particular religious background and socioeconomic status to be authorities on those topics who were therefore able to contribute a different kind of value to the debate than men. As a result, these women appeared to be doing simply what was both obligatory and natural in an exceptional moment of national concern.

But what they did in their petition campaign was neither natural nor obligatory. The power to act collectively as a sociopolitical force emerged through the petition campaign, through the interpretations and declarations made in the texts. This power was neither actively nor conceptually available for these women before Beecher's circular and the subsequent petitions brought it into relief, nor was it presumed after the antiremoval campaign. According to the Jacksonian-era worldview of Beecher and other proto-Whig antiremovalists, women could claim no political rights. Female political actors by definition violated the conventional rules of this community. So, then, the question bears repeating: how did these women articulate or make manifest the right to speak in 1829 to 1831? Their antiremoval texts functioned as constitutive rhetorics.

When I speak of constitutive rhetorics, I mean texts that create exigencies or identities, texts that generate or call forth new, often transcendent or transformational ways of being in or relating to the world. Although rhetorics typically function persuasively as well as constitutively, persuasive functions of discourse can be and often are overt (texts explicitly argue for change), whereas constitutive functions of discourse must be hidden (texts assume the identities and exigencies that they create precede and exist independently of the text) if they are to be successful.

Catharine Beecher's "Circular Addressed to Benevolent Ladies of the U. States" and many of the ladies' federal antiremoval petitions function as constitutive rhetorics by creating exigencies for women's political activism and by crafting identities that used traditional gender roles while transcending them. First, the texts interpreted the crisis in ways that invited women's participation. Instead of accepting dominant interpretations of the issue as legal or political, interpretations that exclusively called forth men's activism, these women wrote United States–Indian policy as, for instance, religiously motivated. In an essay that argues for rhetorical exigencies as created rather than extrarhetorical or existing outside language, Richard E. Vatz explains that "meaning is not discovered in situations but *created* by rhetors." Barbara Biesecker agrees that rhetorical situations are contingent on interpretations, not descriptions of an extrarhetorical scene. Both theorists identify one of rhetoric's constitutive functions: rhetoric constitutes exigence because meanings of events are creations, not reflections of a presumed reality.[56] We can build on this theoretical premise, given the historical documents available to us from the women's antiremoval petition campaign. Constitutive rhetorical theory helps us identify the powerfully creative dimensions of these documents. In turn, or perhaps in return, these documents teach us that rhetorical exigencies can be used to alter balances of power, to justify interventions or transgressions that make available new forms of authoritative political participation.

Second, the texts functioned as constitutive rhetorics in that they articulated a position or persona that had agency in the national political arena. I call that persona the "first persona" of the texts, intentionally provoking comparisons to discourse's "second persona." In a 1970 essay that began the contemporary trajectory of constitutive rhetorical theory, Edwin Black asks rhetorical critics to break the habit of "thinking of discourses as objects" and to start thinking of rhetoric as "active," arguing that rhetorical texts imply their authors and auditors. Black skips over the concept of an implied author—the rhetor—in his essay, mentioning briefly the "probability . . . that the author implied by the discourse is an artificial creation: a persona." Black then quickly moves to an inquiry into a text's "second persona," its audience, auditors implied by the ideology of the text. It is more common to think of "audience" as a rhetorical construct composed of various constituencies than it is to consider "rhetor" as a historically situated composite of identities articulated in discourse. But because these women's antiremoval petitions represented dozens, sometimes hundreds, of voices, they complicate the concept "rhetor" (speaker or writer) and provide critics with compelling reasons to extend theories of constitutive rhetoric by attending to the first personae of their texts. Who did an individual woman appear to be when she acted as an antiremoval petition's rhetor? Who were the implied rhetors of antiremoval petitions? The question in various forms resembles one of Wayne Booth's central questions in *The Rhetoric of Fiction:* who is the implied (rather than the actual) author of a text? Just as discourse constitutes a second persona, it also constitutes a first persona, a rhetor. And that person is as discursively constituted and distinct from the individual speaker as a novel's narrator is from its writer. In the gap between speaker and persona, the space exists for new identities to emerge. In that gap, transformation can occur.[57]

What was the first persona of the antiremoval petitions, the persona that argued for women's "right to speak on the subject"? The first persona was a discursively constructed agent empowered to intervene in United States national policy. This authoritative voice appeared natural and appropriate because of the work that got done in the petitions: the establishment of the circumstances as extraordinary, the reformulation of the issue and the assertion of women's right to speak to elements of the broader question, the employment of particularly gendered appeals. As the petition texts were read—in other words, in the performance of the petitions—some women emerged as people who had power in the national political debate. Female political actors were created by the text.[58] They did not precede the text. Rather, they were brought into being by the text, constituted by its rhetoric.

And yet they appeared extrarhetorical, as if they—their position, authority, power, agency—existed before Beecher's circular and their own petitions. This apparent ontological status of a text's rhetor contributed to the efficacy of the petitions, and it contributes to rhetorical discourse generally. Despite the work required for early nineteenth-century women to be constituted as political actors, the petitions portrayed women's antiremoval political activism as natural, as something anyone who understood women and their roles and responsibilities would have expected in the situation. In fiction, implied authors need not appear as prediscursive, "real," extant before the story's first words. Some storytellers appear as crafted as the character central to their stories, and that creativity contributes to the text's success. Conversely, efficacious rhetoric almost always requires its rhetor to appear not just credible but "real," extant before the text and perhaps even before the rhetorical situation. But identifying the authority of these female political actors as discursive—as rhetorically created, rhetorically maintained, and rhetorically negotiated—affirms a lesson upon which, perhaps unconsciously, Catharine Beecher and her fellow activists capitalized: political agency is a consequence of discourse.

Scholars in disciplines as varied as literary criticism, sociology, history, legal studies, political science, gender studies, and rhetorical studies argue for constitutive functions of discourse, and scholars frequently use that argument to establish, discover, or uncover relationships between language and power.[59] The nineteenth-century texts featured here contribute to that project. Because Beecher's "Circular Addressed to Benevolent Ladies of the U. States" and women's antiremoval petitions modeled a process by which texts function constitutively, a rhetorical reading of the collection throws light on the ways language can be used to mitigate power inequities. Such a reading also opens up other texts, not only texts by women, but also texts by other groups typically seen as passive or having little power. Some texts become active—and their first personae become activists—by seeming to give up or give away political agency. Reading women's antiremoval texts as constitutive rhetorics provides us with an opportunity to generalize from a specific historical case innovative means by which excluded or silenced groups can transcend prohibitions so that they may engage discourses of power.

Petitioning the Federal Government against Slavery

Female abolitionist petitioners began using that same rhetorically constructed authority in 1831, when they started petitioning the United States federal government to end slavery.[60] In December 1831, abolitionist and future woman's rights leader Lucretia Mott submitted to Congress an antislavery petition containing the signatures of 2,312 women. In a letter that accompanied the petition, Mott wrote to the petition's congressional recipients:

> In attempting to address a body of men, who, not by hereditary privileges are qualified to act, but who are the chosen representatives of a free people, and whose practice has proved them capable of governing a nation, we deem it unnecessary to apologise; confident that you; [sic] filling these important stations will discern, that nothing less than a deep conviction of the necessity of the measure your petitioners would recommend, could have induced them to appear in this public manner.[61]

Mott did not apologize even though she acknowledged the irregularity of this intervention. Instead, she underscored how the urgency of the issue justified the rhetorical activism of these two thousand women. In the brief petition, signers admitted "that at this juncture our attempt may be considered intrusive, but we approach you unarmed; our only banner is Peace." Echoing Mott, they called the case "momentous." They did not, however, call the case unique, which both reflected the female intervention in the case of Indian removal and also presaged (though almost certainly inadvertently) an argument female abolitionists began to employ a few years later: women had the right to petition regardless of the nature of the case.

That argument became particularly important for two reasons. First, in 1836 the United States House of Representatives instituted a formal "gag" of abolition petitions. Beginning in May 1836 they passed—to the disgust of a vocal but very small minority of legislators—a resolution each session which immediately tabled the receipt of petitions regarding slavery as representatives introduced them to the House. This resolution (transformed into a standing rule of the House from 1840 to 1844) became known as the gag rule, probably because its most adamant opposition came, session after session, from the former United States president, Representative John Quincy Adams, who in 1836 asked the House Speaker in frustration "if he was gagged or not." The gag rule affected female antislavery petitioners more than male petitioners because women could not vote. Petitions offered women the only means by which they could appeal to Congress for redress of grievances, a basic First Amendment right.[62]

At about the same time women lost the right to petition against slavery because of the gag, congressmen attacked female abolitionists very specifically because they were women. In 1836, Angelina Grimké told women that their appeals were better because of their distinctly female perspective: "It will be a great thing if the subject can be introduced into your legislatures in any way, even by *women,* and *they* will be the most likely to introduce it there in the best possible manner, as a matter of *morals* and *religion,* not of expedience or politics."[63] Congressmen found it easier to debate slavery on questions of expedience and politics than morality and religion, and they targeted women's authority to petition so as to avoid responding to their moral and religious appeals. Senator Isaac Hill of New Hampshire explained: "it is to the *esprit de corps* that has been moved of late years in whole religious bodies, directing benevolence away from home to distant objects— it is to the concentration of religious efforts, sometimes to useful and salutary objects, but often to objects altogether impracticable, that we may attribute the present abolition movement."[64] Hill's remarks emphasized the ongoing Whig-Jacksonian debates about the relationship between church and state. Women frequently were imagined as the arm of the church, bringing a topic about which they had authority into the domain of politics, where, according to Jacksonians, it did not belong. Some congressmen thus did what they could to exclude women, including insulting female petition-ers. North Carolina Representative Jesse A. Bynum, for example, "could not conceive a more degrading condition than this House would be placed in, by consuming its time, at an enormous expense to the Treasury, in receiving and listening to the petitions and memorials of old grannies and a parcel of boarding-school misses, in matters of state and legislation. What light could they throw on the subject?"[65] This attitude toward women reinforced the idea that congressmen simply should ignore women's petitions. Virginia Senator Benjamin Watkins Leigh captured profoundly the biggest challenge to the constructed authority women invoked in their petitions:

> One of these [petitions] is from men; the other is signed by women only. That from the men is comparatively moderate; they only intimate their opinion that the holding of slave property, and the transfer of it by sale, as practised in this country, is alike detestable with the African slave trade, which has been declared piracy by law. But the memorial from the softer sex contains as much matter of offence, insult, and vituperation, applicable to all the slaveholding portions of their fellow-citizens, as could possibly have been put into a paper of the same compass. These ladies probably thought (or rather, perhaps, the person who prepared the memorial for them thought) that their sex would give them a title to indulgence. But, in my sense of things, their sex, instead of furnishing a motive for treating them with indulgence, is an aggravation of their fault. They have unsexed themselves.[66]

Leigh's short tirade illustrated the frustration congressmen particularly felt at the seemingly apolitical arguments women employed in their petitions. But claiming that by petitioning women "unsexed themselves," Leigh and his colleagues who argued this same point damaged women's authority to pe-tition against slavery in ways more severe than the complaints against their topics of argument or the insults about their beauty and common sense. By arguing that women unsexed themselves when they petitioned, congress-men attacked the fundamental authority constituted in their petitions.

The first personae of antiremoval petitions, the personae that had agency in the national debate about Indian removal, were discursively constructed. The authority to petition the federal government did not inhere in individual women who signed the petitions: female signers specifically told congress-men that they had no political authority and readily assured congressmen that they had no interest in setting a precedent for women's intrusion into the arena of national politics. In the particular instance of the delivery of their antiremoval petitions to Congress, they achieved authority and status as agents in national politics because of the work their petitions did to construct that provisional authority. Critical to the efficacy of that authority, though, was its appearance as extrarhetorical. Their authority had to appear natural and real, as a natural extension of their roles, responsibilities, even identities. Maurice Charland calls this feature of constitutive rhetoric an "ideological trick," and Barbara Biesecker, following Gayatri Spivak, says it "marks the rhetoricity of the text."[67]

When Senator Leigh told women they "unsexed themselves" by petitioning, he exposed the ideological trick of constitutive rhetorics. He robbed female petitioners of their discursively constructed authority by suggesting that in the act of petitioning they lost access to the qualities that made them distinctly feminine, which was the constructed authority on which they relied to petition. Basically, Leigh and many of his congressional colleagues argued that petitioning was an unnatural act for women. More than arguments contravening their abolitionist arguments or declaring their abolitionists arguments irrelevant to the national political debates about slavery, that "unsexing" argument voided the authority women used to demand their right to speak on the subject.

Women responded by supplementing or even turning away from an overtly gendered authorization to petition. They declared themselves citizens, only briefly (sometimes not at all) mentioning their sex. The Boston Female Anti-Slavery Society addressed this civics lesson to the women of Massachusetts in 1837:

> Who have the power to abolish [slavery] in the District of Columbia, and to prevent its further progress by forbidding the introduction of slaveholding Texas? Our northern senators and representatives, who form a majority of Congress.—Why do they not use this power? Because they are not sure that it would meet the wishes of their constituents. Who are their constituents? YOU: women of the North! You, with your husbands and brethren, are their constituents. Remember that the *representation of our country is based on the numbers of the population, irrespective of sex.*[68]

That same year, the Anti-Slavery Convention of American Women's *Appeal to the Women of the Nominally Free States* declared "the principle that *women are citizens,* and that they have important duties to perform for their country."[69] A few years later, Angelina Grimké Weld (she had married Theodore

Weld by this point) explained: "We urge upon you, women of America, the duty of petitioning our National and State Legislatures, because your voices as citizens of this republic can be heard only through this medium. It is your solemn duty, as citizens of the United States, to throw a saving influence into the councils of our nation. We urge upon you the duty of petitioning—because, as wives and mothers, daughters and sisters, you can feel for the female slaves of the South."[70] Repeatedly in their addresses to women of the United States, abolitionist leaders tried to convince women to do their duty as citizens by petitioning the federal government against slavery. They did not deny the uniqueness of their gender, and they continued to use arguments particularly suited to female intervention. But they much less frequently invoked the uniqueness of the case as a reason to petition. Increasingly, they argued for that right by arguing for their authority as citizens.

In addition to invoking Queen Esther as a model, for example, some abolitionists began invoking the founding fathers as their models. Grimké told Beecher in 1837, "I trust my sisters may always be permitted to *petition* for a redress of grievances. Why not? The right of petition is the only political right that women have: why not let them exercise it whenever they are aggrieved? Our fathers waged a bloody conflict with England, because *they* were taxed without being represented . . . If, then, *we* are taxed without being represented, and governed by laws *we* have no voice in framing, then, surely, we ought to be permitted at least to remonstrate."[71] The founding fathers and Queen Esther made for an interesting combination, and Angelina Grimké was happy to use both. Esther worked for Grimké because she was petitioning on behalf of an oppressed group to save the nation; the founding fathers worked because they suggested an authority by which women could declare citizenship. Gender still provided women with sources of abolitionist argument—the kind of arguments that congressmen and slave owners particularly feared—but citizenship, rather than womanhood, legitimized their participation in the political arena to make those female-gendered arguments. In 1836, the Boston Female Antislavery Society offered yet another civics lesson:

> We are bound to the constant exercise of the only right we ourselves enjoy—the right which our physical weakness renders particularly appropriate—the right of petition. We are bound to try how much it can accomplish in the District of Columbia, or we are as verily guilty touching slavery as our brethren and sisters in the slaveholding States: for Congress

possesses power 'to exercise exclusive legislation over the District of Columbia in all cases whatsoever,' by a provision of the Constitution; and by an *act* of the *First* Congress, the right of petition was secured to us.[72]

Whether female petitioners in the 1830s declared their right to speak because they were women or because they were citizens, they did declare that right. That they shifted the primary justification for their intervention from womanhood in antiremoval and early antislavery petitions to citizenship in later antislavery petitions brings into relief the constructed nature of their authority.

When some United States women began to act rhetorically in the political domain in the 1830s, their authority to speak existed only discursively. The antiremoval and antislavery petition campaigns provide us with a remarkable opportunity to study the ways people typically excluded from a discourse community gained entry, and the combination of these movements spans enough time to let us explore the ways those strategies shift over time and across varying rhetorical situations. These cases together point to a larger argument for political agency as a product of discourse. People eventually take their agency for granted and no longer need to argue for it, so that it seems inherent or essential: they embrace the "ideological trick" of the language we use to make sense of and participate in our worlds. But initially, as this study of women's emergent rhetorical activism illustrates, that agency must be constructed discursively. It is one of language's most powerfully constitutive functions, and it helped secure to United States women in the early 1830s their "right to speak on the subject."

— 3 —

"The Difference between Cruelty to the Slave, and Cruelty to the Indian"

Imagining Native and African Americans as Objects of Advocacy

> The Whites consider the Indians as in some sort their inferiors; but in no respect their slaves.
>
> —ESSAY, *NATIONAL INTELLIGENCER* (15 APRIL 1829)

In 1829, an unnamed writer of an essay published in a Virginia newspaper, the *Richmond Compiler,* attempted to define the complicated relationship between European and Native Americans. In the essay, which was picked up by the *National Intelligencer,* the writer declared, "The Whites consider the Indians as in some sort their inferiors; but in no respect their slaves—as tribes having some right, but not as a *nation,* having complete rights. This state of things often produces very singular relations between them."[1] The commentator used slavery to clarify the relationship between European and Native Americans, a relationship of inferiority, but not one of property. Native Americans did not belong to white Americans as "their slaves"; Native Americans had "a government of their own," and they had rights, even if the nature and extent of those rights were not clear. African Americans, especially slaves, figured as a constitutive other, another group by which European Americans more precisely could define their relationship with Native Americans. Simply, the relationship between Native and European Americans became more understandable when whites eliminated the possibility of the master-slave relationship from the equation. In fact, one thing Native and European Americans had in common was the ownership of Africans and African Americans. The United States recognized the right of Native Americans to own slaves and even protected that right on occasion. When

87

in 1837 a U.S. general had "reason to believe that the interference of un-principled white men, with the negro property of Seminole Indians, if not immediately checked, will prevent [Seminole] emigration, and lead to a re-newal of the war" between the United States and the Seminoles, he used his federal authority to bar all whites from Seminole territories and to compel "all negroes now at this place, the property of citizens of the United States" to report to him so that their owners could collect them.[2]

One might think, then, that a Jacksonian-era European American hierar-chy of these groups would locate African Americans beneath European and Native Americans. Thomas Jefferson wrote about that hierarchy in his 1787 *Notes on the State of Virginia.* Because of its (and Jefferson's) popularity, his position continues to get cited as an authoritative perspective, sometimes *the* authoritave perspective, on white-black relations through the antebellum period.[3] But Henry Clay—a United States representative, Speaker of the House, United States senator from Kentucky, three-time candidate for United States president, candidate for vice president, and in 1836 unanimously elected president of the American Colonization Society (ACS)—offered an-other perspective. His status as a prominent public leader, his roles in the ACS and in the United States Congress, and the consistency of his position over time indicate some popular approval of this Jacksonian-era challenge to Jefferson's view. In an 1829 speech to the Colonization Society of Kentucky, Senator Clay located African Americans between European and Native Americans in a hierarchy of intelligence:

> The European is the most numerous; and, as well from that fact, as from its far greater advance in civilization and in the arts, has the decided as-cendency [*sic*] over the other two, giving the law to them, controlling their condition, and responsible for their fate to the Great Father of all, and to the enlightened world. The next most numerous and most intelligent race, is that which sprung from Africa, the largest portion of which is held in bondage by their brethren, descendants of the European. The aborigines, or Indian race, are the least numerous, and, with the exception of some tribes, have but partially emerged from the state of barbarism in which they were found on the first discovery of America.[4]

Many European Americans in the 1820s and 1830s could imagine with Clay that African Americans possessed greater intellect than Native Americans. Colonizationists believed that African Americans could and would establish a highly successful, economically solvent, and morally uplifted nation in

Africa, a nation with which the United States could enjoy mutually benefi-
cial trade relations. Native Americans, on the other hand, were a dying race
who could be helped but not saved, with whom the United States could
maintain relations but always in a paternalistic way epitomized by Andrew
Jackson's named role in United States–Indian relations, a title used by Native American chiefs and Jackson alike: Great Father.[5] And yet while many
European Americans experienced African Americans as slaves, European
Americans could not imagine Native Americans as slaves. That distinction
must be taken into account in any history of women's political activism in
the United States.

One of the central questions I seek to answer is why a popular, nationally
prominent figure would initiate a women's petition campaign on behalf of
Native Americans and denounce, without compromise or exception, women's
petitioning on behalf of African Americans in 1837. What changed concerning woman's "right to speak on the subject"? Catharine Beecher and most of
the women who petitioned in 1830 and 1831 rejected political power for
women, but they made an exception for the "unique" and "extraordinary"
case of removal. Why did Beecher refuse the exception for slavery? In the
second chapter, I argue that the antiremoval petition campaign emerged
using gender-specific arguments that appealed to cultural norms and ideologies and that these arguments could not be sustained in abolition petitions. In the fifth and sixth chapters, I argue that Beecher and Angelina
Grimké offered competing perceptions of abolition and colonization as well
as democratic processes and participation, and that Beecher's model followed from a tradition of Evangelical democracy simply incapable of supporting Grimké's politics. In this chapter and the next, I argue that the ways
many European Americans imagined Native and African Americans precluded immediate abolition as an appropriate topic of women's advocacy.

Most European Americans imagined Native and African Americans very
differently, and so the logics of antiremoval and procolonization arguments
are consistent even though one argument concludes with appeals to leave the
group within the United States and the other concludes with appeals to remove them. During the 1830s, most northern whites had no way to imagine African Americans in ways that could fuel or sustain abolitionist
rhetoric—rhetoric that would advocate both immediate emancipation and
the integration of African Americans into what European Americans be-

lieved to be their nation—a point that becomes especially clear when we compare the discursive imaginings of African and Native Americans circulating at the time. Instead, colonization—gradual emancipation and immediate emigration for free Africans and their descendants—emerged as a viable alternative to slavery, immediate emancipation, and the troubled relationships between European Americans and "free people of color" (an expression that at this time always meant African Americans, never Native Americans, Mexican-Americans, or other non-European Americans).[6] Colonization was consistent with antiremoval rhetorics, and in fact the antiremoval and colonization movements shared leaders. Since colonizationists believed that slavery was wrong (often calling it evil) but constitutional and also that slavery was less dangerous and less evil than immediate emancipation, they did not and could not sanction political intervention on behalf of the abolitionist cause—whether those methods of political advocacy came from men or from women. This position rendered impossible any sort of petitioning intended to persuade the national legislature to emancipate the nation's two million slaves.

To understand, then, why women such as Catharine Beecher argued against women's antislavery activism, we need to bring questions about woman's rights and woman's sphere into political and ideological frameworks including gender but not exclusively or even dominantly focused on it. Beecher did not categorically deny women's right to petition in a vacuum. The articulation of that position occurred during an incredibly turbulent decade, a decade that included fierce local and national debates about Indian removal and Indian wars, African American slavery, black codes and other racist restrictions on the movement and rights of free blacks in the northern states, colonization of free people of color to Liberia, and immediate emancipation.

Surprisingly, scholarship on this period rarely considers Native and African Americans together, despite their linkages in United States consciousness at the time. In 1826, for instance, James Madison wrote, "Next to the case of the black race within our bosom, that of the red on our borders is the problem most baffling to the policy of our country."[7] In 1829 Clay made his point about the three races sharing much of the North American continent. In an 1830 congressional debate about the constitutionality of slavery, Senator Thomas Hart Benton from Missouri suggested that the Supreme Court soon would decide about the limits of federal law on states' rights, either in a case about the Georgia Cherokees or in a case about slavery.[8] Also in 1830, President Andrew Jackson signed the Indian Removal bill into law, although petitions poured in on the topic between 1829 and 1831. In 1831

Representative Starling Tucker from South Carolina sarcastically taunted his opponents by asking, "What was the difference between cruelty to the slave, and cruelty to the *poor Indians?*"[9] Also in 1831, Lucretia Mott and more than two thousand other women together submitted the first women's anti-slavery petition to Congress.[10] In an 1833 letter to the *National Intelligencer* it was argued that, unfair though it was, the federal government could not side with the Cherokees because slavery had become such a divisive issue: the federal government had to stand with Georgia and other southern states against Native Americans to show solidarity, given the sectional tensions prompted by slavery. "The Slave and Indian questions," the writer explained, "are the only themes of deep interest," and so they could not be considered independently.[11]

Associations between the issues of Indian removal and slavery continued throughout the decade. Many founders of and participants in the American Board of Commissioners for Foreign Missions (the organization that sent Jeremiah Evarts to Washington, D.C., to lobby on behalf of Native Americans) actively participated in debates about slavery, and most of them advocated colonization as the only viable, Christian response. Popular men including Henry Clay, Lyman Beecher, and Senator Theodore Frelinghuysen spoke publicly on behalf of both causes. Reports, editorials, and advertisements about Native Americans and African Americans filled newspapers during these years, often on the same pages. Abolitionists, too, brought the two groups together, as this sarcastic rant about the American Colonization Society from William Lloyd Garrison illustrates: "Give them a slate and pencil, and in fifteen minutes they will clear the continent of every black skin; and, if desired, throw in the Indians to boot."[12]

In the 1830s it would have been impossible to isolate one's opinions about Native Americans from one's opinions about African Americans. Their association in the minds of many European Americans is beautifully reflected by a question for debate posed by the Social Circle of the Female Seminary in Charlestown, Massachusetts, in the following decade: "Which has the white man most injured, the Indian or African?"[13] And yet most of our histories of the era treat Native and African Americans in isolation and consider separately issues of Indian removal, Negro slavery, and challenges facing free people of color. Given the similarities between the issues and the simultaneity of the controversies, how can we think about antislavery activism—including abolition—in a context that omits the Indian removal debates?

Even more surprisingly, colonization appears to have fallen out of our histories of the era. The same dozen or so books and articles on colonization get cited (however briefly) in the many books and essays on abolition written in the past three or four decades, and a scholar who complained in 1997 that colonizationists "have received very limited scholarly treatment" would be no more satisfied now.[14] This dearth of scholarship on colonization, the American Colonization Society, and the free blacks and whites who actively opposed colonization exists despite the availability of extensive records of the ACS and its auxiliaries, transcripts of state and federal legislative debates about the value and possible funding of the ACS, and significant coverage of the issue in newspapers easily accessible on microfilm. These records are available in part because colonization was so popular in the 1820s and 1830s. Speaker of the House Henry Clay, General Andrew Jackson, Supreme Court Justice Bushrod Washington (President George Washington's nephew), and other prominent political and military leaders added legitimacy to the ACS at its founding in 1817; in the 1820s, James Madison, Daniel Webster, Stephen Douglas, and many others added their names as supporters; and in the 1820s and 1830s the ACS often held part of their annual meeting in the Hall of the House of Representatives.[15] In 1819 President James Monroe interpreted a congressional act as authorization to spend one hundred thousand dollars to found an African colony with the assistance of the ACS. Within ten years most European Americans advocated colonization, and by 1831 the *National Intelligencer* reported that "twelve States have, through their Legislatures expressed their belief that the design of the Colonization Society is worthy of national patronage, while others have recently had the subject under consideration. There are sixteen State Colonization Societies, and more than two hundred other auxiliaries, numbering among their officers many of the first men of the nation."[16] During the 1830s state legislatures in states including Connecticut, Delaware, Indiana, Kentucky, Massachusetts, New Jersey, and Pennsylvania passed resolutions advocating colonization (many specifically praising the ACS); states including Maryland, Tennessee, and Virginia appropriated funds to colonize free blacks or their states' recently manumitted slaves.[17]

In his study on gender in antebellum reform, Bruce Dorsey calls colonizationists "the abolitionists' greatest rivals for northern whites' sympathies."[18] Nationally, colonizationists played an even larger role than they did in the northern states. They opened discussions and then provided an option for southerners who wanted either to emancipate their slaves or to advocate a gradual end to slavery; they offered northerners a way to hope for an eventual nationwide end to slavery without dissolving the Union; they enabled Christian evangelicals to coalesce around a huge international project, the conversion of Africa; and for several years they mitigated the intense anger southerners directed at northerners once the Garrisonian abolitionists became a force on the national scene. Because of its ability to accommodate wide-ranging views, in the 1820s and the early 1830s the ACS attracted people across the political spectrum, including slave owners and political rivals such as Andrew Jackson and Henry Clay as well as future abolitionists such as Theodore Weld and even William Lloyd Garrison, who did not renounce colonization until 1832.[19] But despite colonization's extensive popularity, most histories of the period seem to suggest that there were just two sides to the story in the antebellum United States: slavery and antislavery.

Perhaps it should come as no surprise given this general absence of colonization from historical work on the early nation that scholarship on women's activism often fails to situate antislavery work in the context of colonization and Indian removal. But if we are to understand more completely the process by which women came to acquire political rights and power in the United States, we cannot maintain these dissociations. In this chapter and the next, I argue that the ways antiremovalists imagined African Americans made it impossible for them to petition the federal government for immediate emancipation. Colonization offered a significantly more attractive option for these women and men.

Too often, we limit our study of advocacy to the advocates, and implicit in these two chapters is a methodological argument: we need to include the objects of advocacy in our scholarship. Those objects, even if they are discursive constructs—especially if they are discursive constructs, as I argue the objects of northern antiremoval and antislavery advocacy were—affect advocacy.[20] Advocates have agency, but they are constrained in that agency by, among other things, the available ways to imagine the people they believe they are helping.[21] What imaginings circulated in various discourse communities? What images, relationships, identifications would have been possible for people reading—or talking with people who were reading—popular novels such as Hope Leslie or The Pioneers or daily newspapers such as the National Intelligencer or religious organs such as the Christian Advocate and Journal and Zion's Herald? If we are going to make a serious attempt to understand women's national political activism on behalf of Native Americans or African Americans, and especially if we seek to understand the rhetorical connections between those campaigns, we need to consider the ways Native Americans and African Americans may have appeared in the lives of these women and the men with whom they lived.

By "imaginings" I mean, simply, portrayals that people imagine, write, speak, or believe to be true, representative, or descriptive, especially of other people. These images are not "real" in the sense that they do not exist materially, nor do they objectively reflect material reality—though they often achieve power because people assume that they are real or that they reflect reality. But these images are "real" in the sense that they have consequences: they matter, and they matter materially. Elaine Scarry opens an essay called "The Difficulty of Imagining Other People" with the premise that "the way we act toward 'others' is shaped by the way we imagine them." In an essay called "Imagining the Public Sphere," Robert Asen studies "images of current and potential public assistance recipients" in late twentieth-century United States welfare debates and uses evidence from these debates to "argue that imagining affects participants in public discussions differently, often disadvantaging socially and historically marginalized people and groups while tacitly aiding the appeals of others." And in *Imagined Communities*, Benedict Anderson says matter-of-factly, "All communities larger than primordial villages of face-to-face contact (and perhaps even these) are imagined. Communities are to be distinguished, not by their falsity/genuineness, but by the style in which they are imagined."[22]

The constitutive power of "images" (Asen) or "imaginings" (Scarry) frequently rises to the degree that the images or imaginings appear true to the people doing the imagining. But the products of imagining are always fictions. To say that imaginings are fictitious is not to say that they are false. Rather, it is to claim that they are made up, artificial, constructed—that they are discursive (and I include visual as well as linguistic texts in "discursive").[23] They are textual descriptions or interpretations or even creations of objects, not the material manifestations of those objects. Yet their power declines to the degree that their textuality is unmasked.

In the 1820s and 1830s, discursive imaginings of Native Americans and African Americans would have been very important to northern white women as they considered advocacy on behalf of these "other" races. By the 1820s, few Native Americans remained among whites in the northern states. Also by the 1820s, all of the northern states had enacted gradual emancipation, but even when slavery was legal in the north, William Lee Miller explains, the population of slaves ranged from 7.5 percent to 14 percent of the general population. At the time of the Beecher-Grimké exchange in 1837, Kwando M. Kinshasa reports that, "the free black population stood at 137,000; at the same time there were more than 2 million slaves in the United

States. Less than one percent of the slave population lived in New England and the Middle Atlantic states, and most of those lived in New Jersey. Few northern whites had regular contact with African Americans outside the major cities, and even in those cities races were frequently segregated. Furthermore, when there was interaction, it was limited."[24] By the time Angelina Grimké asked women to support slaves, there were few slaves in northern communities and slavery as a practice had not been legal for at least a decade. When Beecher asked women to support Native Americans, there were no large, stable communities of Native Americans in the north for comparison. Women were petitioning on behalf of Indians they did not know and with whom they had no experience. These women relied predominantly on discursive imaginings to engender sympathy as well as identification with the objects of their advocacy. To understand women's political advocacy during removal, colonization, and abolition, we have to consider what imaginings were available to white northern women of privilege concerning Native Americans and African Americans, especially enslaved African Americans.

Three discursive sites recorded and also shaped these imaginings: popular literature, represented in this study by six of the best-selling books of the period; mainstream news, represented by a decade's issues of the influential daily newspaper the *National Intelligencer;* and religious news, as illustrated in a decade's issues of the widely circulated Methodist newspaper the *Christian Advocate and Journal and Zion's Herald,* the organ that printed in full Catharine Beecher's antiremoval "Circular Addressed to Benevolent Ladies of the U. States" in 1829.[25] In its vehement arguments against these imaginings, abolitionist discourse—including two influential texts published early in the 1830s, William Lloyd Garrison's *Thoughts on African Colonization* (1832) and Lydia Maria Child's *An Appeal in Favor of That Class of Americans Called Africans* (1833), and one from later in the decade, *American Slavery As It Is* (1839), compiled by Theodore Weld and Angelina and Sarah Grimké—illustrates how much power imaginings had in shaping public opinion and public activism. A short history of colonization and immediate abolition provides a historical context with which to read the comparative study that forms the bulk of these two chapters and the heart of their argument: women who intervened in the Indian removal debates in 1829 to 1831 likely avoided the women's antislavery petition campaign not because of a conservative stance on gender but rather because the ways that they imagined African Americans, particularly in contrast to Native Americans, led them to embrace removal of African Americans rather than abolitionism as a benevolent solution to the challenges free and enslaved people of color posed to the nation.

The Early Decades of African Colonization

On January 31, 1820, the ship *Elizabeth* departed from New York, carrying to Africa tools, arms, eighty-six people, and a year's worth of provisions to support three times that number of people. The U.S. government supplied and funded this excursion by using money that Congress allocated to President James Monroe. Monroe had discretionary use of these funds, and they were given to him so that he might establish some means by which the United States could provide for—or, more accurately, deal with—"recaptured" Africans, Africans kidnapped to be sold into slavery but rescued before the sale was made.[26] Congress did not authorize Monroe to establish a colony for free people of color, so he sent a ship full of laborers to prepare a place that would facilitate the return of rescued Africans to their homes. But of the eighty-six people on board, two thirds were women and children—not laborers. And no one planned for any of the passengers to return "home" to the United States after they completed their work. Officers of the American Colonization Society appreciated the *Elizabeth*'s mission for what it was: an attempt at United States colonization of Africa, and one funded by the federal government at that.[27]

The *Elizabeth*'s 1820 passage occurred three years after the founding of the American Colonization Society in early January 1817. But colonization as an idea had been circulating for years. At the end of the seventeenth century, Virginia restricted emancipation within its borders: freed slaves had to be removed "beyond the limits of the colony within six months from the date of manumission."[28] In the late eighteenth century, several plans for colonization were put forward by coalitions of African Americans, including the African Union Society of Newport, Rhode Island; the Masonic African Lodge of Boston; and a group of slaves who petitioned the Massachusetts state legislature for resources so they could establish a colony in Africa.[29] Thomas Jefferson researched the idea as president in 1801 but deemed it untenable because of the financial troubles gripping the British colony of Sierra Leone.[30] Ten years later, Paul Cuffe, who was of African American and Native American descent, arranged to transport free African Americans from the United States to Sierra Leone. Cuffe succumbed to illness in 1817, managing only one trip to Sierra Leone with thirty-eight colonists in 1816.[31] But the American Colonization Society, which formed months before Cuffe died, used his plans as evidence of black support for the establishment of an African American colony in Africa.

Yet almost all free people of color aggressively resisted the ACS. The founders of the ACS were white men chiefly concerned with seemingly "benevolent" ways to secure a white nation. Virginia state legislator Charles Fenton Mercer envisioned colonization as a solution to what he predicted would be a permanent lower class comprising free blacks marked by their color and the prejudice of whites. Worried that such a class would endanger the economy and safety of the region and the nation, Mercer proposed removal as the only solution.[32] If colonization led to gradual emancipation, even better: like many colonizationists, Mercer viewed slavery as a great evil but thought immediate emancipation even more problematic. So Mercer, like Robert Finley, another force in the establishment of the ACS, offered colonization primarily as a means to separate the races by removing free blacks from the United States, not as a means to end slavery.

At around the same time that Mercer became enamored with colonization, Reverend Robert Finley embraced the cause as a benevolent means by which the quality of life for Africans and their descendants currently residing in the United States could be improved. Because the Presbyterian minister imagined that the federal government would embrace and therefore fund his scheme, Finley traveled to Washington, D.C., in December 1816 to promote it. With some well-established Washingtonians as friends and supporters and the popular *National Intelligencer* willing to advertise the cause, Finley called a meeting. The twenty or so men who responded included men of great wealth and political and religious stature. Henry Clay, then Speaker of the House, presided. The speeches made that evening articulated colonization as a means to improve the United States by removing a portion of the population that attendees believed degraded and even threatened American ways of life (including the ongoing practice of slavery) and that exposed cracks in the principles upon which the nation was founded. Henry Clay made it clear that the organization had to steer clear of slavery, working only with blacks already free. In early 1817, the managers of the ACS began advertising, researching, and seeking federal support for their plans.[33]

The 1819 Slave Trade Act, authored by Charles Fenton Mercer, gave President Monroe one hundred thousand dollars to use at his discretion to enforce the abolition of the international slave trade. With some assistance from the ACS, Monroe found a way to use the funds to establish an African colony for free people of color in Liberia (a point that explains why the capital of Liberia is called Monrovia). As the ACS and its auxiliaries grew, funded by individual and also state donations, some slave owners included the granting of freedom and money to support emigration in their wills, acts which the ACS enthusiastically reported.[34] Although the ACS repeatedly made clear their position on ending slavery—it had to be accomplished by slave-state legislatures and slave owners (according to ACS doctrine, victims of an institution they did not create), and any sort of immediacy would be dangerous—they also acknowledged slavery to be evil and so took pride in manumissions linked to their work.

According to the ACS, colonization was a program designed to separate the races and to provide increased opportunities for Africans and their descendants to thrive—and it also was a means to Christianize and civilize the African continent. This benefit especially attracted northerners who worried that the largely southern ACS advocated colonization as a means by which to protect, not end, the institution of slavery. Most reports from the colony mentioned the morality and piety of the colonists, and some letters even suggested that in Africa "the Sabbath is more strictly observed than I ever saw it in the United States."[35] Native Africans, too, were learning about and being converted to Christianity and schooled in things American, which fueled increasingly ambitious plans for converting that part of the world. The ACS-appointed governor of Liberia enthusiastically reported in 1831, "Our influence over the native tribes in our vicinity is rapidly extending . . . [A]s they expressed it, 'they want to be made Americans,' and to be allowed to call themselves 'Americans,' is, I can assure you, deemed no small privilege."[36]

Few people disputed the aims and activities of the American Colonization Society in its first dozen years. Its principles had broad appeal for European Americans. Advocates of slavery envisioned colonization as a means by which the south could protect its human property from the bad influence of freed slaves. Opponents of slavery saw colonization as a means by which the United States gradually could be rid of the institution while preventing the perpetuation of a permanent underclass, class warfare, and vengeful uprisings of freed slaves. Christians embraced its Evangelical program. And most European Americans appreciated its goal to separate the races by removing blacks from the United States. But this broad appeal could not be sustained.

Free blacks spoke against the ACS from the time of its founding, and their opposition grew both louder and less easy to ignore when free people of color refused to be colonized. In the years 1820 to 1833, two-thirds of the people transported to Africa by the ACS were manumitted on the condition of their removal; only one-third were free African Americans who chose to emigrate.[37] Leaders and advocates of the ACS could not understand the resistance of free people of color to return to "the land of their ancestors." They reacted with "astonishment . . . that so much indifference should prevail among them on this subject, in which their real prosperity, happiness, and freedom, are so deeply concerned."[38] Colonizationists argued that removing Africans and their descendants from the United States benefited the colonists as much as the European Americans who got to stay, since blacks never truly could be free in a society in which the dominant group predominantly imagined them as inherently inferior: "experience proves that there is no condition of humanity, which begets more wretchedness, more vice, more premature disease and mortality, than that of emancipated negroes who remain without political rights, in the midst of a free white population."[39] People including James Madison and Lyman Beecher knew that European American prejudice motivated the social, political, and economic inequities confronting blacks, but they reasoned that the prejudices ran so deep that colonization was the only practical solution.[40]

So colonizationists (including many slave owners and politicians from slave states) who wanted to establish a nationally monochromatic population believed that their program also benefited blacks, and some even identified colonization as primarily a benevolent act: colonization returned to Africa free blacks who had been transported violently to the United States, and colonization gave people of color an opportunity to experience equality in their communities. But free blacks who opposed colonization argued that the United States, not Africa, was their homeland. They, their fathers, and often their fathers' fathers had been born in the United States, so a journey to Liberia hardly was repatriation, and exile, no matter how benevolent, was hardly an adequate solution to white prejudice. (The irony of patriarchal lineage as the basis for this argument must be noted.) David Walker summarized this position in his aggressively critical *Appeal . . . to the Coloured Citizens of the World* (1829): "What our brethren could have been thinking about, who have left their native land and home and gone away to Africa, I am unable to say. This country is as much ours as it is the whites, whether they will admit it now or not, they will see and believe it by and by. They tell us about prejudice—what have we to do with it? Their prejudices will be obliged to fall like lightening to the ground, in succeeding generations."[41] Walker's *Appeal*, a harsh critique of slavery and a stern disavowal of colonization, simultaneously scared many southern slaveholders and persuaded some northern colonizationists actively to embrace immediate abolitionism.[42] Both of those consequences proved troubling for the American Colonization Society. But one part of Walker's influence in the north especially caused the ACS tremendous anxiety: the inspirational effect it had on the founder of the *Liberator* and the relentless advocate of immediate emancipation, William Lloyd Garrison.[43]

Garrison was one of several supporters of colonization who turned instead to immediate abolitionism in the 1830s. Some defections hurt because of the legitimacy they took away from the ACS, like the 1834 defection of James G. Birney, an agent of the ACS's national organization and a vice president of his state's auxiliary colonization society. Others hurt because of the financial resources that defectors took from colonization and put toward abolition, as when the wealthy Arthur Tappan and Gerrit Smith, who donated and raised thousands of dollars for the ACS, switched allegiances to American Anti-Slavery Society (AAS). Still other defections hurt because of the important roles the defectors played in the rhetorical leadership of the abolition movement. One example of such a convert is Theodore Weld. A second is Garrison.

Ironically the *National Intelligencer,* which more than once in the 1830s would refer to Garrison as a fanatic and lump all of the troublesome abolition activists under the heading "Garrisonians," advertised Garrison's groundbreaking antislavery newspaper before the *Liberator*'s first issue rolled off the press. As a courtesy to a new publisher, the *National Intelligencer* printed an announcement in which Garrison laid out his beliefs, including deep commitments against slavery, drink, and war. Garrison promised to use moral and religious precepts as standards of judgment in society and politics and to include in the *Liberator* some literature as well as national and international news. He disavowed Andrew Jackson and his administration, declaring his "dignified support" for Henry Clay. The only hint of his radical disposition occurred when Garrison declared "that he who persists in doing injustice aggravates it, and takes upon himself all the guilt of his predecessors." But other than that sentence incriminating contemporary white participants in the peculiar institution of slavery as equally guilty with those who established it, his pronouncements probably met with cautious approval: peace, temperance, Christ, Henry Clay, and even an end to slavery (assuming it was gradual). Easy as it is for us to see it now, it would have been very difficult for the editors of the *National Intelligencer,* Joseph Gales Jr. and William Winston Seaton, to predict how much trouble Garrison would generate for one of their favorite causes, colonization, in the years to come.[44]

The history of the United States abolition movement and Garrison's role in that movement are well documented elsewhere.[45] Important to explain here is the threat that colonizationists believed immediate emancipationists posed to their program. A complaint in the *National Intelligencer* about misguided and misplaced generosity demonstrates the magnitude of one problem: loss of financial support. In May 1835 the *Commercial Advertiser* (New York) reported that "the enormous sum of *fourteen thousand dollars* was subscribed" to the American Anti-Slavery Society. This money "is to be paid out to circulate incendiary publications, papers filled with bitterness, and wrath, and strife, and to support a swarm of heartless agents to prowl about the Northern States, endeavoring to kindle the angry passions of the People against their brethren at the South" instead of being used to free slaves. "Yes, FIVE HUNDRED AND SIXTY SLAVES might be emancipated with the aid of this money; whereas it is destined to be worse than wasted," rebuked the writer.[46] Another problem was that abolitionists made available public spaces for black resistance to and denunciation of colonization, including space in newspapers such as Garrison's *Liberator.* The biggest problem "Garrisonians" caused the ACS, though, highlights for us the pervasiveness of antislavery rhetoric in the 1830s. Over and over ACS advocates bemoaned the trouble immediatists created for their cause in the southern states. They organized their complaints primarily around three issues: abolitionists scared slave owners into restricting the abilities of missionaries to do their jobs among southern slaves; they dramatically damaged the credibility of colonization in the south because southern slave owners associated all northerners as one group, a group that appeared to them more and more fanatical every day; and abolitionists threatened the very foundation of the Union by asking Congress to intervene in an issue colonizationists believed to be constitutionally designated as one belonging to the states.[47]

The American Colonization Society worked hard to dissociate from and denounce as harmful immediate abolitionists, as it simultaneously urged individuals to abandon that cause and return to colonization. The group also persistently attempted to convince free blacks to embrace colonization. But the inability of the ACS to appeal to these constituencies—free blacks and abolitionists, many of whom had defected from colonization's front lines—dramatically decreased the effectiveness of the organization by the middle of the 1830s.

A third group for whom the ACS lost its appeal by the early 1830s was slave owners in the deep south. These men began to believe that colonization was creeping toward an end of slavery without the permission of the southern states or of slave owners. This belief exposed a widening divide between southerners in the upper and deep south. Men from the upper south—many of them slave owners—composed most of the ACS, and in fact the ACS had a harder time in the north because northerners suspected the motivation of its southern leadership.[48] But these southerners from the upper south—men like Virginia's Charles Fenton Mercer—saw colonization as a means to enable gradual emancipation and the transformation of the southern economy from agriculture to industry. Yet slave owners in the deep south earned their living through agriculture. Many of them initially bought into colonization as a way to protect slavery by removing free blacks from their neighborhoods. As the ACS's emancipatory goals increasingly became clear, support from the nation's deep south withered and in some cases transformed into heated critique.

By the middle of the 1830s, the American Colonization Society had lost much of its steam. Advocates divorced themselves from the cause, worried either that it was too radical or not radical enough. But a core group of antislavery activists stayed with the program in the northern states. They abhorred slavery but could not embrace immediate emancipation. Much of their commitment to colonization had to do with the ways they imagined the objects of their advocacy in the 1820s and the 1830s.

Literary Imaginings of Native and African Americans

Imagine, then, possible interpretations of a scene from *The Pioneers* (1823), the first of James Fenimore Cooper's best-selling *The Leatherstocking Tales.* Sheriff Richard Jones, a main character in the novel, returned from several days' duty to a remarkably quiet homestead. He called out simultaneously to his black slave, Agamemnon, and to the family dog, Brave:

> "Holla! Aggy!" shouted the Sheriff, when he reached the door; "where are you, you black dog? will you keep me here in the dark all night?—Holla! Aggy! Brave! Brave! hoy, hoy—where have you got to, Brave? Off his watch! Every body is asleep but myself! poor I must keep my eyes open,

that others may sleep in safety. Brave! Brave! Well, I will say this for the dog, lazy as he's grown, that it is the first time I ever knew him let any one come to the door after dark, without having a smell to know whether it was an honest man or not. He could tell by his nose, almost as well as I could myself by looking at them. Holla! you Agamemnon! where are you? Oh! here comes the dog at last."

By this time the Sheriff had dismounted, and observed a form, which he supposed to be that of Brave, slowly creeping out of the kennel; when, to his astonishment, it reared itself on two legs, instead of four, and he was able to distinguish, by the star-light, the curly head and dark visage of the negro.

An earlier scene in the novel prepared readers for this ambiguous scene in which Aggy morphs from dog to slave. On Christmas morning, Jones called out to his slave, "Holla! Aggy!—merry Christmas, Aggy—I say, do you hear me, you black dog!" If Aggy already appeared as a "black dog" to Jones, were readers to understand the confusing scene that came later as a pun on the synonymy between Aggy and Brave? What was the relationship between Aggy and Brave, slave and dog? More to the point, how did Cooper's Jones imagine Aggy relative to Brave?[49]

There is only one other named African American in Cooper's three tremendously popular 1820s novels in *The Leatherstocking Tales,* and he, too, appears in *The Pioneers.* Abraham "Brom" Freeborn was "a free black" who owned a bird farm and sold chances to shoot the birds for sport (189). During a moment of excitement, Brom "danced, until his legs were wearied with motion, in the snow; and, in short, he exhibited all that violence of joy that characterizes the mirth of a thoughtless negro." Although his shouts sounded "like the outcries of a tribe of Indians," Brom demonstrated none of the nobility, intelligence, nor even Christianity of several Native Americans encountered in Cooper's popular novel (197–198). Only once in Cooper's three 1820s novels did readers see someone who was black by nineteenth-century conventions (though she appeared and passed for white) and who resembled admirable Indians, someone of African descent who exhibited characteristics worthy of imitation or identification: *The Last of the Mohicans*'s Cora Munro, a character born not in the United States but in the West Indies.

Native Americans in 1820s Popular Literature

In the 1820s, literary critics celebrated the emergence of United States literature, fiction that distinguished itself from literatures of European countries, especially England. Critics called for nationalist literature that marked the United States as unique, and Indians quickly became a key marker of American literature.[50] The most celebrated novels of the 1820s featured Indians: Lydia Maria Child's *Hobomok, A Tale of Early Times* (1824); Catharine Maria Sedgwick's *Hope Leslie; or, Early Times in the Massachusetts* (1827); and James Fenimore Cooper's *The Pioneers, or the Sources of the Susquehanna; A Descriptive Tale* (1823), *The Last of the Mohicans; A Narrative of 1757* (1826), and *The Prairie; A Tale* (1827), three of the five novels that came to be known as *The Leatherstocking Tales.* In the middle of the 1820s, the captivity narrative returned to best-seller status as well with the publication of *A Narrative of the Life of Mrs. Mary Jemison* (1824). The extraordinary popularity of these books propelled them to become part of the cultural conversations in literate communities.[51]

These texts have something in common besides their popularity. Five are historical novels, and one is a historical narrative. They aim to convey plausibility and even sometimes fact. Unsurprisingly, the historical narrative, *A Narrative of the Life of Mrs. Mary Jemison,* purported to be "an accurate account" of Mary Jemison's life. In his preface, author James E. Seaver explained that "strict fidelity has been observed in the composition" and that errors entered into the narrative only as a result of the subject's memory— excusable, given her age—not neglect nor an attempt to exaggerate or dull the events on Seaver's part.[52] Towards the end of his introduction, as he prepared to lead readers into Jemison's life, Seaver employed a useful strategy for projecting realism: enargia, the rhetorical figure that denotes vivid descriptions of visual images. Seaver described in great detail Jemison's clothing, stockings, moccasins, gown, Indian blanket, and head covering. Readers also got a detailed description of Jemison's house, barn, and property (56–57). Enargia worked in the *Narrative* as it so often does. Mary Jemison appeared as more than words on a page. She appeared as a woman, interestingly dressed and living in a house that resembled one her readers probably had seen before. In fact, if they were passing through the town of Castile in New York's Genesee County, they might even have spotted her walking between her house and her barn.

In a historical narrative, vivid descriptions authenticate the story. In historical fictions, they create an aura of authenticity or at least plausibility. And Child, Sedgwick, and Cooper used them to that end. But the historical fictions of these three writers moved beyond vivid descriptions. They imported historical facts—even people—into their fiction. Catharine Maria

Sedgwick famously revised the Pequod War through her Indian heroine Magawisca's eyes, but Sedgwick used histories to tell the tale. In the novel, Massachusetts's first governor, John Winthrop, interacted a great deal with Sedgwick's characters Hope and her father, and in fact the "real" Governor Winthrop's journals, compiled as *The History of New England, 1630–1649*, were an important source of historical information for the story.[53] As with *Hope Leslie*, Lydia Maria Child's *Hobomok* included events and people who were a part of the nation's history. At one point, for example, the writer's ancestors traveled from England to New England with Francis Higginson and a Mr. Skelton, men who were mentioned by "Puritan chroniclers" including Thomas Morton and William Bradford; in the novel, Governor Bradford visited Salem from Plymouth to honor Higginson and Skelton.[54]

James Fenimore Cooper's *The Leatherstocking Tales* used landscape and history rather than "real" people to communicate plausibility. Cooper's novels relied on his audience's finding his characters and their stories recognizable.[55] To aid in that identification, Cooper provided the sorts of fictional details Child, Sedgwick, and Seaver provided to varying degrees as historical fact. Cooper opened the third Leatherstocking novel, *The Prairie*, by discussing the Louisiana Purchase. Particularly interesting is his use of first-person pronouns, which seduced readers into wanting to believe the story as real:

> Much was said and written, at the time, concerning the policy of adding the vast regions of Louisiana, to the already immense, and but half-tenanted territories of the United-States . . . It soon became apparent, to the meanest capacity, that, while nature had placed a barrier of desert to the extension of our population in the west, the measure had made us the masters of a belt of fertile country, which, in the revolutions of the day, might have become the property of a rival nation. It gave us the sole command of the great thoroughfare of the interior, and placed the countless tribes of savages, who lay along our borders, entirely within our controul.[56]

Cooper spent the next few pages describing the settlement of these "vast regions," narrowing his focus until he set his sights on particular wagons moving across the prairie (*Prairie*, 889). Those wagons, of course, held some of the novel's main characters.

These six books have at least two things in common: cultural presence, as illustrated by their immense popularity and best-seller status, and a "real" sense of plausibility. The books have a remarkable third thing in common:

many opportunities for their readers to witness strong, admirable, noble Native Americans and no opportunities—none—to imagine African Americans in those ways.

A good deal has been written about these texts and these writers in various combinations, and my object is neither to review that criticism nor to present my own reading of these novels. I seek in these novels images of Native Americans and African Americans. Elaine Scarry suggests that "there is a place—namely, the place of great literature—where the ability to imagine others is very strong."[57] Scarry qualifies the power of literature to influence people's behaviors towards others, especially strangers, as insufficient on its own, and I agree with her. But literature requires imagining as fundamental feature of its engagement. The relative discrepancy, then, between Native Americans and African Americans in United States literature at a key sociopolitical moment in United States history helps explain why many northern whites considered political advocacy for the former group but not the latter to be acceptable womanly behavior.[58] None of these texts were optimistic about the future of Native American nations, and none of them protested loudly against the accepted view of Indians as both savage and vanishing. But each of these texts at least entertained the possibility that Native Americans (in small and steadily decreasing numbers) could join European American communities without threatening the European American way of life. Nowhere was the same case made for African Americans.

First, these popular books included exemplary Native American characters. James Fenimore Cooper's character Uncas earned so much respect from white characters in *The Last of the Mohicans* that a central white character in *The Prairie,* Duncan Uncas Middleton, was named after him. At various points throughout *Mohicans,* Uncas "den[ied] his habits, we had almost said his nature" by turning away from the chance to scalp his victims; assisted sisters Cora and Alice Munro in "an utter innovation on the Indian customs, which forbid their warriors to descend to any menial employment, especially in favour of their women"; found the trail of the sisters and their cocaptive, David Gamut, when others had lost the way; and several times acted to save Alice and especially Cora despite grave danger, his final courageous act ending in his death. At one point in the tale, after a battle in which Uncas, his father Chingachgook, and Natty Bumppo rescued Duncan Heyward, David, Alice, and Cora from a warring group of Indians, "Uncas stood, fresh and blood-stained from the combat, a calm, and apparently, an unmoved looker-on, it is true, but with eyes that had already lost their fierceness, and were beaming with a sympathy, that elevated him far above the intelligence, and advanced him probably centuries before the practices of his nation." Even as it raised Uncas well above his compatriots, this interpretative picture of Uncas expressed an evolutionary possibility for Indians on a scale that Cooper and his audience assumed to be universal.[59]

Magawisca played a similar role in Sedgwick's *Hope Leslie.* Magawisca entered the Fletcher family as a fifteen-year-old servant. She, her brother, and her mother—the family of an Pequod Indian chief—had been captured in an attack on her tribe, and Governor Winthrop sent Magawisca and her brother Oneco to assist the Fletchers with their new charges, Hope Leslie and her sister Faith, daughters of Mr. Fletcher's dead cousin Alice. Magawisca grew close to the Fletchers' son Everell and in fact saved his life. Mononotto, Magawisca's father, captured Everell and Faith as he rescued his daughter and son. Mononotto planned to sacrifice Everell, and at the moment the weapon was to strike, Magawisca, "springing from the precipitous side of the rock, screamed—'Forbear!' and interposed her arm." Magawisca lost her arm and Everell escaped (93). They met again several years later when Magawisca brought word to Hope of her sister Faith, who had integrated into the tribe and married Oneco. Although this brief summary necessarily ignores subplots and oversimplifies the story, basically Magawisca was accused falsely of plotting against whites in Boston and was arrested and jailed. Everell and Hope Leslie facilitated Magawisca's escape, and in the process admitted their love for each other. The novel ends with Magawisca's safe return to her father and Everell and Hope's marriage.

From the moment of her introduction Magawisca was marked as exemplary. When Mr. Fletcher told his wife about the addition to their household and she doubted the assistance an Indian servant could provide, he remarked, "These Indians possess the same faculties that we do. The girl, just arrived, our friend [Governor Winthrop] writes me, hath rare gifts of mind—such as few of God's creatures are endowed with" (21). Magawisca's sincerity, integrity, wisdom, and heroism were on display throughout the novel. In the end, Hope and Everell watched the boat that safely carried Magawisca away: "for a few moments, every feeling for themselves was lost in the grief of parting for ever from the admirable being, who seemed to her enthusiastic young friends, one of the noblest of the works of God—a bright witness to the beauty, the independence, and the immortality of virtue" (334). From her introduction until her departure, Magawisca proved the possibility of exemplarity among Indians—and even among whites.

Hobomok, the title character of Lydia Maria Child's 1824 novel, sacrificed for his love, Mary Conant, as Sedgwick's Magawisca sacrificed for

Everell, and Hobomok rose above his compatriots like Cooper's Uncas. Briefly, in Child's novel Hobomok served as an intermediary between his tribe and the whites who lived in Plymouth. He spent time with the Conant family and fell in love with Mary Conant. When Mary's mother died of illness, Mary's lover seemingly died in a shipwreck, and Mary's father emotionally alienated his beloved daughter, the young, white protagonist decided the only chance she had to be loved was to marry Hobomok. Three years into the marriage, Mary's white lover, Charles Brown, returned, released from a post-shipwreck captivity. The first person he met was Hobomok, who decided to forgo Mary and their son rather than kill Charles or otherwise come between the white lovers. Hobomok divorced Mary and left town that evening. Sad about Hobomok's departure but happy to be reunited, Mary and Charles married several weeks later. Charles adopted the junior Hobomok as his own son, Mary and her father were reconciled, and they lived happily ever after.

The sacrifice Hobomok made for his wife is just one of many instances for which the Indian was praised, his deeds illustrating a moral, caring, honorable character. Mary and her mother, for instance, "were indeed well protected" when Mr. Conant was away, "for Hobomok, the moment his errands were hastily delivered, had returned to guard them with the quick eye of love, and the ready arm of hatred" (41). (Notice that his hatred morphed into an admirable emotion when employed in the service of protecting white women from danger.) In an exchange between Mr. and Mrs. Conant and the newly arrived Lady Arabella Johnson, Hobomok more closely resembled Uncas than Magawisca but was admired nonetheless:

> "I have heard great reports about Hobomok," said [Lady Arabella], turning to Mr. Conant. "They say he is a clever Indian and comely withal, and that he hath been of great use to our Plymouth brethren."
>
> "You must ask Mary about him," replied Mrs. Conant, smiling. "She loves to hear his long stories about the Iroquois, which he learned of one of their chiefs who came hither many years ago; and his account of the ancestors of some neighboring tribe, who, as he saith, were dropped by an eagle on an island to the south."
>
> "It's little I mind his heathenish stories," rejoined her husband; "but I have sat by the hour together, and gazed on his well fared face, till the tears have come into mine eyes, that the Lord should have raised us up so good a friend among the savages." (98)

Lady Arabella's inquiry indicates the esteem in which the colony held Hobomok and also his importance to them, and the reactions of Mr. and Mrs. Conant indicates the varied ways he had endeared himself to the white community. Given Mr. Conant's tendency toward criticism, too, rather than praise, his words particularly illuminate Hobomok's worth. Ironically, or perhaps prophetically, until Mary married Hobomok, Mr. Conant spoke more highly of the him than of Charles.

Admirable characters such as Hobomok and Magawisca enriched the lives of European Americans. Native Americans also had things to teach European Americans. Hobomok reminded white settlers that they should put their trust in their God as they worried about warring Indian nations. Chastised, Mr. Conant said to other male heads of households at the community meeting, "It is a shame on us that an Indian must teach us who is 'our shield and our buckler'" (37). When Hobomok told Charles he would leave Mary and his son so that Mary and Charles could reunite, Charles was amazed at the sacrifice. Charles's friend John Collier was amazed that Charles came upon Hobomok in the forest and lived to talk about it. Charles replied to his friend, "I have a story to tell of that savage, which might make the best of us blush at our inferiority, Christians as we are" (145). For most of the novel, Charles and Mary's father disagreed. On the possibility of learning from the behavior of an Indian, however, their beliefs coincided.

Child's characters suggest that whites could learn from the behavior of a particularly admirable Indian. Cooper's narrator and characters learned lessons in the customs of different tribes. Natty Bumppo, the central character in all five Leatherstocking novels, had been "exposed to the customs of barbarity, and yet perhaps more improved than injured by the association" (*Last of the Mohicans*, 475). Time after time, lessons Natty learned from Indians, including patience, courtesy, and attentiveness, saved the day. At other times, Cooper's narrators overtly marked as didactic a scene describing Native American custom:

Notwithstanding the increasing warmth of the amicable contest, the most decorous [C]hristian assembly, not even excepting those in which its reverend ministers are collected, might have learned a wholesome lesson of moderation from the forbearance and courtesy of the disputants. The words of Uncas were received with the same deep attention as those which fell from the maturer wisdom of his father; and so far from manifesting any impatience, neither spoke, in reply, until a few moments of silent meditation were, seemingly, bestowed in deliberating on what had already been said. (700)

Imagine the possibility of whites—political and religious leaders—learning how to deliberate from Indians. Although those most in need of the lesson would have scoffed at the suggestion, Cooper presented it seriously. Given the admiration with which writers including Cooper portrayed Native Americans, the absence of respectable African Americans, individually or as a group, cannot be dismissed.

African Americans in 1820s Popular Literature

Three of the most popular books in the United States in the 1820s did not include any reference at all to African Americans: *Hobomok, Hope Leslie,* and *The Prairie.* Three included "black" characters: *The Pioneers, The Last of the Mohicans,* and *A Narrative of the Life of Mrs. Mary Jemison.* Given how central Native Americans were to the popular literature of the 1820s, as represented by some of the best-selling books of the decade, it is amazing that African Americans resided at the margins or were completely invisible. Critics challenged U.S. writers to create a distinctly "American" literature, and Native Americans suited that work much more easily and much less controversially than African Americans and the institution of slavery. But the absence of African Americans cannot be interpreted to mean the world was "raceless." As Toni Morrison argues, "The act of enforcing racelessness in literary discourse is itself a racial act."[60]

When writers included African Americans in U.S. literature, the differences in the portrayals between the races were striking. Of the three best-selling works from the 1820s that included African Americans, Seaver's *Narrative* treated them the most neutrally. After U.S. soldiers pillaged lands owned by Mary Jemison's tribe, she worked for "two negroes, who had run away from their masters," helping them harvest their corn. They "were kind and friendly" if perhaps somewhat foolish. As Seaver reported Mary's story, she "laughed a thousand times" recalling the ways one of the men watched over her to protect her from Indian attacks, so that he "lost as much labor of his own as he received from me, by paying good wages." Mary and her children stayed with them for a winter, then built shelter and lived on the same land as them for several years until the men moved on (105–106). The only other mention of African Americans occurred when Mary talked about a group of prisoners that included two white men and "two negroes." Mary named the white men and disclosed what happened to them (one eventually moved to Niagara, the other enlisted in the U.S. Army). She neither named nor subsequently mentioned the two African Americans. They simply disappeared from the narrative, exiled to irrelevance (107–108).

Cooper marginalized all of the African Americans in his first Leatherstocking novel, *The Pioneers*. He named two of them: a slave, Agamemnon, and a free black man, Abraham "Brom" Freeborn. The others were grouped as servants in Judge Temple's house, and their presence was felt on three occasions. First, when her father brought Elizabeth home after a five-year absence, Cooper's narrator described in detail the housekeeper, a white woman named Remarkable Pettibone, and the butler, a white man named Benjamin Penguillan. After several lengthy paragraphs in which Remarkable and Ben were described, the narrator remarked, "In addition to these, were three or four subordinate menials, mostly black, some appearing at the principal door, and some running from the end of the building, where stood the entrance to the cellar-kitchen" (58–60). These "subordinate menials" were almost as invisible when Ben attempted to seduce Remarkable. Elizabeth had gone to bed, Judge Temple and Richard were at the local pub, and, as Ben told the housekeeper, "the niggers [were] snug stowed below, before a fire that would roast an ox whole" (171). One learned more about the status of the black servants in the Temple household when Oliver Edwards accepted a position as Judge Temple's assistant. Elizabeth, perturbed by Oliver's "airs," asked her father in which part of the house Oliver would live, and with whom he would eat:

> "With Benjamin and Remarkable," interrupted Mr. Jones; "you surely would not make the youth eat with the blacks! He is part Indian, it is true, but the natives hold the negroes in great contempt. No, no—he would starve before he would break a crust with the negroes."
>
> "I am but too happy, Dickon, to tempt him to eat with ourselves," said Marmaduke [the judge], "to think of offering even the indignity you propose."
>
> "Then, sir," said Elizabeth, with an air that was slightly affected, as if submitting to her father's orders in opposition to her own will, "it is your pleasure that he be a gentleman."
>
> "Certainly; he is to fill the station of one; let him receive the treatment that is due to his place, until we find him unworthy of it." (204–205)

Despite being what Richard Jones had moments before disparagingly called a "half-breed," in the judge's mind Oliver's education and background raised him above even the white servants, Ben and Remarkable. But everyone believed "the negroes" to be at the bottom of the social structure. These sorts of comparisons emerged subtly as well. Reverend Grant, for instance, hosted Indian John and Oliver for dinner and made sure they came to church. Indian John seemed comfortable during the services, taking a seat next to the judge "in a manner that manifested his sense of his own dignity" (124). Ben and Remarkable attended services, as well. But the African American "menials" did not figure in Reverend Grant's mission, and they were the only group not mentioned as having attended Christmas services.

Only two African Americans figured in the narrative enough to be named: Judge Temple's slave Aggy (actually owned by Richard because of Temple's Quaker commitments) and Brom, who arranged a turkey shoot for sport. Neither received much respect from the narrator or the novel's characters. Several times in the novel Richard displayed affection for Aggy, but Richard also quickly threatened Aggy with a whip when he suspected his slave was hiding the truth (54–55). Richard knew Brom by his proper name and got involved in a dispute at the turkey shoot in which Richard and Elizabeth took Brom's side. But these African Americans played fools in *The Pioneers*, marginalized in different ways than Native Americans. "Playing in the dark" as fools or as ghosts, African Americans "snug stowed below" rarely even got near the edges of European American society that Native Americans occasionally crossed.[61]

Only one character of African descent in any of these novels played a role central to the story: *The Last of the Mohicans*'s Cora Munro, whose West Indian mother was "descended, remotely" from Africans (653). Cora was strong and wise. During the novel she took care of her younger sister, Alice; stood up to Magua, the Indian bent on revenge against her father; and took charge as hostile Indians prepared to capture her, Alice, Heyward, Natty, Uncas, and Chingachgook. But Cora had no future: doomed to be set apart in Cooper's world, she died by the sword of an Indian. Readers learned of Cora's lineage when Heyward confessed his love for Alice to their father, Colonel Munro. Munro assumed that Heyward loved Cora, and when Heyward corrected him Munro assumed the young man shunned his older daughter because of prejudice, even though Cora passed as white and Heyward had yet to learn of her ancestry. Munro explained to his future son-in-law that, while in the West Indies, he had "form[ed] a connexion" with a remote descendent of the class "so basely enslaved" in the United States. Munro accused Heyward of prejudice, which Heyward denied despite being "conscious of such a feeling" (653–654). Cooper's narrator portrayed Heyward as typifying and Munro as flouting popular sentiment. Cora was caught in the middle. Too white to marry an Indian (Cooper hinted at Cora and Uncas as a pair), too black to marry a white, to preserve narrative fidelity Cora—and Uncas—had to die.

Native Americans frequently appeared in popular fiction—novels such as *The Leatherstocking Tales* as well as short stories—from the 1820s and 1830s. Of the most popular texts of the 1820s, five novels and a captivity narrative, Native Americans featured prominently in all six; African Americans appeared in only three, and there they were forced to live on the margins or, as with the case of Cora Munro, die rather than face ostracism or the failure to integrate into white or Native American culture. The differences between Native Americans and African Americans in terms of plausible imaginings and relationships was astounding, and we see even more of it in the newspapers from the Jacksonian era, featured in the following chapter.

— 4 —

"Merely Public Opinion in Legal Forms"

Imagining Native and African Americans in the Public and Political Spheres

> It was public opinion that *made him a slave*. In a republican
> government the people make the laws, and those laws are merely
> public opinion *in legal forms*.
>
> —THEODORE WELD, *AMERICAN SLAVERY AS IT IS:*
> *TESTIMONY OF A THOUSAND WITNESSES* (1839)

On January 8, 1830, the *National Intelligencer* reprinted from the *New York American* a report that a large group of gentlemen recently had met to protest the U.S. government's plans to forcibly remove southern Indians from their lands. The *National Intelligencer* included in the article a resolution that these men had passed urging people to protect the "national and social rights" of Indians and also "the honor and good faith" of Americans composing the United States: "*Resolved,* That it be recommended to our fellow citizens, in different parts of the country, to petition Congress on behalf of the Cherokees and other southern tribes of Indians, that they may be sustained in the undisturbed enjoyment of their national and social rights, and that the honor and good faith of this nation may be preserved." On the same page, one column to the right and a little bit lower than the report of the New York meeting, appeared this advertisement for a runaway slave:

TWENTY DOLLARS REWARD.

RAN away on the 28th ult. Negro Tom Jefferson, from the Subscriber; he had on when he went away a country pair of Kersey pantaloons filled in with black yarn, a green pea coat, an old fur hat with black sash round it, and a new cotton shirt; his hands have got some scars on them, and very chubby thumbs, and a scar on one of his legs, occasioned by the cut of an axe; he is very full of talk . . .

The above reward will be given if taken and secured in Jail, so that I can get him again. All persons are hereby notified not to harbor or employ said runaway at their peril.

Negro Tom Jefferson had no rights, national or social, to protect, and if anyone believed otherwise they acted "at their peril" rather than with "honor and good faith."[1]

These two texts were published on the same day in January 1830, within a week of the moment Charlotte Cheever and other women from Hallowell, Maine, prepared and submitted that first petition from a group of women demanding of the U.S. Congress a voice in the Indian removal debates. In the decade that included the wide distribution in 1829 of Catharine Beecher's "Circular Addressed to Benevolent Women of the U. States" and Beecher and Angelina Grimké's debate over women's antislavery petitioning in 1836 to 1838, there were many other days on which the *National Intelligencer* printed stories, advertisements, or reports from Congress on both Native Americans and African Americans. Because of the high number of advertisements about slaves (people wanting to buy or sell slaves, people hoping to recapture their runaway slaves, law enforcement agencies alerting slave owners that allegedly runaway slaves had been captured), on most of the days when readers encountered both African and Native Americans on the pages of the *National Intelligencer,* Indians appeared as citizens of other nations whereas "negroes" appeared as property.

Even reports about African colonization frequently appeared near slave ads, creating an odd juxtaposition of texts that both celebrated the self-government and freedom of colonists in Africa and perpetuated the institution of slavery in the United States. Telling, too, are the times when people of color and Indians are subjects of articles in issues without slave ads, as when in June 1836 Congress simultaneously debated appropriations to facilitate Indian removal and the admission of Arkansas to the Union as a slave state.[2] Some congressmen called Indians savages and barbarians, but all congressmen recognized Indians as a free (though sometimes conquered) people. On the other hand, even congressmen such as John Quincy Adams who abhorred the institution of slavery saw no constitutional way to compel Arkansas to treat people of color as free people rather than as property.

But convincing European Americans to imagine African Americans as people rather than property was only part of the battle. People sympathetic to Native and African Americans, people who agreed that European Americans caused both races enormous trouble, perceived Native Americans as warriors who fought back or gentlemen who became increasingly civilized but free people of color as degraded and desperate outcasts. Reports of an extended visit by dozens of Native Americans to Washington, D.C., make this disparity exceedingly clear. The *National Intelligencer* described negotiating sessions in which hundreds of whites gathered in a church to witness Indian and white leaders share a peace pipe and then discuss an impending treaty, a meeting between the Indians and the U.S. president, a demonstration of Indian dance that drew white crowds numbering in the thousands, and a night at a popular D.C. theater in which the visiting Indians were introduced to an elegant element of white culture. Analogous institutional negotiations and cultural exchanges did not occur in the United States between "whites" and "people of color" in the Jacksonian era.[3]

These implicit and sometimes explicit comparisons between African and Native Americans filled the pages of the *National Intelligencer*. In 1831 a North Carolinian wrote to the editors of the newspaper, Joseph Gales Jr. and William Winston Seaton, requesting that they publish his editorial against Indian removal. In his letter, which the editors published, the southerner urged Gales and Seaton to advocate more strongly on behalf of Indians in their newspaper: "you stand preeminent among those who direct public opinion in this country; and therefore it is, that an expectation is entertained in this momentous crisis of our country's honor, that you will, upon reflection, find it obligatory upon you, to guide the nation's sense of justice more pointedly than heretofore, to view in its true and glaring colors the conduct of Georgia and of the present Administration of the United States Government towards the Cherokees."[4] Flattery? Of course. But Gales and Seaton played an important national role from their offices in Washington, D.C. When they purchased the newspaper in 1810, they inherited as their primary area of coverage the business of the federal government. Newspapers around the country relied on the *National Intelligencer* for national news. Until Jackson was elected, Gales and Seaton's newspaper had no competition. For almost two decades their daily was the capital's and the nation's sole source for coverage of national politics. Even when Jackson's supporters established their own newspapers, the *National Intelligencer* maintained its preeminent status as the primary Whig paper in the nation's capital.[5]

Politicians living in the District of Columbia, too, relied on the *National Intelligencer* for its political news—but they also needed the daily to provide sociopolitical news from around the country. Besides its federal news, Gales and Seaton filled their newspaper the same way most editors did at the time: they reprinted extensively from other newspapers sent to them as part of a national news exchange. During Jackson's presidency, reprints from at least six dozen newspapers published in towns located in more than eighteen states (and at least three foreign countries) filled their pages.[6] Given the extensive list of newspapers from which the *National Intelligencer* pulled material and its nearly exclusive role as the nation's source for federal news, in the pages of their daily newspaper Gales and Seaton reflected and also shaped people's perceptions of national politics and culture for years.

The phenomenon did not go unnoticed. In a remarkable letter to two men clearly opposed to his politics, former member of the House of Representatives, former governor of Georgia, and then member of the Senate Wilson Lumpkin acknowledged Gales and Seaton's pervasiveness and influence when he publicly asked them to print an essay refuting charges of Georgian and United States oppression of Cherokees. Lumpkin wrote to the *National Intelligencer* editors:

> In order, therefore, that the readers of the Intelligencer, *now and hereafter,* as well as the *historian* who may collect materials from the preserved files of the newspapers of the present day, may find the means of making up a correct decision on this subject, I have, therefore, respectfully to request of you, as faithful journalists, to publish in the Intelligencer, at as early day as practicable, the reply . . . Should any cause whatever prevent your compliance with my request herein contained, I then have to request that you will at least publish this letter, in order that those who may read and examine the files of the Intelligencer after the present generation shall have passed away, may find this letter as an index to point to a more correct history of facts.[7]

Two pieces of Lumpkin's formal appeal are especially noteworthy. First, Lumpkin recognized the contemporary importance of the *National Intelligencer;* the Senate published the reply in question, but this Georgia senator knew he had to ask Gales and Seaton to reprint or at least record the document for word to get out. Second, Lumpkin took seriously the *National Intelligencer*'s nearly exclusive role as documenter of national business.[8] To study national policy in the late eighteenth and early nineteenth century, he knew that historians necessarily would rely on the *National Intelligencer* for its public records, and he provided detailed technical information to guide them to documents telling his side of the story.

Lumpkin was right: the *National Intelligencer* reflected and also helped shape sociopolitical discourse in the 1820s and 1830s, especially in the middle and northeastern states, and especially concerning issues central to the ideologies of the women active in the antiremoval, colonization, and immediate abolitionism movements. Gales and Seaton supported Whiggery, antiremovalism, and colonization. The *National Intelligencer* reprinted the William Penn essays, endorsed the presidential candidacy of Henry Clay, frequently published material from the *African Repository* of the American Colonization Society (ACS), and regularly reproached Garrison and immediate abolitionism as the newspaper reported the business of Congress and news from around the nation.

In the logics of the 1820s and 1830s, it is, however, not surprising that the newspaper also printed advertisements that reinforced, even supported, the institution of slavery. These advertisements make for odd twenty-first-century reading experiences, as when, for example, the *National Intelligencer* ran a column celebrating the anniversary of the abolition of the slave trade in the United States next to an advertisement for a runaway slave or when a report advocating the ACS's program as a means to gradual emancipation ran next to an ad offering cash for hundreds of slaves. But the ads reinforce the degree to which colonizationists including Gales and Seaton refused to call for immediate emancipation and the end of institutionalized slavery or to interfere with what they imagined to be the property rights of their fellow U.S. citizens, and these advertisements must be read as a part of, rather than a digression from, the whole text. Careful reading of the whole text of this daily newspaper—including its many slave advertisements—published over a period of more than ten years makes it possible to trace and to compare the ways members of this particular discourse community encountered and imagined Native and African Americans as its objects of advocacy in the 1830s.

Such a longitudinal, comparative study of this discourse community makes clear several things. These European Americans defined people of color inside the slave system in the United States, whether the African Americans they encountered were enslaved or free. The system, and its correlative prejudices, would not permit African Americans to be anything but degraded and subservient in the United States. Native Americans not only were not imagined as property but were imagined as property owners.[9] Furthermore, Native Americans belonged to nations, and African Americans were imagined as having no national belonging. European Americans treated with Native American governments and traded for Native American cultural artifacts. As Michael Gomez argues, the Middle Passage stripped Africans of their nationality and national artifacts as part of their enslavement.[10] Although Africans maintained some of their cultural and national identities and passed them on to their children, those identities remained invisible to most European Americans during the antebellum period. Because Native Americans had national status (even if that status was as a dependent rather than a foreign nation), they could respond officially to the United States as well as to European Americans.[11] Enslaved African Americans had no representation, no redress for grievances, and most free African Americans lost the few rights they had during the 1820s and 1830s with the imposition of black codes in many states.[12] The only place from which African Americans had voice in the United States was, ironically, Liberia, when they physically were located there.

Because African Americans dramatically outnumbered Native Americans and because most European Americans understood their treatment of slaves as inhumane and ruthless, European Americans continually protected themselves against servile wars and insurrections by silencing even suspected dissent. Native Americans, on the other hand, were celebrated by many antiremovalists and colonizationists as warriors who were strong and independent. In the pages of the *National Intelligencer*, Native Americans often were justified in fighting European American hostilities, but African Americans never were. Again, African Americans were imagined inside the slave culture: no matter the injustices they faced, African Americans had to remain subservient. Native Americans faced very different constraints and therefore were the objects of very different imaginings in the 1830s. Tracing these imaginings explains why there was no way for antiremovalists turned colonizationists rhetorically to sustain arguments for permitting African Americans to remain in the United States.

Indians and "Negroes" or Free People of Color

It virtually is impossible to begin a discussion of these imaginings without beginning with slave advertisements. The kind of writing about non-European Americans that most distinguishes Native and African Americans in the

National Intelligencer is the hundreds and hundreds of slave advertisements on the newspaper's pages. The ads fall primarily into four categories: ads from people wanting to sell slaves, ads from people wanting to buy slaves, ads from slave owners offering rewards for runaway slaves, and ads from law enforcement agents announcing the apparent capture of runaway slaves. As classified advertisements, these texts conveyed a lot of information in a short space. Despite this constraint, ads almost always mentioned a slave's color and used the word "negro." "Negro" did not signify blackness. It didn't even signify nonwhiteness; it did not include Native Americans, nor did it include nonwhites who owned nonwhite slaves in the United States nor nonwhites who emigrated to Africa. It was an interpretive and formative label that emerged inside a system in which people legally could be enslaved as someone else's property.

In the ads, "negro" appeared as a category to mark one's status as a participant in the slave culture before it became fully a marker of one's color in the antebellum period. What is particularly striking about this category is that it was defined situationally rather than essentially in the Jacksonian era. "Negro" was not about being black; it was about one's role or state of being inside the slave culture. Many colonizationists predicted that blacks would always be degraded in the United States not because of their color, but because of the widespread prejudice against people of color that colonizationists believed inevitably followed from legalized slavery. For colonizationists, Africans and their descendants were not defined by color but rather positioned within a culture constituted by and organized around slavery. And if African Americans were imagined as degraded only inside a slave culture and if that culture could not be transformed, the benevolent—in fact, the only—solution was to remove these objects from the culture that constituted them so negatively and therefore so oppressively.

Many European Americans, then, who formed the discourse community in question imagined people of color living in the United States as defined by—one might say colored by—slavery, rather than by inherent qualities or characteristics entailed by their skin color or race. But before I draw conclusions about the ads as a means by which to understand the constructed category "negro" and its relationship to colonizationists' imaginings of the objects of their advocacy, I present several ads in succession to create a sense of the genre. A typical advertisement offering a reward for a runaway slave read this way:

ATTENTION! $100 REWARD.

RANAWAY from Parsons' shoe shop, (Georgetown) [t]he 26th of November last, a negro slave by the name of BOB, (calls himself Robert Diggs.) It is apprehended that said fellow has made for Pennsylvania, or some of the free States, as he absconded without provocation. He is about 28 years of age, about five feet nine or ten inches high, stutters, his front teeth, particularly the lower ones, very wide asunder, has a scar on the ridge of his nose, just between his eyes, which he received when a boy by the kick of a horse. His clothes were, a drab roundabout, and surtout coat also drab, and a variety of other clothes. He is by trade a good shoemaker, and has taken his tools with him. Whoever will apprehend said fellow, and secure him so that I get him again, shall receive the above reward, if taken in Pennsylvania; 50 if taken in any of the upper counties of Maryland; and 10 ten [sic] if taken in any of the Southern counties of Maryland, and secured as above. Masters of vessels, stage properties, and all others, are cautioned against harboring or aiding said fellow in making his escape, as the law will be rigidly enforced against all such.

JOHN E. KEECH.[13]

Advertisers began with the reward amount listed in bold and capital letters, and proceeded with descriptions and information that might assist in finding and capturing the runaway. Owners of "runaways" often warned people against aiding or harboring their slaves, acts which infringed upon the rights of advertisers to get back their property. Most of the ads about runaway slaves included the phrase "so that I get him again," a phrase which emphasized possession, as did the regular use of the possessive pronoun "my" in phrases such as "my negro man BILL" and "my negro man John."[14] Almost always, owners proposed levels of reward amounts depending on how far from home someone captured the slave; in this advertisement, the especially high reward for capture in the state of Pennsylvania indicated the state's reputation as a haven for escaped slaves.[15] A typical ad announcing the capture and commitment of a slave to jail by law enforcement officials read this way:

RUNAWAY

WAS committed to the jail of Allegany county, as a runaway, a negro boy, who calls himself THOMAS KICK, about 5 feet 10 inches high, 20 or 21 years of age, stout and well made; has a scar on his left temple occasioned by a burn, scar on the left leg near the knee; had on a light roundabout and pantaloons—says he belongs to Nathaniel Benton, and that he was at work for Mr. Clemmens on the 26th Section of the Chesapeake and Ohio Canal, 20 miles above Georgetown. The owner of said negro boy is requested to come forward, prove property, and take him away, otherwise he will be discharged agreeably to law.

RICHARD BEALL,
Sheriff of Allegany County.[16]

More often than not these ads claimed that the captured slave had named his or her owner (how else, of course, would the law enforcement agent know for sure that his prisoner was a runaway and not a free person of color wrongly imprisoned?), and the ads almost always ended with a reminder that the slave would be sold according to applicable laws if his or her owner did not "prove property" within a specified amount of time. Slavery was, after all, a business.

Ads from people wanting to purchase slaves make that point clear. Very rarely did people advertise in the *National Intelligencer* to purchase one or two slaves. Instead, people advertised to buy dozens or even hundreds of slaves—"likely negroes"—usually between the ages of twelve and twenty-five. On one day in March 1836, these three ads appeared in the *National Intelligencer* in succession:

CASH FOR 500 NEGROES,

INCLUDING both sexes, from 12 to 25 years of age. Persons having likely servants to dispose of, will find it to their interest to give us a call, as we will give higher prices, in Cash, than any other purchaser who is now, or may hereafter come into the market.

FRANKLIN & ARMFIELD,
Alexandria.

CASH FOR 300 NEGROES.—The highest cash price will be given by the subscriber for Negroes of both sexes, from the ages of 12 to 28. Those wishing to sell, will do well to give me a call, at my residence, or at A. Lee's Lottery Office, five doors east of Gadsby's Hotel. Letters addressed to me, through the Post Office, shall receive the earliest attention.

WM. H. WILLIAMS,
Washington.

CASH FOR 400 NEGROES, including both sexes, from twelve to twenty-five years of age. Persons having servants to dispose of will find it to their interest to give me a call, as I will give higher prices, in cash, than any other purchaser who is now in this market.

I can at all times be found at the MECHANICS' HALL, now kept by B. O. Sheckle, and formerly kept by Isaac Beers, on Seventh street, a few doors below Lloyd's Tavern, opposite the Centre market. All communications promptly attended to.

JAMES H. BIRCH,
Washington City.[17]

The repetition in these advertisements suggests the standardization or normalization of established business practices. Likely some men took or shipped slaves south in time for harvesting. Others operated as agents for selling as well as buying slaves (and other merchandise) in or near the nation's capital. For example, the agents in the first of the 1836 ads listed above, Franklin and Armfield, had hosted a sale a few months earlier:

70 LIKELY NEGROES.—The subscribers will sell at Messrs. Franklin & Armfield's establishment in Alexandria, D.C., on Tuesday, the 5th day of January next, seventy likely negroes of different ages, male and female. They will be sold without reserve (to the highest bidder) in families. The negroes are now at Messrs. Franklin & Armfield's, where they can be seen till they are sold. Purchasers are invited to call and examine these negroes. The sale will commence at 10 o'clock A.M., on Tuesday, the 5th day of January next.

THOS. S. HERBERT,
H. CAPRON,
Administrators W. W. A. of T. Snowden.[18]

More common than ads like this one were ads that sold one, two, or a few slaves, often as part of an estate sale. Edwin Dyer, an auctioneer and frequent advertiser in the *National Intelligencer* who sold everything from furniture to food to slaves, ran advertisements like this one:

BY EDWARD DYER.—Cook and House Servant, Negro Girl, Furniture, &c.—On SATURDAY, the 23d instant, at 11 o'clock A.M. I shall sell, to the highest bidder, a Female Servant, 20 years of age, who has eight years to serve; said to be an excellent cook and a house servant, and perfectly honest. Also, a Negro Girl, 12 years old, slave for life, raised in the country, active and handy at house work, very docile and obliging. A good Cutting Box, Awning and Frame, Stoves, &c. Also, good Household Furniture, as Feather Beds, Hair Mattresses, Chairs, Bedsteads, Washstands, Candlestands, Mahogany Tables, Carpets, China and Crockery Ware, Sideboards, Waiters, &c. with a great many other articles. Terms of sale, cash.

EDW. DYER,
Auctioneer.[19]

Notice the inclusion of both of these females in the broad category of property to be bought and sold. Even when people named slaves in advertisements, they still grouped them with other property:

MARSHAL'S SALE.

BY virtue of two writs of fi. fa. issued from the Circuit Court of this District, for the county of Washington, and to me directed, I shall expose to public sale, for cash, on Tuesday, the 28th instant, at the house of Hezekiah Langley, one negro woman named Jane Bowie, one negro girl named Elizabeth, aged about seven years, two mahogany breakfast Tables, two mahogany end Tables, one hair Sofa, twelve rush bottom Chairs, two gilt Looking-glasses, one pair brass Andirons, Fender, Shovel, and Tongs, one Carpet and Rug, two Waiters, one small mahogany Sideboard, one do Candle Stand, one set of Castors, one lot of Glass, China and Crockery, one small passage Lamp, nine old Chairs, one curl maple Bedstead, Bed, and Furniture, one Toilet, one mahogany Bureau, and Kitchen Furniture; seized and taken in execution as the property of Hezekiah Langley, and will be sold to satisfy debts due by him to Elijah Parsons. Sale to commence at 10 o'clock, A.M.

TENCH RINGGOLD,
Marshal D. of Co.[20]

Part of the incredible power of these advertisements is their repetition. Over and over, advertisements include slaves in their lists of objects for sale. A cursory look at even half a dozen advertisements concerning slaves illustrates the degree to which slavery's European American participants imagined slavery as a business with buyers, sellers, agents, owners, and property. No one hid the nature of the business or the status as property of the African American men, women, and children forced to participate.

An intense study of these advertisements and their surrounding essays, letters, and articles over more than a decade, though, reveals a more nuanced and complicated means by which the people paying for the ads—and paying for the men, women, and children described in the ads—articulated their human property. They were "negroes," a classification made possible only because slavery existed. In other words, millions of Africans and their descendants living the United States were constituted for many white Americans from within, rather than external to or accidentally involved with, the institution of slavery. Simply, "negro" in the 1820s and 1830s meant more than "not white." African Americans who lived in the northern states and colonists in Africa almost exclusively were called "free people of color," whereas "negro" meant a particular group of people defined by their roles within the United States slave culture. "Negro" was an attitude or state of being imposed by whites. And if people believed that "negro" was a position articulated inside a slave culture—a constitutionally sanctioned culture for which no end was in sight—then the way to eradicate what European Americans imagined as "the negro problem" was to remove the people who, because of their skin color and the prejudice of whites, inevitably filled the role "negro." This premise enabled colonizationists to argue that the Africans and descendants of Africans who "returned" to Africa eventually would thrive together as a successful, moral, well-educated, civilized, and Christian society—despite their inability to perform in that way in the slave-based culture of the United States. "Negro" was a concept about people based not only on their color but on the interpretations and projections of people who had the power to label them.

Ads for runaway slaves contributed to the articulation of "negro" as a concept rather than a color. Advertisers almost always described a slave's skin color: yellow, mulatto, very black, tolerably black, copper, dark mulatto, tawny, quite black. In the south, one simultaneously could be "a negro man" and also "not very black."[21] One could even be "negro" and "white":

FORTY DOLLARS REWARD.

RAN AWAY from the subscriber, living about three miles from Piscataway, Prince George's county, Maryland, my Negro Woman, LETTY BROWN, taking with her, her two children, Bob and Dave . . . I have no doubt but she is now either in Washington (where she has a great number of negro acquaintances, both white and black) or lurking about some of Calvert's negro quarters, near Bladensburgh.[22]

The extension of "negro" to include whites as well as blacks in this advertisement appears to be an exception to typical usage. But even as the ad captures the outer limits of the term's use, it suggests the word's breadth and complexity as well as its ambiguity.

In this period "negro" sometimes described a class and began to signify a race. But the term still was used widely to describe a type of people implicated in the slave culture. For example, the word "negro" was used in ads when people provided descriptions of their slaves' skin color—so, for example, a yellow slave or a copper slave or a very dark or a black slave *also* was a negro. Using a nonwhite color to describe a slave did not render the adjective "negro" redundant. In this period, "negro" added information to a text that color did not convey. Among other things, "negro" implied bondage in epithets such as "my negro man Bill" or "Negro man John." People often used the noun "negro" as a synonym for "slave." One advertisement published in 1833 announced "LAND AND NEGROES FOR SALE." A group of about forty people lived and worked as slaves on this plantation, but they were not identified as slaves. Instead, they were identified collectively as "the Negroes," a category that presumed that all negroes were slaves: "The Negroes consist of Men, Women, and Children, young and likely, and among them a first rate Boot and Shoemaker and a Carriage Driver."[23]

The normal status of negroes in the southern states in the 1820s and 1830s was enslaved, and this normality actually was marked grammatically. When people used "negro" to refer to someone who was not enslaved, they modified the noun: "Free Negroes and Slaves," "The whole subject of slaves, free negroes, and mulattoes," and "Emigration of Free Negroes to Africa."[24] When people talked about bound negroes, they needed no modifier on the noun. In fact, with few exceptions European and African Americans referred to Africans and their descendants in the northern states as well as colonists in Africa not as "free negroes" but as "free people of color," a telling linguistic variation that illustrates the extent to which "negro" implied a state of being intimately connected to slavery before the word became exclusively a marker of race.

The point that in the 1820s and 1830s "negro" and the degraded qualities it both encompassed and signaled were articulated as a product of slavery rather than as essential to people of color can be made using discourses of colonization as well as slave advertisements. For instance, in an 1828 letter he wrote to the American Colonization Society, a Virginia clergyman requested that his slaves, for whom he said he cared deeply, be put on a list for colonization. To minimize their few faults, he explained that "in a land of freedom they would avoid many habits incidental to a state of slavery."[25]

The assumption that slavery incited degradation was echoed the following year in a call to support the ACS:

> Will not national pride conspire with promptings of humanity, the precepts of justice, and the charity of religion, to rouse us, and induce us to remedy those evils which our fathers and ourselves have inflicted upon a now degraded and wretched portion of our fellow creatures? Let us, as we have ability, lift them from their abasement—enlighten their minds—tell them that they like us are men, and entitled to the respect and the privileges of men—and, bidding them "God speed," generously restore them to the home of their ancestors, from which they have been mercilessly dragged away.[26]

Three words in particular argue for the degradation as situated, rather than natural: "now," "abasement," and "restore." Africans and their descendants were lowered into their current condition by the horrific slave trade, but the condition was not essential nor should it be permanent. In an 1830 fund-raising letter from the ACS to clergy and congregations, the ACS argued, "If to relieve our country from a class injurious to the public welfare, because destitute of motives for industry and enterprise and distinction; if, by changing the circumstances of this class, to elevate its character, and confer upon it the most precious social and political blessings . . . if these are worthy objects, the society which now makes its appeal, is deserving both of individual and national aid."[27] African Americans were "injurious to the public welfare," but they committed these injuries because the system had failed them. According to colonizationists, immediate abolitionists greatly underestimated these prejudices:

> Towards the accomplishment of the ends which they have in view, there are obstacles, obvious to the eye of reason, but which [abolitionist] fanaticism cannot see. Prejudices of color, prejudices of habit, differences of physical conformation, inequalities arising from unequal intellectual cultivation, a dissimilarity of moral sense—the inevitable result of a state of freedom and a state of bondage—all these, in the frenzied brains of agitators, are to vanish in the twinkling of an eye, and, on the instant, such an assimilation is to take place as would eclipse all recorded miracles.[28]

Time and time again members of the ACS point to the coexistence of European and African Americans, not something essential about African Americans, as the problem. In an argument that very specifically made this point, a New York reverend reported at the eighteenth annual ACS meeting in 1835 that "the facts had demonstrated that the African race, if kept in communities by themselves, were capable of the highest degree of civilization, moral elevation, and social improvement; while on the other hand, all attempts to elevate them while in a country where their race was in slavery, had proved utter failures."[29] Later that same year, the New York City auxiliary of the ACS used the same argument once again to persuade free people of color to emigrate:

> It may safely be left to the judgments of such persons to determine for themselves, whether a greater degree of comfort, welfare, respectability and happiness may be attained and enjoyed by them in this country, where they are surrounded by a more numerous population of a distinct race and different color, by the great majority of whom they will, so long as slavery endures in any portion of the Union, be regarded as an inferior *caste*, and excluded from all equality of social intercourse, even when admitted to an equal participation of political and civil privileges, than in the colony of Liberia, where no such distinctions, prejudice, or degradation, can exist; where they will be secure of perfect equality in the enjoyment of all social advantages as well as of political freedom, civil liberty, and religious privileges.[30]

These colonizationists invoked race as an important marker, given that Africans and their descendants formed a minority based on their race and color. But color and race alone failed to explain the disparity in status between whites and blacks. The mitigating factor was the peculiar institution of slavery ("so long as slavery endures in any portion of the Union"), illustrating once again that this discourse community of European Americans imagined African Americans—Africans in America, free and enslaved—as constitutionally defined by their relationship to slavery, rather than as essentially degraded. This belief about the objects of their advocacy grounded a fundamental principle of the ACS: free blacks in the United States who could not succeed in the United States could thrive in Africa.

Nations and Individuals

By the 1830s white Americans had a stable category for Indians but competing categories for "people of color." Those categories had important implications for benevolent activism. So, too, did questions of national belonging.

In a controversial 1831 decision, the United States Supreme Court defined Indians as dependent, not foreign, nations.[31] Although the decision dramatically disempowered the Cherokees, it did solidify some degree of national status for the various tribes. This point was significant: "nation" implied rights, political presence, shared culture among members, and entitlement to a homeland, even if the location of the homeland was up for debate. Blacks who lived in the United States, according to the dominant slave ideology held by most whites, whether pro- or antislavery, had no national belonging. They were individuals who had been kidnapped from various African countries (sometimes by their own rulers) and sold into slavery, or they were descendants of those captured individuals, and so they had ancestors who were African. But they had no contemporary collective structure, unlike Indians, who belonged to different tribes or nations. Slavers erased the national identities of people of color during the Middle Passage, and so—according to the dominant white ideology—millions of people of color in the United States had no shared culture, no collective rights, no homeland. That is, these millions of people of color were expected (and were thought) to exist as disconnected individuals without shared culture, collective rights, and a homeland until colonizationists embraced expatriation as a solution to the problem they imagined that people of color posed in the United States. Then colonizationists nationalized people of color as Africans (using the continent rather than the country, Liberia, to which they sent emigrants), despite intense protest from many free people of color who believed their home was the United States, not Liberia.

It is true that the status of Indian nations and the breadth of their rights were tenuous during the Jacksonian era and that some people of color were free to own their own property (including nonwhite slaves), obtain an education, and keep the money they earned—rights some of which women would not have in the United States for decades. But a comparative study of the ways these two groups were talked about by white Americans rather than the ways Indians and people of color experienced their lives, and a comparative study across rather than within these groups, throws into stunning relief the significance of the differences between the ways European Americans imagined Native and African Americans as objects of advocacy, as people whose situations warranted some sort of benevolent response.

The messages created not simply by the texts but also by the adjacency of the texts—something that can only be experienced in a comparative study of the two groups—simply is remarkable. The messages are clear, for example, in a reading of the *National Intelligencer* on a random day, say, August 5, 1829. In the first, second, and third columns of the second page, the first William Penn essay discussed the "present crisis in the condition of the American Indians." As Penn, Jeremiah Evarts framed the crisis between the United States and Indians as one between nations: "It has been truly said," he wrote, "that the character which a nation sustains, in its intercourse with the great community of nations, is of more value than any other of it[s] public possessions." Two columns to the right of Evarts's essay, the bottom third of the page is filled with three short texts on "negroes": two runaway slave ads and one announcement that a runaway slave "was committed to the jail of Washington county, MD." Three days later, on August 8, two short, adjoining articles on Indian emigration were published, one referring to "men, women and children, from the Creek Nation," another quoting a Cherokee who promised to "hold to my country" rather than emigrate west. In the very next column, abutting the second piece on Native Americans, one comes across an ad headed "NEGROES WANTED": "The subscriber wishes to purchase from fifty-five to sixty young NEGROES, of both sexes, from ten to twenty-five years of age, for which the most liberal prices will be given."[32]

A month later, a text was published about people of color that did not express a desire to purchase, sell, hunt, or return a slave to his or her master. On September 9, the paper published a two-column essay on African colonization written for the *National Intelligencer,* an essay in which the writer described people of color in the United States as "descendants of the ill-fated natives of that section of the globe [Africa], who, in violation of the plainest principles of honor, honesty, justice, and humanity, were torn by cupidity, and avarice, and cruelty, from their homes, their parents, their husbands, their wives, their children, and from every thing near and dear to human nature." This essayist wrote sympathetically about captured Africans and their descendents, focusing on the individual act of kidnapping and the horrible impacts of that theft as measured by the destruction of individual relationships between victims and their homes, parents, spouses, and children. In the next column, readers were reminded again of the *National Intelligencer*'s position on Indians as belonging to nations. Gales and Seaton reprinted from a Georgia newspaper this attack against the editors: "With regard to the position taken by the writers in the National Intelligencer, and other papers, that the Indian nations are free and independent, we

shall not offer one remark upon it, its absurdity is sufficient for its refuta-
tion." But the editors, men who clearly opposed forced removal of Cherokees and other southern Indians from their lands, refused to back down.
They continued to identify Native Americans as nations or members of
nations—just as they continued, in their own editorials and the texts and
advertisements they included in their daily newspaper, to portray people of
color living in the United States as individuals without any rights entailed
or protected by national belonging.[33]

This juxtaposition of Native Americans and African Americans continued on the pages of the *National Intelligencer* through the 1830s. My analysis
here highlights days on which Native and African Americans were included
in one way or another in a single day's issue, but it is important to remember that there were many more days when one or the other nonwhite group
was represented. So, for example, in the three days between the publication
of the sixth and seventh William Penn essays in August 1829, there were
several runaway slave advertisements, a report on the Cherokee alphabet,
and a statement from members of the Creek Nation; in the three days between the publication of the seventh and eighth essays, there were several
notices about runaway and recaptured slaves (as well as runaway slave ads
on the days that both essays were published); in the four days between the
tenth and eleventh essays, again, the only intervening texts about either
Native or African Americans were slave ads.[34] So even if in a particular
month few or no issues of the *National Intelligencer* included pieces on both
African and Native Americans, daily readers still found comparative imaginings of those groups over short periods of time.

Given the numbers of advertisements about slaves in this Whig daily,
most frequently whatever was being written about Native Americans came
before or after texts that defined people of color as property. In January 1831,
on the same page as information about import taxes on "Indian Blankets,"
a report which took for granted the concept of international trade, was a
runaway slave ad, an ad which took for granted the individual and unpro-
tected status of the slave.[35] After an extensive report on an 1832 House of
Representatives debate about a Chickasaw treaty, typesetters placed a runaway slave ad; the following month the newspaper continued its coverage of
the same debate and placed an ad offering "twenty-five negroes for sale" on
the facing page.[36] The same thing happened when the *National Intelligencer*
reported on, for example, wars between Native Americans and the United
States, cultural exchanges between the several nations, and congressional

debates about appropriations to various Native American nations or tribes.[37] Over and over readers encountered information that affirmed collective and national belonging for Indians and individual and isolated status for "negroes."

Conceiving Indians as nations or members of nations and blacks as individuals devoid of any citizenship status profoundly affected resources allocated by United States government. In 1834, the *National Intelligencer* reported that the federal government aimed to decrease "the expenditure of the Indian Department by more than one-half," from nearly $150,000 to almost $62,000—bad news for Native Americans, and yet evidence of an "Indian Department" and allocations of funds nonetheless. This report lies adjacent to a report of another ACS-sponsored excursion to Liberia, this time delivering "three physicians and three teachers, and supplies to the amount of 7,000 dollars, a large portion of which has been contributed by the citizens of New York."[38] There were no federal departments dedicated to African Americans, and the occasional federal funds used to support colonization still came from the 1819 Slave Trade Act. Consequently, most of the money for colonization came from individuals and was used to support individual emigration, whereas most of the money flowing to Native Americans came from the federal government and was used to support the development of other nations. Most of the congressional discussions about Native Americans reported in the *National Intelligencer* focused on treaties between the United States and Indian nations and allocations of funds to nations for improvements or for removal. Most of the congressional discussions about African Americans, conversely, focused on abolishing slavery in the District of Columbia or on handling antislavery petitions from abolitionists.

The United States also dealt on a national level with Indian aggression. The U.S. military fought against various Indian tribes (especially the Seminoles in Florida), and state governments frequently called on the federal government to send troops to manage conflicts, including border skirmishes, between Indians and white Americans. But violence between white Americans and black slaves occurred as "insurrections," not wars. When writers predicted rebellions between slaves (or former slaves) and their masters, these large-scale conflicts were called "servile" wars. Those wars were imagined as class-based, not nation-based. Southerners responded to insurrections by arresting as many blacks, including free blacks, as they figured might be involved in the uprising. Almost always, local townspeople and law enforcement agents handled slave rebellions. When abolitionists created suspicion on the part of southerners as to the loyalties and motivations of most northerners (were all northerners abolitionists?), most northerners, including colonizationists, tried to reassure southerners by promising that they would travel south to protect southerners from uprisings caused by the incendiary literature and ideas championed by fanatical abolitionists. Even when northerners planned to fight with southerners against people of color, though, northerners made those promises as civilians rather than as soldiers. When free negroes and slaves challenged white southerners, white Americans imagined those conflicts as local and personal—on a very different scale than fights with Indians which almost always involved state or national troops, even though some skirmishes with Indians involved just a few dozen foreigners encroaching on United States lands.

Colonizationists considered United States–born people of color neither as foreign nor as American. In more than ten years of newspaper stories about people of color and colonization, only a few times did colonizationists call free people of color "American." In March 1831, for example—ironically, just to the right of a report of the landmark Supreme Court case in *Cherokee Nation v. State of Georgia*—the *National Intelligencer* printed a report from Africa that conveyed news of emigrant arrivals to the colony and a clear reminder that the colony was American: "Another of the native Chiefs had placed himself and his people under the protection of the Colony, and two other chiefs were seeking the same benefit, and ready to submit to the Laws of the Colony. They deem it a great privilege to be allowed to call themselves *Americans*."[39] Indians may have been dependent on Americans, but Africans—native Africans—could become Americans in Africa. In fact, the only place people of color were called Americans by this discourse community was in Africa, in "those little American African communities."[40] Colonizationists and colonizers alike, though, anticipated the day when the ACS would transfer the colony to its "colored" citizens, relinquishing U.S. ownership. Two free people of color born in the United States and "deputed by their brethren" to examine life in the African colony prepared a glowing report upon their return in the fall of 1832. They "felt, for the first time, what it was to be free and independent," and they concluded their report by encouraging "a removal to Liberia. There alone can the black man enjoy true freedom; and where that freedom is, shall be our country."[41]

This report reveals two important beliefs in the 1830s: freedom and national belonging were invariably linked, and both freedom and national belonging categorically were unavailable to people of color in the United

States during this period. But it is significant that the writers of this report, Gloster Simpson and Archy Moore, did not speak of the move to Liberia as a repatriation. They accepted Liberia as "our country" not for genealogical reasons but for the quality of life available to people of color there. They called themselves black and imagined as their nation Liberia, not Africa. It was colonizationists who most frequently referred to this group of people as Africans.

Perhaps it is not surprising given the symbolic power of national belonging that just as people of color were being nationalized by colonizationists so they could be "repatriated" to Africa, the Jackson administration attempted to strip the Cherokee nation (and thus, by precedent, other Native American nations) of its nationhood. In the column to the left of the Liberian report from Simpson and Moore, the *National Intelligencer* reprinted a report from the *Cherokee Phoenix:*

> The President of the United States, we understand, has instructed Colonel Montgomery to deposit the annuities due the Cherokee nation, and now in his hands, in the Branch Bank of the United States at Nashville. It will be recollected by our readers, that during the administration of Secretary Eaton, he instructed the agent to pay the annuities to the individuals of the nation, and not to the nation, and in no instance to depart from this rule. The Cherokees have, with some exceptions, refused to receive the money under that regulation.[42]

President Jackson attempted to rupture the national collective by offering individual Cherokees who agreed to move west payment for their lands. Nationhood meant power, and Cherokee and U.S. leaders, removalists and antiremovalists alike, recognized the importance of that equation. It was in this context that most white Americans imagined national belonging as nonexistent for people of color in the United States—and in this context that the ACS nationalized people of color as Africans.

Free people of color affirmed their African ancestry but denied the argument that their ancestry entailed African citizenship. Colonists like Simpson and Moore adopted Liberia as their home because in that country they were free, not because they were African, and they referred to themselves as black men, not Africans. In 1833, Colvert Barker called Liberia "the land of our forefathers," but called himself and his friends "colored" people, not Africans or even Liberians.[43] Free people of color who opposed colonization repeatedly denied Africa as their home, including denials in resolutions such as the following, passed during what the *National Intelligencer* called a "meeting of colored persons" in 1831: "Resolved, That it is the declared opinion of the members of this meeting, that the soil which gave them birth is their only *true and veritable home*, and that it would be impolitic, unwise, and improper, for them to leave their home without the benefits of education." In their other resolutions this group protested the ACS, explaining that they "distrust[ed] the efforts made by the Colonization society." They also "acknowledge[d] with gratitude the efforts made in our behalf" by abolitionists, including Benjamin Lundy and William Lloyd Garrison.[44] Garrison vehemently opposed labeling people of color born in the United States "Africans" or members of the African race. If a Garrisonian abolitionist read the New York *Commercial Advertiser* editorial reprinted by the *National Intelligencer* in May 1833 that called "misguided fanatics"—abolitionists— "the greatest foes to the best interests of the African race," they would have argued against not just the interpretations of their actions but also the idea that people of color in the United States were Africans, either by race or nationality.[45] This distinction meant that, whereas abolitionists aimed to aid their "colored brethren" in the United States, throughout the 1830s the ACS imagined all people of color as African and aimed to do "good towards the whole African race."[46] In the 1820s and 1830s, for people who condemned Indian removal and advocated the removal of free people of color from the United States, "African" became synonymous with "colored" as a name for the nonwhite, non-Indian race who lived among them.

According to colonizationists, members of the "African" race acquired their racial affiliation based on their geographical heritage, a process that did not apply to whites. Whites who were born in the United States did not belong to a British or an Irish or a French race, even if their descendants were British, Irish, or French. Once, in 1829, Henry Clay called whites the Anglo Saxon or European race to contrast them with blacks, which he called the African race.[47] But the exception proves the rule. Otherwise, people of color were racialized by color or geographic heritage—the colored race or the African race—whereas whites were racialized only by color—the white race. Consider this assessment: "The climate of Africa, though evidently congenial to the constitution of the African race, whether native or foreign, is much less so to the constitution of the white man."[48] The writer used "white" and "African" as parallel modifiers, although one word racialized a group by color and the other by geographic ancestry. Too, the clause "whether native or foreign" emphasized that "African" was not the same as

"American"; one could not be American and foreign in the United States at the same time, but one could be African and foreign in Africa at the same time. During the 1830s, ACS discourse uniquely nationalized—without citizenship—people of color not to a country, but to a continent based on their color and ancestry (ignoring, of course, how many descendants of Africans living in the United States also descended from European Americans). Over and over, whites in the "American" Colonization Society—a national organization—declared ACS efforts "to improve the condition of the African race" in the United States and in Africa.[49] By nationalizing the race as "African," colonizationists made it possible to argue that these non-Indian people of color belonged on a continent an ocean away. As one colonizationist explained at the 1835 annual meeting of the ACS:

> It had been proposed to effect the good of the African race by giving them freedom *here*. But who that was acquainted with the condition of those called *free* among us, could suppose for a moment that they were free indeed? . . . It was impossible, in the nature of things, that anything that deserved the name of freedom could be enjoyed by the colored man on any part of this continent. But let him be transported to a land where there were no white men, superior in numbers, in wealth and refinement, lords of the soil, and dictators of the laws; there we might hope to see him a free man.[50]

Whites were not confined to a geographic location by their race, unlike people of color, for whom the colonizationist ideology assigned a circumscribed geographical space. Geographic location assured "Africans" freedom—in Africa. By the end of the decade, people of color, like Indians, were nationalized—with a major difference: when antiremovalists argued that Indians should live in their homelands, they got to stay put; when colonizationists argued that people of color should live in their homelands, they had to leave.

Resistance and Compliance

Monday, February 6, 1837, began peacefully in the U.S. House of Representatives. Members of the House briefly discussed a resolution about how to count votes in presidential elections, and then they returned to hearing petitions from their constituents—Mondays being petition days in the House. The House proceeded through the presentation of petitions by state and territory, as directed by House rules. A minor controversy occurred when first Caleb Cushing and then John Quincy Adams, both representatives from Massachusetts, presented abolition petitions sent to them from residents of other states. The Speaker of the House reminded the chamber that this practice was standard, a few representatives spoke on the issue, some asked that the chair's decision be challenged, and the House voted to support the Speaker (and, by extension, Cushing and Adams).

One imagines Adams smiling to himself because some unsuspecting (although probably belligerent) congressman started that little game of one-upmanship. It gave Adams a chance to call attention to someone else causing trouble in the House, and to imply his own innocence. He returned to the business of his petitions, but only after "wish[ing] the House to recollect that more time, thrice told, had been consumed in debating this appeal than he had taken up, or should take up, in presenting all his petitions. He hoped, therefore, the House would not hold him responsible for the consumption of time."[51] Little did the House know Adams was about to create a controversy that would take a week to settle. But first, Adams presented a petition against slavery in the District of Columbia, which, according to the gag rule, was laid on the table. Then, calmly and respectfully, the former United States president asked the Speaker of the House for some advice. This request—and the subsequent debate—was printed in page after page of the *National Intelligencer.* It began:

> Mr. ADAMS said he held in his hands a paper on which, before it was presented, he desired to have the decision of the Speaker. It was a petition from twenty-two persons, declaring themselves to be slaves. He wished to know whether the Speaker considered such a petition as coming within the order of the House?
>
> The SPEAKER said he could not tell until he had the contents of the petition in his possession.
>
> Mr. ADAMS said that if the paper was sent to the Clerk's table it would be in possession of the House, and if sent to the Speaker he would see what were its contents. Now, he (Mr. A.) wished to do nothing except in submission to the rules of the House.

There were no rules to deal with this case, as Adams knew. When he agreed to send the petition to the speaker, protests erupted. A representative from South Carolina "hoped that no further discussion would be had on the it could only lead to excitement and disorder in the House."[52]

The discussion went not as that representative hoped, but rather as he predicted. Very quickly—in the next column, for *National Intelligencer* subscribers reading at home—amid cries for Adams's expulsion, one of Adams's colleagues proposed a resolution to censure the former U.S. president for disrespecting the House. And so it began. The House spent the rest of the day on Monday, all day Tuesday, and all but the last few minutes of the day on Thursday debating whether to censure Adams for asking whether House rules allowed its members to present a petition from slaves. (They skipped Wednesday: the House had to tally the votes and announce the next president and vice president of the United States.) Late Thursday, the House voted 137 to 21 against censuring Adams and then briefly introduced business to be conducted on Friday. On Saturday, the House returned to Adams's original question: could slaves petition? At the end of the day, they voted 162 to 18 to affirm the resolution "that slaves do not possess the right of petition secured to the people of the United States by the constitution." On Monday, representatives returned to the business of hearing petitions from their constituents.[53]

Theodore Frelinghuysen had a very different experience than did John Quincy Adams when the New Jersey senator presented a petition from Cherokees to the Senate on January 21, 1835. According to the record of the session in the *National Intelligencer,* in their petition the Cherokees asked the House to facilitate the purchase of their lands by the federal government and their own acquisition of U.S. citizenship so that they could remain in Georgia under the state's jurisdiction. Frelinghuysen summarized the petition and moved that the House refer it to the Committee on Indian Affairs. The motion passed and, without any debate, the Senate went on to its next piece of business. None of the senators questioned whether the United States Congress would accept or act upon a petition submitted by the Cherokees.[54] Several times during the Jacksonian-era removal debates Native Americans petitioned the federal government, sometimes writing to the national legislature, sometimes writing to President Jackson or members of his cabinet, and sometimes bringing suit before the Supreme Court. Although the three branches of the federal government usually denied Native American appeals, typically they attended and responded to those appeals.

Though they did not have rights as citizens of the United States (they were, after all, citizens of other nations), Native Americans could engage white American leaders and participate in political negotiations. People of color rarely could, whether they were enslaved—as the astonished reactions of Adams's colleagues in the House made clear—or free. Interestingly, not only did slaves have no right to engage the federal government, but according to many congressmen, Congress had no right to engage, or even hear from, slaves. One legislator declared, "Slaves have no right to petition. They are property, not persons; they have no political rights; and even their civil rights must be claimed through their masters. Having no political rights, Congress has no power in regard to them, and therefore no right to receive their petitions."[55] Congress could do nothing to intervene in the property rights of slaveholders, so they had no right to hear grievances from slaves. In most states, African Americans also had no rights to engage local or national policy. Some states, like North Carolina, took away the right to vote from its free black men during this time. Others charged one hundred times more in poll taxes for blacks than for whites. Still others forced all African Americans living within their borders to register and even post bond assuring their good behavior but then made the bond unaffordable or passed laws making it extremely difficult for African Americans to make a living. Many state governments passed these sorts of laws explicitly to discourage free people of color from settling in their states.[56] Aaron Vanderpoel, a congressman from New York, explained his state government's position during the 1837 congressional debate on slaves' right to petition:

> Sir, what has the Legislature of New York lately done to indicate its abhorrence of the movements of modern abolitionists? A petition was there very recently presented to enlarge the political rights of free negroes—emanating, no doubt, from the same sources that are constantly agitating us here; and, *eo instanti* that it was presented, its prayer was indignantly rejected by an almost unanimous vote of the popular branch of the New York Legislature. There was little or no sympathy for abolitionists there.[57]

With pride, Vanderpoel declared that his state quickly and nearly unanimously denied any expansion of rights for free African Americans.

Vanderpoel also assigned responsibility for the petition to abolitionists. The charge illustrates the perception that the fate of African Americas living in the United States was up for grabs in the fight between abolitionists and colonizationists; African Americans simply did not have a political presence to combat their oppression as Native Americans did during this period. We see this situation in the petitions Native Americans submitted to the federal government; in the treaties they signed; in the responses they received from President Andrew Jackson, Secretary of War John Eaton, and other members of the administration; and in the nearly complete absence of this sort of interaction between African Americans and the federal government. We also see it on the pages of the *National Intelligencer.* As part of the newspaper exchange so prevalent in the 1830s, Gales and Seaton received copies of the *Cherokee Phoenix,* and they reprinted stories and reports from the *Phoenix* in their daily. Most of the texts written by Native Americans that appeared in the *National Intelligencer* came from the *Phoenix,* and many of the texts appeared without comment from Gales and Seaton when they were reprinted. These texts are informative and, especially in the late 1820s and early 1830s, often belligerent. In August 1828, the *National Intelligencer* reprinted this brief article:

FROM THE CHEROKEE PHOENIX.

NEW ECHOTA, JULY 23.—We have heard much of late, in many of the Southern papers, of the degraded state of our neighbors, the Creeks, and their rapid decline. This may be true; but we protest against associating the Cherokees with them, under the general name of "Southern Indians," as we have noticed in some of the Northern prints. We know, that, in the late session of Congress, we were denounced by some of our neighbors, as miserable and degraded as the Creeks now are: but the public have been told that all was misrepresentation, intended merely to *electioneer* us out of our present homes. We repeat again, that the Cherokees are not on the decline, in numbers and improvement, and we hope we shall, for this once, be believed, and that the friends of Indian emigration will urge the necessity of our removal on some other reason than that of our degraded condition.[58]

These Cherokees dissociated themselves from the Creeks, a rhetorical move available to them because of their nationalized status in the white imagination. They also directly addressed and refuted as disingenuous claims of their degradation. At no point in the decade beginning in 1828 were African Americans seen refuting claims of degradation in the *National Intelligencer,* even though "degraded" was one of the most common adjectives assigned to them at that time, it was one of the most potent arguments for their removal, and people such as William Lloyd Garrison easily marshaled significant contrary evidence in the early 1830s.

The theme of white deception persisted in the *Phoenix,* and antiremovalists Gales and Seaton gave voice to Cherokee complaints. In the summer of

1829, a member of the Cherokee nation accused the United States of falsely reporting Indians who had emigrated as being happy with their move: "We are even told that the Creeks, many of whom have already removed, and the Choctaws and Chickasaws who have explored it, are pleased with it, and prefer it to their old homes. All this shows how determined interested persons are to misrepresent the Indians, and mislead the public. From all we can learn, the truth of the case is entirely different."[59] The picture Native Americans were allowed to draw in the *National Intelligencer* was highly sympathetic to their antiremoval case, and they appeared honest compared to United States government agents and politicians. On the other hand, African Americans were used in the *National Intelligencer* to authenticate the claims of the ACS about the virtues of removal in the face of charges of deception made by free black and white abolitionists. Native Americans appeared resistant to an outside force compelling removal whereas African Americans appeared complicit with the ACS and its removal program.

On the pages of the *National Intelligencer*, Native Americans also appearred principled and heroic in the face of their oppression. In June 1830, the *Intelligencer* reprinted a rallying cry from the *Phoenix*: "We hope we are not yet at the end of our row . . . Let then the Cherokees be *firm* and *united.*— Fellow citizens, we have asserted our rights, we have defended them thus far, and we will defend them yet by all lawful and peaceable means.—We will no more beg, pray and implore, but we will *demand* justice . . . Let us then be *firm* and *united.*" A similar but more sympathetic piece was reprinted a few months later: "We and our people are under the screw, and one turn has already forced tears from our eyes. If the Indian Bill is not repealed by next Congress, the second turn will draw from our agonized bodies, life preserving blood. But let us remain still innocent, and pray the lord to change the hearts of the Rulers of these United States." Ironically, the writer of this text, David Vann, metaphorically employed a mechanism used to torture negro slaves. But there were no anguished cries from African Americans on the pages of the *National Intelligencer.*[60]

On several occasions during the height of the Indian removal debates, the *National Intelligencer* opened its pages to pieces written by Cherokees especially for distribution among white Americans. Twice in four months Gales and Seaton published letters written to them from W. S. Coodey, a member of the Cherokee nation identified by the editors as "one of the Cherokee delegation who spent some time in this city during the last session."[61] The first letter quoted and then argued against a derogatory paragraph about the southern tribes published in the *New York Evening Post*. In his letter, clearly written for publication in the *Intelligencer*, Coodey complained about the unjust portrayal and declared, "I must therefore be allowed to speak with some certainty of facts, which throughout may differ with the plain & positive statements" made in the *Post* article. Coodey was allowed to speak, in a way unmatched by black Americans at the time. He described his fellow citizens as "industrious and laboring" people, as farmers who regularly attended church and school. Coodey also defended the Choctaws, Chickasaws, and Creeks as being prosperous and not at all degraded as the *Post* article implied.[62] A few months later, Gales and Seaton published another letter to the editors written by Coodey. That letter, too, specifically and forthrightly defended the Cherokees against accusations about his nation that Coodey believed to be false.[63] Significantly, both of these letters appeared unmediated. The first one stood alone without editorial comment. The second letter had appended to it only the explanation about Coodey's identity and an explanation about the timing of the letter's publication. In the following month the *Intelligencer* published the "Address of the Committee and Council of the Cherokee Nation, in general council convened, to the People of the United States." That address urged white Americans to advocate on behalf of the Cherokees, using logical as well as pathetic appeals grounded in precedent, democratic principles, and Christian teachings. The committee summarized its position: "We wish to remain on the land of our fathers. We have a perfect and original right to remain without interruption or molestation. The treaties with us, and laws of the United States made in pursuance of treaties, guaranty our residence, and our privileges, and secure us against intruders. Our only request is, that these treaties may be fulfilled, and these laws executed."[64] Gales and Seaton respected the writers of the address enough to let the document stand on its own, without commentary, as they did a year later after the Supreme Court made its landmark decision in *Cherokee Nation v. State of Georgia*.[65] At the same time, state after state passed restrictive laws on its free black residents and on slave owners, who increasingly were not permitted to manumit slaves without providing for their emigration out of the state. Needless to say, black Americans had no access to channels of communication to defend themselves or appeal to the *National Intelligencer*'s white readership. Their silence, especially when compared to the protests of Native Americans, contributed to very different imaginings by these white Americans of the objects of their advocacy.

When black Americans appeared as speakers or writers on the pages of the *National Intelligencer*, their texts almost always were explicitly mediated by whites. Usually, when the *National Intelligencer* included African Americans on its pages it did so by reprinting, from the *African Repository* (the ACS organ) or other newspapers, colonists' letters home to friends and family. In June 1833, for example, Gales and Seaton reprinted an article from the *Winchester Virginian*. The article included a paragraph introducing the letter, and then a letter from Reuben Moss to his brother Benjamin. Moss's letter is fairly typical: it noted the health of his family, the ease with which he found employment and could support himself, the prominence of religious activity and ideals, some details about native plants and peoples. It also encouraged more free people of color to emigrate: "I believe an industrious man can live here easier than in the United States . . . I wish very much that you were here with me. I feel that I am in a land of great privileges and freedom." Also typical in this article is the paragraph that introduced Moss's letter. The introduction marked the letter as an argument for colonization. It began, "The accounts of prosperity attending the colony of Liberia have been so imposing through the letters that have been received from that place, that doubts of their authenticity have existed in the minds of some of our colored population." Like many other letters home, the introduction continued, this one "speaks for itself—indeed the colonization society now meets with little opposition."[66] Of course most of the letters, including Moss's, did not speak for themselves—editors insisted on introducing them and framing them as arguments for colonization. In September 1834, the *National Intelligencer* extracted two paragraphs from a letter extolling the governor and teachers in the colony. But the first paragraph of the article belonged to Gales and Seaton: "We rejoice to notice that each arrival from the Colony affords new proofs of the benefits conferred on long-suffering Africa by the wise and philanthropic labors of the American Colonization Society. The following extract from the letter of an old and highly respectable colored colonist to a gentleman of Philadelphia, will, we are sure, gratify the friends of the cause."[67] In 1836, when the colonizationist-abolitionist conflict neared its peak, those introductory paragraphs situated letters home as crucially relevant to the debate. In September, Gales and Seaton wrote this introduction:

We give below another letter on the same subject, from an intelligent Mississippi emigrant, whose statements are equally favorable to the climate, healthiness, and fertility of the colony . . . If the abolitionists, instead of agitating the country with their mischievous assumptions, and worse than vain abstractions, would employ their efforts in assisting to remove all the free and emancipated Negroes to the land which Nature has made their peculiar home, and which is their most suitable asylum, they would contribute at once to a work of practical philanthropy and public utility. The only effect of their present misguided efforts is to do harm to the Negro, mischief to society, and good to nobody.[68]

In November, the editors presented a letter "as conveying information which may be relied on with certainty, and as contradicting falsehoods which have been widely circulated in relation to this prospering colony."[69] The introductions to the letters directed readers to interpret the letters as arguments for colonization, and so the letters themselves—which were fairly redundant—looked like set pieces and represented their writers, free people of color, as grateful beneficiaries of the ACS program.

Another way the *National Intelligencer* gave voice to African Americans on its pages was by extracting reports and information from the colony's newspaper, the *Liberia Herald*. But the excerpts looked nothing like the pieces taken from the *Cherokee Phoenix*. For instance, in June 1830, the *Intelligencer* reprinted a story from the *Liberia Herald* just as it did stories from dozens and dozens of United States newspapers. This five-paragraph long story compared the death rate in Liberia to that of other colonies and noted how very well Liberia compared. In 1834, Gales and Seaton extracted seven paragraphs from the *Liberia Herald*. Five of those paragraphs sang the praises of the colony and the wonderful quality of life experienced by its residents. The writer could not understand the resistance to African emigration by his brethren living in the United States, especially given the full citizenship rights free people of color enjoyed in Liberia. Other extracts from other days in other years included items of news. But there was no protest, only unwavering support for colonization in the words of these people of color.[70]

Only once in the more than ten years of the issues examined did the *National Intelligencer* include on its pages free people of color voicing dissent against the colonization project or oppression more broadly. In that one instance, the *Intelligencer* published a brief overview of "a large and very respectable meeting of the colored citizens of Washington, D.C.," a meeting called "for the purpose of expressing their views upon the subject of African Colonization." Their views were very unfavorable, and these "colored citizens" expressed their views in five resolutions that not only condemned colonization and the ACS but also thanked abolitionists for their support. On the same page Gales and Seaton offered a corrective to the free people of color and the conclusions of their meeting:

> In publishing the proceedings of certain colored citizens of Washington, which appear in another column, we accord to them the privilege of making their opinions known, to which they are entitled by their general respectability and morality of deportment. We cannot give them a place in our columns, however, without expressing our belief that they are not well informed on the subject of their resolutions, and are, (under the influence of misapprehension,) endeavoring to diffuse a groundless prejudice against emigration among their brethren. Their first and principal resolution is based upon an erroneous assumption.

The editors went on to explain the mistakes these people made.[71] Simply, except for this 1831 case—and a corrected case at that—the only times *National Intelligencer* readers heard black voices were instances when they advocated colonization and the ACS, and even then commentary from *African Repository* or *Intelligencer* editors surrounded their words. On the other hand, *Intelligencer* readers frequently encountered Indian voices that argued for Native American independence and rights and that argued against United States oppression and usurpation of their lands and resources.

Abolitionists Imagine the Objects of Their Advocacy

"I have heard it asserted," remarked Lydia Maria Child in *An Appeal in Favor of That Class of Americans called Africans* (1833), "that the Indians were evidently superior to the negroes, because it was impossible to enslave *them*." Almost certainly Child had read Catharine Sedgwick's comparison in her preface to *Hope Leslie*: "The Indians of North America are, perhaps, the only race of men of whom it may be said, that though conquered, they were never enslaved. They could not submit, and live." Child took issue with the point, arguing first, that slave laws designed to protect owners from insubordination, insurrection, and escapes proved that negroes resisted captivity; second, that Indians only fought "with but one nation at a time," whereas "the whole world have combined against the Africans"; and third, that no one reported on negro resistance. She emphasized this last point by sharing a fable with her readers: "We are told in the fable that a lion, looking at a picture of one of his own species, conquered and trampled on by man, calmly said, 'We lions have no painters.'"[72] Child in her *Appeal*, William Lloyd

Garrison in his *Thoughts on African Colonization: Or An Impartial Exhibition of the Doctrines, Principles and Purposes of the American Colonization Society. Together with the Resolutions, Addresses and Remonstrances of the Free People of Color* (1832), and Theodore Weld (with assistance from the Grimké sisters) in his *American Slavery As It Is: Testimony of a Thousand Witnesses* (1839) attempted to paint some of those missing pictures. Garrison actually provided canvases in different forms for people of color: as he did in his abolitionist newspaper the *Liberator*, in his aptly named 1832 tome Garrison published antislavery and anticolonization texts written by people of color.[73]

These three texts—Garrison's *Thoughts on African Colonization*, Child's *Appeal*, and Weld's *American Slavery As It Is*—were three of the most important and influential abolitionist texts of the 1830s. But most of the thousands of colonizationists did not abandon the ACS for the American Anti-Slavery Society (AAS), and in fact the ACS's popularity and success peaked in the early 1830s in part because of backlash against the "incendiary" texts and ideas of abolitionists. Abolitionist texts, especially the three by Garrison, Child, and Weld, threatened most European Americans by aggressively contesting whites' imaginings about people of color as articulated and reproduced by the American Colonization Society and its advocates. So although *Thoughts on African Colonization*, the *Appeal*, and *American Slavery* provide windows into fundamental abolitionist principles, they also can be read as mirrors: in their aggressive opposition they reflected and thereby captured the most basic colonizationist principles and practices.

All three books argued that the discourse about Africans and their descendents in the United States—free people of color as well as slaves—was remarkably one-sided and therefore produced grossly inaccurate understandings. They argued that the classification of a group of people as property prohibited the humanization of people of color. All three texts also deplored the definition of descendants of Africans born in the United States as African nationals rather than as U.S. citizens. Central, then, to their abolitionist rhetoric was a critique of the ways colonizationists imagined the objects of their advocacy in the 1820s and 1830s. In their critiques Garrison, Child, and Weld powerfully confirmed the pervasiveness of these imaginings and the persuasive power the imaginings entailed in colonizationist discourse. Their texts punctuate this chapter's central argument: the ways antiremovalist-colonizationists imagined Native and African Americans as objects of their advocacy in the 1830s precluded that community from embracing abolition and its tactics, including a national petition campaign and other forms of protest against U.S. federal and state policies.

Theodore Weld's *American Slavery As It Is* was premised on the rhetorical force of what its compiler called "corroborative testimony,—facts, similar to those established by the testimony of others" (iv). Weld designed a project that proved the horrors of slavery to be regular, even normal, not exceptional. After an introduction in which Weld promised several times to provide evidence about "the actual condition and treatment of slaves in the United States" (9), the text primarily comprised personal narratives written by people involved with slavery and documents that detailed the atrocities condoned within the slave system produced by slave owners, including advertisements for runaway slaves described by the harm done to their bodies. One of *American Slavery*'s contributors explained to northern readers that their understanding of slavery was fallacious because they based it on the 10 percent of the black population with whom northerners often came into contact, slaves who served in roles such as house servant, nurse, or waiter. So the Reverend Horace Moulton, a former brick maker who had lived in Georgia for five years, chose to testify about "*field hands*, who compose much the largest portion of the black population, (probably nine-tenths)" (18). At another point in the text, Weld used testimony that included reports from slavers as well as laws about prison rations to "show that the slaves have insufficient food" (27–28). *American Slavery* continued in this manner for more than two hundred pages, using testimonials to paint detailed pictures of the oppressed, their oppression, and their oppressors. "Look at the slave," Weld wrote, "must not humanity let its voice be heard?" (17). Ironically, no slaves actually spoke in *American Slavery As It Is: Testimony of a Thousand Witnesses*. But the horrors of their lives and their burdens were told as never before, "produced by accumulations of proof, by affirmations and affidavits, by written testimonies and statements of a cloud of witnesses who speak what they know and testify what they have seen, and all these impregnably fortified by proofs innumerable" (9–10). In its concept and its execution, *American Slavery* argued that northern imaginings of slaves and their conditions—imaginings based on biased, fallacious, and absent evidence—were wrong.

After offering hundreds and hundreds of horrific testimonials, Weld refused the opportunity to call for slavery's abolition in the United States. The only paragraph between the book's final testimonial and the book's index begins with this sentence: "Having drawn out this topic to so great a length, we waive all comments, and only say to the reader, in conclusion, *ponder these things*, and lay to heart, that slaveholding 'is justified *of her children*'" (210). Weld's tract clearly aimed to persuade apathetic or colonizationist northerners to embrace the abolitionist cause, but in its design it remained true to its original topic: "The question at issue is not one of law, but of fact—'What is the actual condition of the slaves in the United States?'" (7). Fundamentally, Weld's *American Slavery As It Is*, the most popular nonfiction antislavery tract of the antebellum era, did its rhetorical work by presuming that its opponents profoundly misunderstood the objects of their advocacy in ways that impeded their joining the radical cause of immediate abolition.

That Weld focused so carefully on this issue in 1839 emphasizes the pervasiveness of the problem that both Garrison and Child addressed earlier in the decade. In a chapter of *Thoughts on African Colonization* called "The American Colonization Society is the Disparager of the Free Blacks," Garrison complained that "the leaders in the African colonization crusade seem to dwell with a malignant satisfaction upon the poverty and degradation of the free people of color, and are careful never to let an opportunity pass without heaping their abuse and contempt upon them" (1:124). Garrison proceeded to quote disparaging remarks about people of color from colonizationist documents, including the ACS monthly journal *African Repository*, the ACS's annual reports, and procolonization newspapers. To counter these texts and "repel these charges against the free people of color, as unmerited, wanton and untrue" (1:128), Garrison provided counterexamples from northern communities. For example, he celebrated "the colored inhabitants of Philadelphia," who, in less than three decades, increased their collective real estate holdings from nothing to "hundreds of thousands of dollars," a stunning increase that "speaks volumes in praise of their industry and economy" (1:129). Garrison also contradicted the ACS claim that people of color could succeed only if they left the United States. He listed by name three wealthy black Philadelphians who could "buy out" Francis Devany, the wealthiest black emigrant in Liberia. James Forten, for instance, could "*buy him out* three or four times over" (1:129). The ACS bias against Garrison's countrymen deeply disturbed the abolitionist leader, and Garrison allotted significant space in the *Liberator* for critique and counterexamples, including pieces written by black men and women. Recognizing the importance of this work, many anticolonization meetings held by black Americans in the early 1830s passed resolutions thanking Garrison and other abolitionist editors such as Benjamin Lundy. For example, "a large and very respectable meeting of the colored citizens of Washington, D.C." adopted this resolution in May 1831: "That we believe the PRESS to be the most efficient means of disseminating light and knowledge among our brethren; and that this meeting do acknowledge with gratitude the efforts made in our behalf, by the editors of the Genius of Universal Emancipation, and the Liberator;— and do most earnestly recommend their respective papers to our brethren generally, for their approval and support" (2:22–23). But few colonizationists read the *Liberator* or Lundy's paper, the *Genius of Universal Emancipation,* in the early 1830s. Colonizationists continually and vehemently derided abolitionist papers, especially the *Liberator,* as dangerous, inflammatory, and fanatical, and abolitionists' competing imaginings about people of color failed to influence—probably failed to reach—most ACS advocates. In his *Thoughts on African Colonization,* Garrison perceptively admitted the critical hurdle in their path: "The truth is, the traducers of the free blacks have no adequate conception of the amount of good sense, sterling piety, moral honesty, virtuous pride of character, and domestic enjoyment, which exists among this class" (1:131). Garrison recognized that colonizationists and their prominent leaders could not (or would not) imagine people of color who remained in the United States as anything but degraded. This imaginative failure on their part played an important role in ACS arguments for the removal of free people of color to Liberia.

Whereas Garrison primarily denounced the one-sided reports about free people of color and Weld primarily contested the one-sided reports about slavery, Child addressed both problems in *An Appeal in Favor of That Class of Americans Called Africans.* U.S. newspapers and other media, Child argued, circulated only troubling reports about free and bound people of color. These one-sided reports, not anything essential in the nature of people of color, led to erroneous imaginings about African citizens of the United States. Child explained, "In Brazil, people of color are lawyers, clergymen, merchants and military officers; and in the Portuguese, as well as the Spanish settlements, intermarriages bring no degradation. On the shores of the Levant, some of the wealthiest merchants are black. If we were accustomed to see intelligent and polished negroes, the prejudice would soon disappear. There is certainly no law of our nature which makes a *dark color* repugnant to our feelings" (127–128). And so in her ongoing commitment "to prove that the present degraded condition of that unfortunate race is produced by artificial causes, not by the laws of nature" (140), Child provided story after story celebrating black men and women who achieved prominence and respectability as scholars, philosophers, architects, mechanics, rulers, officers, soldiers, physicians, priests, lawyers, legislators, shopkeepers, farmers, orators, poets, preachers, professors—men and women who were courageous, talented, magnanimous, brave, intelligent, perseverant, benevolent, prudent, industrious, faithful, skilled, eloquent, and well educated (140–167). Child admitted the bias of her own text and in fact argued that her bias should be construed as her point. She predicted that she "shall be told that in the preceding examples I have shown only the bright side of the picture. I readily grant it; but I have deemed it important to show that the picture *has* a bright side" (162).

Slavery, too, had another side—one that Americans hardly ever saw. Over and over, Child claimed, Americans heard stories told by slave owners. Rarely did Americans "hear of the grievous wrongs which provoke the vengeance of the slave" (183). So, for instance, "negroes" had earned a reputation as being "a very unfeeling race." But if newspapers would print the whole of each story, Americans could see that slaves' callousness resulted from the institution of slavery, not their natures. The Georgia slave who stabbed his overseer three times appeared as a monstrous murderer in a newspaper report of the incident. But "the Georgia editor viewed the subject only on one side," charged Child. He failed to mention that the overseer was brutally and mercilessly whipping the slave's wife at the time (179). On the final pages of her *Appeal,* in a chapter called "Prejudices Against People of Color, and Our Duties in Relations to This Subject," Child explicitly lamented the devastating bias of American media:

> It is true we *hear* a great deal more about West Indian cruelty than we do about our own.—English books and periodicals are continually full of the subject; and even in the colonies, newspapers openly denounce the hateful system, and take every opportunity to prove the amount of wretchedness it produces. In this country, we have not, until very recently, dared to publish anything upon the subject. Our books, our reviews, our newspapers, our almanacs, have all been silent, or exerted their influence on the wrong side. The negro's crimes are repeated, but his sufferings are never told. Even in our geographies it is taught that the colored race *must* always be degraded. (201)

The problem was so pervasive that the first thing Child urged her readers to do on behalf of "that class of Americans called Africans" was to counter negative imaginings. Child very specifically told her readers that "we can speak kindly and respectfully of colored people upon all occasions; we can repeat to our children such traits as are honorable in their character and history; we can avoid making odious caricatures of negroes; we can teach boys that it is unmanly and contemptible to insult an unfortunate class of people by the vulgar outcry of 'Nigger!—Nigger!'" (206). She also urged "our almanacs and newspapers [to] fairly show both sides of the question," a practice that could make clear the intolerable conditions of free and enslaved people of color in the United States (206). Child focused significant energy in her *Appeal* on the portrayals of African Americans, the stories that white people told about them and the conclusions drawn from those stories, and how much those conclusions mattered to the politics of slavery. Like Garrison before her and Weld after her, Child recognized that the Jacksonian–era logics of slavery, colonization, and abolition fundamentally relied on the ways that European Americans imagined the objects of their advocacy.

Unfortunately for abolitionists, those imaginings developed inside a culture that classified more than two million people of color as property. Slavery hinged on this classification, and one of Garrison's chief "allegations" against the ACS, as he said in the title to the third section of *Thoughts on African Colonization*, was that "The American Colonization Recognises Slaves as Property" (1:68). Garrison called this belief disgraceful in the eyes of man and God, even as he acknowledged its rhetorical force: "The Society, if language means any thing, does unequivocally acknowledge property in slaves to be as legitimate and sacred as any other property, of which to deprive the owners either by force or by legislation, without making restitution, would be unjust and tyrannical" (1:68). Child also acknowledged the consequences of the classification when she declared that "slave holders try to stop all the efforts of benevolence, by vociferous complaints about infringing upon their *property*" (93). Imagining slaves as property rendered most abolitionist arguments irrelevant, since abolitionists refused to recognize the relationship between slave masters and slaves as possessive. "I wish it settled in your minds, as a fixed and immutable principle, that there is and can be no property of man in man," wrote Garrison, quoting from a speech by an Edinburgh minister. Garrison agreed with the minister, who explained that "the whole question may be said to hang upon this point. If the slaves are not property, then slavery is at an end" (1:78). But of course slavery was decades away from its end, and the classification of slaves as property dominated proslavery and colonizationist discourses throughout this period.

Child recognized the ways that this classification debased all people of color living in the United States. Child reminded her readers that "people of their color only, are universally allowed to be slaves" (126). Since people used color to identify human property, since United States laws protected property rights, and since more than two million people of color were enslaved while less than half a million were free, many European Americans nationally and most European Americans who lived in the southern states operated as if the people of color they encountered were slaves or escaped slaves. European Americans normalized all people of color as slaves. Child pointed out that "every colored man is *presumed* to be a slave, till it can be provided otherwise; this rule prevails in all the slave States, except North Carolina, where it is confined to negroes" (59). Even language conventions reflected the tenacity of this racist ideology: in popular discourse "negro" was used interchangeably with "slave" and people spoke of "free people of color" but never "enslaved people of color," since "people of color" almost always meant slaves. To perpetuate this racist ideology, advocates of slavery debased people of color institutionally and systematically. Child described one manifestation: "Even in the *laws*, slaves are always mentioned before free people of color; so desirous are they to degrade the latter class below the level of the former" (62). Slaves were property; people of color who were not property might as well have been property; if they proved they were not property, they were degraded because they were presumed to be property. Each of these beliefs pointed its adherents toward removal under the guise of colonization, rather than abolition.

Garrison, Child, and Weld clearly believed that as long as European Americans imagined slaves as property, the logic of abolition remained conceptually unavailable to them. But in the Jacksonian era, European Americans had few opportunities to rethink those beliefs. Popular literature reinforced imaginings of African Americans as slaves and offered few respectable possibilities for people of color outside that role, even as literature made it virtually impossible to imagine Native Americans as property. Mainstream media reinforced the sanctity of the propertied relationship between master and slave. Garrison and Child attempted to create dissonance by presenting their readers with successful people of color whom it would be impossible to imagine as someone else's property, but they failed to replace or even disrupt the ways most people imagined people of color during the 1830s. At the end of the decade, Weld tried a different strategy.

Weld capitalized on the idea of slaves as property. He used it to explain the horrible cruelty exposed by the graphic testimonials amassed in *American Slavery As It Is*. Weld anticipated seven objections to the book, and the first one he addressed was the skeptical response that "such cruelties are incredible" (110). Weld had to make it impossible for his readers to dismiss *American Slavery* as too terrible to be true. His explanation was elegant in its simplicity:

> The enormities inflicted by slaveholders upon their slaves will never be discredited except by those who overlook the simple fact, that he who holds human beings as his bona fide property, *regards* them as property, and not as *persons;* this is his permanent state of mind toward them. He does not contemplate slaves as human beings, consequently does not *treat* them as such; and with entire indifference sees them suffer privations and writhe under blows, which, if inflicted upon whites, would fill him with horror and indignation. (110)

Weld reminded his (primarily northern) readers that slave owners grew up watching family and friends habitually treat slaves "as domestic animals" so that "such practices have become to him a mere matter of course," analogous to kicking a dog off the porch or out of a church (110). In his best-selling tract Weld explained how pervasively the concept of slave as property had infiltrated the belief systems of slaveholders:

> The same terms are applied to slaves that are given to cattle. They are called "stock." So when the children of slaves are spoken of prospectively, they are called their "increase;" the same term that is applied to flocks and herds. So the female slaves that are mothers, are called "breeders" till past child bearing . . . when moved from one part of the country to another, they are herded in droves like cattle, and like them urged on by drivers; their labor is compelled in the same way. They are bought and sold, and separated like cattle . . . those who bid upon them examine their persons, just as purchasers inspect horses and oxen; they open their mouths to see if their teeth are sound; strip their backs to see if they are badly scarred, and handle their limbs and muscles to see if they are firmly knit. Like horses, they are warranted to be "sound," or to be returned to the owner if "unsound." A father gives his son a horse and a *slave;* by his will he distributes among them his racehorses, hounds, game-cocks, and *slaves.* (110)

Weld assured his readers that his explication could go on. But instead of continuing that line of proof, Weld supplied testimony from respected leaders, including several congressmen and President Thomas Jefferson, to make his point that slave owners imagined slaves as dehumanized property.

Because slave owners imagined slaves as property, they could commit acts against people of color that others found nauseating, intolerable, and monstrous. Weld counted on his readers to be disgusted, overwhelmed, shocked—and to be so repulsed by the consequences that followed from treating slaves as property that they would resist that equation, insisting that slaves were human beings and should not be treated with such cruelty. Weld knew that people who imagined slaves as property would find it nearly impossible to switch their allegiance from colonization to abolition, and *American Slavery As It Is,* like *Thoughts on African Colonization* and *An Appeal in Favor of That Class of Americans Called Africans,* included as part of its project the dismantling of that idea for European Americans who advocated on behalf of people of color.

On one hand, the belief that slaves were property made it nearly impossible for most Americans to embrace immediate emancipation in the 1830s. On the other hand, the belief that people of color were African nationals made it easy for people to embrace colonization, and the attention prominent abolitionist leaders gave to that nationalist discourse reinforces for us how important it was to ACS doctrine. The ACS relied on a repatriation argument to justify the colonization of free blacks in Africa. In response, Garrison, Child, and Weld insisted that free blacks born in the United States were citizens of the United States. "Twenty-seven hundred thousand free born citizens of the U.S. in slavery," declared a subheading of *American Slavery*'s table of contents (v). Child attacked the ACS specifically on this point: "Neither the planters nor the Colonization Society, seem to ask what *right* we have to remove people from the places where they have been born and brought up,—where they have a home, which, however miserable, is still their home,—and where their relatives and acquaintances all reside. Africa is no more their native country than England is ours,—nay, it is less so, because there is no community of language or habits" (122–123). Garrison called the idea "that our free blacks are natives of Africa" absurd and charged the ACS with dishonesty based primarily on their promotion of that idea (1:10–11). Abolitionists recognized U.S. people of color as descendants of Africans. Child's first chapter, for example, is a history of slavery that goes back to Africa, she turned to African history when she celebrated people of color, and she occasionally referred to United States people of color as members of the "African race." But abolitionists clearly understood bound and free people of color born in the United States as countrymen.

Garrison used that appellation and otherwise marked people of color as citizens repeatedly in his monograph, as when he reported that white

Americans "are determined to deprive millions of their own countrymen of every political and social right, and to send them to a barbarous continent, because the Creator has given them a sable complexion" or when he declared, "Thus, and thus only, shall we be able to liberate our enslaved countrymen" (1:14, 105). One of Garrison's most virulent criticisms of the ACS was that its members "represent the colored inhabitants of the United States as aliens and foreigners" (1:117). Because nationalizing of U.S. people of color as African propelled one of the strongest colonizationist arguments being made during the Jackson presidency, abolitionists attacked the argument from as many angles as possible. Garrison and Child reminded their readers that people of color fought in the Revolutionary War and the War of 1812:

> But our colored population are not aliens; they were born on our soil; they are bone of our bone, and flesh of our flesh; their fathers fought bravely to achieve our independence during the revolutionary war, without immediate or subsequent compensation; they spilt their blood freely during the last war; they are entitled, in fact, to every inch of our southern, and much of our western territory, having worn themselves out in its cultivation, and received nothing but wounds and bruises in return. Are these the men to stigmatize as foreigners? (*Thoughts*, 1:12)

Both Child and Garrison quoted Andrew Jackson's proclamation delivered at the end of the War of 1812, in which Jackson acknowledged black soldiers for nobly loving and defending what he called "the land of your nativity" (*Appeal*, 123; also *Thoughts*, 2:6). Garrison's opposition to the ACS on this point moved between belligerent and belittling:

> The great mass of our colored population were born in this country. This is their native soil; here they first saw the light of heaven, and inhaled the breath of life; here they have grown from infancy to manhood and old age; from these shores they have never wandered; they are the descendants of those who were forcibly torn from Africa two centuries ago; their fathers assisted in breaking the yoke of British oppression, and achieving that liberty which we prize above all price; and they cherish the strongest attachment to the land of their birth. Now, as they could not have been born in *two* countries, and as they were certainly born here, it follows that Africa is not their native home, and, consequently, that the Society has dealt in romance, or something more culpable, in representing them as strangers and aliens. It might as rationally charge them with being natives of Asia or

Europe, or with having descended from the regions of the moon. To see ourselves gravely represented in a British periodical as natives of Great Britain, I doubt not would create great merriment; and a scheme for our transportation would add vastly to our sport. (1:117–118)

ACS imaginings of U.S. people of color as African nationals pervaded and animated colonizationist arguments. Along with the ideas that slaves were property and that people of color could not rise above perpetual degradation in the United States, the idea that people of color belonged in Africa strongly divided colonizationists and abolitionists.

People of color, too, realized the rhetorical significance of the argument. In the second part of *Thoughts on African Colonization,* which Garrison turned over almost entirely to black Americans, anticolonizationist blacks focused their attention on it. Garrison's introduction to this section addressed the three recurrent issues separating abolitionists and colonizationists: people of color were Americans, not Africans; people of color were freemen, not property; and people of color were peaceful, not degraded. In the part of the book that Garrison called "Sentiments of the People of Color," groups of African Americans picked up these themes. By far, though, because many of these texts emerged at anticolonization meetings, the two primary messages were that the ACS had done and continued to do great harm to people of color living in the United States and that people of color born in the United States were American, not African. In their meeting's resolutions, for example, a group of "colored citizens of New-York . . . claim *this country, the place of our birth, and not Africa,* as our mother country, and all attempts to send us to Africa we consider as gratuitous and uncalled for" (2:14). This same group attacked the ACS because "it has produced a mistaken sentiment toward us. Africa is considered the home of those who have never seen its shores" (2:16). At meetings in towns across Connecticut, Delaware, Maryland, Massachusetts, New Jersey, New York, Pennsylvania, Rhode Island, and Washington, D.C., free blacks made similar declarations. Interestingly, in self-descriptions these groups frequently employ the appellation "Afric-American," which called attention to the Americanization of these descendants of Africans. In New Haven, for instance, "a meeting of the Peace and Benevolent Society of Afric-Americans" passed in 1831 a series of resolutions, including these two:

Resolved, That we know of no other place that we can call our true and appropriate home, excepting these United States, into which our fathers were brought, who enriched the country by their toils, and fought, bled and died in its defence, and left us in its possession—and here we will live and die.

Resolved, That we consider the American Colonization Society founded on principles that no Afric-American, unless very weak in mind, will follow; and any man who will be persuaded to leave his own country and go to Africa, as an enemy to his country and a traitor to his brethren. (2:30–31)

In Pittsburgh the local meeting as adamantly embraced the United States as home and also as adamantly denounced the ACS as troublesome. The similarities in the Pittsburgh and New Haven resolutions suggest that texts circulated across state lines, which presupposes a network joining African American communities in the northern states. Members of one of those communities, working together as "a large and respectable meeting of the colored citizens of Pittsburgh," unanimously adopted this resolution: "Resolved, That we, the colored people of Pittsburgh and citizens of these United States, view the country in which we live as our only true and proper home. We are just as much natives here as the members of the Colonization Society. Here we were born—here bred—here are our earliest and most pleasant associations—here is all that binds man to earth, and makes life valuable" (2:34–35). In 1832 in Lewistown, Pennsylvania, "free people of color" invoked the Declaration of Independence and also attacked the ACS in an address explaining their position:

We, the undersigned, . . . beg leave to present to the public, in a calm and unprejudiced manner, our reasons for opposing the scheme of African colonization. This is the land of our birth. The Declaration of Independence declares, that 'all men are born free and equal:' it does not say that the *white* man or the *black* man is free,—but all, without respect to color, tongues, or nation. We therefore consider all laws to enslave or degrade the people of color as contrary to the letter and spirit of this Declaration; and that according to it we are freemen, and have as indisputable a right to enjoy our liberty as any white man. To deny it to us, because we differ in color, is oppression. To say that Africa is our native country is untrue. Here we were born, and here we mean to die; for all men are born free . . .

We would say to colonizationists that we consider them our foes instead of our friends. It is vain for them to say that we would do better in Liberia; for we do not believe it. There is room enough in this country for us; and if they be our friends, let them meliorate our condition here. Let them join in the work of immediate abolition of slavery. (2:49–50)

In their brief address (the whole amounted to five paragraphs), this group from Lewistown identified colonizationists as a very real threat, accusing them not just of hypocrisy but also of dishonesty. They identified central disagreements between abolitionists and colonizationists and illustrated clearly how distinct the fundamental premises of both groups were.

As these abolitionist texts demonstrate, we cannot divide the slave debates of the 1830s into two sides, one for and one against slavery, and expect to understand the politics of the era. At least two prominent discourse communities identified slavery as evil. Most of our histories leave out colonizationists—the dominant group at that time. But if we leave out colonizationists, we leave out an important element of the logics of antislavery doctrine in Jacksonian America. Those logics fundamentally incorporated the ways European Americans imagined the objects of their advocacy. These imaginings divided colonizationists from abolitionists, and the Beechers from the Grimké-Welds. To understand more fully antislavery doctrine in the 1830s—when the abolitionist movement was born—we have to recover colonizationist as well as abolitionist discourses about African Americans. More broadly, to understand the concomitant debates about rights, freedom, and power in the 1830s, we have to recover simultaneously discourses about the two groups European Americans simultaneously oppressed: Native and African Americans.

Theodore Weld understood the constitutive power of language. In his *American Slavery As It Is,* he explained how a man comes to be a slave: "It was public opinion that *made him a slave.* In a republican government the people make the laws, and those laws are merely public opinion *in legal forms.* We repeat it,—public opinion made them slaves, and keeps them slaves; in other words, it sunk them from men to chattels, and now, forsooth, this same public opinion will see to it, that these *chattels* are treated like *men!*" (143). Weld pointed to the power of discursive imaginings. Constructions of African and Native Americans carried tremendous power in the 1830s, especially since so few European Americans had actual contact with members of these groups, since descendents of Africans and tribal nations did not have their own representation or access to representation in U.S. legislatures and courts, and since debates over their presence in the United States were so prevalent in national conversations during and immediately following Andrew Jackson's presidency. Because these discursive imaginings circulated in tandem, analyzing them independently cannot capture their rhetorical force. When they are analyzed together, the logics of removal, colonization, and abolition become increasingly clear. The imaginings by most European American antislavery activists of African Americans, especially compared with their imaginings of Native Americans, neither could fuel nor sustain abolitionist rhetoric. The rhetorical force of these discursive imaginings, as Theodore Weld, William Lloyd Garrison, and Lydia Maria Child knew, had to be contravened before colonizationist men and women could be persuaded to advocate for the immediate abolition of slavery in the United States.

— 5 —

"On the Very Eve of Coming Out"

Declaring One's Antislavery Affiliations

What has become of Dr. Hawes of Hartford. He was on the very
eve of coming out when I left him.

—JAMES BIRNEY, LETTER TO LEWIS TAPPAN
(NOVEMBER 1835)

Catharine Beecher said "she had never expected to say a word to us on the
subject," Angelina Grimké wrote in her diary on the evening of July 12, 1831.
Beecher and Grimké had met five days earlier, and they were up late talking
with another friend one evening. A poem Grimké read aloud reminded
Beecher of her fiancé who died at sea eight years earlier. Beecher revealed to
her new friends how, upon hearing "the sad intelligence [of his death], she
could compare the state of her mind to nothing but a large manufacturing
establishment in which the whole machinery was suddenly stopped, such
was the perfect vacuum, the entire cessation of interest in everything she
experienced." The event altered "the whole course of her life," bringing to
her a sense of discipline and a deep commitment to religion. Beecher and
Grimké had known each other for just a few days, and yet this personal rev-
elation hardly seemed out of place. Grimké's diary suggests that she and
Beecher enjoyed each other's company and became fast friends.[1]

In July 1831, Grimké visited Beecher during a monthlong journey through
several northern states. Grimké considered becoming a teacher, and so a
visit to Beecher's Hartford Female Seminary made good sense. Grimké
spent several days observing classes, recording in her diary that Beecher
told her "she tho't I might prepare myself to become a teacher in 6 months."
But clearly Beecher viewed Grimké as a friend more than as a potential student or even a colleague, and Grimké shared the sentiment. Grimké's diary
reveals an admiration for Beecher, a sense of pleasure in the company of her
"kind friend Catharine."[2]

160

When she returned to Philadelphia in 1831 Grimké's Quaker friends discouraged her from becoming a teacher, and so Grimké did not return to Hartford. In 1832, Beecher moved from Hartford to Cincinnati with her father, the new head of that city's Lane Seminary. By 1833, Grimké embraced public activism on behalf of slaves. In 1834, antislavery activist Theodore Weld led what would be known as the "Lane Rebellion" against Catharine's father, Lyman; in 1835, Grimké became famous after sending a letter to William Lloyd Garrison that used her experiences in South Carolina to decry slavery; in 1836, Weld trained Angelina and Sarah to be antislavery "agents"; and in 1837 Beecher challenged Grimké to a public debate about colonization, abolition, and women's role in bringing slavery to an end in the United States.

But a historical master narrative of the events that came before the Beecher-Grimké exchange does justice neither to the participants nor to the positions they defended. Simply, the web that enmeshed these two people is just too tangled and too interesting in its tangles to be reduced to a linear, chronological history. The positions Beecher and Grimké espoused in 1837 cannot be separated from the ideologies that colored colonization-abolition debates. Because ideologies are dynamic processes, they best can be studied within relationships rather than as ornaments attached to events. Focusing on interwoven relationships rather than a linear list of events, one could enter the web of ideologies from any number of points—say, a poem written by Sarah Forten, or an endorsement for Henry Clay, or a resignation letter written by James Birney—and emerge with a holographic image of the web's composition. In that sense, my presentation of the history leading to the 1837 polemics is itself an argument for a feminist reading of history coincident with a rhetorical reading of the colonization-abolition debates. Wherever we choose to begin, what develops is a respect for Beecher's *Essay on Slavery and Abolitionism, with Reference to the Duty of American Females* and Grimké's *Letters to Cath[a]rine E. Beecher, in Reply to An Essay on Slavery and Abolitionism, Addressed to A. E. Grimké* as strategic expressions of long-standing and contradictory philosophies about reformist and antislavery politics in the United States. This chapter begins, then, by venturing into an 1830s web of antislavery reform. It ends by locating the colonization-abolition debate of the 1830s within the sociopolitical understandings and commitments of Catharine Beecher and Angelina Grimké. When we put these women at the center, rather than at the margins, of one of the most important rights debates of the nineteenth century, what emerges is a rich, complicated picture of public deliberation in one of the most volatile moments of United States history.

A Web of Antislavery Reform

Sarah Forten's Poem

On the title page of the 1837 *An Appeal to the Women of the Nominally Free States, Issued by an Anti-Slavery Convention of American Women* is a poem written by Sarah Forten, an African American woman who credited the abolition movement with "arousing me from apathy and indifference." Forten's poem reminded readers that, although "our skins may differ," African and European American women were bound as sisters "in a Christian land." That sentiment ran through the *Appeal,* a document generated at the United States' first national women's antislavery convention. The *Appeal* urged northern women to advocate on behalf of immediate emancipation. It also argued against colonization, and in fact in her epistolary debate with Beecher, on the topic of colonization Grimké chose to refer her interlocutor to the *Appeal to the Women of the Nominally Free States* rather than repeat its critique in full.[3]

Ironically, or perhaps fittingly, Sarah Forten participated in that antislavery convention and prominently affixed her name to its version of a manifesto almost exactly two decades after her father, James Forten, chaired a large anticolonization meeting of African American men in Philadelphia and, as chair, signed the meeting's public and widely circulated address. Both Fortens, James in 1817 and Sarah in 1837, condemned the prejudice inherent in colonization schemes. James seemed swayed briefly in early 1817 by the American Colonization Society (ACS). But by August 1817, when Forten chaired a meeting of African American men gathered to discuss colonization, he emphatically denounced the scheme and the ACS. The anticolonization addresses produced at meetings Forten chaired in January and August 1817 made deep impressions on white abolitionists. William Lloyd Garrison included both statements in his 1832 indictment of the ACS, *Thoughts on African Colonization: Or An Impartial Exhibition of the Doctrines, Principles and Purposes of the American Colonization Society. Together with the Resolutions, Addresses and Remonstrances of the Free People of Color.* Theodore Weld and the Grimké sisters considered Forten's later writings for publication in their antislavery journals. James Forten sent one such letter right around the time that Sarah Forten sent her first letter to Angelina Grimké.[4]

Grimké solicited that letter from James's daughter. Grimké wanted to know about the "effect of Prejudice" on Sarah Forten, and in 1837 Forten replied candidly. Even though her father's financial success and standing in the community meant that the Fortens escaped some forms of prejudice, they restricted their travel and otherwise proceeded cautiously to avoid prejudice when possible. Sarah Forten found it impossible to avoid prejudice altogether, which made her quite "embittered." As "you are well aware," Forten wrote to Grimké, "it originates from dislike to the color of the skin, as much as from the degradation of Slavery." This argument—for it was an argument—called to task northerners who believed themselves innocent because they owned no slaves. Forten admitted "feelings of discontent and mortification" when others received advantages for which she, too, was qualified, "THEIR sole claim to notice depending on the superior advantage of being *White*."[5]

A few years earlier, Lyman Beecher assured benefactor Arthur Tappan that such discrimination did not occur at his prominent school, Lane Seminary. Tappan agreed to endow Beecher's chair at Lane in October 1830, and in 1833 Tappan asked Beecher whether Lane excluded students of color. Beecher assured Tappan that "our only qualifications for admission to the seminary are *qualifications* intellectual, moral, and religious, without reference to color, which I have no reason to think would have any influence here." Few students of color attended Lane, however, and in other ways Lyman Beecher made it clear that he believed that fighting against prejudice wasted time, energy, and other resources that more effectively could be spent materially improving the lives of the oppressed. When Lane students not only taught free blacks who lived near the school but also socialized with them, Beecher recalled "repeatedly" telling Theodore Weld, "you are taking just the course to defeat your own object, and prevent yourself from doing good. If you want to teach colored schools, I can fill your pockets with money; but if you will visit in colored families, and walk with them in the streets, you will be overwhelmed." First improve the oppressed, Beecher reasoned, then they themselves become arguments against prejudice and lead to its gradual eradication. That belief grounded Beecher's philosophy of racial reform. In an 1834 speech advocating colonization, Beecher acknowledged the injustice of white prejudice against "the colored race." It was "wicked" and "criminal." But convince "the whites" to give up their racism? Easier and safer first to improve the "intellectual and moral character" of those giving offense. The same philosophy drove Lyman Beecher's antiremoval commitments in the late 1820s and early 1830s. Many southern Native Americans, especially among the Cherokees, had converted to Christianity by the early 1830s. They could face prejudice and also stand as arguments against it. Christian missionaries daily educated Native Americans, on tribal lands segregated from European Americans. But African Americans lived among European Americans, and, according to Beecher's world-view, most African Americans were inferior to whites. Beecher believed that their inferiority resulted from "condition and character," not inherent or natural inferiorities. "Had Africans been the oppressors," he explained, "Americans"—in other words, whites—would be inferior in their place. Like Native Americans, African Americans could learn to be more like whites. But immediate emancipation would come too quickly to strip prej-udice of its power: reformers needed time to prepare blacks and whites for equality of opportunity. According to Beecher, forcing confrontations too soon only made things worse.[6]

Antislavery advocates including Sarah Forten considered this response to prejudice indefensible. It excused prejudice. Worse still, it fueled coloniza-tion arguments. But Lyman Beecher liked colonization. He imagined it to be a benevolent program designed to Christianize Africa: "It is not neces-sary that the Colonization Society should be or claim to be an adequate remedy for slavery. Her great and primary object, is the emancipation of Africa, while she anticipated as an incidental result, the emancipation of the colored race at home." Beecher sincerely believed colonization would lead to emancipation in the United States and conversion in Africa. On the other hand, abolition would lead to emancipation but not conversion. He wanted both and was willing to make immediate sacrifices to ensure long-term success: "If the effect of colonization would be to increase the security of the slave property, the effect would be only temporary and limited, and more than balanced by the general and more permanent good, for the diffusion of light and argument, which she could circulate where the agents of aboli-tion could not come." For Beecher, colonization enabled a gradual opening of slave owners' minds as it did God's work, and he held tightly to the idea that it complemented, not contradicted, abolition. For Beecher, coloniza-tion enabled emancipation and evangelical conversion.[7]

For the Fortens and other abolitionists, the only thing colonization en-abled was exclusion. Initially, James Forten believed African Americans would "never become a people until they com[e] out from amongst the white people." Within six months, he changed his mind: "we have no wish to sep-arate from our present homes, for any purpose whatever." The Philadelphia address bearing Forten's signature also argued that before the ACS was founded, when owners emancipated their slaves the newly freed people of color had "opportunities for instruction and improvement" in the United States, but after the ACS formed, slave owners refused to free their slaves unless they promised to emigrate to Africa. Regardless of its professed benevolent ends, the ACS introduced and regularized forced removal for manumitted slaves. Twenty years later, Sarah Forten believed colonization to be a practical manifestation of what she called a "longing desire of a separation . . . and the spirit of 'This is not your Country.'" James Forten's daughter "despise[d] the aim of [the ACS] most heartily" because it provided European Americans with a vehicle for the expression of their prejudice: "No doubt but there has always existed the same amount of prejudice in the minds of Americans towards the descendants of Africa; it wanted only the spirit of colonization to call it into action." When Lyman Beecher looked at the ACS in 1834, he saw an organization converting Africa. In 1837, Sarah Forten saw an organization justifying segregation in and forced exile from the United States.[8]

An Endorsement for Henry Clay

When William Lloyd Garrison announced his plans to publish the *Liberator* and called for subscribers, he endorsed Henry Clay's candidacy for president of the United States. Although Garrison must have come to rue the endorsement, in August 1830 it made sense. Three days after the *National Intelligencer* ran Garrison's announcement, Clay wrote a letter to Jeremiah Evarts on Indian removal in which he complimented Evarts's William Penn essays, encouraged Evarts to keep fighting against forced removal, and urged Evarts to involve women in the campaign. Although Garrison objected to women's antiremoval petitioning (a position he regretted later), he shared Clay's condemnation for Andrew Jackson's removal policies. In 1830, Garrison also shared Clay's support for colonization. At the time, Clay served as a vice president of the ACS; Clay replaced former U.S. president James Madison as ACS president in 1836. The presidency that eluded Clay, though, was presidency of the United States, and it disappointed him deeply that he and his vice presidential running mate, Theodore Frelinghuysen, lost the race in 1844, the third and final time Clay ran for that office.[9]

Henry Clay and Theodore Frelinghuysen played recurring roles in the intersections of Indian removal, colonization, and abolition. At around the same time that Garrison endorsed Clay, Clay instructed Jeremiah Evarts to involve women in the antiremoval fight. In the late 1820s, Garrison and Evarts, with Frelinghuysen, Lyman Beecher, Lewis Tappan, and other Sabbatarians, organized boycotts and a national petition campaign to prohibit mail service on Sundays. In that campaign, Evarts transformed the use of petitions as a protest tool, subsequently influencing their use in the 1830s antiremoval and abolition campaigns.[10]

Sabbatarian petitions failed to persuade Congress to legislate Sabbath prohibitions, even though Theodore Frelinghuysen, an outspoken senator from New Jersey, spoke eloquently on the topic. Lyman Beecher worried little about Congress, though. He believed that the movement had to be grounded in "the moral authority of individual choice," not legislation—a belief that soon reverberated in his arguments to persuade slave owners, not federal legislators, to bring an end to slavery.[11] Beecher and Evarts aligned on a moderate path toward their goals, which distinguished them from Lewis Tappan and another Sabbatarian, Josiah Bissell Jr. Beecher "favored the use of quiet persuasion, conversations with leading men, and firm tugs at the levers of power." Bissell and Tappan, on the other hand, "believed that Sabbatarians had to fight the agencies of darkness with every weapon available." Evarts and Beecher tried to restrain Tappan and Bissell, without much luck. When the Sabbatarian movement folded in 1832, Tappan admitted that his zealotry contributed to its failures. Nonetheless, the pattern manifested again during the antislavery movement. In 1834 Beecher appealed to Lewis Tappan for help ameliorating the antislavery tension at Lane Seminary. But, as Tappan reported to Theodore Weld, Tappan responded by chastising Beecher for his moderate support of gradual emancipation.[12]

Like Clay, Frelinghuysen shared Evarts's and Garrison's Indian sympathies in 1830. People called Frelinghuysen "the Christian Statesman" because of his Evangelical position on reform, and he piously advocated for Sabbath observance, Native American rights, and the Christianization of Africa during Jackson's presidency. In April 1830, Frelinghuysen gave a six-hour antiremoval Senate speech that spanned three days. Frelinghuysen inspired many people by speaking for the oppressed. William Lloyd Garrison even wrote a poem about Frelinghuysen from his Baltimore jail cell.

Garrison had joined Benjamin Lundy as an editor of Lundy's antislavery newspaper, the *Genius of Universal Emancipation,* in September 1829. In the six weeks before he arrived in Baltimore, Garrison converted from gradual to immediate abolitionism. Garrison still advocated colonization—it would be three years before he would author his scathing attack, *Thoughts on African Colonization*—but he advocated colonization only as a benevolent program, not as a solution to slavery. In his first editorial for the *Genius,* he explained that colonization could "never entirely relieve the country. It may pluck a few leaves from the Bohon Upas [sic], but can neither extract its roots nor destroy its withering properties. Viewed as an auxiliary, it deserves encouragement; but as a remedy, it is altogether inadequate." Then he explained his views on slavery, which, despite his acceptance of colonization as a benevolent program, marked a radical break with colonizationists. Garrison's position privileged right over expedience and denied the right of slave owners to decide when to free their slaves. It also exposed important logics of removal. Garrison condemned the coerced removal of black Americans "born on American soil." This was an early version of one of the most significant abolitionist arguments against colonization: people of color born on American soil, abolitionists argued, were Americans.[13]

Garrison promised readers that he would "give no quarter to the open advocates of slavery, nor easily excuse those pseudo-philanthropists who find an apology for its continuance in the condition of the slaves." He established a regular column called "Black List" in which he "recorded each week some of the terrible incidents of slavery,—instances of cruelty and torture, cases of kidnapping, advertisements of slave auctions, and descriptions of the horrors of the foreign and domestic slave trade." On November 13, less than two months after his arrival at the *Genius,* Garrison accused the *Francis,* a ship owned by Francis Todd, of carrying seventy-five "unfortunate blacks" into slavery, transporting them from Baltimore to New Orleans. Todd promptly sued the *Genius* and its editors for libel. Garrison was found guilty and could not pay the fine of $100, so he began his jail sentence on April 17, 1830.[14]

Friends visited Garrison in jail, and he kept up with national news and continued to write from his cell. Five weeks into his incarceration, Garrison wrote the poem in honor of Senator Theodore Frelinghuysen on the occasion of the Christian Statesman's three-day congressional denunciation of the Indian removal bill. The six-stanza poem began by suggesting that senators unconvinced by Frelinghuysen's speech were more inanimate than "marble statues" and had hearts colder than "icy hearts congeal'd by polar years." In the next two stanzas Garrison accused the Senate of breaking treaties, usurping "rights which nature's God bestowed" on "the red men," and submitting to "PARTY POWER." The fifth and sixth stanzas praised and honored Frelinghuysen for "stand[ing] boldly." In between stanzas about the Senate and Frelinghuysen, Garrison portrayed Indian removal as a national sin and, significantly, linked it to slavery:

Our land—once green as Paradise—is hoary,
　　E'en in its youth, with tyranny and crime;
Its soil with blood of Afric's sons is gory,
　　Whose wrongs eternity can tell—not time;
The red man's woes shall swell the damning story,
　　To be rehearsed in every age and clime!

Garrison fought for no other cause as he fought for immediate emancipation. But if he believed slavery the greater crime, he acknowledged a shared oppression between African and Native Americans. His disgust with the Indian removal bill was noted in this poem for Frelinghuysen. More forcefully, Garrison represented his argument with a recurring visual image: the masthead of the antislavery newspaper he founded in January 1831, the *Liberator*.[15]

The *Liberator's* initial masthead was plain: the newspaper's title stood out in solid block letters. But on April 23, 1831, Garrison introduced a controversial image that remained for the duration of the paper's existence. The scene featured a slave auction in which a black family—a man, a woman, and two children—and an additional black man are being sold in front of the United States Capitol under signs that read "HORSE-MARKET" and "SLAVES HORSES & OTHER CATTLE TO BE SOLD AT 12 00." The Capitol building itself bears a flag that reads "Liberty." In the background a white man is whipping a black man tied to a post. In the foreground immediately to the left of the slave auction, between the words "The" and "Liberator," are documents carelessly tossed on the ground. These documents say "Indian Treaties," and they lie at the feet of slave traders and masters. Although slavery appears the greater tragedy, the masthead of the United States' primary abolition newspaper indisputably and controversially linked the nation's sins against African Americans with its sins against Native Americans.

Two weeks after he wrote his poem in honor of Senator Frelinghuysen, Garrison was released from prison. In May 1830, Lewis Tappan's brother Arthur, a New York merchant who through the early 1830s donated thousands of dollars to the ACS, who in October 1830 endowed Lyman Beecher's professorship at Lane, and who, in a few short years, would undergo a complete transfer of allegiance from colonizationism to abolitionism, sent Benjamin Lundy two checks. Tappan—who had never met Garrison and Lundy but knew them from their antislavery newspaper—directed that Garrison's fine be paid and offered one hundred dollars to reinvigorate the

Genius. Tappan's simultaneous donations to the ACS, his endowment of Beecher's chair, and his bail for Garrison indicate that people across a broad range of positions on the abolition of slavery—Beecher at the "gradual" end, Garrison at the "immediate" end, and Tappan likely in the middle—all believed colonization was a sound program in 1830. But even in 1830 Tappan showed signs of an impending full denunciation of colonization. In August, at the same time that Garrison endorsed Clay, Garrison proposed the *Liberator,* and Tappan made a generous contribution to it. Within a few years Tappan concentrated all of his efforts and all of his financial resources on immediate emancipation, and reports in the *National Intelligencer* indicate that the ACS felt that defection deeply.

In the meantime, the hero of Garrison's poem, Theodore Frelinghuysen, continued to work against Indian removal until his Senate term ended in 1835. But Frelinghuysen lost one of his most important partners in that work in 1832 when Jeremiah Evarts died. The senator's famous three-day speech that inspired Garrison relied heavily on arguments culled from Jeremiah Evarts's William Penn letters, originally published in the *National Intelligencer* between August and December 1829. Evarts enrolled women as well as men in the antiremoval cause. Frelinghuysen's friend Evarts was also Lyman Beecher's friend Evarts (all three worked together on the Sabbatarian movement), and Evarts encouraged Catharine Beecher, Lyman's eldest daughter, to advocate on behalf of Native Americans. Lyman reinforced Evarts's appeal to Catharine, as when on November 21, 1829, he wrote to his daughter, "Mr Evarts has sent on some things & will send more on Monday. You can do much I believe by this circulating. Such a circular may be made out & sent, or [you can do much] by making one of your own." With the support of her father and her father's close friend, Catharine returned to Hartford and initiated a sizeable women's antiremoval petition campaign.[16]

That Frelinghuysen and Clay had other connections with participants in the Indian removal, colonization, and abolition movements reinforces again the intricate details of the web that extended through these concomitant programs. For instance, while preparing to transfer his allegiance from the ACS to the American Anti-Slavery Society (AAS) in 1834, James Birney complained to Theodore Weld that Senator Frelinghuysen still supported colonization (Frelinghuysen was a vice president of the ACS at the time). On May 28, Weld wrote to Birney, "You speak of Mr. Frelinghuysen's piece—it is indeed most superficial. But he will come right just as soon as he understands the subject and he cannot remain long in ignorance. There is a large class of men of high standing, great influence, spotless integrity and real benevolence who are precisely in Frelinghuysen's situation. All they want is light." Weld, Birney, the Tappans, and other abolitionist leaders often targeted specific men for conversion, a process they sometimes called a person's "coming out." In November 1835, for example, James Birney asked Lewis Tappan about a Connecticut pastor named Joel Hawes: "What has become of Dr. Hawes of Hartford. He was on the very eve of coming out when I left him."[17]

James Birney, who himself had repudiated colonizationism for the immediate emancipation movement in the summer of 1834, played an active role in Gerrit Smith's conversion. Smith's conversion ranked as a tremendously important opportunity for the nascent AAS. Smith donated thousands and thousands of dollars to the ACS. He served as one of the ACS's officers and traveled to promote it. By the middle of the 1830s, Smith also turned an eye toward abolition. Like Lyman Beecher, Smith believed that the ACS program benefited untold numbers in the southern United States and in Africa. Like Theodore Weld, Smith believed that the United States would have to mandate an end to slavery. Smith did not so much bridge Beecher's and Weld's beliefs as much as he exposed their differences. Beecher thought the abolitionist methods were wrong but felt that the two organizations could exist simultaneously, each focusing on their own projects. Smith valued the programs of both organizations and thought that they could coexist but also admitted that colonization was inadequate to the task of even a gradual abolition. Weld, Birney, and Garrison believed that colonization was immoral and nationally corrosive and that it precluded emancipation.

Weld knew it would be a coup for the AAS if Smith renounced the ACS, and in October 1834 he urged Birney to engage Smith on the issue. Weld's exhortation illustrates the strategic targeting of a key player in the ACS-AAS rivalry as well as the intensity of that rivalry: "If that man could be divorced from the delusive sorcery of Colonizationism, an immense and incalculable influence would be secured to the cause of Abolition. Do take the subject into serious consideration. From what I hear of his regard for you—on account of your letter—I am persuaded that a private letter from you to him just at this juncture would operate more powerfully upon his mind than any other instrumentality." Soon after receiving Weld's letter, Birney wrote to Smith. In his November 1834 letter Birney argued for the "*immediate* abandonment" of slavery and against gradualism. He defended abolitionists (despite their occasional "errors") and denounced colonizationists. His arguments against African removal illustrated key contradictions between abolitionist and colonizationist doctrine: according to Birney, colonization relied on arguments of expedience rather than justice, and so failed "to lay hold of men[']s consciences" against the sins of slavery. Because colonization had "done more to rock the conscience of the Slaveholder into slumber, and to make this slumber soft and peaceful, than all other causes united," Birney called it "the greatest obstacle in the way of the advocate of freedom."[18]

The letter Birney wrote to Smith at Weld's behest exposed philosophical differences between the ACS and the AAS. It also exposed the rivalry between the two groups. Despite Lyman Beecher's interpretation of the ACS and AAS programs as complementary, ACS and AAS leaders considered the programs mutually exclusive. For leaders of both causes, as long as Smith advocated colonization and contributed money to the ACS—even if he advocated abolition at the same time, believing one tied to Christianizing Africa and the other tied to ending slavery in the United States—his ACS advocacy damaged the abolitionist cause.[19] Birney aggressively urged the philanthropist to renounce colonization as part of his abolitionist commitment. Smith and Birney discussed the issue in their letters for more than a year: did an acceptance of abolitionist principles require condemnation of colonization?

In a November 1835 letter to Smith (before Smith renounced colonization), Birney reported using an antislavery speech Smith wrote to push a member of Lyman Beecher's congregation toward abolition. Birney said he stopped by the office of a friend on the way home from the post office. This friend, "an Elder in Dr. Beecher's Church," agreed with Birney on principles of slavery but refused "to be called an abolitionist, and to become of 'no reputation.'" Smith's speech—and Smith's credibility—helped matters:

> I handed him your speech, saying—"here, friend Starr, regale yourself with a speech of your Colonizationist, G. Smith, who gives $1000 a year to your cause, whilst I look over these letters." Whilst he was reading it, I paid more attention to him than to my letters. As he advanced, he would remark, "it is right,—no man can dispute this doctrine—every man, woman, and child in this country ought to read this" etc. etc. When he had finished it,

he said "I will at once write a note to Hammond (Editor of the 'Cin'i Gazette'—the leading paper of the city) requesting him to republish it." This he did, accordingly, before I left his office.

To Birney's surprise, Hammond reprinted Smith's speech. Birney had thought "it was too warm and glowing and strong" for Hammond, but Smith's association with the ACS sanctified its arguments. The ACS held a privileged position in 1835, especially relative to the AAS. As this anecdote illustrates, the label "abolitionist" stained one's character. The contrast is an important one, especially as part of the context in which the Beecher-Grimké debate occurred. Frequently, it was abolitionist radicalism, not antislavery principles, that troubled northerners.[20]

But James Birney convinced Smith that colonization dulled men's consciences and was incompatible with abolition.[21] Birney even may have used Henry Clay as an example. Birney recorded in September 1834 that Clay, an active officer in the ACS, "had no *conscience* about the matter" of slavery. A few months after Birney complained to Weld about Frelinghuysen's allegiance to colonization, Birney breakfasted with Senator Clay. According to Birney, like most colonizationists Clay believed that slave owners possessed constitutional rights to their property, that their property rights proved "an insurmountable barrier to gradual emancipation," and that "the case was hopeless by any direct effort, and was to be left to the influence of liberal principles as they should pervade our land." Birney concluded that Clay "would swim with the popular current" on the matter, and Birney was right on both counts. First, Clay proudly declared his moderation. In his first ACS presidential address, delivered in 1837, Clay echoed Lyman Beecher's 1834 argument: "The roads of colonization and abolition lead in different directions, but they do not cross each other. We deal only with free persons of color; their efforts are directed towards the slave." Hoping for benevolent reform initiated by the slaveholding class, the ACS avoided alienating calls for emancipation. "No, gentlemen," he declared, "we are no ultraists." (Months earlier, Theodore Weld gave six reasons why Angelina and Sarah Grimké should focus on slavery and not woman's rights; the fifth reason was, simply, "Ultra Abolitionists." For Weld and the Grimkés, "ultraist" was a compliment.) Second, the popular current was—and would remain, for several years more at least—colonization.[22]

That was one reason why a few years later Senators Clay and Frelinghuysen (who, contrary to Weld's optimistic prediction, never embraced immediate abolitionism) had a chance in the presidential election of 1844. These Whig candidates embraced rhetorics of African removal, not African American emancipation. Their colonization politics appeared consistent with Jacksonian-era antiremoval rhetorics that defended Native American rights fifteen years earlier, whereas to moderate opponents of slavery, abolition was a radical departure from reasonable and just reform. These divergent paths of radical and moderate antislavery reform had been foreshadowed in 1830, when Garrison endorsed Clay as the next U.S. president and memorialized Frelinghuysen for his speech against Indian removal. But during the summer of 1830, Clay's and Frelinghuysen's convictions landed them in the national spotlight. Garrison's convictions landed him in jail.

James Birney's Resignation Letter

On July 15, 1834, James G. Birney resigned from his job. To explain his resignation, Birney wrote a letter that amounted to nearly fifty pages. Hardly the ravings of a disgruntled employee, Birney's letter was a thoughtful anti-colonization polemic. The letter detailed why Birney no longer wished to serve as a paid agent for the American Colonization Society nor as a vice president for the Kentucky Colonization Society, the auxiliary to which Henry Clay had strong ties. Birney argued that southern apathy to the ACS rendered it ineffective for Christianizing Africa. He objected to the ACS's declaration that it was "the only effectual and appropriate remedy for slavery," given the "utter inadequacy of colonization" to end that horrible institution. After almost a decade of volunteer work and nearly two years as a paid ACS agent, Birney publicly declared the basic principles of colonization "unsound, imperfect and repugnant."[23]

Birney's *Letter on Colonization, Addressed to the Rev. Thorton J. Mills, Corresponding Secretary of the Kentucky Colonization Society* was not the first anticolonization tract to energize the abolition community. David Walker's *Appeal, In Four Articles, Together with a Preamble, to the Coloured Citizens of the World, but in Particular, and Very Expressly, to Those of the United States of America* (1829–1830), William Lloyd Garrison's *Thoughts on African Colonization* (1832), and Lydia Maria Child's *An Appeal in Favor of That Class of Americans Called Africans* (1833) challenged the rhetorics of African colonization as part of their authors' deeply held commitments to immediate emancipation and social justice. But Walker's intervention was unique. Many African Americans spoke or wrote against slavery and colonization, yet none had the impact or the weight of Walker's *Appeal . . . to the Coloured Citizens of the World.* Of the four widely circulated antislavery and anticolonization texts written during Jackson's presidency, Walker's created the biggest stir in the south. States passed laws to prevent its distribution, and local authorities arrested men in whose possession they found copies of the *Appeal.*[24] One wonders what kinds of activist interventions Walker would have made had he not died in 1830.

Despite his early death, Walker's influence continued. His *Appeal* inspired abolitionists including Garrison, Maria Stewart, and Frederick Douglass. Garrison, like Child and Birney, initially embraced colonization, and Walker's *Appeal,* which Garrison clearly admired, almost certainly hastened his renouncement of the ACS. In turn, Garrison persuaded Lydia Maria Child and her husband David to advocate for the more radical cause. By 1830, Lydia Maria Child was famous for her 1824 novel *Hobomok,* her stories, her domestic and parenting advice manuals, her children's literature, and the popular children's magazine she began in 1826, the *Juvenile Miscellany.* Garrison knew Lydia Maria Child could help the cause and he targeted her as Weld and Birney targeted Gerrit Smith. He flattered Child on the pages of the *Genius of Universal Emancipation* and the *Liberator,* and he reprinted in the *Liberator* stories and articles she wrote for her husband's newspaper. Their positions aligned by 1832 (David Child attended the first meeting of Garrison's New England Anti-Slavery Society in January of that year), and in fact Garrison quoted from one of Lydia Maria Child's antislavery essays in *Thoughts on Colonization.*[25] In 1833, Child published a book that had immediate and long-term impact on the United States slavery debates: her *Appeal in Favor of That Class of Americans Called Africans.*

Birney's letter of resignation from the ACS was the fourth extended, influential antislavery and anticolonization polemic published in five years. Theodore Weld was so excited by it that he planned to "have thirty or forty thousand of them struck off and sent all over the Country."[26] Not only did Birney's family, like the Grimké family, own slaves, but Birney himself owned slaves while he served as an agent for the ACS. There was no precedent for his conversion to abolitionism, and he and Weld conspired to maximize the public impact of his arguments.

When the ACS appointed Birney as an agent in 1832, even Weld embraced colonization. Weld encouraged Birney to accept the ACS job, and a few months later Weld called the ACS the nation's only hope in its fight against slavery: "I am ripe in the conviction that if the Colonization Society does not dissipate the horror of darkness which overhangs the southern country, we are undone. Light breaks *in from no other quarter.*"[27] Weld's belief epitomized the idealistic views of the ACS as an emancipatory organization that some northerners held during Jackson's first presidential term. At the same time, many northern and southern gradualists refused to identify the ACS as either for or against slavery, arguing instead that the benevolent organization's primary mission was to enable (or compel) free blacks to emigrate; through African repatriation, the United States would become the all-white nation these gradualists believed it was destined to be, and Africans actually could have the freedom they never would have in the United States.[28] A third group saw in the ACS an organization uniquely positioned to disseminate the Christian gospel throughout Africa. These Evangelicals feared losing that opportunity if the ACS became entangled in slave debates.

Just as non-slave-owners read different missions into the ACS, so too did slave owners. By the early 1830s, some southern states had laws that prevented slave owners from manumitting their slaves without providing for their removal from the state.[29] Slave owners who wanted to free some or all of their slaves viewed African colonization as the most viable (even the only viable) mechanism for individual emancipation. Another group of slave owners believed the ACS scheme protected their human property. The ACS provided a means by which slave owners could dispose of rebellious or even incompetent slaves without worrying about the corruption of loyal, amenable, and competent slaves.

The ACS enjoyed widespread support and popularity because people could read multiple, even competing, missions in its design until the early 1830s. But in 1832 committed antislavery activists ("fanatics") proposed an alternate plan: immediate emancipation. In December 1832, just three months after Weld wrote to Birney that the ACS was the nation's only hope, Birney became aware of abolition as an alternate antislavery reform. But because Birney believed the ACS was the only organization that safely and constitutionally could end slavery and because he believed that the removal of blacks from the southern states was in the best interest of blacks and whites, he resisted immediacy. He also advised ACS agents to put southern fear of abolition to work for their cause: "the opposition of the Abolitionists I consider one of the strongest grounds for recommending [colonization] to the people of the South."[30] Birney believed—as Catharine Beecher would argue a few years later—that the main difference between northern abolitionists and colonizationists was the methods of their programs. He was prepared to defend colonization, even if that defense included deception. In April 1833, Birney admitted what abolitionists found so odious about the

ACS: "The *selfish* principle is the only one to which an appeal can be made in the South. Our cause is approved by many under the very just impression, that its success will give them a more quiet and undisturbed *possession* in their slaves."[31] Abolitionists detested this colonizationist argument of expediency. But Birney had yet to embrace abolition. Although he recently had expressed a desire to manumit his slaves and send them to Liberia, in 1833 he identified much more strongly with European Americans than with African Americans. And so he catered to white men's psyches rather than black men's and women's freedom.

But abolition continued to advance in the north. The ACS had competition, and they had to shift their methods of persuasion to accommodate Garrison's northeastern popularity. Within a few months, ACS leaders began to admit that the south had to demonstrate a commitment to gradual emancipation or colonization would lose significant northern support. Soon the slaveholding south would call all northerners abolitionists, and northern abolitionists would claim that all nonimmediatists were apologists for slavery. Colonizationists hated being caught in the middle, and they blamed abolitionists for triggering their loss of moral, political, and cultural authority.[32]

In June 1833, as Birney and other colonizationists adjusted their rhetoric to account for abolitionism's growth in the northeast, Theodore Weld enrolled as a student at Lane Seminary. Weld's role at Lane was unusual. Thirty years old, Weld already had earned a national reputation as a brilliant Christian reformer and public speaker. He had turned down several pastorates and had declined to head several seminaries—including Lane.[33] But in 1831 he did serve in an advisory capacity to Lane's trustees.[34] Weld's affiliation with Lane, Lyman Beecher's commitment to head the institution and serve as one of its professors, and the endowment trustees acquired from Arthur Tappan and other northeastern reformers marked the Cincinnati seminary as the premier national institution of its kind, and it attracted smart, enthusiastic, committed men from around the country to its student body. Years after the Lane rebellion—one of the most embarrassing events in Lyman's Beecher's career—Beecher remained respectful of that stellar class of students and the man they considered their leader and president, Theodore Weld.[35]

Weld's commitment to his studies might have looked like a temporary retirement from his life as a prominent Evangelical reformer, but Lane, a seminary located in Cincinnati, a northern city deeply connected to the southern states, figured prominently in Weld's zealotry.[36] At Lane, Weld had access to some of the best and brightest young Christian minds in the country—the core of the nation's future ministers and leaders of Christian reform. Many were from slaves states, most advocated colonization, and few (if any) embraced abolitionism. Weld set about persuading every Lane student to support the cause of immediate emancipation, and during the course of his only academic year at Lane, he very nearly succeeded.

In July 1832, Weld urged Birney to become a paid advocate of the ACS. Sometime during the fall of 1832, Weld decided that the colonization project was morally bankrupt, and he committed himself to immediate abolitionism. At around the same time, Birney worked against what he considered abolition's deleterious effects in his assigned ACS territory. In January 1833, Weld wrote to Garrison: "no condition of birth, no shade of color, no mere misfortune of circumstances, can annul that birth-right charter [of freedom]." Significantly, he also wrote that anyone who perpetuated the crime of slavery, even when crying "expediency or necessity . . . is joint partner in the original sin."[37] Weld had come to embrace not just the antislavery cause but also the abolitionist cause, which required that he renounce colonization because it delayed complete and immediate emancipation. At around the same time that Weld wrote Garrison, Birney wrote to ACS officer Ralph Gurley about his own colonizationist plans to free his slaves and send them to Liberia.[38] Birney worked through the spring of 1833 to mitigate abolition in the southern states while Weld preached the abolitionist cause. But in the fall, Birney and Weld met again.

In the fall of 1833, Weld worked earnestly to convince Lane students to join the abolition movement. As he told the tale, his first important conversion was of William Thomas Allan, "from Alabama; born, bred, and educated in the midst of slavery; his father an owner of slaves, and himself heir to a slave inheritance." The conversion involved a weeklong conversation in Allan's Alabama home about slavery and abolition. Allan's neighbor and Weld's friend James Birney participated in those talks. Birney did not switch allegiances that fall, but his letters reveal changes in his philosophy. By December 1833, Birney gave up on making any headway in states south of Tennessee. He accused southern plantation owners of being "blind to the natural rights of their Slaves" and exhibited much less tolerance of them than he had earlier that year. Birney also gave up on colonization as a "means of ridding us of *Slavery*" and admitted he was "pleased to see all engines at work for the extirpation of Slavery from our land." But he refused to embrace immediate abolition. Instead, like many others in the middle of the 1830s, he accepted that colonization "w[ould] be the mode under Divine providence of enlightening and [C]hristianizing robbed and spoiled AFRICA." Then he drafted a constitution for the Kentucky Society for the Gradual Relief of the State from Slavery. Believing that slave owners had retreated from genuine plans to abolish slavery, Birney helped devise a plan for gradual abolition and urged southerners to prepare people of color for their eventual freedom. At the same time, in a letter to the founders of the AAS, Weld confirmed his resolve against slavery and his abolitionist view that anything besides immediacy was inadequate.[39]

Then came the Lane debates. According to Weld, most of Lane's students had pledged their allegiance to abolitionism by January 1834. Prompted by the enthusiastic talk about abolition and colonization on campus, students proposed a debate to weigh the antislavery alternatives. Lyman Beecher initially supported the debate, but members of the faculty soon convinced him of its controversial nature, and as a body they advised students to postpone indefinitely the event. Students decided to proceed. Since Lane faculty saw their role in the matter as advisory, they took no further steps to prohibit the proceedings.[40]

The Lane debates began in early February and lasted for eighteen days. For each of nine evenings, participants debated one of two questions: "Ought the people of the Slave holding States to abolish slavery immediately?" and "Are the doctrines, tendencies, and measures of the American Colonization Society, and the influence of its principle supporters, such as render it worthy of the patronage of the Christian public?" Most of Lane's students and faculty and some of Cincinnati's residents attended part or all of the debates, and on the first question they heard from students who had lived in slave states—and even one student who had been a slave, James Bradley. At the end of deliberations on the question of immediate emancipation, with the exception of a few abstentions the vote was unanimous support for immediacy. That posed a problem for the next nine days of debate. Who would defend the ACS? Students originally scheduled to speak on the organization's behalf had been persuaded by abolitionist arguments during the debate's first nine evenings. Instead of testimony from student members of the ACS and its auxiliaries, students relied on textual analysis of ACS reports, issues of the *African Repository*, documents from the AAS, and a report on the Liberian colony provided by a Cincinnati doctor who visited the colony in 1831. In the end, only one student voted to affirm the ACS as an organization "worthy of the patronage of the Christian public."[41]

Effects of the debate were widespread and controversial. Locally, Lane students organized an antislavery society and began working with the black population in Cincinnati. Most white Cincinnatians rebelled against their philanthropic and collaborative efforts. Cincinnati had close ties, economic and familial, with neighboring slave states, and extensive abolitionist activity threatened those ties. Additionally, given its proximity to the slaveholding south, emancipated slaves often settled in Cincinnati. Many white citizens refused to integrate or even treat with respect the city's free blacks. The city was known for its enforcement of Ohio's ruthless black codes, which restricted the freedoms of African Americans and made it difficult for them to live in the state. In 1829, the same year David Walker first published his *Appeal . . . to the Coloured Citizens of the World* and the U.S. House of Representatives Committee on Indian Affairs recommended the emigration of Native Americans from their national lands to areas west of the settled United States, Cincinnati became famous for forcing (predominantly through riots) the removal of more than one thousand free African Americans from the city.[42] Its leading white citizens abhorred Lane students' zealous advocacy of abolition. These white citizens tolerated schools and other forms of aid arranged to benefit African Americans but condemned social interaction between whites and blacks and the implications of racial equality that threatened the racist hierarchies governing the city's social, political, cultural, and economic structures.

Nationally, the debate received a remarkable amount of attention. Lane— conceived as a paradigmatic example of a Presbyterian seminary in the new west—had as its head one of the most famous nineteenth-century preachers and reformers in Lyman Beecher, had as its student leader the popular reformer Theodore Weld, and had as its primary benefactors the renowned Lewis and Arthur Tappan. Beecher hardly could avoid national attention because of his cultural prominence. The Tappans and Weld drew as much attention to Lane as they could in the spring of 1834 because the debate outcomes so overwhelmingly favored abolition and because they needed to raise money to fund student activities in Cincinnati. In all of this national attention, abolitionists and abolitionist newspapers found it easy to praise Lane students. As easily, though, nearly everyone else blamed the students as well as the faculty and trustees of this school of theology for such an apparently irresponsible and politically partisan series of events.

Lyman Beecher thought things would settle down over the 1834 summer break.[43] He left Lane in July to see his eastern friends and benefactors, and he assumed most of his students would return to their homes for the summer. But some stayed at Lane, working with black Cincinnatians and using Lane's resources to print and mail abolitionist materials. In the meantime, many white Cincinnatians continued to stew about the events of the academic year. One Lane professor found the students' activism offensive, and he urged the seminary's trustees to act quickly during the summer months on behalf of the institution. As he must have known, that meant acting without Beecher's calming influence. The trustees agreed with the professor's urgency, especially when they discovered students using Lane virtually as an abolitionist publishing house. Lane's trustees were prominent leaders in Cincinnati, and they shared concerns that abolitionist activity at the seminary would hurt the town's financial prospects and inspire riots (not a small concern, given the antiabolition riots that occurred in New York in July).

During the summer and into the fall, the trustees generated a new set of rules for Lane Seminary. They designed the rules to stifle all abolitionist advocacy—word and deed—and to encourage the most rebellious of the students to quit Lane. The rules outraged Lane students and a few of the Lane trustees, including a local abolitionist pastor, Asa Mahan. Mahan and Weld wrote to Beecher, urging him to return as quickly as possible to intervene. Underestimating the situation's urgency, Beecher returned on schedule in October, at the start of the term. Beecher accepted the new rules but promised his students that his faculty would not enforce them. Because the trustees gave themselves the power to dismiss any Lane student and because most Lane students found the rules to be immoral in principle, Beecher's attempts to broker a compromise were insufficient. Because of the trustees' intervention, seventy-five of approximately one hundred students left Lane or failed to return that fall, and many of the financial pledges Beecher secured during his trip east were withdrawn.

Beecher's antislavery beliefs went through a profound transformation because of the abolitionism of Lane's student body and the rise of abolition nationally in 1833 and 1834. Beecher's transformation mapped onto the experiences of thousands of other colonizationists at the time and so provides us with a remarkably useful case study. In April 1833, eight months before the AAS was formed, Beecher responded to Arthur Tappan's question about Beecher's stance on slavery. This explanation indicated his own position and also his misunderstanding of Tappan's. First, Beecher admitted he saw no "controversy between the Colonizationists and the Abolitionists. I am myself both, without perceiving in myself any inconsistency."[44] Beecher was hardly alone. Lewis Tappan, Arthur's brother and partner, for example, was still a couple of months away from renouncing colonization. Abolitionists would name their organization the American Anti-Slavery Society, but northern colonizationists considered their own program antislavery too. Although Beecher had not heard much about their doctrine yet (besides the "fanatic" rants of Garrison, which most northerners dismissed), abolitionists denied the ACS its claims to antislavery. Abolitionists argued that southern colonizationists refused to commit one way or the other on slavery and that colonization indefinitely postponed true emancipation. But the ACS listed the rosters of every ship that sailed from the southern states to Liberia, and its officers counted the colonists on board who had been freed to "repatriate." The numbers of slaves liberated and sent to Africa might have been small relative to the number of slaves who remained in chains, the ACS admitted, but the ACS reminded the listening public with increasing frequency that their program was the only program that actually emancipated slaves.

Second, Beecher believed the best way to end slavery was "to make emancipation easy instead of difficult." Colonization offered slave owners "an easy, practicable way of doing their duty," whereas Beecher worried that abolitionists hardened the hearts of slave owners by confronting them with the possibilities either of slave insurrections or the complete chaos that many people expected would manifest if two million slaves they believed to be uneducated, uncivilized, and unprepared suddenly became free. Beecher suggested that abolitionists and colonizationists could learn from each other, perhaps aligning to realize the soundest, quickest, and safest means to end slavery in the United States. Even if the organizations did not work together, there was "no need that the two classes of philanthropists should fall out by the way." Beecher favored colonization because he believed it the kindest and most expedient means to the end that both organizations sought. But he was not opposed to the other organization, given that he shared its goals and saw no immediate harm in its founding. His third point in the spring of 1833, then, was that both the ACS and the AAS contributed to "a great work, which will not stop until not only the oppressed here are free, but Africa herself shall have rest in the Lord," even if they approached that work differently.[45]

As abolitionist doctrine began to spread—Arthur Tappan started publishing his abolitionist newspaper the *Emancipator* in the spring of 1833, Child's *Appeal in Favor of That Class of Americans Called Africans* was published that August and almost immediately was widely reviewed, Garrison continued to accuse everyone who did not advocate immediate emancipation of advocating the sin of slavery—colonizationists tried to figure out what to make of the new movement. Birney decided to use southern irritation with abolitionists to promote the ACS. Gales and Seaton began to dissociate their position from abolitionism. What would Lyman Beecher do? He believed in gentle and friendly persuasion, lived in a town sympathetic to the southern way of life, and worked for a man who had abandoned colonization and was spending thousands of dollars to promote abolition. In September 1833, Elizur Wright hardly said hello to Theodore Weld before he asked, "Where stands our beloved Dr. B now that the lines are forming between the cringing EXPEDIENCY on the one side, and ETERNAL TRUTH on the other?"[46] But Beecher probably had yet to see the conflict. The question, after all, was posed by an abolitionist. Colonizationists believed their doctrine attended to expedience and truth, and few thought it necessary to abandon it.

When Lane students proposed a series of debates on the questions of immediate emancipation and colonization, Beecher initially welcomed the free exchange of ideas. Even when his faculty convinced Beecher that the debates would be controversial, he did not prevent the debate, nor did Beecher prevent the subsequent organization of a campus antislavery society. According to Weld, after the debate Beecher reviewed an admittedly heated essay Weld wrote for the *Cincinnati Journal* defending Lane students. Beecher "told (me) he had no fault to find with it."[47] Beecher also advised his students about their antislavery activism. It was too radical to be practical, Beecher told Weld, and Beecher could not help as long as his students continued to integrate so publicly with African Americans who lived in Cincinnati. He advise the student body to learn from his own reformist practices. "I made it a fixed maxim of my life," he explained, "never to take a public stand in favour of any new subject that is likely to excite controversy, until I was fully assured that public sentiment was so far advanced in its favour as to sustain me in its advocacy. I earnestly commend my example to your imitation in the perilous circumstances in which we are now placed."[48] But still in the spring of 1834 Beecher saw no need to shut down forcefully their organization or stifle their activism. As abolitionists they were overly zealous but not harmful.

Then two of Lane's students gave speeches at the AAS annual convention in May 1834, and Lane acquired a national reputation as a hotbed of abolitionist activity that did not tolerate colonization. Beecher had to respond. In a June address that colonizationists distributed throughout the nation, Beecher repeated his initial claim that abolitionists and colonizationists

could coexist. But this time he publicly condemned the methods of abolitionists. "Both associations are agreed," he said, "that slavery is wrong, and
a great national sin and national calamity, and that as soon as possible it is
to be brought to an end; not however, by force, nor by national legislation,
nor by fomenting insurrection, nor by the violation of the constitution and
the dissolution of the union, but by information, and argument, and moral
suasion—and by the spontaneous action of the slave-holding states." As he
distinguished the differences between the ACS and the AAS as methodological rather than philosophical, he also criticized the agonistic attitude of the
AAS toward the ACS: "we ought by no means to denounce one another as
the abetters [sic] of slavery, because we do not accord in all respects as to the
ways and the means of accomplishing emancipation." He warned abolitionists not to force colonizationists to choose between the two programs. Inevitably and categorically, he and others like him would not relinquish their
Christian mission:

> We oppose not the emancipation or elevation of the colored race. We de-
> sire it sooner than it can come, we fear, by the means relied on by many.
> We have only to say to our brethren, hinder us not. Commend your cause
> to public confidence in your own way, and we will do the same with ours,
> and let the people judge; but let there be no controversy between us. But
> if, after all, the abandonment of Colonization is demanded, as the only
> condition of peace, then we have made our election. If it be possible, as
> much as in us lieth, we will live peaceably, but we cannot abandon the one
> hundred millions of Africa.[49]

Like many European Americans who denounced slavery, Beecher initially
was tolerant of abolition. But he believed that abolitionists forced him to
choose between the two programs. He resented the AAS for attacking the
ACS, he disagreed with abolitionists' radical tactics, and he believed emancipation would come but that it should not be rushed. In June 1834,
Beecher declared his allegiance to the ACS. In typical Beecher fashion, he
continued to seek middle ground between the two groups, especially when
he visited his eastern benefactors. But abolitionists refused to be palliated,
and by the end of 1834 the split between colonizationists and abolitionists
had grown from a crevice to an irreparable chasm. Beecher remained on the
side of colonization.

Some abolitionists never gave up on Lyman Beecher. James Birney and
other abolitionists who lived in Cincinnati looked for signs of his conversion

as they worked on members of his church and the new students at Lane Seminary.[50] Birney knew how persuasive a well-timed and well-orchestrated conversion could be. Not only had he advised Smith on his "coming out" in 1835 and pursued Beecher's conversion for years after that, but he and his friend Theodore Weld carefully plotted Birney's own public disavowal of the ACS. Birney admitted in early 1834 that colonization would not end slavery. But he still advocated gradualism, so he founded the Kentucky Society for the Gradual Relief of the State from Slavery; and he still loved the Evangelical mission of the ACS, so he remained loyal to that group. Two months after the Lane debates, though, almost all of that changed. In 1834 Birney gave up on gradualism and he gave up on the ACS.

What did abolitionists do when someone who owned slaves, preached colonization and condemned abolition throughout the southern states as a paid ACS agent, and regionally and nationally published dozens of essays, addresses, and letters supporting colonization admitted he was wrong— and decided he wanted to tell the world why? Theodore Weld and Lewis and Arthur Tappan built for Birney the largest platform possible. First, they leaked the news. Weld told Birney, "I have *followed the course* which you suggested and the 'Magnus Rumor' will be ringing in the public ears within a few days, from different papers on both sides of the Alleghany, but of course *only as something* REPORTED *not definitely known.*"[51] Second, Weld advised Birney as the new abolitionist prepared the strongest possible arguments for his "coming out." Birney sent Weld drafts of his 1834 resignation letter, the *Letter on Colonization.* Weld shared the letter with some of his trusted classmates at Lane and then sent detailed feedback to Birney. Recognizing the significance of Birney's experience and national reputation, in their feedback Weld and his friends repeatedly urged Birney to criticize the ACS more specifically as an organization that perpetuated slavery.[52] Third, when this leading colonizationist told Weld he was giving up on colonization, Weld orchestrated the printing and distribution of Birney's polemic. Weld promised Birney that Lane students would contribute financial and manual assistance, and the Tappans bankrolled some of the expenses. Thousands of copies of the *Letter* went out across the country as extras in abolitionist newspapers. People mailed hundreds, even thousands, to family, friends, and acquaintances. Elizur Wright, who personally mailed about two hundred, hoped "for an edition of 100,000."[53]

The massive distribution and also the general plan for Birney's "coming out" went as planned. A review of Birney's *Letter on Colonization* in the

November 1834 issue of the ACS's *African Repository* is telling. It began by reminding readers that they regularly had been reprinting Birney's colonization letters, even though some "intelligent friends" believed that parts of Birney's letters had "a PRO-*slavery* tendency." Birney had advocated gradual emancipation and appealed to the selfish desires of southern slave owners in 1833, and the criticism expressed here exposes the rift forming between northern and southern colonizationists at the time. The *African Repository* planned to defend Birney until, to their surprise, he defected. The *Repository*'s narrative of the defection captures the ACS's surprise and the abolitionist orchestration of the defection:

> Our anxiety [about how to defend Birney against his critics] was soon, however, interrupted most unexpectedly by rumours that the party for whom we were meditating an apology had surrendered to his assailants, and was about to fulminate from their camp charges against the Colonization Society, similar to those which had been made against himself. The flourishes with which the organs of Immediate Abolition announced, in advance, Mr. BIRNEY's abjurement [*sic*] of the Colonization cause, were in due season followed by the appearance of the letter, of which the title is given at the head of this article. Instead, therefore, of defending the officer of the Society against his adversaries, we are placed in the sudden necessity of defending the Society against the Parthian warfare of the fugitive officer.

The ACS imagined itself as at war and under attack. According to its advocates, the ACS was a cautiously productive organization limited by finances as well as prudence. Abolitionists, on the other hand, developed and articulated their doctrine against the ACS. ACS failings, abolitionists claimed, called the AAS into being. Given how intimately connected the fall of the ACS and the rise of the AAS were, it would be a shame not to note the ironic placement of the *African Repository*'s review of Birney's letter. It immediately preceded the reprint of Lyman Beecher's June 1834 pledge of allegiance to the ACS. Immediately before it turned to Beecher's address, the *Repository* closed its review of Birney's *Letter on Colonization*: "between an enterprise so chimerical or revolutionary, and the practical, inoffensive, and Constitutional system of Colonization, it is for an enlightened people to decide."[54]

After his resignation from the ACS and the Kentucky Abolition Society, Birney needed another job. The AAS hired him as an agent, and he frequently wrote and spoke on their behalf. He also founded an antislavery newspaper, the *Philanthropist*. Birney and his family moved to Cincinnati, and the new abolitionist began publishing the *Philanthropist* there despite threats of violence against him. During the summer of 1836, Cincinnati citizens rioted, destroying the press and offices of the *Philanthropist*. Birney believed his life spared only because he had been out of town.

Riots like these frequently threatened abolitionists. Arthur and Lewis Tappan lost property to rioters in New York; William Lloyd Garrison was tarred and feathered by rioters; hundreds of African Americans lost churches, homes, and property in the middle of the 1830s because of riots that began as attacks on white abolitionists and turned into rampages against blacks living in northern cities.[55] Although newspapers such as the *National Intelligencer* and the *Christian Advocate and Journal and Zion's Herald* denounced the rioters, they placed some of the blame with the abolitionists and their "fanatical" and aggressive words and deeds, which lead to vociferous calls for public and state censorship, even the silencing, of abolitionist discourse. Perhaps the most egregious violation of First Amendment rights of abolitionists by the state occurred in 1836, when the U.S. House of Representatives denied abolitionists their right to petition the federal government. In the context of this aggression, Angelina Grimké and her sister Sarah publicly began urging women to form and join abolitionist antislavery societies—and petition the federal government to abolish slavery. Catharine Beecher publicly said no. In that moment of call and response, these women arrived at the center of the antislavery debates raging between abolitionists and colonizationists.

Prelude to the Debate

Catharine Beecher and her father Lyman arrived in Cincinnati on November 14, 1832. By turns exhausted, bored, and frustrated by her work at the Hartford Female Seminary, excited by the challenge of educating the west, and pleased to accompany her father—to whom she was very close—Catharine made the move from Hartford to Cincinnati in good spirits. She soon set to work integrating herself into Cincinnati's leading social network and building support for her western school, aptly named the Western Female Institute. The school opened in 1833, though Beecher excused herself from its daily operations. The school never quite satisfied her: she desired a permanent female seminary that had its own classroom buildings and dormitories, but her plan to establish such an institution in Cincinnati stalled because she could not raise seed money. Then, because of the Lane debates and subsequent rebellion, an unrelated charge of religious heresy against her father, and Catharine's miscalculation of the loyalties of some of Cincinnati's elites, Catharine and her father became controversial figures in Cincinnati. Most female schools relied on local support, and the Western Female Institute grew smaller as the social elites grew colder toward the Beechers. Unable to attract local students, Catharine Beecher's school failed in 1837.[56]

But neither Catharine nor Lyman had given up their northeastern ties, which helped Catharine survive the failure of the Western Female Institute. In 1835, Catharine traveled to New York to present *An Essay on the Education of Female Teachers*. Thousands of copies of that essay, "written at the request of the American Lyceum, and communicated at their annual meeting," were printed simultaneously in New York and Cincinnati.[57] Local editors in Cincinnati held more traditional views on education than Beecher, so it was important that she had an enthusiastic northeastern audience for her work. In the summer of 1836, Beecher toured the northern states to advocate her program of western education (conveniently forgetting the troubles of her own western institution). Enrolling potential teachers in city after northern city, Beecher biographer Kathryn Kish Sklar writes, she "was received as a spokeswoman for the West" and "welcomed into the homes of prominent clergymen and educators at each of her stops in the East." Especially compared to the difficulties she faced in Cincinnati, the seven months Beecher spent in the northeast were "exhilarating."[58] Before embarking on her northeast trip, Beecher published a lengthy book called *Letters on the Difficulties of Religion*. Dedicating it to "an honored and beloved father," Beecher hoped the book would quell some of the controversy swirling around her father and her family, given the heresy charges Lyman faced in the Presbyterian General Assembly. The book explained various theories about religion, including why one should behave as if God existed, what counted as proof that God existed, and how Christian denominations differed from one another.[59] When she took on Angelina Grimké in 1837 after the publication of the *Essay on the Education of Female Teachers* and *Letters on the Difficulties of Religion* and her successful tour of the northeast, Beecher was practiced in thinking about her purview as national, rather than local.

In 1837, Beecher personally was committed to a particular resolution of the colonization-abolition rivalry. But she also used the conflict to buttress arguments for the status of women as integral to the Christian and democratic project that was the United States and thus to warrant her ambitious plans for female education. This use of the conflict is consistent with the work Beecher did in her 1835 and 1836 publications. Beecher's 1835 *Essay on the Education of Female Teachers* carefully articulated the plans and ideas she promulgated in her 1836 tour of the northeast. Ostensibly, Beecher argued that the nation needed teachers and that women were ideally suited to serve the nation in that capacity. But implicitly, Beecher argued for women's power within the Christian democracy that men like her father, Henry Clay, and Theodore Frelinghuysen hoped to build.

First, Beecher did what she does so masterfully in all of her texts from this period: she established exigence for her program by identifying and strategically interpreting national problems that were both particular to the United States and particularly urgent at the moment in which she wrote. Worldwide, Beecher explained, intellectual power was superseding physical power. It was time for people to "decid[e] whether disenthralled intellect and liberty shall voluntarily submit to the laws of virtue and of Heaven, or run wild to insubordination, anarchy, and crime" (14). "The great crisis" was "hastening on" even more quickly in the United States, and Beecher's response in a seemingly simple essay about female education was deeply political: "The necessity of *virtuous* intelligence in the mass of the community is peculiarly felt in a form of government like ours, where the people are not held in restraint by physical force, as in despotic governments, but where, if they do not voluntarily submit to the restraints of virtue and religion, they must inevitably run loose to wild misrule, anarchy, and crime" (9–10, 14). Beecher used the proto-Whig, anti-Jackson anxiety about the separation between church and state to make urgent the relationship between piety, morality, and politics. Beecher also used middle- and upper-class anxieties about the ignorant and immigrant vote to declare another crisis: "All these ignorant native and foreign adults are now voters, and have a share in the government of the nation. All these million children, in a very few years, will take the same stand; while other millions, as ignorant and destitute, are hastening in their rear. What is the end of these things to be?" (16). A Christian democracy required education, virtue, and piety, and the United States was wavering on all three. For Beecher, these crises naturally demanded that United States women be equipped and empowered to intervene.

Women's "*peculiar* duties," after all, revolved around developing "the character, of the future citizen of this great nation" (5). This development occurred in the nursery. But Beecher believed it also could and should happen in the classroom: "mankind are not aware how much might be effected by teachers, in the most important part of education, were they properly trained for these duties, and allowed sufficient time and opportunity for the discharge of them" (13). Properly trained teachers could be as effective, perhaps more effective (especially in the homes of "all these ignorant native and foreign adults"), than parents in instilling moral and religious commitments in children. And, according to Beecher, those properly trained teachers had to be women. First, men had no patience for elementary education and could not support a family on a teacher's salary. Second, women were best "fitted by disposition, and habits, and circumstances, for such duties." Third, the training and experience prepared women "for that domestic relation she is primarily designed to fill" (18).

This division of labor was oppressive for women. But if one believed in the version of Christian democracy Beecher inherited from her father (or at least believed it was the game that would be played), this division of labor could entail a very powerful role for women—just as giving up power to gain power worked for the women who petitioned the federal government against the forced removal of Native Americans in the early 1830s. In 1835 Beecher, too, gave up power: "Give us the opportunity of aiding to preserve the interests and institutions of our country. Send us to the thousands of destitute children whom we should rejoice to train up in virtue, and prepare for Heaven. We relinquish the pursuit of wealth, the paths of public honor, and the strife for patronage and power; give us the humble, sacred, delightful pleasures of benevolence" (22). But what did she aim to get in return? Education, authority, and power—in massive quantities. "Aroused to a sense of danger" like that caused by the ignorant vote, "the wealthy and intelligent must pour out their treasures to endow seminaries for teachers," Beecher declared (17). She wanted permanent buildings, textbooks and lab equipment, teachers specialized in a limited number of subjects. She wanted female seminaries equivalent to male seminaries such as Lane, Oberlin, and Yale College. Beecher had a plan: "Men of patriotism and benevolence can commence by endowing two or three seminaries for female teachers in the most important stations in the nation, while to each of these seminaries shall be attached a model school, supported by the children of the place where it is located" (19). And the numbers she imagined were remarkable. From each village Beecher needed "one, two, three, and in some cases ten or even twenty, laborers for this field" (19). She highlighted the urgency of the crisis:

In New England, we hear of one solitary institution for the preparation of teachers; and, in New York, eight are just starting into being; and this is all! Now, at this moment, we need at least thirty thousand teachers, and four thousand every year in addition, just to supply the increase of youthful population. And we must educate the nation, or be dashed in pieces, amid all the terrors of the wild fanaticism, infidel recklessness, and political strife, of an ungoverned, ignorant, and unprincipled populace. What patriot, what philanthropist, what Christian, does not see that all that is sacred and dear in home, and country, and liberty, and religion, call upon him to waken every energy, and put forth every effort? (17–18)

Beecher described a group of thirty thousand female teachers, seventy thousand within a decade. She imagined all of these teachers as highly educated according to her own plan for female education (Beecher's students at Hartford were placed as teachers all over the country, so she had done this work before on a smaller scale). These women would have a tremendous influence as the shapers of the nation's citizenry. Grown men would have greater respect for their opinions and ideas because female education of the kind Beecher described would "elevate and purify" its students (5). Beecher returned to these arguments in her 1837 polemic against abolition. Beecher wanted education for women and the power it brought, and she used crisis after crisis to argue for it. In important ways, the slave debates were another crisis Beecher could shape to warrant her national program for female education.

Important elements of Beecher's 1836 *Letters on the Difficulties of Religion* also made their way into Beecher's 1837 *Essay on Slavery and Abolitionism, With Reference to the Duty of American Females.* Little came through in terms of the content of the argument. Whereas arguments for female education carried from Beecher's 1835 essay to her 1837 monograph, Beecher did not incorporate the fundamental arguments about Christianity from her 1836 book into the *Essay on Slavery and Abolitionism.* But because in 1836 Beecher aimed to convince her invoked interlocutors to accept God and live a Christian life, *Letters* also was in many ways a treatise on argumentation. Fundamentals of argumentation—for instance, methods of good debate, the ways one should treat an opponent, and the criteria with which to judge controversial questions—bridged the 1836 *Letters* and the 1837 *Essay on Slavery and Abolitionism.* These fundamentals are significant because they help us understand *Essay on Slavery and Abolitionism* as much more than a gendered dismissal of the abolitionist movement.

Catharine Beecher taught rhetoric, and her *Letters* and *Essay on Slavery and Abolitionism* reveal strategic methods of engagement. In *Letters,* for example, Beecher paused her epistolary debate to confirm that she and her interlocutor agreed before moving on:

> I do not wish to proceed any farther till it appears whether we agree so far. The question under consideration is, what is that character which is revealed as indispensable to future eternal happiness? As a preliminary, we must first determine what it is that is regarded as constituting human character, in order to learn what it is that can be made the subject of divine legislation. Will you examine what I have written, and see if there is anything included in human character that could be made the subject of legislation, which I have not herein specified and described. (121–122)

Beecher took herself seriously as a skilled debater and she was comfortable engaging in public argument and even dictating the terms of those arguments. She refuted arguments as diligently as she constructed them, and, by spending time on definitions of concepts such as "human character," "Christian," and even "what a contradiction is," affirmed the centrality of definition to public debate (a key point for her in her 1837 exchange with Angelina Grimké) (96, 112–114, 269–270). Beecher welcomed intelligent debate about controversial issues, at one point writing in *Letters* that she picked up a pen because she and her disputant repeatedly were interrupted during their face-to-face discussions (107).

Beecher found it deeply troubling that men (and, presumably, women) had so much difficulty expressing unpopular ideas because people would rather silence debate than consider for a moment that their positions might be faulty—and because people increasingly tended to insult, rather than treat respectfully, people with whom they disagreed. Beecher wondered, "If he shows what he deems wrong and injurious, in a calm, kind, and [C]hristian way; reasons fairly, states well supported facts, uses no opprobrious epithets, and impeaches no man's motives, is he not to be justified, is he not to be honored for this course?" (322). This point personally was important to her because her father was under such attack in the Presbyterian church during his heresy trial. Additionally, the ideal of a Christian democracy was harder to advocate if people talked about denominational differences as grounds for attack. Beecher explained that she "lament[s] the practice now so common, of speaking, of all religious discussions, as *quarrels.* Is there not a distinction between free and animated discussion and quarreling? If men can keep their temper, and treat their antagonists with courtesy, fairness, and benevolence, they may earnestly contend for principles and doctrines, and yet be free from the charge of being engaged in a quarrel" (347). This maintenance of a public space for debate was very important to Beecher, especially given the methods of governance in the United States. Beecher dedicated most of the preface of *Letters on the Difficulties of Religion* to "the best method of promoting *right intellectual views* of truth and duty, and that *right state of heart* which will lead men to practice what they know to be right" (v–vi). There were two things important to Beecher in that inquiry: convincing people what was right, and convincing them to act on that knowledge. For Beecher, results were an important measure of the efficacy of someone's position.

In her preface, Beecher offered two methods of persuasion: what she deemed a correct, Christian way and what she regretted was the more common way. In her 1837 *Essay on Slavery and Abolitionism,* Beecher named as one of the most egregious sins of abolitionists their unchristian method of persuasion. In her 1836 *Letters,* Beecher clearly explained what that meant. In Christian debate, the debater "always g[a]ve credit to an opponent for sincerity, and good motives," for example, and "never use[d] satire, sneers, severe rebukes, or invidious epithets." People who followed the Christian way assigned good motives to their opponents and pointed out what was right as well as what was wrong in opponents' judgments. In contrast, unchristian disputants typically ignored what was good in their opponent's position and exaggerated what was good in their own, insulted their opponents' intelligence and piety, publicly denigrated their opponents, excited them into passion and rage, and even called them names—all sins Beecher attributed to abolitionists in 1837 (vi–viii). Beecher had a tremendous commitment to what she called the Christian methods of persuasion, and she believed no dispute—especially one as urgent as slavery—could be resolved safely and quickly if disputants employed unchristian argumentative practices. Given her ideas about the nature of public debate as she expressed them in 1836 and in 1837, it virtually was impossible for Beecher either to defend abolitionists or to imagine their methods as a viable route to the controversy's resolution.

A third element of *Letters* that presaged Beecher's participation and position in her exchange with Angelina Grimké is the criteria Beecher offered to judge controversial questions. Beecher argued against moral absolutes. Reason and common sense, explained Beecher, should be one's guide. Several times Beecher admonished her invoked interlocutor because his principles or behaviors were "at war with common sense" (25, 35). Beecher directed her readers to evaluate a position based on whether it had "the *balance of evidence* in its favor" and whether it was the choice that "*involves the least risk*" (75). Beecher explained that all positions "involve[d] some *incidental evils*" and had to be evaluated in context. "It is right for a physician to stay out nights, to go through storms, and to do without sleep in cases of sickness and danger," Beecher reasoned, "when it would be folly and wickedness to do it, to gain amusement, or trifling emolument" (44, 323–324). In 1837, Beecher accused Grimké of falsely dividing the slavery issue into two sides: proslavery and abolition. Beecher argued against the absolutism she saw in abolitionist doctrine, telling Grimké that gradual emancipation was a more reasonable, safe, and sensible solution to the evils of U.S. slavery than immediate emancipation. To draw that conclusion, Beecher used the criteria she outlined in her 1836 *Letters on the Difficulties of Religion*. That book offers a reference point for Beecher's philosophies of argumentation, and those philosophies simply were incompatible with abolitionist methods. Beecher believed that gradualism was a safer, more expedient means by which the United States could end slavery, and therefore abolitionist doctrine violated the common sense criteria with which Beecher evaluated controversial questions.

By 1837, Beecher had founded a successful female academy in Connecticut, which placed teachers all over the nation. She had moved to Cincinnati, where she founded another school and got involved in public issues, standing in for her father one night during the 1834 Lane debates and personally witnessing the negotiations in Cincinnati at which James Birney refused to move his abolitionist paper from that city. She publicly and nationally advocated female education, including her own specific plans for recruiting, educating, and placing a corps of thousands of teachers throughout the nation in 1835 and 1836, and in 1836 she published her 350-page book on contemporary religious controversies. Catharine Beecher knew how to argue, she was used to intervening in national issues, and she believed abolition to be disastrous in myriad ways. As with most challenges, Beecher faced this one head on. She picked up a pen and wrote her 1837 *Essay on Slavery and Abolitionism, with Reference to the Duty of American Females.*

Like Catharine Beecher, Angelina Grimké came from a well-known family. Her father, John Grimké, was a wealthy and well-connected South Carolinian judge as well as a plantation and slave owner, and her mother, Mary

Smith Grimké, was herself born to well-established, wealthy, and prominent parents. Unlike Catharine, who was the first of Lyman and Roxanne Beecher's children, Angelina was the youngest of her family, one of thirteen children. As a young child Angelina neither understood nor tolerated slavery, and she often created strife over the peculiar institution in the Grimké household. When Angelina was twenty-four, her mother agreed with her youngest daughter that it would be best for everyone if Angelina moved away from the slaveholding south, and in 1829 Angelina took up residence with her older sister Sarah in Philadelphia and began her conversion to the Quaker faith (Sarah had moved to Philadelphia in 1821 and converted to Quakerism in 1823). Angelina's move away from Charleston has been called an "exile," though self-imposed—at least until 1836, when her *Appeal to the Christian Women of the South* drew such ire in Charleston that threats of mob violence prevented her ever from returning home.[60]

Sarah and Angelina were not the only two Grimké children to resist slavery. Their older brother Thomas, to whom Sarah had been especially close while growing up, actively advocated colonization as a means to the end of slavery. Angelina and Sarah were in the process of converting Thomas from colonization to abolitionism when he died of cholera in 1834, which gives us an indication of the degree to which Thomas's sisters themselves embraced the radical cause by 1834.[61] Angelina and Sarah's mother, Mary, resisted Angelina's antislavery appeals for years. But Mary, Sarah, and Angelina stayed in touch despite Angelina's 1836 abolitionist *Appeal* and her banishment from Charleston by its angered citizens. In fact, when Angelina decided to become an agent for the American Anti-Slavery Society, Mary Grimké urged the wavering Sarah to join her youngest daughter rather than to send Angelina "on such a mission alone." Sarah said her mother's request "was like a voice from the Lord," and so Sarah and Angelina headed to New York to meet with Elizur Wright and other AAS leaders in October 1836, almost seven years after Angelina forever left the Grimké plantation.[62]

By the time the Grimké sisters arrived at AAS headquarters, Angelina was renowned for an 1835 letter she wrote to William Lloyd Garrison and her 1836 *Appeal to the Christian Women of the South*. Angelina wrote both of those documents by herself, immersed in the abolitionist discourse she read in the *Liberator* and heard at several abolition meetings. Angelina did not know the letter to Garrison would be a public piece, although her diary reveals that she suspected Garrison might publish it.[63] Despite the tremendous consternation with which she knew her Quaker community and even her sister Sarah—not to mention members of her South Carolina circle—would receive the letter, Angelina felt compelled to address the abolitionist who quickly was earning the appellation "fanatic" in northern as well as southern cities. Garrison was so excited about her letter that he immediately published it in the *Liberator*, noting in an introduction that Grimké grew up in South Carolina and was the sister of Thomas Grimké (another stab at colonizationists, given Thomas's advocacy of that cause).[64]

After a series of riots in the fall of 1835, Grimké's letter and some other AAS texts were published together as a pamphlet, and the young exile from South Carolina gained notoriety for her courageous antislavery activism.[65] Her Quaker community hoped to discourage Grimké's public advocacy and suggested that she become a teacher; at around the same time, in the summer of 1836, Elizur Wright offered her a position as an abolitionist agent. Grimké quickly dismissed the Quaker offer, but the AAS offer gave her pause. Not yet ready to commit herself to the American Anti-Slavery Society but still compelled to intervene, Angelina decided to write an appeal to the Christian women she left behind when she emigrated north.[66] That letter, written in two weeks during her summer vacation in New Jersey, became the infamous 1836 *Appeal to the Christian Women of the South*, printed and widely distributed by the American Anti-Slavery Society. Once that essay reached South Carolina, there was no going back to Charleston for the youngest Grimké. But also, once that essay entered into abolitionist discourse, there was no turning away from abolitionism for Angelina. Within a few months, she and Sarah joined forty other abolitionists for three weeks of AAS agent training under the tutelage of Theodore Weld.

Angelina Grimké's first public abolitionist text, the page-long 1835 letter to Garrison, was inspired by an essay Garrison himself wrote and published in the *Liberator* in August 1835, during a summer remarkable for its antiabolition mobs and riots. In his essay, Garrison defined the horrors of slavery and resolved to stand against the evil institution even if entrenchment led to martyrdom.[67] Grimké was relieved to read of Garrison's resolve against the violence, thrilled to read that, as she explained it, Garrison "stoodest firm in the midst of the storm, determined to suffer and to die, rather than yield one inch." This uncompromising, extremist position—"*not* that we may escape suffering, but that we may be willing to endure unto the end . . . *this is a cause worth dying for*"—remained central to Grimké's abolitionist doctrine and became a source of conflict between Grimké and Beecher. Grimké imagined the abolitionist mission as analogous to radical religious reform and drew confidence that abolitionists were on track because their persecution was so violent:

> Religious persecution always begins with *mobs:* it is always unprecedented in the age or country in which it *commences,* and therefore there are *no laws,* by which Reformers can be punished; consequently, a lawless band of unprincipled men determine to take the matter into their hands, and act out in *mobs,* what they know are the *principles* of a large majority of those who are too high in *Church* and State to *condescend* to mingle with them, though they *secretly* approve and rejoice over their violent measures.[68]

Grimké understood that antiabolitionist sentiment was institutionalized in the United States—in church and in state—and that mobs foretold the passage of laws aimed at silencing the radical reformers. In that sense she was correct: states passed laws to prevent the distribution of abolitionist literature, to further limit emancipation, and increasingly to restrict the education and movement of slaves. In 1836 the United States House of Representatives passed the gag rule, which prevented the national legislature from receiving petitions relating in any way to the abolition of slavery.

In her 1836 *Appeal,* Grimké urged her southern Christian sisters to ignore all of those laws and rules. She appealed to them to teach their slaves to read, to free their slaves, and to petition Congress against slavery despite the gag rule. Grimké bypassed any sort of secular debate about whether state laws were fair, just, and reasonable, instead setting "*human* law" against God's law (10). Grimké constituted the choice she offered to those Christian women as one between God and man: "*we* will assuredly be condemned and punished for obeying *Man* rather than *God*" if we remain passive, she warned her readers (10). According to Grimké the Bible neither contained a model for nor sanctioned U.S. slavery, an institution that so fundamentally and dramatically differed from biblical instances of Jewish and Christian servitude that comparisons categorically cast United States slavery as evil. In fact, Grimké told her readers that the Bible alone provided enough evidence against United States slavery to compel Christians resolutely to oppose it (17). In her 1836 *Appeal,* Grimké amplified her 1835 argument that antislavery activism was a religious reform, more radical than but in the same group as Sabbath education, temperance advocacy, and Christian missions (27).

Labeling abolition a religious reform, especially a radical religious reform, made viable arguments that would have been unavailable to Grimké if she considered abolition a strictly political or benevolent reform. It enabled the binary between God's law and man's law, and it gave Grimké access to the stories of Esther, Miriam, Jael, and other biblical women who could serve as models for her Christian sisters (20–22). It allowed Grimké to affirm the suffering her readers likely would experience as southern abolitionists and still to encourage their activism:

> But you will perhaps say, such a course of conduct would inevitably expose us to great suffering. Yes! my [C]hristian friends, I believe it would, but this will *not* excuse you or any one else for the neglect of *duty*. If Prophets and Apostles, Martyrs, and Reformers had not been willing to suffer for the truth's sake, where would the world have been now? If they had said, we cannot speak the truth, we cannot do what we believe is right, because the *laws of our country or public opinion are against us,* where would our holy religion have been now? (20)

Grimké suggested that *"religious duty"* be women's inspiration. When Grimké told her southern sisters about the horrible crowd that mobbed the anniversary meeting of the Ladies' Anti-Slavery Society of Boston, she explained that those women remained determined in spite of the mob because of their religious commitments (23–24). Calling abolition a religious reform also provided Grimké with a response to the series of questions that antiabolitionists asked about the aftermath of emancipation: How would freed slaves survive European American prejudice? How would they survive and thrive having been denied secular and religious educations? Drawing an analogy between southern women who would free their slaves and Peter and John who preached the gospel, Grimké explained: *"Consequences,* my friends, belong no more to *you,* than they did to these apostles. Duty is ours and events are God's. If you think slavery is sinful, all *you* have to do is to set your slaves at liberty, do all you can to protect them, and in humble faith and fervent prayer, commend them to your common Father" (19). On the enlightenment of free people of color, Grimké wrote:

> Yes, some may be ready to say of the colored race, how can *they* ever be raised politically and intellectually, they have been dead four hundred years? But *we* have *nothing* to do with *how* this is to be done; *our business* is to take away the stone which has covered up the dead body of our brother, to expose the putrid carcass, to show *how* that body has been bound with the grave-clothes of heathen ignorance, and his face with the

napkin of prejudice, and having done all it was our duty to do, to stand by the negro's grave, in humble faith and holy hope, waiting to hear the life-giving command of "Lazarus, come forth." (28)

This disregard for the consequences of immediate emancipation invited sharp criticism from antiabolitionists who focused on the expediency of antislavery methods. Yet Grimké confidently maintained the position. In the *Appeal*'s argument for women's antislavery petitions, Grimké claimed for women a particularly appropriate role as petitioners of the national legislature: "*they* will be the most likely to introduce it [the subject of abolition] there in the best possible manner, as a matter of *morals* and *religion,* not of expediency or politics" (26). Here, too, was another binary for Beecher to refute: in the antislavery debate Grimké opposed morals and religion to expedience and politics. In important ways this binary was a key to the dispute over women's abolitionist activism for Beecher and Grimké. Beecher imagined the controversy primarily as an issue of expedience guided by morality and thus as offering no public role for women, whereas Grimké saw the controversy as primarily religious and thus as virtually demanding women's public intervention.

Grimké also appealed to women to act in less public ways—to read the Bible and pray in their private rooms, for instance, and gently and calmly "to persuade your husband, father, brothers, and sons" of the sins of slavery (18). Grimké asked her readers to think for themselves whether the Bible sanctioned U.S. slavery, and she asked them to identify with the victims of that evil institution:

> I appeal to you, my friends, as mothers; Are you willing to enslave *your* children? You start back with horror and indignation at such a question. But why, if slavery is *no wrong* to those upon whom it is imposed? why, if as has often been said, slaves are happier than their masters, free from the cares and perplexities of providing for themselves and their families? why not place *your children* in the way of being supported without your having the trouble to provide for them, or they for themselves? Do you not perceive that as soon as this golden rule of action is applied to *yourselves* that you involuntarily shrink from the test; as soon as *your* actions are weighed in *this* balance of the sanctuary that *you are found wanting?* (13–14)

Some of the subversions Grimké asked southern Christian women to undertake occurred in private spaces, such as teaching slaves to read and write. But of course Grimké also appealed to the Christian women of the south to act publicly. They should free their slaves, and if their freed slaves were captured and sold back into slavery, they should declaim the crime publicly (18–19). Southern women should write pamphlets and use crafts such as paintings and needlework continually to advocate abolition, urged Grimké, and they should join abolition societies and petition state and national legislatures protesting slavery (23, 26). From her desk in Shrewsbury, New Jersey, Grimké informed her southern sisters that already "there [were] sixty female Anti-Slavery Societies in operation" (23), and she refused to let womanhood function as an excuse for meaningful action: "But you may say we are *women*, how can *our* hearts endure persecution? And why not? Have not *women* stood up in all the dignity and strength of moral courage to be the leaders of the people, and to bear a faithful testimony for the truth whenever the providence of God has called them to do so? Are there no *women* in that noble army of martyrs who are now singing the song of Moses and the Lamb?" (21). With a committed, impassioned sincerity, Grimké told her readers that "the *women of the South can overthrow* this horrible system of oppression and cruelty, licentiousness and wrong" (26). Catharine Beecher concurred—perhaps even more adamantly, given the ways Beecher argued against northern intervention in this peculiar business of the south. But Beecher decried abolitionist methods, calling the public and political interventions Grimké advocated illegal, aggressive, irritating, and inexpedient. The antagonism of these interventions decreased women's status in all domains of public and private life, Beecher maintained, rendering them less effective as antislavery advocates and guardians of the nation's moral and religious future.

Grimké anticipated these arguments because they dominated public antislavery debates. In addition to constituting abolition as a moral and religious issue and using biblical warrants for women's active intervention in controversy, in her 1836 *Appeal to the Christian Women of the South* Grimké defended abolitionists and articulated slavery as a national rather than a southern problem. First, Grimké acknowledged the prevailing beliefs about abolitionists: "Doubtless you have all heard Anti-Slavery Societies denounced as insurrectionary and mischievous, fanatical and dangerous. It has been said they publish the most abominable untruths, and that they are endeavoring to excite rebellions at the South. Have you believed these reports, my friends? have *you* also been deceived by these false assertions?" (28). Then Grimké used her own credibility and her articulation of abolitionists as radical religious reformers to defend the organization to which she now belonged. Grimké reasoned that she had family in the south and would not join an organization that had any sort of insurrectionary or incendiary motives, and that her own continued study of abolitionist principles, newspapers, pamphlets, and other materials uncovered absolutely nothing but that which was pacific, moral, and true. But Grimké knew from experience what slavery was like: "They cannot deceive *me*, for I lived too long in the midst of slavery, not to know what slavery is . . . I am not at all afraid to assert, that the Anti-Slavery publications have *not* overdrawn the monstrous features of slavery at all" (29). Because of the truths Grimké knew, pacifism and morality for her were about martyrdom in the face of mobs and personal sacrifice to prevent servile wars, whereas for Beecher pacifism and morality were about compromises and patient, private means of suasion. Within Grimké's understanding of moral antislavery action, though, the South Carolinian personally was able to affirm the morality of antislavery societies. Grimké also defended abolitionists by drawing again on the articulation of abolitionists as radical religious reformers who, like hundreds of reformers before them, spoke unwelcome truths. She told her southern Christian sisters that abolitionists "know that the greater the sin is, which is exposed, the more violent will be the efforts to blacken the character and impugn the motives of those who are engaged in bringing to light the hidden things of darkness. They understand the work of Reform too well to be driven back by the furious waves of opposition" (31). Grimké made the claim more plausible by comparing it with a very familiar story: "Abolitionists have been accused of abusing their Southern brethren . . . No man will *now* accuse the prophets and apostles of *abuse,* but what have Abolitionists done more than they? No doubt the Jews thought the prophets and apostles in their day, just as harsh and uncharitable as slaveholders now, think Abolitionists" (32). By using this analogy, Grimké relieved herself of having to make the (false) argument that abolitionists were waiting patiently for the south to act on its own. Instead, she let take shape a correlative equation in which increased violence against abolitionists proved the morality of abolitionist acts.

Grimké knew that most northerners assailed abolition societies. But, as she did with violence against abolitionists, Grimké used northern dissent for her own rhetorical ends. Instead of arguing that northerners were wrong (just as she did not argue that the violence against abolitionists was inexplicable), Grimké argued that northern interests were aligned with southern interests—and thus, intervening in a crucial national debate, Grimké argued that slavery was a national, not a regional, issue. Grimké explained to her southern readers that "northern merchants and manufacturers are making *their* fortunes out of the *produce of slave labor;* the grocer is selling your rice and sugar; how then can these men bear a testimony against slavery without condemning themselves?" (30). Grimké repeatedly called slavery an American, not a southern, institution, as when she asked her readers "to draw the *parallel* between Jewish *servitude* and American *slavery*" (12). Grimké also echoed one of Garrison's and Child's most aggressive arguments against slavery: American slavery enslaved American citizens. In Texas, "citizens of the United States," reported Grimké, "are now engaged in deadly conflict, for the privilege of fastening chains, and collars, and manacles—upon whom? upon the subjects of some foreign prince? No! upon native born American Republican citizens" (25). Issues like that one—whether territories including Texas should be admitted to the Union as slave states—were political issues, and northern politicians knew that their political careers still required acceding to southerners on these issues (29–30). Rather than denying northern aggression toward abolition, Grimké used it to make national what many people, including Catharine Beecher, hoped to circumscribe as an exclusively southern debate.

In fact, Grimké's 1836 *Appeal to the Christian Women of the South* took the nation by storm. Likely more northerners than southerners read the essay; almost immediately upon its arrival in Grimké's hometown of Charleston, the essay was labeled incendiary and copies were burned. But with the 1836 *Appeal* and Angelina and Sarah's "parlor talks" (the sisters' speaking engagements soon became lectures in large halls), the Grimké sisters increasingly persuaded northern women to form or join female antislavery societies and publicly as well as privately to advocate for the immediate emancipation of the nation's two million slaves. The Grimké sisters became well-known speakers and writers, and Angelina especially threatened Catharine Beecher, who had very specific plans for women's role in the Christian democracy her father was so involved in constructing. Actually, the Grimké sisters threatened many people's ideas about Christian and American ways of life, and they frequently were subjected to taunts, rebukes, and violence in their three years on the lecture circuit. In July 1837, several months after Beecher's *Essay on Slavery and Abolitionism* was published, two months after the first national Anti-Slavery Convention of American Women (for which Angelina and Sarah each wrote popular and widely circulated essays and at which both were elected to serve as officers of the national society), and one month after Angelina began responding to

Beecher's *Essay*, the General Association of Congregational Ministers of Massachusetts released a pastoral letter that called women's public reform efforts "mistaken conduct." People widely interpreted the pastoral letter as a targeted indictment of the Grimké sisters. They had become that famous. Besides Frances Wright, few United States women other than fiction writers and poets were as well-known nationally as Catharine Beecher, until Angelina and Sarah Grimké dedicated themselves to the work of United States abolition.[69]

— 6 —

"Coming from One Who Has a Right to Speak"

Debating Colonization and Abolition

It is a law of experience, that when wrong is done, if repentance
and reformation are sought, then love and kindness, mingled with
remonstrance, coming from one who has a *right* to speak, are more
successful than rebuke and scorn from others who are not beloved,
and who are regarded as impertinent intruders.

—CATHARINE BEECHER, *AN ESSAY ON SLAVERY AND
ABOLITIONISM, WITH REFERENCE TO THE DUTY OF
AMERICAN FEMALES* (1837)

In her autobiography, Catharine Beecher remembered being inspired by
her father's friend Jeremiah Evarts to write her 1829 "Circular Addressed to
Benevolent Ladies of the U. States." Evarts told Beecher that "American
women might save these poor, oppressed natives."[1] Evarts, Lyman Beecher,
and many other Christian reformers were convinced that Native Americans
would be lost forever if the U.S. government forced them to leave their
homelands. When Beecher took up her pen to call European American
women to action, she invoked a potent symbol of a woman "sent to supplicate for a nation's life": the Bible's Queen Esther. Beecher predicted that
some people initially might resist women petitioning the federal government. But she believed that Native American nations were at stake, as was
the United States, which was threatened by an angry God who cursed "all
who oppress the poor and needy." Esther seemed an especially relevant
model for appropriate female behavior in the face of these multi-national
crises. Beecher wrote in her "Circular," "We remember the Jewish princess
who, being sent to supplicate for a nation's life, was thus reproved for hesitating even when *death* stared her in the way: 'If thou altogether hold thy
peace at this time, then shall deliverance arise from another place; but thou

203

and thy father's house shall be destroyed. And who knoweth whether thou art come to the kingdom for such a cause as this?'" The story of Esther suited the urgency of the moment, in its activist tendency as well as in its implications that Esther's supplication was not a transgression of woman's appropriate and, according to Beecher, divinely ordained sphere.[2]

Beecher was not the only woman to embrace Esther in the turbulence of the 1830s. Angelina Grimké invoked Esther in her 1836 *Appeal to the Christian Women of the South*. In fact, the epigraph of her *Appeal* summarizes Esther's story. Like Beecher, Grimké had an oppressed group in mind in her invocation of Esther. But for Grimké, that group was African American slaves. She asked her readers, "Is there no Esther among you who will plead for the poor devoted slave?" Also like Beecher, Grimké predicted the United States was doomed to destruction. Unlike Beecher, Grimké believed colonization was of no use as an antislavery program. Abolition and abolitionist tactics were in order, and those tactics included petitioning the federal government as Esther petitioned her king: "if there were but *one* Esther at the South, she *might* save her country from ruin; but let the Christian women there arise, as the Christian women of Great Britain did, in the majesty of moral power, and that salvation is certain."[3]

Beecher found Grimké's use of Esther completely inappropriate. Beecher believed that colonization would bring slavery to a gradual end, and she believed its peaceful, Christian methods would save the United States whereas abolition was sure to tear it apart. When Beecher responded to some of Grimké's abolitionist principles and methods in her 1837 *Essay on Slavery and Abolitionism, with Reference to the Duty of American Females*, she explained the proper use of "the case of Queen Esther": "when a woman is placed in similar circumstances, where death to herself and all her nation is one alternative, and there is nothing worse to fear, but something to hope as the other alternative, then she may safely follow such an example." By these criteria, given the aggression of abolitionists and the safe alternative of colonization, Beecher declared that, with regard to antislavery petitioning, "the case of Queen Esther is not at all to be regarded as a suitable example for imitation."[4]

In *Letters to Cath[a]rine E. Beecher, in Reply to An Essay on Slavery and Abolitionism, Addressed to A. E. Grimké*, Grimké responded to Beecher's criticism by telling her old friend that Beecher had "conceded every thing I could wish, and proved beyond dispute just what I adduced this text to prove in my Appeal." Grimké described the terrible "condition of our country" and predicted a massively destructive servile war if the federal government failed to end slavery and end it immediately. She bemoaned that "Church and State [were] deeply involved in the enormous crime of slavery" and used her southern background to tell Beecher "that reflecting slaveholders expect their peculiar institution to be overthrown in blood." As Grimké defined the situation, Beecher's version of Esther made women's political intervention in the slave debates imperative as well as God-ordained.[5]

Beecher and Grimké's disagreement over the use of Esther as a model for 1830s activism in many ways epitomized the larger disputes they had about slavery, colonization, and abolition. Both women agreed that Esther's acts had been motivated by tremendous urgency, including threats of national destruction and the exhaustion of every other alternative. But they adamantly opposed each other's antislavery programs and discounted each other's imagined paths to the nation's destruction.

There were few points of agreement in the exchange that took place in 1837 between Catharine Beecher and Angelina Grimké. In the preface of her *Essay on Slavery and Abolitionism,* Beecher explained the aim of her monograph, an open letter to Grimké. Prompted by a man who asked Beecher "why he should not join the Abolition Society" and by Grimké's popular 1836 *Appeal* as well as Grimké's "intention to visit the North, for the purpose of using her influence among northern ladies to induce them to unite with Abolition Societies," Beecher desired to present to the public "another aspect [of] the cause [Grimké] advocates" (3–4). Grimké deemed Beecher's "main design . . . to counteract the effect of my testimony at the north" so urgent that she published her response serially as each letter to Beecher was completed (3).

The exchange between these two women appears to be one of the only sustained conversation between adherents of intensely competitive, antagonistic rival organizations, the American Colonization Society (ACS) and the American Anti-Slavery Society (AAS). But the debate between Beecher and Grimké gets little contemporary attention as representative of that aggressive rivalry. Instead, scholars typically read the exchange as a debate "on the role of women in the antislavery struggle" or on "the role of women in American society."[6] Gerda Lerner is one of two early exceptions. She writes that "Angelina, in her *Letters to Catherine Beecher,* was making herself one of the foremost spokesmen for abolition" and that Beecher decided to respond to

Grimké's recruitment of women into the cause "while she was preparing an essay against abolition societies." Lerner also calls attention to the fact that the first ten of the thirteen letters written by Grimké focused on abolitionism, and Lerner's brief summary of the exchange follows suit. Lorman Ratner associates Catharine with her father Lyman's formation of "the American Union, a group claiming to stand for 'moderate abolition'" and describes Catharine's *Essay on Slavery and Abolitionism* as "a tract in which she further developed the American Union's argument against the abolitionists."[7]

As women's history emerged as a field, though, the exchange was claimed as an early debate about feminist principles. In her groundbreaking 1968 anthology of U.S. feminist documents, for example, Aileen S. Kraditor limits her coverage of the exchange to excerpts from Grimké's eleventh and twelfth letters, the letters that concentrate on woman's rights and women's roles in the antislavery movement. The headnote introduces the letters as a response to Beecher, "one of the attackers" who wrote about the Grimkés' "'unfeminine' behavior in lecturing in public." In her very thorough and informative biography of Beecher, Kathryn Kish Sklar introduces Beecher's 1837 *Essay* as the text that "began the task that was to occupy her for the rest of her career—that of interpreting and shaping the collective consciousness of American women." Mary Hershberger simplifies Beecher's *Essay* by calling it "a lengthy treatise on the role of women in the antislavery struggle," one that resulted from her "retreat from political activity" and her critique of "women's political rights." Mark Perry notes in his history of the Grimké family that Beecher's *Essay* "defended the policy of gradualism, endorsed the work of the American Colonization Society, and criticized women abolitionists for acting outside their moral and domestic 'sphere.'" And yet his brief reading of Beecher's monograph exclusively features Beecher's commentary on women's role, whereas his reading of Grimké's *Letters* reveals the more complicated nuances of the debate. For Perry, Beecher was the conservative woman who provided Grimké with the opportunity to articulate radical feminist and abolitionist ideas. Describing the reaction to one of Angelina Grimké's protofeminist speeches delivered in 1837, Perry writes, "The women in her audience did not politely applaud this statement, as they had been instructed to do in such situations by Cath[a]rine Beecher; instead, a number of them did something very unladylike indeed: they cheered." Like Grimké's 1837 audience, we, too, implies Perry, are to cheer the feminist Grimké and scorn the conservative Beecher.[8]

Stephen Howard Browne warns against the conventional casting of Beecher "as an easy target for Grimké's finely edged skills as a public disputant" in his analysis of the exchange between these two public activists. Browne argues that Beecher's *Essay* and Grimké's *Letters* must be read together to appreciate the richness of each text, and he concludes that the exchange "represents a serious and systematic discussion of the language of reform, the province of public action, and the role of women in the work of the early republic." Browne appreciates that "Beecher represents her position first as an attack on the methods of abolitionists and then, only then, as a defense of woman's sphere," and he contextualizes Beecher's *Essay* by first considering two of her earlier publications (one on female education, the other on religion). But he almost completely overlooks colonization—its principles, its organization, its popularity, and its status as an alternative to immediate abolition in the 1830s.[9] So, for example, when Browne claims that "Beecher believed she could offer a superior alternative [to abolitionist rhetoric], a language grounded in community, enriched through private expression, made sensible through the laws of mind and experience," he imagines that alternative as "a categorically different language of reform" rather than a twenty-year-old system its advocates believed would promote gradual emancipation without threatening the Union: colonization.[10]

Beecher's attack on abolition was not an isolated attack. Beecher—and members of her family, including her famous father—participated in a movement that involved thousands of people, raised thousands and thousands of dollars, and listed as members and officers of its national organization men who also served as members of the clergy, members of Congress, justices of the U.S. Supreme Court, and presidents of the United States. Beecher echoed arguments that colonizationists regularly employed against abolitionists, and she addressed men as well as women. She was an intelligent, well-educated, well-connected, well-known advocate of moral reform who taught rhetoric and who knew how to compose a strong and persuasive case. She imagined the complicated, contentious debates about slavery as a conversation in which she authoritatively could intervene, and in her rhetoric she articulated the situation as one that invited the sort of arguments she wanted to make. That is the frame in which we need to read her *Essay on Slavery and Abolitionism, with Reference to the Duty of American Females*.

Grimké, too, was intelligent, well-educated, well-known, and rhetorically sophisticated. True, her arguments about woman's rights created dissent among abolitionists. Even she and her future husband angrily debated the things she and her sister Sarah said and believed about their rights to speak and to be heard and the role of those beliefs within their abolitionist advocacy. But her arguments for immediate emancipation united abolitionists, and we seem to have lost track of the authority abolitionists gave Angelina Grimké to represent them against Catharine Beecher's very public attack. Beecher's *Essay* was an open letter to Angelina Grimké, and in it she argued that women should not join abolition societies. Yet Beecher listed as the essay's first inspiration a gentleman who asked Beecher "why he should not join the Abolition Society," and much of the essay attacked the AAS (3). Beecher herself divided the essay after it was nearly two-thirds complete: "The preceding are some of the reasons which, on the general view, I would present as opposed to the proposal of forming Abolition Societies; and they apply equally to either sex. There are some others which seem to oppose peculiar objections to the action of females in the way you would urge" (96).[11] Theodore Weld knew Beecher's audience would not be limited to women. He worried that "it will catch the great mass of *prejudiced* mind and be likely to do mischief," and he urged Grimké to sharpen her doctrinal arguments and definitions of terms such as liberty, freedom, power, man–stealing, and slaveholding, especially as Grimké revised her letters for compilation in a book. James Birney, too, recognized that "Miss Beecher's Book" would be read widely, not restricted to the hands of women. He wrote to fellow abolitionist Lewis Tappan that abolitionists should use the book to abolitionist advantage. He engaged "this little *hand grenade*" in his abolitionist newspaper the *Philanthropist,* but only briefly—freed of more extensive critique because, he explained, Angelina Grimké was in the process of "exposing in a manner so effectual" the fallacies of the book.[12]

That process entailed serial publication (a point easy to forget, since now the letters are accessible as a book), and it was not until the eleventh letter, published two and one-half months after Grimké commenced her response, that she specifically addressed women's rights and responsibilities. The delay afforded her the time to argue about woman's rights with Weld, and in a moment of tremendous frustration she wrote to him, "Dost thou really think in my answer to C. E. B.'s absurd views of woman that I had better suppress my own? If so I will do it, as thou makest such a monster out of a molehill; but my judgment is *not* convinced that in this incidental way it is wrong to throw light on the subject."[13] Perhaps Grimké taunted Weld a bit by calling the point incidental, or perhaps she called it incidental so he would be more amenable to her engagement with Beecher's "absurd views of woman" in the midst of their colonization-abolition debate. Nonetheless, for neither Grimké, nor Weld, nor Birney, nor Beecher, nor for many other antislavery advocates, was the exchange between these two women predominantly about woman's rights. Nor was it marginalized because its inter-locutors were women. In 1837, people treated this exchange between Catharine Beecher and Angelina Grimké as a high-stakes confrontation between compelling rhetorical advocates seeking to persuade their readers that their organization, their methods, and their principles would rid the nation of its most dangerous and despicable evil, and that their organization, methods, and principles would do this great deed most effectively.

Ironically, only by returning to this perspective can we fully understand the role of this exchange in the United States woman's rights movement and Jacksonian-era judgments about woman's right to speak. Once we situate the exchange amid the rivalry and triangulate it inside the movements, then we see that the exception of political intervention was acceptable on behalf of Native Americans in 1829 but not African Americans in 1837 because Catharine Beecher refused to view abolitionism as a peaceful, Christian, and benevolent reform and thus as an appropriate vehicle for women's rhetorical advocacy.

Catharine Beecher's 1837 polemic enumerated fault after fault of abolition societies and argued adamantly against women's public, political advocacy of immediate emancipation. At the same time, Beecher stressed that slavery challenged the United States in urgent and far-reaching ways and that, as an urgent and wide-reaching cause, slavery demanded women's private, modest, decorous intervention:

> The question of slavery involves more pecuniary interests, touches more private relations, involves more prejudices, is entwined with more sectional, party, and political interests, than any other which can ever again arise. It is a matter which, if discussed and controlled without the influence of these principles of charity and peace, will shake this nation like an earthquake, and pour over us the volcanic waves of every terrific passion. The trembling earth, the low murmuring thunders, already admonish us of our danger; and if females can exert any saving influence in this emergency, it is time for them to awake. (*Essay,* 135–136)

In the sentences immediately preceding and following this passage Beecher told women to act but to act differently than abolitionists and even to act against them. She asked readers who were "surrounded by those who favour the Abolition measures" gently but diligently to question their beliefs, and she listed the questions readers should use (136). This prodding was consistent with everything else Beecher wrote in her *Essay on Slavery and Abolitionism.* As Angelina Grimké explained in the first paragraph of her *Letters* to Beecher, Beecher clearly intended to discredit abolitionists and prescribe an antislavery role for women defined by its opposition to abolitionist methods.

Imagine, then, how disgusted Beecher must have been when the first national Anti-Slavery Convention of American Women, led by Grimké, implied that Beecher endorsed their abolition organization and its methods. On the first page of the *Appeal to the Women of the Nominally Free States,* published immediately after the May 1837 convention and a couple of months after Beecher's *Essay* rolled off the press, was the title of the abolition address and then an epigraph:

> "The trembling earth, the low, murmuring thunders, already admonish us of our danger; and if females can exert any saving influence in this emergency, *it is time for them to awake.*"—Catharine E. Beecher.[14]

Beecher must have been mortified that her urgent call headed this abolitionist appeal to northern women. But this decontextualized rallying cry was only one of many barbs these women exchanged. It angered Grimké that Beecher said in her *Essay on Slavery and Abolitionism* that the transplanted South Carolinian was "not sufficiently informed in regard to the feelings and opinions of Christian females at the North" (6). Beecher also spoke disparagingly of abolitionists in her 1837 monograph. Repeatedly Beecher argued that the AAS was "neither peaceful nor [C]hristian" (28), that the group's methods were "most calculated to awaken anger, fear, pride, hatred, and all the passions most likely to blind the mind to truth" (56) and "calculated to generate party-spirit, denunciation, recrimination, and angry passions" (a pointed rebuke from a benevolent, anti-Jackson, proto-Whig reformer) (17, repeated on 46), that their premises were "not only illogical, but false" (10), and that they "rejoice[d]" in "illegal acts of violence" (36). As was typical of the Beechers, Catharine dissociated individual abolitionists from the AAS, ascribing good intentions to individuals as she berated the organization (14). But she accused the group of being dangerous, ineffective, and irresponsible, sometimes actively and intentionally.

As an abolitionist leader, Grimké responded to Beecher with charges of her own. Beecher's book strengthened Grimké's conviction that the northern states required as much antislavery work as the south: "a more subtle defence of the slaveholder's right to property in his helpless victims, I never saw" (*Letters*, 20). Confirming Beecher's critique of abolitionists as confrontational and therefore more likely to engender wrath than cooperation, Grimké wrote to Beecher, "I cannot help thinking how strange and unaccountable thy soft excuses for the *sins of prejudice* will appear to the next generation, if thy book ever reach their eye" (51). According to Grimké "not a word of compassion for *him*," the slave, appeared in Beecher's *Essay* nor did Beecher once "ask [herself], what the free man of color would think of it" (128–129). Beecher's monograph was "paralyzed and spell-bound by the sorcery of a worldly-minded expediency." "Perhaps on a dying bed," Grimké wrote at the very end of her *Letters*, "thou mayest vainly wish that '*Miss Beecher on the Slave Question*' might perish with the mouldering hand which penned its cold and heartless pages" (129).

These attacks were personal, and there were important personal as well as philosophical and doctrinal exigencies weighing on this heated exchange for both women. Grimké's public persona threatened Beecher's national leadership and widespread public support of her passion, female education. Beecher's public intervention threatened Grimké's national credibility and widespread public support of her passion, immediate emancipation. Grimké's AAS colleagues generated one of the most embarrassing moments in Lyman Beecher's career at Lane in 1834, and Beecher insulted Grimké's friends and associates explicitly in her *Essay*.

In other words, the public dissolution of Beecher and Grimké's friendship also was symptomatic of the larger rivalry between the ACS and the AAS. In 1833, procolonization newspapers began to note the antagonism between the ACS and the AAS. The *National Intelligencer* reprinted a letter in May 1833 from ACS secretary Ralph Gurley "intended as an answer to the objections which have been urged against the society by zealous anti-slavery men." That summer, the newspaper noted that AAS agents were traveling, lecturing, and writing to "create prejudice against the Colonization Society" and drew its own comparisons between the ACS and the AAS: "the scheme of Colonization compared with premature efforts to force abolition, was like the gentle and refreshing dews, renovating the earth in its beauty, compared to the tornado, breaking up its foundations, and covering it with ruins."[15]

Particularly sensitive to the growing antagonism, the *Christian Advocate and Journal and Zion's Herald* (*CAJZH*) called abolitionists "the *anti-colonization class of our citizens*" and compared the "two rival institutions": "without giving offence, or infringing upon the constituted rights of an individual, the Colonization Society has already accomplished more in behalf of emancipation than could ever have been done by the wild scheme of the abolitionists." In 1834 the *CAJZH* continued to call the AAS "an *anti-colonization society*" and added the labels "anti-American" and "anti-republican" to its list. Because slave owners emancipated hundreds of slaves each year to emigrate to Liberia, colonizationists increasingly pointed to the results of the two organizations as a means of comparison. According to ACS dogma, their program set slaves free whereas the AAS spent all of their time and money publishing incendiary papers and making incendiary speeches. The comparison played well at ACS events, including an 1835 New York Colonization Society meeting:

> An anti-colonizationist now rose in the gallery at the extremity of the church, and said that he would give one hundred [dollars] on condition that one question should be answered to his satisfaction. "That, probably, will be impracticable," said Mr. Duer: "however, we will hear your question." "I want Mr. Bethune to say," replied the man, "whether he ever knew or heard of a confirmed drunkard who was reformed by gradual drinking?" (A few clapped at this question, but the clapping was soon drowned in hisses, and some voices cried, "Put him out—turn him out!") "I will answer the gentleman's question," responded Mr. Bethune: "and I will answer it as my Lord and Master sometimes replied to questions of no meaning, or such as were irrelevant and improper, by asking the gentleman another: Can that gentleman tell me whether he ever knew or heard of a single slave who was set free by the anti-slavery society?" (Tremendous cheering.)

Whether the story was told by colonizationists or abolitionists, the story was that the AAS emerged in 1833 in large part as a hostile alternative to the ACS. Within a couple of years the rivalry between the two organizations, their programs, and their proponents was fierce. Catharine Beecher and Angelina Grimké epitomized the strife between these antislavery coalitions.[16]

Peaceful Christian Benevolence or Radical Religious Reform?

Catharine Beecher and Angelina Grimké agreed in 1837 that the United States faced an emergency. For Beecher, the emergency was the national breakdown of Christian methods of deliberation concerning the issue of slavery. In her *Essay on Slavery and Abolitionism* she had just outlined seven "maxims of peace and charity": one should be protected to express not only one's advocacy of but also one's opposition to ideas; one should allow one's own ideas to be debated; one should not accuse others of false or hidden motives and interests; when assigning motives, one should always give opponents the benefit of the doubt; one should avoid any sort of unchristian retaliation or retribution regardless of the wrongs incurred; one should guard others from temptation; and one should refrain from gossiping about, slandering, or hurting the feelings of others (128–135). These principles had to be maintained in a Christian democracy: "with our form of government, and our liabilities to faction and party-spirit, the country will be safe and happy only in proportion to the prevalence of these maxims among the mass of the community" (135). Everywhere Beecher turned, though, these principles were being violated, especially in the political and religious arenas. And amid the unmannered chaos of Jacksonian democracy, the most stunning and insidious violations were executed by abolitionists.

Beecher was not isolated in her disdain for abolitionists. In the *Essay on Slavery and Abolitionism* Beecher detailed a widespread complaint that abolitionism was destructive. Newspapers such as the *National Intelligencer* and the *CAJZH* regularly lambasted abolitionists as deluded fanatics doing harm and making things worse for Americans (they meant European Americans), slaves, free people of color, and the United States, even though abolitionists had no business intervening in slavery in the first place. Beecher also voiced the popular conviction that the only safe and legal way to end slavery was by working with southern slave owners, not by rebelling against or ostracizing them. To this distillation of popular antislavery discourse, Beecher added a discussion of Christian means of persuasion and an articulation of a special role for women as mediators of public debate in what she concluded was the safest, most expedient program to rid the nation of slavery, a program of gradual emancipation.

Since Beecher aimed to derail the Grimké sisters' 1837 lecture tour, Grimké felt compelled to answer Beecher. Actually, as several abolitionist leaders including the Grimkés saw it, Beecher offered Grimké an opportunity to defend abolitionism against a litany of erroneous abuses. In response to Beecher, Grimké said that abolitionists were doing God's work and effecting change in the northern and southern states. She accused antiabolitionists of privileging human law over God's law, she rebuked Beecher specifically and gradualists generally for their prejudices, and she declared it immoral to own people as property. She argued that abolitionist methods resembled those of earlier radical religious reformers, and, matching the pattern of Beecher's polemic, Grimké articulated (again) the role she envisioned for women in this national crisis, a politically interventionist role that invited agitation and excitement. Thus, within their exchange about slavery—or, more accurately, their exchange about antislavery programs—Angelina Grimké and Catharine Beecher assigned women distinct activist roles, rights, and responsibilities.

Antislavery Debates

Beecher primarily argued in her *Essay on Slavery and Abolitionism* that neither men nor women should affiliate with abolitionists or embrace abolitionism. Never one to mince words, Beecher explained that abolitionists frequently were unreasonable, irresponsible, and extremist (Beecher did avoid the word "fanatics" in the monograph, despite the frequency with which most northerners used it to refer to the "deluded advocates of immediate emancipation").[17] No less than six times Beecher accused abolitionists of willfully creating strife, dissension, and violence (14, 28, 32–36). She declared it to be "a fact, that Abolitionists have taken the course most calculated to awaken illegal acts of violence, and that when they have ensued, they have seemed to rejoice in them" (35–36). This accusation against abolitionists was so common in public discourse that the same words were repeated in a kind of rote pattern: Beecher spoke about choices "most calculated to excite wrath and strife" (28); the *National Intelligencer* quoted the New York *Commercial Advertiser*'s report that AAS funds were used "to circulate incendiary publications, papers filled with bitterness, and wrath, and strife, endeavoring to kindle the angry passions of the People." Beecher considered it irresponsible for abolitionists to act without concern for these and other consequences (49–50), as when Grimké in her 1836 *Appeal* told her southern readers to free their slaves and leave the aftermath to God. At around the same time that Grimké published that provocative essay, writers in the *National Intelligencer* also bemoaned what they called "the reckless efforts of these disturbers of social order." Beecher reflected widespread animosity when she wondered how abolitionists could be so unreasonable as to believe slavery would ever end if the northern and southern states ceased "mingling on those fraternal terms that existed before the Abolition movement began" (89–90). But the AAS refused to consider alternatives, the *CAJZH* complained: "the Anti-Colonization Society disclaim every other method" that might end slavery in the United States. The *CAJZH* marked its aggression against the AAS by calling it the "Anti-Colonization Society," and that small but highly visible act of resistance was a reminder of the ways antiabolitionists unceasingly felt as if they were under attack by the AAS. Beecher also criticized abolitionists for inflexibility and excessive righteousness, as when abolitionists collapsed all positions on slavery into a pro and con binary or refused to consider anything besides their own program: "Abolitionists very extensively have endeavoured to make the impression that all who do not join their party, or who object to their measures, are in the same class with the advocates of slavery. But this is a mistake" (93–94). Given the "discourteousness, uncharitableness, denunciation, misjudgment, and reckless ultraism" Beecher cataloged among abolitionists (92), her deeply entrenched resistance to the AAS and Grimké's appeals hardly can be reduced to a conservative position on gender roles.[18]

This charge of reckless ultraism was just one of many charges Beecher made against abolitionists in her 1837 *Essay on Slavery and Abolitionism*. Like many European Americans, Beecher blamed abolitionists for harming slaves, free people of color, and whites with their antislavery program. Abolitionists so annoyed and scared southerners that antislavery discussions that had been possible even a few years earlier were silenced:

> While Abolition Societies did not exist, men could talk and write, at the South, against the evils of slavery, and northern men had free access and liberty of speech, both at the South and at the North. But now all is changed. Every avenue of approach to the South is shut. No paper, pamphlet, or preacher, that touches on that topic, is admitted in their bounds. Their own citizens, that once laboured and remonstrated, are silenced; their own clergy, under the influence of the exasperated feelings of their people, and their own sympathy and sense of wrong, either entirely hold their peace, or become the defenders of a system they once lamented, and attempted to bring to an end. (82)

Furthermore, because of abolitionists, Beecher argued, southerners harassed and expelled whites who attempted to comfort and legally aid slaves (84). Colonizationists who remembered the Christian missionaries who had been harassed, jailed, and expelled from the Cherokee nation under Georgia laws had a very real, very disappointing set of experiences against which they interpreted and condemned the hostilities they believed abolitionists caused in the southern states.

Not only, though, did antiabolitionists believe that abolitionists rendered nearly impossible any conversations in the southern states about emancipation, but also antiabolitionists blamed abolitionists for the ways slave

owners increasingly restricted slaves' movements, education, religious practices, and other behaviors. The correlation was predictable, according to
Beecher: "How will the exasperated majority act, according to the known
laws of mind and of experience? Instead of lessening the evils of slavery,
they will increase them. The more they are goaded by a sense of aggressive
wrong without, or by fears of dangers within, the more they will restrain their
slaves, and diminish their liberty, and increase their disabilities" (*Essay*,
83–84). One *CAJZH* article explained to its readers that, as a result of abolitionist activities, slaves "must be subjected to more rigorous discipline—their
privileges curtailed—their congregations dispersed—their improvement
stayed—their Christian teachers silenced" because slave owners worried that
"these privileges are very capable of being perverted to ruinous purposes."
And reports like this one from a Christian mission near Nashville, Tennessee, infuriated gradual emancipationists: "The mission is in a prosperous condition, although we have been deprived of many privileges this year,
in consequence of the great excitement on the subject of abolition; by this
we have been deprived of our Sunday school, and night meetings." That
particular report was published in the *CAJZH* just a few months after
Grimké's *Appeal to the Christian Women of the South* circulated, and surely
made many northern Christians more sympathetic to Beecher's arguments.
Most northerners believed with Beecher that abolitionists made life harder
for slaves. Abolitionists repeatedly were told that they were "riveting more
closely the bonds which they seem so anxious to sever" and that the AAS's
"only effect will be to have the fetters of the slave welded stronger."[19]

According to antiabolitionist logics, abolition was bad for free blacks
also, although ironically (perhaps unsurprisingly) this argument rested on
white prejudice against African Americans. Abolitionists forced African
Americans upon northerners by doing things such as proposing schools for
free blacks in cities populated by whites, Beecher explained, and then abolitionists attacked whites who resisted these developments because of their
prejudices (*Essay*, 30–32). Like her father, Beecher argued that prejudice
was odious, but, also like her father, Beecher condemned abolitionists for
taunting racist European Americans into increasing their prejudice rather
than patiently working with them to excise it (26). Moreover, in "incendiary" abolitionist papers such as the *Liberator*, free people of color "were
taught to feel that they were injured and abused, the objects of a guilty and
unreasonable prejudice" (28). Beecher did not dispute the existence of these
prejudices, but she blamed abolitionists for exacerbating the problem by

"generat[ing] anger, pride, and recrimination, on one side, and envy, discontent, and revengeful feelings, on the other" (28). The *National Intelligencer* reported the same phenomenon:

> Stimulated by the writing of the prominent officers of the Anti-Slavery Society,—writings which that Society has adopted as its own,—the colored inhabitants of these free States have occasionally manifested a spirit of hostility towards the whites, fatal to the harmony of the two races in its immediate effect, and in its remote effect adapted to render the condition of the free blacks doubly uncomfortable, and to discourage and counter-act all philanthropic designs in their behalf.

Antiabolitionists argued that giving free people of color "impracticable hopes" of equality was one of the most ruthless errors of the AAS:

> We have long been of the opinion, and frequently expressed it, that the Abolitionists are *the worst enemies* the blacks of this city have. They are holding out to them the prospect of amalgamation, feeding their pride with impracticable hopes, exclaiming and denouncing the prejudice against color, leading them to believe that they are unjustly and cruelly treated by the whites, by denial of *equal political* and SOCIAL privileges, fomenting their passions, denouncing all who will not join them in their absurd cru-sade as kidnappers, villains, manstealers, thieves, and pirates, inviting them to sit with the whites indiscriminately.

Because antiabolitionists believed that abolitionists "compelled [slave own-ers] to multiply restraints upon their slaves, and thus increase the rigors of slavery" and pushed "public policy [to] be harsh and vindictive," antiaboli-tionists concluded that "no one body of men have ever inflicted a deeper in-jury on the other than have the abolitionists on the blacks of the United States." Beecher did not have to look far for public incriminations of aboli-tionists in 1837. They were everywhere.[20]

Everywhere, too, abolitionists were said to provoke violence harmful to whites. Abolitionists regularly and frequently were blamed for "excit[ing] insubordination and insurrection among the slaves," offenses for which abolitionists were called treasonous. Abolitionists also were assigned blame for antiabolitionist mobs and riots—in other words, for riots against them-selves. Reports of mob violence never absolved white "mobocrats" from their responsibility, but neither did these reports defend without qualification the abolitionists who came under attack. One Cincinnati newspaper concluded its mob report by condemning the mob but also blaming abolitionists for its provocation: "Thus have the abolitionists brought upon our hitherto peaceful city a highly disreputable mob." Several reports blamed abolitionists for provoking a particularly extensive riot in New York: abolitionists "gave occasion for the expression of mobocratic feelings" and the mob "grew out of the absurd and outrageous project of the abolitionists to force public sentiment."[21] Beecher explained the fault of abolitionists in these mobs by invoking the Christian principle that people should not lead others into temptation. As far as Beecher was concerned, "where Christians could foresee that by placing certain temptations in the way of their fellow-men, all the probabilities were, that they would yield, and yet persisted in doing it, the tempters became partakers in the guilt of those who yielded to the temptation" (*Essay*, 33).

Beecher also accused abolitionists of interfering inappropriately and even dangerously in other people's business—in the north as well as in the south. Slavery was an issue for slave owners and slave states to manage. Since all of the northern states legally had abolished slavery there was no point in preaching abolitionist doctrine in the north, Beecher reasoned. Why try "to convince those who are not guilty, of the sins of those who are" (*Essay*, 47)? Abolitionists made worse the conflicts between northern and southern states, regions already "rival, and jealous in feeling," by working in the northern states against slavery, trying to rally the north against the south (12). Instead, Beecher charged, abolitionists should travel throughout the south, persuading slave owners voluntarily to emancipate their slaves and gradually to end the horrible institution—which apparently abolitionists refused to do because they "feared personal evils to themselves" (13). For Beecher, the geography of abolition was anathema: "The distinctive peculiarity of the Abolition Society is this: it is a voluntary association in one section of the country, designed to awaken public sentiment against a moral evil existing in another section of the country" (8). Implicit in Beecher's critique was that this scheme threatened the nation's union. That threat dominated antiabolitionist discourse in the *National Intelligencer*. Interference by northern states in the business of slavery violated southerners' constitutional rights, most European Americans argued. Henry Clay explained the point at the annual ACS meeting in 1835: "He denied the right of discussion on a subject where, politically speaking, there was no power to decide. Discussion was the antecedent to deliberation; deliberation to decision—and the people of the non-slaveholding States had no right to decide on the question of slavery. It was a matter for the slave-holding States exclusively." An address reprinted in the *CAJZH* summarized the claim: "the constitution of the United States solemnly forbids any interference on the part of a state, or of individuals, which would go to infringe upon the legal rights of the slave-holder." According to the Alexandria *Gazette* and many other newspapers reporting on the issue, "the vast majority of the northern people conscientiously believe Slavery to be a great evil; but they also believe it to be an evil which does not affect them, with which they can and ought to have nothing to do, and with which their *interest* alone would prevent them from meddling." The most probable consequence of northern interference in slavery, most northerners and southerners alike acknowledged through the 1830s, was "a dissolution of the republic."[22]

But there were alternatives to Anti-Slavery Societies and their abolitionists practices. Beecher reported that few antiabolitionists—few Americans—believed that "the evil" should or could be sustained. The question was one of means and methods, explained Beecher. She detailed several alternatives, as did newspapers including the religious *Christian Advocate and Journal and Zion's Herald* and the secular *National Intelligencer*. All of the alternatives presumed that the abolition of U.S. slavery required slave owners voluntarily to give up the institution, whether they individually emancipated their slaves or, more realistically, together changed the laws of the state in which they lived. "*The measure*," antislavery antiabolitionists agreed emphatically, "*must originate with their masters.*"[23] Beecher made it clear for her readers:

> The object to be accomplished is:
> First. To convince a certain community, that they are in the practice of a great sin, and
> Secondly, To make them willing to relinquish it. (*Essay*, 53)

Beecher insisted that men and women evaluate their courses of action "entirely on the *probabilities of success*" for the accomplishment of these objects (48). Which means were most expedient—which would most likely, safely, and quickly lead the south to "finally be convinced of her sins, and voluntarily bring the system of slavery to an end" (89)? One had to approach sinners out of love and kindness, in private, with the permission of the sinner to engage the topic: "It is a law of experience, that when wrong is done, if repentance and reformation are sought, then love and kindness, mingled with remonstrance, coming from one who has a *right* to speak, are more successful than rebuke and scorn from others who are not beloved, and who are regarded as impertinent intruders" (54). For those who doubted the viability of these methods, Beecher provided her readers a model to emulate: the British abolitionist Thomas Clarkson. Beecher detailed Clarkson's antislavery career and then summarized the differences between the United States and the British abolition movements. The British movement

> was conducted by some of the wisest and most talented statesmen, as well as the most pious men, in the British nation . . . It was conducted by men who had the intellect, knowledge, discretion, and wisdom demanded for so great an enterprise.
>
> Secondly. It was conducted slowly, peaceably, and by eminently judicious influences.
>
> Thirdly. It included, to the full extent, the doctrine of expediency denounced by Abolitionists . . .
>
> Fourthly. Good men were not divided, and thrown into contending parties.—The opponents to the measure, were only those who were personally interested in the perpetuation of slavery or the slave-trade.
>
> Fifthly. This effort was one to convince men of their *own* obligations, and not an effort to arouse public sentiment against the sinful practices of another community over which they had no control. (78–79)

The U.S. colonization movement and the U.S. antiremoval movement operated according to these criteria. The U.S. abolition movement did not.

In her *Essay on Slavery and Abolitionism,* Beecher systematically proposed methods that promised, as the *CAJZH* described it, "a gradual, but final, and not less complete abolition of slavery, by the influence of moral means." Although Beecher defended the ACS in her 1837 monograph, she stopped short of advocating colonization as the only or the primary means to gradual emancipation and abolition (*Essay,* 23–26). Beecher explained that the most powerful position from which to speak was one unaffiliated with any party or organization, so Beecher sympathized with but did not explicitly endorse the ACS in her monograph (94–95). Generally, though, public antislavery discourse advocated the ACS as the most viable means of ending slavery in the United States. In 1833, an ACS officer claimed that the ACS "[was] most happily *adapted to exert a powerful influence in favor of the voluntary emancipation of slaves*" because its means were kind and nonthreatening: "Such an *indirect influence,* gentle, persuasive, but *mighty,* does the Colonization

Society send forth on the public mind in *favor of emancipation*. Since its origin, it *has done more* to produce *voluntary emancipation than all other causes and influences*." ACS adherents increasingly argued in the mid-1830s that the ACS produced voluntary emancipation and the AAS did not. By 1837, the ACS had "already emancipated from their chains several thousand of slaves." Whereas a twenty-five-dollar contribution to the AAS enabled the production of yet another "incendiary" publication, the ACS "pledge[d] ourselves that for every twenty-five dollars, a slave shall be set free." Colonizationists earned the right to speak about abolition in the southern states, they asserted, and they effected emancipation. Like Catharine Beecher, they had no patience for abolitionists who threatened their opportunities in the southern states: "the men who are agitating the whole community by their publications, and who are accused of riveting instead of breaking the fetters of the slave, are bound at least to come forward, and prove that they have done *some good to somebody*." Antiabolitionists including Catharine Beecher focused on results, on the expedience of reform practices, and they found the AAS completely inadequate to the urgent task at hand.[24]

Beecher's antislavery, antiabolition polemic articulated widespread criticism of the AAS and used that critique to argue against men and women joining abolitionist societies. Beecher also used the opportunity to popularize what she called "peaceful and Christian" methods of persuasion, hoping to raise the general level of debate in the United States. These persuasive strategies closely resembled the methods she presented in her 1836 *Letters on the Difficulties of Religion*, especially in the preface of that book. Her 1837 *Essay on Slavery and Abolitionism* demonstrated the methods as much by talking about and using them as by pointing out the ways abolitionists failed to use them. For instance, Beecher analyzed the ways abolitionists handled their disagreement with colonizationists about ACS practices:

> One of the first measures of Abolitionists was an attack on a benevolent society, originated and sustained by some of the most pious and devoted men of the age. It was imagined by Abolitionists, that the influence and measures of the Colonization Society tended to retard the abolition of slavery, and to perpetuate injurious prejudices against the coloured race. The peaceful and [C]hristian method of meeting this difficulty would have been, to collect all the evidence of this supposed hurtful tendency, and privately, and in a respectful and conciliating way, to have presented it to the attention of the wise and benevolent men, who were most interested

in sustaining this institution. If this measure did not avail to convince them, then it would have been safe and justifiable to present to the public a temperate statement of facts, and of the deductions based on them, drawn up in a respectful and candid manner, with every charitable allowance which truth could warrant. But such was not the course adopted. (23–24)

Beecher overwhelmingly sympathized with colonizationists, but kept her assessment as impersonal as possible given her own acquiescence to the peaceful and Christian methods she advocated. In keeping with this philosophy, Beecher explained that abolitionists would have been justified to make their complaints public if they had followed a different protocol than that which they actually adopted. It is important to note here how extensively Beecher's critique of abolitionists goes beyond their proposed solutions to slavery. Like most antiabolitionists, Beecher deplored the abolitionist methods that she believed to be aggressive, antagonistic, extreme, and dangerous.

Rather than dismiss abolitionists as fanatics, though, Beecher used the colonization-abolition rivalry to promote what time after time she called a "peaceful and [C]hristian method of meeting this difficulty" or a "peaceful and Christian method of encountering such opposition" (*Essay,* 24, 37). When James Birney refused to move his abolitionist newspaper away from Cincinnati despite the appeals of leading citizens and the clear signs of imminent riots, Beecher concluded that abolitionists chose to lead men into temptation instead of accomplishing whatever "good" they intended "in a quiet, peaceable, and [C]hristian way" (34–35). When abolitionists attacked their opponents, they treated antislavery gradualists and colonizationists "as though they were the friends and defenders of slavery" (38). In line with her argument generally that AAS methods were "neither peaceful nor Christian in their tendency," Beecher told her readers that "the peaceful and Christian method of encountering such opposition, would have been to allow the opponents full credit for purity and integrity of motive, to have avoided all harsh and censorious language, and to have employed facts, arguments and persuasions, in a kind and respectful way with the hope of modifying their views and allaying their fears" (37–38). In yet another example, Beecher argued against the means by which abolitionists "attempt[ed] to remove the prejudices of the whites against the blacks" (26). Beecher believed that white prejudice was both "*unreasonable* and *groundless,*" but she believed that abolitionists responded inexpediently:

The best way to make a person like a thing which is disagreeable, is to try in some way to make it agreeable; and if a certain class of persons is the subject of unreasonable prejudice, the peaceful and [C]hristian way of removing it would be to endeavour to render the unfortunate persons who compose this class, so useful, so humble and unassuming, so kind in their feelings, and so full of love and good works, that prejudice would be supplanted by complacency in their goodness, and pity and sympathy for their disabilities . . . Instead of this, reproaches, rebukes, and sneers, were employed to convince the whites that their prejudices were sinful, and without any just cause. (26–27)

In addition to believing abolitionists to be inexpedient and unchristian on this topic, somehow Beecher also believed that she was above the sin of prejudice—a belief for which, of course, Grimké soon reproached and rebuked her. But it was Beecher's prejudice that made possible her acceptance of gradual rather than immediate emancipation, and her prejudice that enabled her to privilege the protection of a public, safe space for debate among European Americans above freedoms for Africans and their descendants. According to Beecher's interpretation of Evangelical and Whig ideologies, for the United States to function as a Christian democracy, the nation needed peaceful, Christian methods of persuasion. For Beecher it was that need, more than black freedom, that required urgent and immediate action.

A Peaceful and Christian Solution

Catharine Beecher constructed a fairly nuanced argument about public debate in the United States. It was an argument that offered limited but, Beecher believed, powerful options for women's advocacy. The young nation was unique in the freedoms it offered its citizens, especially the freedoms of speech, religion, and press. For the first time, neither church nor state restrained "the perfect right of all men to entire freedom of opinion" (*Essay,* 109). (The presumption by Beecher of an all-white citizenry is almost too obvious even to mention.) At the same time, matters of public policy and private interest were "decided by *public sentiment* . . . by the *majority of votes*" (111). In principle, men achieved power not by religious anointment nor by despotic, feudal, or monarchical appointment but by convincing other men to vote for them or for their ideas. But the system already was corrupt because, as much as men asserted their own freedom to speak their mind, they refused other men that same freedom. (In summarizing Beecher's argument, I am using "man" as she did, as a gender-neutral term, though much more ironically than the eldest daughter of the Beecher clan.) To keep their opponents from taking that liberty, men—often as members of a party—refused to listen to their opponents or they attacked their opponents' character or motives. According to Beecher, abolitionists epitomized this behavior. Beecher called it rule by "pains and penalties": "And it is the remark of some of the most intelligent foreign travellers among us, and of our own citizens who go abroad, that there is no country to be found, where freedom of opinion, and freedom of speech is more really influenced and controlled by the fear of pains and penalties, than in this land of boasted freedom" (124). Free discussion and other "fundamental principles of liberty" (110), freedoms absolutely requisite in a Christian democracy—a democracy free from coercion, uninhibited in its pursuit of truth and virtue—had to be protected: "God designs that every intelligent mind shall be governed, not by coercion, but by reason, and conscience, and truth. Man must reason, and experiment, and compare past and present results, and hear and know all that can be said on *both* sides of every question which influences either private or public happiness, either for this life or for the life to come" (126). The alternatives were unthinkable:

> What is the end of these things to be? Must we give up free discussion, and again chain up the human mind under the despotism of past ages? . . . Must we be distracted and tortured by the baleful passions and wicked works that unrestrained party-spirit and ungoverned factions will bring upon us, under such a government as ours? Must we rush on to disunion, and civil wars, till all their train of horrors pass over us like devouring fire? (125–126)

Beecher passionately warned of the temptations posed by unrestrained freedoms of opinion and speech coupled with a system of government in which the majority ruled. She predicted an insurmountable proliferation of corruption and vice. She argued for the situation's magnitude, and she detailed its immediate urgency. At the climax of her amplification of the problem, Beecher declared a salve for the nation:

> There is an influence that can avert these dangers—a spirit that can allay the storm—that can say to the troubled winds and waters, "peace, be still." It is that spirit which is gentle and easy to be entreated, which thinketh no evil, which rejoiceth not in iniquity, but rejoiceth in the truth, which is not

easily provoked, which hopeth all things, which beareth all things. Let this spirit be infused into the mass of the nation, and then truth may be sought, defended, and propagated, and error detected, and its evils exposed; and yet we may escape the evils that now rage through this nation, and threaten us with such fiery plagues. (126–127)

This was a sudden and, in the *Essay,* an unusual turn to biblical inflection. But women had the religious authority to advocate the spirits of charity and peace that Beecher deemed fundamentally requisite for the constitution of a Christian democracy.

That religious authority required a very clear separation of men's and women's spheres, a prescriptive demarcation we certainly would label conservative by today's standards. But Beecher's solutions to the unique challenges facing the United States involved new interventions, new power dynamics. They altered, rather than conserved, the status quo. Inside a rubric of Christian democracy Beecher inherited from her father and his national cadre of theocrats, a rubric perpetuated by Whigs into the 1840s, Beecher posited a particularly Christian system of persuasion whose very viability relied on women. Beecher identified an emerging problem entailed by the coupling of unrestrained freedoms and a democratic system of government as a refusal of men to respect those same freedoms in other men. She reasoned, "This method of resisting freedom of opinions, by pains and penalties, arises in part from the natural selfishness of man, and in part from want of clear distinctions as to the rights and duties involved in freedom of opinion and freedom of speech" (*Essay,* 114). This causal explanation of the "pains and penalties" derailing Christian democracy was masterfully strategic. Where should the nation turn for solutions? To religion and education, both domains appropriate for the assertion of women's power.

To get power, Beecher gave up power (again). Beecher affirmed a divinely ordained relationship between men and women in which "woman holds a subordinate relation in society to the other sex" (99). But that affirmation, that acceptance of God's plan, entailed "mode[s] of gaining influence and of exercising power" that could not be stripped from women by man (99). So Beecher accepted the relegation of women to what she called "the domestic and the social circle" (100). She also understood powerful and influential women to be defined by the qualities of peace, benevolence, and love. Essentially those qualilties precluded women from acting as "combatants" or "partisans" (102). But, according to the "Divine economy" that assigned to human beings their relations and roles, women had the responsibility of acting "as the advocate[s] of charity and peace": "There are certain prominent maxims which every woman can adopt as peculiarly belonging to her, as the advocate of charity and peace, and which it should be her especial office to illustrate, enforce, and sustain, by every method in her power" (128). Those maxims were the seven "maxims of peace and charity" Beecher delineated, the "principles which alone can protect and preserve the right of free discussion, the freedom of speech, and liberty of the press" (135). Beecher assigned to women the job of maintaining a safe, public, peaceful, and Christian space for debate. Without that space, the United States would fail as a Christian democracy: "with our form of government, and our liabilities to faction and party-spirit, the country will be safe and happy only in the proportion to the prevalence of these maxims among the mass of the community" (135). If the United States were to survive as a Christian democracy, Beecher reasoned, women had to participate, and they had to participate powerfully.

One site of participation was the classroom, where women could intervene in the national crisis as teachers of the nation's future citizens and the future teachers and mothers of those citizens. In her 1837 antiabolition polemic, Beecher abridged the argument she introduced in her 1835 *Essay on the Education of Female Teachers*. Children needed intellectual, moral, and religious education to ensure "the safety and happiness of this nation," Beecher repeated in 1837 (*Essay*, 104). Already the nation was short thirty thousand teachers, Beecher explained, "but if we allow that we need not reach this point, in order to save ourselves from that destruction which awaits a people, when governed by an ignorant and unprincipled democracy; if we can weather the storms of democratic liberty with only one-third of our ignorant children properly educated, still we need *ten thousand* teachers at this moment, and an addition of *two thousand every year*" (105). Beecher invoked again, as she had done in 1835, the dangers of "democratic liberty." Individual freedoms available only to citizens of the United States required unique measures and practices. To accommodate that extraordinary exigence, the nation needed educated teachers of young children. Men, Beecher reminded her audience, rarely would accept such low-paying, intellectually unsatisfying jobs. Women, on the other hand, were ideally suited to fulfill the incredible demands Beecher reported. In return for their sacrifice, "women will more and more be furnished with those intellectual advantages which they need to fit them for such duties." Not only would they become better educated, but they would become more influential in "the general interests of society" (106).

Just as she was in 1835, in 1837 Beecher was willing to give away power to get power. She reminded her readers, "If females, as they approach the other sex, in intellectual elevation, begin to claim, or to exercise in any manner, the peculiar prerogatives of that sex, education will prove a doubtful and dangerous blessing" (*Essay*, 107). Beecher knew that "American females [had to be] peculiarly sensitive in reference to any measure, which should even *seem* to draw them from their appropriate relations in society" or they would lose this avenue to increased rights, influence, and power (104). Consider, then, Beecher's strategy. She used what she identified as a national emergency—the breakdown of the public sphere—to acquire rights, influence, and power for women through their careers as teachers. By warning women against violating cultural expectations appropriate for women, Beecher was not protecting gender as a construct, nor was she limiting women's power simply because of their gender. She was using gender to protect, even creatively to increase, women's access to power.

At no point in her treatise did Beecher presume women to be apathetic to or ambivalent about slavery and the distressing state of national affairs, and at no point did Beecher expect women to remain neutral. Beecher explained that "it [was] not necessary that a woman should in any manner relinquish her opinion as to the evils or the benefits, the right or the wrong, of any principle or practice." What was necessary was that women remained calm in their advocacy and that they promoted peaceful and Christian public discussion rather than "exciting or regulating public sentiment." Given the national state of emergency (a breakdown of deliberative democracy regarding slavery), women had "instantly to relinquish the attitude of a partisan" and instead "assume the office of a mediator" (*Essay*, 127–128). What did those constraints mean, in practical terms? Beecher advised women to ask abolitionists in their domestic and social circles questions such as these:

> Is not slavery to be brought to an end by free discussion, and is it not a war upon the right of free discussion to impeach the motives and depreciate the character of the opposers of Abolition measures? . . . Is not the only method by which the South can be brought to relinquish slavery, a conviction that not only her *duty*, but her highest *interest*, requires her to do it? And is not *calm, rational Christian* discussion the only proper method of securing this end? (136–137)

As mediators, "women among those who oppose Abolition movements" should ask these sorts of questions:

Ought not Abolitionists to be treated as if they were actuated by the motives of benevolence which they profess? . . . If Abolitionists are censurable for taking measures that exasperate rather than convince and persuade, are not their opponents, who take exactly the same measures to exasperate Abolitionists and their friends, as much to blame? If Abolitionism prospers by the abuse of its advocates, are not the authors of this abuse accountable for the increase of the very evils they deprecate? (138–139)

None of these questions were neutral. All illustrated an antislavery, and also an antiabolition bias. Beecher's *Essay on Slavery and Abolitionism, with Reference to the Duty of American Females* was not an etiquette manual for women, nor did it remove women from public debate. The *Essay on Slavery and Abolitionism* was an antiabolitionist polemic that categorically insisted on peaceful and Christian public debate as integral to a Christian democracy, and it strategically located women as integral to that project.

Women and Their Right to Speak

In that context, why did Beecher deny women the right to petition the federal government against slavery? Beecher told her readers, "In this country, petitions to congress, in reference to the official duties of legislators, seem, IN ALL CASES, to fall entirely without the sphere of female duty" (*Essay,* 104). She urged women to help "bring this national sin of slavery to an end" (108), so why not petition? For the same reason Beecher argued that women—and men—should not join abolition societies. Antislavery petitions submitted to Congress generated wrath and strife, and moved the United States farther from, not closer to, ending slavery. Beecher applied the same standard to this question as she did to all of the questions she asked in her monograph: "the rectitude and propriety of any such measure, depend entirely on its probable results" (102). Beecher reasoned that women's antislavery petitions, even on behalf of enslaved women, would be remarkably inexpedient and therefore had to be stopped:

If petitions from females will operate to exasperate; if they will be deemed obtrusive, indecorous, and unwise, by those to whom they are addressed; if they will increase, rather than diminish the evil which it is wished to remove; if they will be the opening wedge, that will tend eventually to bring females as petitioners and partisans into every political measure that may tend to injure and oppress their sex, in various parts of the nation, and under the various public measures that may hereafter be enforced, then it is neither appropriate nor wise, nor right, for a woman to petition for the relief of oppressed females. (102–103)

Beecher's argument clearly is gendered. Basically, she offered three measures: first, whether the petitions would annoy or otherwise confront their recipients; second, whether the petitions would help rather than hurt the cause; and third, whether the petitions would establish a precedent for regular female intervention into politics. The gender of the petitioners especially dominated the first and third measures.

Beecher believed antislavery petitions generally hurt the antislavery cause because they increased the jealousies, tensions, and defenses that got in the way of gently persuading slave owners voluntarily to give up the institution and their property. But women's petitions particularly damaged the cause by drawing attention away from the issue at hand—slavery—and calling attention to a different threat, what many men and women perceived to be violations of divinely ordered gender relations. And the idea that women's political intervention might become regular rather than extraordinary not only threatened conventional notions of gender but also threatened one of Beecher's most common arguments for women's political power and influence: the extraordinary nature of the case. Indian removal was an extraordinary crisis. The shortage of teachers was an extraordinary crisis. Slavery and its correlative breakdown of public debate were extraordinary crises. Inside the model of Christian democracy, the more women resembled men by acting and responding like men, the less authority they had and the less relevant they became to issues of public policy and private interest.

But why would Beecher emphatically prohibit women from petitioning the national legislature "IN ALL CASES" when she had urged women to petition Congress eight years earlier? In her 1829 "Circular Addressed to Benevolent Ladies of the U. States," Beecher urged women to petition Congress in protest of the federal government's Indian removal policies, and she deemed that legislative intervention appropriate: "It may be, that female petitioners can lawfully be heard, even by the highest rulers of our land." Mary Hershberger argues that Beecher "retreat[ed] from political activity" because of gender-based "congressional attacks" on female antiremoval petitioners, but only one congressman attacked women for their antiremoval activism. Furthermore, Beecher retreated only from national petitioning.

Beecher did not absent herself nor the women she represented from U.S. politics. What Beecher did was change strategies.[25]

If we place Beecher's 1829 essay next to her 1837 monograph and evaluate them through a lens colored only by gender, or if we evaluate Beecher's *Essay on Slavery and Abolitionism* only to get a sense of the ways her ideas about women differed from Angelina Grimké's, it is easy to conclude that Beecher retreated to a more traditional position on women's roles, rights, and responsibilities when she and Grimké briefly shared the national spotlight in 1837. What happens when we use the criteria Beecher herself advocated— context and expedience?

In 1829, Beecher acted at the behest of Jeremiah Evarts and her famous father, with the enthusiastic support of leading women in Hartford—and Congregational, Methodist, and Presbyterian communities as well as Whig politicians, including Henry Clay and Theodore Frelinghuysen. Catharine Beecher and the fifteen hundred women who petitioned Congress against the forced removal of Native Americans appealed to the national legislature to conserve decades-old policies and to enforce treaties men such as George Washington and Thomas Jefferson had signed. "Removal" of Native Americans meant forced exile from their homelands and very likely the extinction of their nations, their cultures, and their peoples. It was easy to cast the issue as more than merely political, as moral and religious as well. The nation had a responsibility to honor its agreements and protect the oppressed. Additionally, the objects of antiremovalists' advocacy numbered about sixty thousand; they belonged to "civilized tribes" and were easy for northern European Americans to romanticize as noble and vanishing; they owned property; many spoke English, practiced Christianity, farmed, and subscribed to a constitution modeled after the U.S. Constitution. Furthermore, because female antiremovalists were not singled out for "unsexing themselves" and their political intervention was not perceived as threatening to men (it was "extraordinary"—and, frankly, easy to ignore), their influence and power as women were unharmed by their participation in the national petition campaign.

In 1837, most Americans considered abolitionists fanatics. In contrast, colonizationists were led and supported by former presidents of the United States, national and state legislators, U.S. Supreme Court justices, respected clergymen from all of the major Christian religions, and influential editors of secular newspapers. Angelina Grimké and the thousands of women who petitioned Congress to end slavery appealed to the national legislature to change radically the way its citizens lived and were governed. The objects of their advocacy numbered two million; many were uneducated and unconverted; most owned no property and all were considered (by most European Americans) someone else's property. For most European Americans, the "removal" of Africans and their descendants (who were not imagined as African Americans nor as Americans) meant repatriation to their homelands, freedoms and equality unavailable to them in the United States, and possibly the Christianization of Africa. Removal was a moral and religious solution to the evils of slavery. Even gradual emancipation lessened the threats of insurrection and perpetual degradation that antiabolitionists believed surely would follow immediate emancipation. And because women used the moral and ethical arguments congressmen found it so difficult to defeat (as Angelina Grimké noted in her 1836 *Appeal*), female abolitionists were decried for "unsexing themselves" and abused for acting out of their sphere. Their national petition campaign, so widely despised, threatened the influence and power of all white women in the United States.

Between 1829 and 1837, slavery emerged as an issue large enough and contentious enough to destroy the Union. Closer to home for Beecher, there was dissent among some of the major Christian denominations. Jacksonian democracy threatened Christian democracy, and Christian leaders were losing power to partisan political leaders. Even closer to home, Lyman Beecher had been embarrassed by Theodore Weld and the Lane rebels, many of whom trained to become AAS agents with the Grimké sisters in November 1836. Catharine Beecher's plans for female education needed nationwide support, and Catharine Beecher needed some personal reassurance as to her status as a public intellectual.

What remained consistent for Beecher over time was a fundamental belief in the divine distinctions of purpose and place for men and women. Although we might want to call that belief conservative, for Beecher it was simply Christian. There was no changing it. And so Beecher used it, just as she used gender to achieve increased education, influence, and power for women. Beecher wanted female education, influence, and power, and, given her attachment to expedience, she made choices about women's interventions according to their probabilities for success. In 1837, she imagined colonizationism would be more successful than abolitionism. She also believed that a backlash against women would compel restrictions on their power and

influence, not to mention limit the support of her national program for female education. How women could gain the most power was as the facilita-
tors of peace and charity and viable public discussion in the Christian
democracy. Within the rhetorical situations as she interpreted and even
constructed them, Beecher creatively used gender as a source of power and
authority for women.[26] Frequently, that strategy required giving up power
to get power. Most of the female antiremovalists who petitioned in 1830
and 1831 gave up regular or consistent political power to claim power in the
particular and extraordinary case facing the nation. In 1837, women like
Catharine Beecher gave up the right to petition the federal government on
slavery. Women like Beecher had no choice: they could not petition the federal government against slavery because of their beliefs about race, nation,
and religion. Given that constraint, Beecher did her best to get United States
women as much political power as she could regarding the most significant
issue to face the nation in its history.

Grimké's Response

Angelina Grimké's response to Beecher helps us understand why we cannot
simplify a rejection of women's abolitionist petitioning as a retreat into traditional, conservative constructs of women. Neither Grimké nor Beecher
began with women's roles, responsibilities, and rights. They began with
heated, contested interpretations of the issues and then argued for women's
participation within those rival interpretations.

In even the most basic ways, Angelina Grimké's and Catharine Beecher's
articulations of slavery and abolition conflicted. Beecher, for example, told
her readers that abolitionists really meant "gradual emancipation" when
they said "immediate emancipation":

> The meaning which the Abolitionist attaches to his language is this, that
> every man is bound to treat his slaves, as nearly as he can, like freemen;
> and to use all his influence to bring the system of slavery to an end as soon
> as possible . . . The great mistake of Abolitionists is in using terms which
> inculcate the immediate annihilation of the relation, when they only in-
> tend to urge the Christian duty of treating slaves according to the gospel
> rules of justice and benevolence, and using all lawful and appropriate
> means for bringing a most pernicious system to a speedy end. If Aboli-
> tionists will only cease to teach that *all* slave-holding is a sin which ought

to be *immediately abolished*; if they will cease to urge their plan as one of *immediate emancipation*, and teach simply and exactly that which they do mean, much strife and misunderstanding will cease. (*Essay*, 43–44)

Beecher could not imagine a group of people blaming slaveholders for the institution of slavery if laws forbid slaveholders to emancipate their slaves, if slaveholders worked toward an end of the pernicious institution, and if they treated their slaves as the Bible ordained people should be treated. Instead, she concluded that abolitionists used "immediate" when they meant "gradual" to provoke anxiety, fear, and anger. Following the same logic, Beecher disputed the abolitionist use of "man-stealer" to signify slaveholder as well as slave trader because the magnitude of their sins and their agency in the perpetuation of the institution differed so dramatically (44). A common defense of southern slave owners was that they were victims of a system instituted by their forefathers and even by the British crown, so for abolitionists to call slaveholders "manstealers" proved how aggressively antagonistic abolitionists meant to be.

Abolitionists, though, really believed in "immediate" rather than gradual emancipation, and they were convinced that "man–stealer" was an accurate appellation for men who held other men as property. At the start of her first letter to Beecher, Grimké explained why men who owned slaves were "man–stealers": "to *begin* to hold a slave is man-stealing—to *keep on* holding him is merely a *repetition* of the first act—a doing the same identical thing *all the time*" (*Letters*, 5). At the start of her second letter (titled "Immediate Emancipation"), Grimké called Beecher's "statement of what Abolitionists mean by immediate emancipation . . . a novelty" (9). Abolitionists understood the difference between immediate and gradual emancipation, and they commanded slaveholders "to cease to do evil *now*, to emancipate his slaves *now*" (12). Grimké denied that abolitionists used "immediate" or "man–stealer" to antagonize their opponents. Rather, those terms accurately indicated the "fundamental principle of Abolitionists": "man cannot rightfully hold his fellow man as property" (4, 12). Because Beecher's antislavery doctrine recognized that right, she understood abolitionist methods to be dangerous, unprincipled, and illegal.

Because Beecher respected the right of men to own other men as property, she believed that the only safe, legal means to the abolition of slavery was through voluntary manumission and legislation in the southern states. Beecher believed the northern states were free of the sins of slavery, and she could not understand why abolitionists conducted all of their work in the northern states. She concluded that abolitionists aimed to provoke wrath and strife between northern and southern states by convincing one community of another's sins, and she argued that the only way abolitionists would make any real progress toward emancipation was by traveling through the south benevolently talking with slave owners until they were convinced of their sins and ready to give them up. Of course Grimké understood the situation very differently.

First, the AAS called slavery "a *national* sin" and "h[e]ld that the North is guilty of the crime of slaveholding" (*Letters*, 7). Grimké directed Beecher to another one of her essays in which she "pointed out fifteen different ways in which the North was implicated in the guilt of slavery" (18). The northern and southern regions of the nation were so integrated—through business, through religion, through family, through politics—that it was impossible to consider the north innocent of a crime it not only refused to stop but in fact supported by, for instance, buying slave-produced goods and holding mortgages on southern "property." Grimké believed that European American prejudice against African Americans prevented northerners from demanding immediate emancipation and lulled them into supporting colonization, which the AAS firmly held to be an impediment to abolition. "When public opinion is rectified at the North," Grimké reasoned, "it will throw a flood of light from its million of reflecting surfaces upon the heart and soul of the South" (54). In yet another stinging rebuke, Grimké made this point at Beecher's expense: "The *North was the right place to begin Anti-Slavery efforts*. Had I not been convinced of this before, surely thy book would have been all-sufficient to satisfy me of it; for a more subtle defence of the slaveholder's right to property in his helpless victims, I never saw" (20). If northerners like Beecher believed slavery to be a sin and believed the only way to eradicate it was to travel through the south convincing owners to change their ways, Grimké wondered, why did Beecher remain in the free state of Ohio? Grimké had this to say to her old friend: "you, I say, have no excuse to offer, and are bound to go there now" (25). With that, Grimké repeated the AAS conviction that work remained to be done in the north.

Second, Grimké explained to Beecher and the rest of her readers, "By all our printing and talking at the North, we *have actually reached the very heart of the disease at the South*" (25). Grimké revealed that some of the mail sent to the southern states did get past censors, especially in smaller towns (64). She provided testimony from former slaveholders who emancipated their slaves because of abolitionist literature, she listed southern converts to abolition who attributed their conversion to AAS materials, and she shared appeals from antislavery southerners who called the AAS their only hope. Grimké also reasoned that southern outrage against abolitionists proved abolitionist efficacy. Southerners worried about the AAS, not the ACS. The South Carolina delegation in Congress recently had ordered "all the principal bound volumes, pamphlets, and periodicals" of the AAS (64); reports of bounties for William Lloyd Garrison and Arthur Tappan were widespread and easily verified as authentic; southern cities regularly burned abolitionist materials received in the mail. If abolitionists were prolonging the eradication of slavery, as Catharine Beecher and others argued, the south had no reason to be irate and vengeful. But of course they were, a point which Grimké brought close to home for Beecher:

> *Whose* mouths are slaveholders so fiercely striving to seal in silence? Why the mouths of Abolitionists, to be sure—even our infant school children know this. Strange indeed, when the labors of these men are actually rolling back the car of Emancipation for one or two centuries! Why, the South ought to pour out her treasure, to support Anti-Slavery agents, and print Anti-Slavery papers and pamphlets, and do all she can to aid us in *rolling back* Emancipation. Pray, write *her a book,* and tell her she has been very needlessly alarmed at our doings, and advise her to send us a few thousand dollars: her money would be very acceptable in these hard times, and we would take it as the wages due to the unpaid laborers, though we would never admit the donors to membership with us. How dost thou think *she* would receive *such a book?* Just try it, I entreat thee. (95–96)

"The fact is," concluded Grimké, "the South is enraged" (99).

Grimké obviously took that rage to mean that she and the reformers with whom she worked were doing something right. Whereas Beecher claimed that the abuses heaped on abolitionists proved that the methods of the AAS were "neither peaceful nor Christian" and were "calculated to generate party spirit, denunciation, recrimination, and angry passions," Grimké interpreted those same antiabolitionist abuses as signs that their cause was a righteous one: "That others are exasperated, I do not deny . . . Is *this* any cause of discouragement?" (93). Grimké continued the representation she began in her 1836 *Appeal to the Christian Women of the South* of abolitionists as radical religious reformers. In *Letters,* Grimké wrote,

> Why, then, protest against our measures as *unchristian,* because they do not smooth the pillow of the poor sinner, and lull his conscience into fatal

security? The truth is, the efforts of abolitionists have stirred up the *very same spirit* which the efforts of *all thorough-going* reformers have ever done; we consider it a certain proof that the truths we utter are sharper than any two edged sword, and that they are doing the work of conviction in the hearts of our enemies. If it be not so, I have greatly mistaken the character of Christianity. (30)

Over the course of her *Letters,* Grimké compared abolitionists to religious reformers including Moses, the apostle Paul, Isaiah, and Jeremiah (55–56, 59). She admitted that "the most tremendous blows with the sledgehammer of abolition truth" might be necessary to eradicate the United States of its most deeply entrenched sin, and Grimké had little faith that Beecher's form of Christianity would save the nation: "Thou sayest, 'Christianity is a system of *persuasion,* tending by kind and gentle influences to make men *willing* to leave their sins' . . . Thou seemest to think . . . that Christianity is just such a weak, dependent, puerile creature as thou hast described woman to be" (30, 52–53).

Grimké was less interested in gently persuading men than she was in obeying what abolitionists interpreted to be "God's holy command" (*Letters,* 14). She insisted that Beecher's "expedience" might keep the peace, but it privileged men over God: "Expediency is emphatically the doctrine by which the children of this world are wont to guide their steps, whilst the rejection of it as a rule of action exactly accords with the divine injunction, to 'walk by faith, *not* by sight.' Thy doctrine that 'the wisdom and rectitude of a given course depend entirely on the *probabilities of success,*' is not the doctrine of the Bible" (54–55). Grimké had no patience for peaceful and Christian methods, desiring instead what she implied to be Christian principles. Recalling that "when Jehovah commanded Pharaoh to 'let the people go,' he meant that they should be *immediately emancipated,*" Grimké announced, "My Dictionary is the Bible; my standard authors, prophets and apostles" (11). In response to Beecher's argument that slaveholders were not obligated to free their slaves because state laws "forbid emancipation," Grimké categorically declared, "*We* say that all the laws which sustain the system of slavery are unjust and oppressive—contrary to the fundamental principles of morality, and, therefore, null and void" (9). Grimké preferred Christian morality to human laws, and so when Beecher insisted that the Constitution permitted no vehicle for northern intervention and therefore northerners had no power in the matter, Grimké "answer[ed] unhesitatingly, certainly they have, for *moral* evils can be removed only by *moral* power" (26). Repeatedly, Grimké countered Beecher's insistence on Christian democracy with principles of a democratic Christianity.

Whereas Beecher committed herself to securing a peaceful, Christian system of governance in the United States, one that prescribed behaviors for men while accommodating a democratic system of government with its extensive freedoms and majority rule (for and by whites), Grimké committed herself to strong Christian principles applied equally, without prejudice. Abolitionists acted on "the principle of *equal rights*, irrespective of color or condition, instead of on the mere principle of *'pity* and *generosity'* " (*Letters*, 47); the comment was a clear shot at Beecher, who advised abolitionists to better manage white prejudice by appealing to antiabolitionists' "pity, generosity, and [C]hristian feelings" towards African Americans (*Essay*, 27). Other examples are peppered through Grimké's *Letters*, and they move beyond slavery and abolition. Grimké told Beecher that she disagreed "that the station of a nursery maid makes it inexpedient for her to turn reprover of the master who employs her. This is the doctrine of *modern aristocracy*, not of primitive [C]hristianity" (*Letters*, 61). In Beecher's version of a Christian democracy, people respected hierarchies. A Christian democracy provided all white men with remarkable and unprecedented liberties, even as it sustained divinely ordered relations. A democratic Christianity, on the other hand, presumed a democratic distribution of liberties restrained solely by one's moral and ethical commitments. When Beecher looked at the United States, she saw a young nation whose (white male) citizens ran the country by convincing other (white male) citizens to vote for their ideas, for the first time without compulsory controls from the church or the state, and she idealized the project as a Christian democracy. When Grimké looked at the United States, she saw a nation in which "liberty is justly *due* to every American citizen, according to the laws of God and the Constitution of our country" (*Letters*, 11), and she idealized that project as a democratic Christianity.

So Angelina Grimké imagined a democratic Christianity, and Catharine Beecher imagined a Christian democracy. Grimké imagined abolitionists as radical religious reformers hastening emancipation, and Beecher imagined them as irritating, unreasonable, aggressive extremists courting wrath and delaying emancipation. Grimké imagined slavery as a national sin, and Beecher imagined the north as innocent of and removed from the crime. Grimké imagined men holding other men as property to be fundamentally untenable and unchristian, and Beecher imagined it as a right guaranteed in the U.S. Constitution. Grimké imagined ending slavery through immediate emancipation, and Beecher imagined ending slavery through voluntary manumission and state-by-state legislation. What did these competing perspectives mean for women's roles, responsibilities, and rights in the young nation, especially with regard to the antislavery debates?

Beecher confidently decided it was inappropriate for men as well as women to join the AAS, but slavery posed an urgent challenge to the United States. How could women help? They could maintain a peaceful, honest space for public debate of the issue. "While quietly holding her own opinions, and calmly avowing them," Beecher explained, a woman should serve as a "mediator," guiding men to debate rationally and reasonably (*Essay*, 128). Only peaceful, Christian methods of persuasion would yield an expedient, safe abolition of slavery. If southerners refused to talk with northerners and northerners refused to talk with one another, disunion was the only predictable outcome. Men had to be persuaded, not coerced, to give up slavery, and so women had to "illustrate, enforce, and sustain, by every method in her power," fair and gracious debate (128). The implications for women's power and influence, successfully wielded, were huge: they "will most certainly tend to bring to an end, not only slavery, but unnumbered other evils and wrongs" (145). Beecher had in mind a long-term solution to long-standing problems made especially and immediately urgent by the particular and particularly prominent case of slavery.

Grimké also had in mind a long-term solution to long-standing problems thrown into relief by slavery. In her thirteenth and last letter to Catharine Beecher, Angelina Grimké wrote, "The discussion of the rights of the slave has opened the way for the discussion of *other rights*, and the ultimate result will most certainly be, 'the breaking of *every* yoke,' the letting the oppressed of *every* grade and description go free,—an emancipation far more glorious than any the world has ever yet seen" (126). Angelina and her sister Sarah were fighting attacks against their right to speak in public and their right to petition the federal government on issues of national policy, and both of those attacks centrally involved their sex. In July the General Association of Congregational Ministers of Massachusetts published their pastoral letter condemning women's participation in contentious reform efforts such as abolition ("when she assumes the place and tone of a man as a public reformer . . . her character becomes unnatural"), to which Sarah Grimké responded in a series of letters collectively published as *Letters on the Equality of the Sexes, and the Condition of Woman.*[27] Although Congress's

1836 gag rule silenced all antislavery petitions, it weighed more heavily on women since they significantly outnumbered male petitioners and since petitioning was, as Angelina Grimké told Beecher, "the only political right that women have" (*Letters*, 112). In her role as an advocate of immediate emancipation Grimké experienced discrimination based on a personal characteristic she could not change, and it fundamentally colored her ideas about human rights. She explained, "The investigation of the rights of the slave has led me to a better understanding of my own. I have found the Anti-Slavery cause to be the high school of morals in our land—the school in which *human rights* are more fully investigated, and better understood and taught, than any other" (114). Grimké argued that rights inhered in moral beings, not in one's sex—or skin color. Whatever was right for a man to do was right for a woman to do.

Committed to that belief, Grimké disputed Beecher's divisions between the sexes and she reiterated the appropriateness of abolition activities for men and women. First, Grimké told the Reverend Doctor Lyman Beecher's daughter that she had no evidence supporting a divinely ordered hierarchy between men and women and that in fact the proposition was counterintuitive in at least three ways: It circumscribed women's influence against biblical precedent, devalued women, and implied an intolerably low moral standard for men (103). The proposition contradicted biblical precedent by limiting women's agency to the "domestic circle." "I read in the Bible," Grimké shared with her readers, "that Miriam, and Deborah, and Huldah, were called to fill *public stations* in Church and State," and Grimké amplified the point by providing several more examples (105). Grimké significantly misrepresented Beecher on this issue: Beecher insisted on women's agency in the social as well as the domestic circle, and much political debate occurred in that space. But probably most of Grimké's readers would not have caught the discrepancy given how common the ideology of domesticity was in the 1830s.

The proposition that a divine dispensation subordinated women to men also was counterintuitive, Grimké suggested, in that it devalued women. In their accommodating role, Beecher told her readers, women were to ingratiate themselves to men so that men would do as they urged ("yield to *her* opinions" and "gratify *her* wishes," quoted Grimké). Grimké responded to this plan "with holy indignation." It favored "the fashionable belle" by stroking "*her* vanity, by yielding to *her* opinions, and gratifying *her* wishes, because they are *hers*" rather than "the humble Christian, who feels that it is the *truth* which she seeks to recommend to others, *truth* which she wants them to esteem and love, and not herself" (104–105). Beecher also advised women to maintain a dependent, defenseless, nonthreatening status in her relations with men and to revel in their chivalric protection. "I cannot refrain from pronouncing this sentiment as beneath the dignity of any woman who names the name of Christ," Grimké replied (107). How could a woman be that "silly," and how could she insult God by turning her back on the strength he gave her? All kinds of "absurdities" resulted from "draw[ing] a line of separation" (107–108):

> I have often been amused at the vain efforts made to define the rights and responsibilities of immortal beings as *men* and *women*. No one yet has found out just *where* the line of separation between them should be drawn, and for this simple reason, that no one knows just how far below man woman is, whether she be a head shorter in her moral responsibilities, or head and shoulders, or the full length of his noble stature, below him, i.e. under his feet. (117–118)

In tone and argument, Grimké did her best to make Beecher's separation of men's and women's spheres contemptible.

Besides devaluing women, Grimké argued, Beecher's proposition disrespected men. Repeatedly, Grimké complained, Beecher told women they had to be more moral than men, had to resist the combative ways of men, even had to teach young children because men refused the job. Grimké refused to allow men to meet lower standards than women, for man's sake as well as woman's. "*Man* has no more right to appear as *such* a combatant than woman," she explained, "for all the pacific precepts of the gospel were given to *him*, as well as to her" (109). The abolitionist repudiated partisanship "in *both* sexes" and forbade men as well as women from acting on "ambition, or the thirst for power" (111, 106). She even denied men the privilege of opting out of teaching young children, declaring men equally "bound to engage in this sacred employment" (122). Grimké argued that the principle of separate spheres followed from circumstances rather than morality, a critique consistent with her concern that men and women followed human law more frequently than God's law: "Whatever it is morally right for man to do, it is morally right for woman to do. Our duties originate, not from difference of sex, but from the diversity of our relations in life, the various gifts and talents committed to our care, and the different eras in which we live" (115). Rather than arguing which duties, rights, responsibilities, and roles were appropriate for women—a task Grimké was sure had people "committing the grossest inconsistencies on the one hand, or running into the most arrant absurdities [on] the other"—Grimké changed the nature of the debate by demanding a Christian consistency for men and women (108).[28]

Grimké even demanded that consistency in Congress. Beecher denied women the right to petition the federal government against slavery, including the right to petition on behalf of enslaved women, because antislavery petitions incensed most congressmen and because women were supposed to imbue the nation with peace and calm, not wrath and strife. Grimké used one of her standard arguments in response: Beecher's reasoning privileged man over God. Grimké admonished her old friend: "If *thou* canst consent to exchange the precepts of the Bible for the opinions of *such a body of men* as now sit on the destinies of this nation, I cannot. What is this but *obeying man* rather than God, and seeking the *praise of man* rather than of God?" (110). Neither should women refrain from petitioning because of its inherently political function, especially since it was "the only political right they ha[d]" (112). If petitioning the federal government was morally right for men (a point on which Beecher and Grimké agreed in principle, though not in abolitionist practice), it was morally right for women (119). All that remained, then, was to defend one last time the AAS as a moral, efficacious organization for the abolition of slavery in the United States, which Grimké did in her last letter.

By dismissing the proposition of a separate and subordinate sphere for women, Grimké made it unmistakably clear that her program to end slavery in the United States entailed women's full participation in the abolition movement. Yes, Grimké affirmed, that meant women should "keep up agitation in Congress," "promote the excitement of the North against the iniquities of the South," and "coerce the South by fear, shame, anger, and a sense of odium" (quoting Beecher's description of these "labors") (*Letters*, 124–125). Those were moral, nonpartisan, nonviolent acts that Grimké believed most quickly would end slavery, and since Grimké believed Christianity demanded immediate abolition, she prescribed them for all Christians even though they threatened social and political peace. (Abolitionists did, however, denounce all physical violence.) Grimké's articulation of women's roles, responsibilities, and rights inside the nation's slave debates and about the nation's slave policies was influenced by gender, because Grimké denounced any segregation of acts based on sex. But her construction of women's roles, responsibilities, and rights also depended on other factors. Abolitionism as a formal antislavery program relied on ideologies of race, nation, and religion. Since what was appropriate for men was appropriate for women (and vice versa), women appropriately participated in the abolition movement even though it meant that women acted in novel and controversial ways.

The Nature of the Case—and Race, Religion, Nation, and Gender

Ultimately, neither Beecher nor Grimké denied women the right to petition. In her 1837 polemic addressed to Grimké, Beecher argued, "In this country, petitions to congress, in reference to the official duties of legislators, seem, IN ALL CASES, to fall entirely without the sphere of female duty" (*Essay*, 104). Beecher embraced the ideology of separate spheres, and it would be easy to attribute this admonition to gender constraints. Yet she argued for women's antiremoval petitioning as both appropriate and even obligatory for benevolent, Christian women in 1829. She used Queen Esther to make the case and argued that women could and should appeal to a nation's rulers on behalf of an oppressed people if the stability of a nation was at stake. But Beecher never argued that women could petition Congress "in reference to the official duties of legislators." The distinction may seem small now by twenty-first-century standards, but recall the decision of the American Board of Commissioners for Foreign Missions (ABCFM) discussed in Chapter 1. As a missionary rather than a partisan organization, the ABCFM resolved to petition against Indian removal "with the understanding that the petition should not insist upon the treaty rights of the Indians but should dwell on the injurious consequences of removal to the Indians and not upon the obligations of the United States to protect them where they were."[29] Like this religious organization, Beecher relegated telling congressmen how to run the nation to the political domain—a domain belonging to men, not women. Women could intervene in extraordinary cases on behalf of an oppressed people, just like the ABCFM.

Beecher did not deny women the right to petition in 1837. She denied that slavery warranted the kind of exception Queen Esther represented. According to Beecher, colonization was a viable solution to the evils of slavery (and Beecher hardly was alone in this belief), while abolition threatened the United States to a much greater degree than colonization and gradual emancipation. Again, consider Beecher's interpretation of Esther closely—especially the ways Beecher argued against Grimké's use of Esther in 1836. Beecher interpreted the story of Esther to mean that women could appeal to a nation's rulers on behalf of an oppressed people if a nation was threatened. Pair that with Beecher's interpretation of abolition and colonization. Beecher believed, as did many colonizationists, given the ways they imagined the objects of their advocacy, that most enslaved African Americans (all but those owned by the cruelest masters) were likely to suffer more from immediate emancipation than from remaining in slavery until the southern states established programs of gradual emancipation. Beecher also believed, as did many colonizationists given their fierce rivalry with abolitionists, that abolitionists threatened the nation and needed to be silenced as quickly as possible. Within those conditions, to conclude that Beecher refused women the right to petition on behalf of African Americans because she embraced traditional gender roles is to strip this historical moment of nearly all its complexity and explanatory force.

Beecher and Grimké disagreed about women's roles, rights, and responsibilities. But Beecher did not deny women the right to intervene on all issues of national policy. She held women to different standards than men, and in ways that we can only understand inside the rhetorics of the Indian removal, African colonization, and second-wave abolition movements, slavery did not meet the criteria to warrant women's exceptional intervention into men's sphere. Based on the kinds of petitioning abolitionists undertook (by that standard, the ABCFM also would have refused abolitionist petitioning) as well as predominant European American imaginings of enslaved African Americans as an oppressed group and dogmatic ideas about which program would most safely and quickly end United States slavery, abolition as Beecher understood it in the 1830s was an insufficient reason for women to claim a "right to speak on the subject." Ultimately, Beecher's denial of the right on which Grimké insisted had at least as much to do with the ways these women interpreted Jacksonian-era national crises, the nation, race, and religion as it did with the ways they understood gender during the 1830s.

Notes

Introduction

1. Memorial of Sundry Ladies of Hallowell, Maine, praying that certain Indian tribes may not be removed from their present place of abode, 8 Jan. 1830 (endorsed 18 Jan. 1830); Committee on Indian Affairs; Petitions and Memorials Referred to Committees (SEN21A-G8); 21st Congress; Records of the United States Senate, Record Group 46; National Archives Building, Washington, D.C. This citation follows the format published by the National Archives and Records Administration (NARA). In this and other citations, I have neither corrected nor made consistent titles of petitions, as the titles often are crucial to locating a petition in the NARA collection. In future citations I omit redundant information as follows. The call number (here SEN21A-G8) designates the legislative house ("SEN" indicates the Senate; "HR" indicates the House of Representatives) and the Congress (here the 21st). Senate petitions belong to Record Group 46. House petitions belong to Record Group 233. Petitions referenced are housed in the National Archives Building in Washington, D.C.

2. Catharine E. Beecher, "Circular Addressed to Benevolent Ladies of the U. States," *Christian Advocate and Journal and Zion's Herald* (New York), 25 Dec. 1829, 65. Subsequent references are to page 65 unless noted.

3. Catharine E. Beecher, *An Essay on Slavery and Abolitionism, with Reference to the Duty of American Females,* 2nd ed. (Philadelphia: Perkins and Marvin, 1837), 104.

4. Angelina Emily Grimké, *Letters to Cath[a]rine E. Beecher, in Reply to an Essay on Slavery and Abolitionism, Addressed to A. E. Grimké* (1838; repr., Freeport, N.Y.: Books for Libraries Press, 1971), 115.

5. Mary Hershberger relies on gender norms as the sole explanation for what she claims is a change of Beecher's mind on the question. Hershberger reasons that, because congressmen attacked women for their antiremoval petitions and be-

cause Beecher took a health-related leave of absence from the Hartford Female Seminary immediately after she wrote the circular, Beecher retreated from political activism because she found her initial venture out of woman's sphere so distressing. But only one congressman attacked women for their antiremoval activism over the course of the two-year petition campaign, and Beecher attributed her leave to work-related stress. For a longer discussion, see Alisse Theodore Portnoy, "'Female Petitioners Can Lawfully Be Heard': Negotiating Female Decorum, U.S. Politics, and Political Agency, 1829–31," *Journal of the Early Republic* 23 (2003): 573–610. Mary Hershberger, "Mobilizing Women, Anticipating Abolition: The Struggle against Indian Removal in the 1830s," *Journal of American History* 86 (1999): 15–40.

6. *National Intelligencer* (Washington, D.C.), 5 June 1830.

7. William Lloyd Garrison, *Thoughts on African Colonization: Or An Impartial Exhibition of the Doctrines, Principles and Purposes of the American Colonization Society. Together with the Resolutions, Addresses and Remonstrances of the Free People of Color* (1832; repr. New York: Arno Press, 1968), 2:44–45.

8. On first-wave abolitionism (beginning in the 1770s) and the identification of the abolition movement dating from the early 1830s as second-wave, see Richard S. Newman, *The Transformation of American Abolitionism: Fighting Slavery in the Early Republic* (Chapel Hill: University of North Carolina Press, 2002).

9. In *Fighting for American Manhood: How Gender Politics Provoked the Spanish-American and Philippine-American Wars* (New Haven, Conn.: Yale University Press, 1998), Kristin L. Hoganson argues for a revisioning of these wars within a frame that includes ideologies of gender, given the importance of gender to United States politics and policies at the time. I admire Hoganson's basic question: "What happens if we start from the beginning and reconstruct the narrative with gender as a basic building block?" (14). In its argument that we conceive gender as just one of several ideologies crucial to the Beecher-Grimké debates, my methodology mirrors Hoganson's. Instead of laying gender on top of 1830s antislavery debates, I put women at the center of volatile rights debates and argue that these women were crucially influenced by, and that they crucially influenced, ideologies of nation, race, class, and religion as well as gender. Gender was a basic, but not the only, building block for women's intervention. To fully understand the dynamics of gender as an ideological process, we must situate it within rather than above the complex, complicated network of ideologies within which Beecher and Grimké advocated on behalf of Native, African, and European Americans in the 1830s.

10. Hugh Davis complains about the lack of scholarship on colonization in a 1997 essay, and Bruce Dorsey notes in 2002 that few histories of abolition attend to colonization despite its popularity at the time the abolitionist movement

emerged. Priscilla Wald's work on Supreme Court cases involving Native and African Americans is an exception to the segregation of these debates in scholarship about the early nineteenth century. See also David Murray, "Representation and Cultural Sovereignty: Some Case Studies" in *Native American Representations: First Encounters, Distorted Images, and Literary Appropriations,* ed. Gretchen M. Bataille (Lincoln: University of Nebraska Press, 2001), 80–97; Hugh Davis, "Northern Colonizationists and Free Blacks, 1823–1837: A Case Study of Leonard Bacon," *Journal of the Early Republic* 17 (Winter 1997): 651–675; Bruce Dorsey, *Reforming Men and Women: Gender in the Antebellum City* (Ithaca, N.Y.: Cornell University Press, 2002); Priscilla Wald, *Constituting Americans: Cultural Anxiety and Narrative Form* (Durham, N.C.: Duke University Press, 1995); Priscilla Wald, "Terms of Assimilation: Legislating Subjectivity in the Emerging Nation," *boundary 2* 19 (1992): 77–104.

11. Henry Clay to Gentlemen of the Colonization Society of Kentucky, 17 Dec. 1829, *Papers of Henry Clay,* vol. 8, *Candidate, Compromiser, Whig,* ed. Robert Seager II and Melba Porter Hay (Lexington: University Press of Kentucky, 1984), 138; Madison quoted in Jane Tompkins, *Sensational Designs: The Cultural Work of American Fiction, 1790–1860* (New York: Oxford University Press, 1985), 109; *National Intelligencer,* 9 Oct. 1833.

12. From 1830 to 1834 the ACS sent 1,873 colonists to Liberia; from 1835 to 1839, 674; from 1840 to 1844, 625. P. J. Staudenraus, *The African Colonization Movement 1816–1865* (New York: Columbia University Press, 1961), 251.

13. Speaking specifically of antislavery historiography, Nancy A. Hewitt notes that "women's histories of the cause marginalize conservative women" because of a scholarly interest in the woman's rights movement. More broadly, scholarship of this period tends to focus on the radical positions and voices that frequently led more quickly to advances in minority rights. Hewitt, "On Their Own Terms: A Historiographical Essay," in *The Abolitionist Sisterhood: Women's Political Culture in Antebellum America,* ed. Jean Fagan Yellin and John C. Van Horne (Ithaca, N.Y.: Cornell University Press, 1994), 25.

14. Theodore Weld to James G. Birney, 27 Sept. 1832, *Letters of James Gillespie Birney, 1831–1857,* vol. 1, ed. Dwight L. Dumond (New York: D. Appleton-Century, 1938), 27.

15. Not until the 1970s do we again see such simultaneous attention to rights debates (black freedom, women's liberation, gay liberation), and a comparison between the 1830s and the 1970s highlights the need to study removal, colonization, abolition, and woman's rights concomitantly.

16. I came across two petitions from this collection as a volunteer for "Our Mothers Before Us" at the National Archives and Records Administration, a project that aimed to recover women's appeals to Congress before women achieved suffrage in the United States. Independently researching the antiremoval cam-

paign, I encountered the full collection. Susan Zaeske introduces the two peti-
tions featured in "Our Mothers Before Us" in *Signatures of Citizenship: Petition-
ing, Antislavery, and Women's Political Identity* (Chapel Hill: University of
North Carolina Press, 2003). For a detailed explication of the collection, see
Alisse Theodore, "'A Right to Speak on the Subject': The U.S. Women's Antiremoval
Petition Campaign, 1829–1831," *Rhetoric and Public Affairs* 5 (2002): 601–624.

17. This formulation of the case is modeled on Michel Foucault's rules of discourse:
who can speak about what topics under which circumstances. Michel Foucault,
"The Discourse on Knowledge," in *The Archaeology of Knowledge and the Discourse
on Language*, trans. A. M. Sheridan Smith (New York: Pantheon Books, 1972),
215–237.

18. *National Intelligencer*, 11 Apr. 1833.

19. In rhetorical studies, see for example Kenneth Burke, *A Rhetoric of Motives*
(1950; repr., Berkeley: University of California Press, 1969); Kenneth Burke,
Language as Symbolic Action: Essays on Life, Literature, and Method (Berkeley:
University of California Press, 1966); Wayne C. Booth, *The Rhetoric of Fiction*,
2nd ed. (Chicago: University of Chicago Press, 1983); Maurice Charland, "Con-
stitutive Rhetoric: The Case of the *Peuple Québécois*," *Quarterly Journal of
Speech* 73 (1987): 133–150; Barbara A. Biesecker, "Rethinking the Rhetorical
Situation from within the Thematic of *Différance*," *Philosophy and Rhetoric* 22
(1989): 110–130; Sharon Crowley, *A Teacher's Introduction to Deconstruction*
(Urbana, Ill.: National Council of Teachers of English, 1989); Ronald Walter
Greene, "Another Materialist Rhetoric," *Critical Studies in Mass Communication* 15
(1998): 21–44; James Jasinski, "A Constitutive Framework of Rhetorical Historiography: Toward an Understanding of the Discursive (Re)constitution of 'Constitution' in *The Federalist Papers*," in *Doing Rhetorical History: Concepts and
Cases*, ed. Kathleen J. Turner (Tuscaloosa: University of Alabama Press, 1998),
72–92, 261–267; Steven Mailloux, *Reception Histories: Rhetoric, Pragmatism,
and American Cultural Politics* (Ithaca, N.Y.: Cornell University Press, 1998); Sharon
Crowley and Debra Hawhee, *Ancient Rhetorics for Contemporary Students* 3rd
ed. (New York: Longman, 2003); Robert Hariman, ed., *Prudence: Classical
Virtue, Postmodern Practice* (University Park: Pennsylvania State University
Press, 2003); Edward Schiappa, *Defining Reality: Definitions and the Politics of
Meaning* (Carbondale: Southern Illinois University Press, 2003). Scholars in
disciplines as varied as literary criticism, sociology, history, legal studies, political science, and gender studies also argue for constitutive functions of discourse, and scholars frequently use that argument to establish, discover, or
uncover relationships between language and power. See for example Anthony
Giddens, *Central Problems in Social Theory: Action, Structure and Contradiction
in Social Analysis* (1979; repr., Berkeley: University of California Press, 1994);

Stephen Greenblatt, *Renaissance Self-Fashioning: From More to Shakespeare* (1980; repr., Chicago: University of Chicago Press, 1984); Judith Butler, *Gender Trouble: Feminism and the Subversion of Identity* (1990; repr., New York: Routledge, 1999); Joan W. Scott, review of *Heroes of Their Own Lives: The Politics and History of Family Violence* by Linda Gordon, *Signs: Journal of Women in Culture and Society* 15 (1990): 848–852, 859–860; James Boyd White, *Justice as Translation: An Essay in Cultural and Legal Criticism* (Chicago: University of Chicago Press, 1990); Anne Norton, *Republic of Signs: Liberal Theory and American Popular Culture* (Chicago: University of Chicago Press, 1993); Wald, *Constituting Americans.*

20. Richard E. Vatz, "The Myth of the Rhetorical Situation," *Philosophy and Rhetoric* 6 (1973): 154–161; Biesecker, "Rethinking."

21. Vatz and Biesecker differ in that Biesecker argues that texts, not rhetors, are the source of interpretations, but both scholars agree that exigencies are not simply reflections or functions of material conditions. I find Biesecker's model theoretically more attractive but difficult to use in critical analysis. As a compromise between their positions, I use "we" rather than "rhetor" to signify that meanings are constructed by participants in the rhetorical event—auditors as well as rhetors.

22. The question resembles one of Wayne Booth's central questions in *The Rhetoric of Fiction*: who is the implied (rather than the actual) author of a text?

23. I use "first personae" to evoke audience studies in constitutive rhetorical theory, which refer to the audience as the "second persona." See for example Edwin Black, "The Second Persona," *Quarterly Journal of Speech* 56 (1970): 109–119; Charland, "Constitutive Rhetoric"; Cynthia Duquette Smith, "Discipline—It's a 'Good Thing': Rhetorical Constitution and Martha Stewart Living Omnimedia," *Women's Studies in Communication* 23 (2000): 337–366.

24. Memorial of Sundry Ladies. On the seemingly magical power of signing one's authority into existence, see Jacques Derrida, "Declarations of Independence," *New Political Science* 15 (1986): 7–15.

25. Edward W. Said calls the result of this mediation "textual attitude": "people, places, and experiences can always be described by a book, so much so that the book (or text) acquires a greater authority, and use, even than the actuality it describes." *Orientalism* (1978; repr., New York: Vintage Books, 1994), 93.

26. I prefer "imaginings," a term Elaine Scarry uses, rather than terms including representations, images, and portrayals, because "imaginings" emphasizes the construction of others as an active and creative process and because "imaginings" connotes a high degree of artifice or construction. Elaine Scarry, "The Difficulty of Imagining Other Persons," in *The Handbook of Interethnic Coexistence*, ed. Eugene Weiner (New York: Continuum, 1998), 40–62.

27. On the use of Native Americans, African Americans, and European American women by European American men in the constructions of their subjectivities, see Carroll Smith-Rosenberg, "Dis-Covering the Subject of the 'Great Constitutional Discussion,' 1786–1789," *Journal of American History* 79 (1992): 841–873. On constructing identities in relationship to others, see for example Butler, *Gender Trouble.*

28. Lydia Maria Child, *An Appeal in Favor of That Class of Americans Called Africans* (1833; repr., Amherst: University of Massachusetts Press, 1996), 195.

29. *House Journal,* 21st Cong., 1st sess., 8 Dec. 1829, 24; Beecher, "Circular." Jeremiah Evarts's essays were published in the *National Intelligencer* between Aug. and Dec. 1829.

1. "Causes of Alarm to Our Whole Country"

1. *House Journal,* 21st Cong., 1st sess., 8 Dec. 1829, 23–25. On Georgia's oppressive laws, see Mary Young, "The Exercise of Sovereignty in Cherokee Georgia," *Journal of the Early Republic* 10 (1990): 43–63.

2. John H. Eaton's letter reprinted in Jeremiah Evarts, *Cherokee Removal: The "William Penn Essays" and Other Writings,* ed. Francis Paul Prucha (Knoxville: University of Tennessee Press, 1981), 197.

3. Catharine E. Beecher, "Circular Addressed to Benevolent Ladies of the U. States," *Christian Advocate and Journal and Zion's Herald* (New York), 25 Dec. 1829, 65. Subsequent references are to page 65 unless otherwise noted.

4. *House Journal,* 20th Cong., 2nd sess., 2 Dec. 1828, 16.

5. The history of removal that follows relies on Annie Heloise Abel, *The History of Events Resulting in Indian Consolidation West of the Mississippi* (1908; repr., New York: AMS Press, 1972); Francis Paul Prucha, *American Indian Policy in the Formative Years: The Indian Trade and Intercourse Acts, 1790–1834,* 2nd ed. (Cambridge, Mass.: Harvard University Press, 1970); Ronald N. Satz, *American Indian Policy in the Jacksonian Era* (Lincoln: University of Nebraska Press, 1975); Francis Paul Prucha, "Introduction," in Evarts, *Cherokee Removal;* Michael D. Green, *The Politics of Indian Removal: Creek Government and Society in Crisis* (Lincoln: University of Nebraska Press, 1982); Young, "Sovereignty"; Anthony F. C. Wallace, *The Long, Bitter Trail: Andrew Jackson and the Indians* (New York: Hill and Wang, 1993); Louis P. Masur, *1831: Year of Eclipse* (New York: Hill and Wang, 2001); Robert V. Remini, *Andrew Jackson and His Indian Wars* (New York: Viking, 2001).

6. Robert V. Remini, *The Legacy of Andrew Jackson: Essays on Democracy, Indian Removal, and Slavery* (Baton Rouge: Louisiana State University Press, 1988), 47.

7. Wallace, *Long, Bitter Trail,* 53. See also Remini, *Legacy,* 81.

8. Andrew Jackson to James Monroe, 4 Mar. 1817, *Correspondence of Andrew Jackson,* ed. John Spencer Bassett (Washington, D.C.: Carnegie Institute of Washington, 1927), 2:279–280.

9. Young, "Sovereignty."

10. Several historians caution against imagining Jackson as an evil man who pushed Native Americans toward extinction. Although not "exonerat[ing]" Jackson for "the horrors" of removal, Remini argues for the inevitability of removal and disputes images of Jackson as uncaring. Remini, *Andrew Jackson and His Indian Wars,* 226–238. See also Satz, *American Indian Policy,* 9; Wallace, *Long, Bitter Trail,* 54–56.

11. Daniel Walker Howe, *The Political Culture of American Whigs* (Chicago: University of Chicago Press, 1979), 9, 16.

12. Ronald P. Formisano, *The Transformation of Political Culture: Massachusetts Parties, 1790s–1840s* (New York: Oxford University Press, 1983), 268.

13. Henry L. Watson explains that "church affiliation was itself a reflection of class standing and aspiration, so that cultural and economic concerns were closely intertwined in the creation of party loyalties." Henry L. Watson, *Liberty and Power: The Politics of Jacksonian America* (New York: Noonday Press, 1990), 186.

14. Ronald G. Walters, *American Reformers, 1815–1860* (New York: Hill and Wang, 1997), 33.

15. The term "theocrat" is John R. Bodo's. He explains that theocrats, American Protestant clergy, were "a self-conscious social group . . . ministers and Christian leaders with a college and seminary education or its equivalent." As a group, "anchored firmly in their belief in the universal sovereignty of God and in his particular concern for the United States, they sought to bring the young nation under his rule and into conformity with his will." John R. Bodo, *The Protestant Clergy and Public Issues, 1812–1848* (Princeton, N.J.: Princeton University Press, 1954), viii–ix.

16. Howe, *Political Culture,* 18. See also Bodo, *Protestant Clergy,* 44–45.

17. Bodo, *Protestant Clergy,* 88–89.

18. Gaylord P. Albaugh, *History and Annotated Bibliography of American Religious Periodicals and Newspapers Established from 1730 to 1830 with Library Locations and Microfilm Sources* (Worcester, Mass.: American Antiquarian Society, 1994), 1:xiii; Frank Luther Mott, quoted in Alan Nourie and Barbara Nourie, eds., *American Mass Market Magazines* (New York: Greenwood Press, 1990), viii.

19. *Christian Advocate and Journal and Zion's Herald* (New York), 3 Apr. 1829, 122.

20. Ibid., 13 Mar. 1829, 110.

21. Prucha, *Cherokee Removal,* 21–23.

22. Two additional Penn essays were published in the *National Intelligencer* (Washington, D.C.) on 24 and 27 Nov. 1830, six months after the Indian Removal Act passed but during the time in which antiremovalists worked for its repeal.

23. Francis Paul Prucha claims they were published in forty to one hundred news-papers and printed as pamphlets. John Coward questions the range and there-fore the reliability of Prucha's assessment. Coward interprets pamphleteering by antiremovalists, which included Evarts's Penn essays, as evidence "that their message was not universally published" and therefore not widely disseminated. An alternate interpretation might take as its starting point the popularity of political pamphlets during this era and conclude that pamphlets were a natural, rather than remedial, outlet for the essays. Prucha, *Cherokee Removal,* 11, 43; John M. Coward, *The Newspaper Indian: Native American Identity in the Press, 1820–90* (Urbana: University of Illinois Press, 1999), 75, 95. On pamphleteering, see Joel H. Silbey, ed., *The American Party Battle: Election Campaign Pamphlets, 1828–1876* (Cambridge, Mass.: Harvard University Press, 1999).
24. *Register of Debates in Congress,* 21st Cong., 1st sess., 11 Jan. 1830, 509.
25. *National Intelligencer,* 14 Oct. 1829.
26. Eaton's letter is reprinted in Evarts, *Cherokee Removal,* 195–199.
27. Ibid.
28. Given that Jackson refused to enforce a Supreme Court decision that favored the Cherokees in 1832, Evarts's worry not only was justified but also prescient.
29. *National Intelligencer,* 5 Aug. 1829. Subsequent references to the Penn letters will be provided using the date only. Letters were published in 1829 unless otherwise noted.
30. 24 Aug. See also for example 4 Sept.; 25 Nov.
31. 27 Aug.
32. 30 Sept.
33. 10 Sept.
34. 18 Sept.
35. 15 Sept.
36. 7 Nov.
37. 8 Sept.
38. 14 Oct.
39. 31 Aug.
40. 5 Aug.
41. 8 Aug.
42. 15 Sept.
43. 7 Nov.
44. 8 Aug.
45. 12 Dec.
46. 26 Sept.
47. Ibid.
48. Theda Perdue, *Cherokee Women: Gender and Cultural Change, 1700–1835* (Lincoln: University of Nebraska Press, 1998), especially 136–137.

49. 16 Dec.

50. Ibid.

51. 28 Nov.; 18 Sept.

52. 18 Sept.

53. 19 Dec.

54. 24 Aug.

55. 18 Sept.

56. 19 Dec.

57. 24 Aug.

58. 18 Sept.

59. 30 Sept.; 19 Dec.

60. 25 Nov.

61. 16 Dec. For a discussion of these controversies, see Catherine Allgor, *Parlor Politics: In Which the Ladies of Washington Help Build a City and a Government* (Charlottesville: University Press of Virginia, 2000); Kirsten E. Wood, "'One Woman So Dangerous to Public Morals': Gender and Power in the Eaton Affair," *Journal of the Early Republic* 17 (1997): 237–275.

62. Catharine E. Beecher, *Educational Reminiscences and Suggestions* (New York: J. B. Ford, 1874), 62; Lyman Beecher to Catharine Beecher, 21 Nov. 1829, Schlesinger Library, Radcliffe Institute, Harvard University, A-102, Beecher-Stowe Collection of Family Papers, 1798–1956, folder 4.

63. Beecher, *Reminiscences,* 63.

64. Ibid., 62–65, 69–70. The *Genius of Universal Emancipation* (Baltimore) described and reprinted several paragraphs of the circular in their "Ladies' Repository" on 8 Jan. 1830. The *Christian Advocate,* a Presbyterian press unrelated to the Methodist *Christian Advocate and Journal and Zion's Herald,* reprinted an introductory letter and the text of an actual petition submitted to Congress by women from Burlington, New Jersey, presumably as a model for its female readers to imitate, in Mar. 1830. The circulation of Beecher's exhortation as a pamphlet was typical, given the popularity of political pamphlets during this era and the expanded use of the United States postal system in the late 1820s and early 1830s. On pamphleteering, see Silbey, *American Party Battle.* On the importance of the postal system to Jacksonian politics and culture, see Richard R. John, *Spreading the News: The American Postal System from Franklin to Morse* (Cambridge, Mass.: Harvard University Press, 1995).

65. Beecher, "Circular."

66. Ibid.

67. Ibid.

68. Ibid.

69. Ibid.

70. Ibid.

71. Ibid.
72. Catharine E. Beecher, *Suggestions Respecting Improvements in Education, Presented to the Trustees of the Hartford Female Seminary, and Published at their Request* (Hartford, Conn.: Packard and Butler, 1829), 53, 45–46, 53–54.
73. Beecher, "Circular."
74. Ibid.
75. Beecher, *Suggestions,* 53–54.
76. Beecher, "Circular."
77. Ibid.
78. Ibid.
79. Prucha, *Cherokee Removal,* 33–34.

2. "A Right to Speak on the Subject"

1. J. Arnold to Elizabeth Cheever, 3 Sept. 1829, Cheever Family Papers, c. 1800–c. 1900, American Antiquarian Society, box 2, folder 6. Hereafter referred to as Cheever Family Papers.
2. Charlotte Cheever to George Cheever, 30 Jan. 1830, Cheever Family Papers, box 3, folder 1.
3. George Cheever to Elizabeth Cheever, 10 Feb. 1830, Cheever Family Papers, box 3, folder 1.
4. George Cheever to Charlotte Cheever, 17 Feb. 1830, Cheever Family Papers, box 3, folder 1; Henry Cheever to Elizabeth Cheever, 4 Apr. 1830, Cheever Family Papers, box 3, folder 1; *American Advocate* (Hallowell, Maine), 17 Apr. 1830.
5. Memorial of Sundry Ladies of Hallowell, Maine, praying that certain Indian tribes may not be removed from their present place of abode, 8 Jan. 1830 (endorsed 18 Jan. 1830); Committee on Indian Affairs; Petitions and Memorials Referred to Committees (SEN21A-G8); 21st Congress; Records of the United States Senate, Record Group 46; National Archives Building, Washington, D.C. This citation follows the format published by the National Archives and Records Administration (NARA). In this and other citations, I have neither corrected nor made consistent titles of petitions, as the titles often are crucial for locating a petition in the NARA collection. In future citations I omit redundant information as follows. The call number (here SEN21A-G8) designates the legislative house ("SEN" indicates the Senate; "HR" indicates the House of Representatives) and the Congress (here the 21st). Senate petitions belong to Record Group 46. House petitions belong to Record Group 233. Petitions referenced are housed in the National Archives Building in Washington, D.C.
6. Anne M. Boylan, "Women and Politics in the Era Before Seneca Falls," *Journal of the Early Republic* 10 (1990), 372; Catherine Allgor, *Parlor Politics: In Which the Ladies of Washington Help Build a City and a Government* (Charlottesville:

University of Virginia Press, 2000), 139. On the "discourse of domesticity," see Nancy F. Cott, *The Bonds of Womanhood: "Woman's Sphere" in New England, 1780–1835*, 2nd ed. (1977; repr., New Haven, Conn.: Yale University Press, 1997). On early petitioning, see also Cott, *Bonds;* Anne M. Boylan, "Women in Groups: An Analysis of Women's Benevolent Organizations in New York and Boston, 1797–1840," *Journal of American History* 71 (1984): 497–523; Lori D. Ginzberg, *Women and the Work of Benevolence: Morality, Politics, and Class in the Nineteenth-Century United States* (New Haven, Conn.: Yale University Press, 1990).

7. Individual women occasionally petitioned the United States federal government before 1830 about private issues, including widow's pensions and land claims. Female residents of Washington, D.C., petitioned the national legislature for divorces, since no state mechanism existed for that purpose.

8. On conservative meanings, see Ginzberg, *Women and the Work of Benevolence,* 34.

9. Elizabeth E. Varon, *We Mean to Be Counted: White Women and Politics in Antebellum Virginia* (Chapel Hill: University of North Carolina Press, 1998), 72, 80. See also Norma Basch, "Marriage, Morals, and Politics in the Election of 1828," *Journal of American History* 80 (1993): 890–918; Rebecca Edwards, *Angels in the Machinery: Gender in American Party Politics from the Civil War to the Progressive Era* (New York: Oxford University Press, 1997): 16–18; Ronald J. Zboray and Mary Saracino Zboray, "Whig Women, Politics, and Culture in the Campaign of 1840: Three Perspectives from Massachusetts," *Journal of the Early Republic* 17 (1997): 277–315. For an early definition of the nineteenth-century "cult of true womanhood," see Barbara Welter, *Dimity Convictions: The American Woman in the Nineteenth Century* (Athens: Ohio University Press, 1976).

10. Henry Clay to Jeremiah Evarts, 23 Aug. 1830, *The Papers of Henry Clay*, vol. 8, *Candidate, Compromiser, Whig,* ed. Robert Seager II and Melba Porter Hay (Lexington: University Press of Kentucky, 1984), 255.

11. Basch, "Marriage, Morals, and Politics," 894; Kirsten E. Wood, "'One Woman So Dangerous to Public Morals': Gender and Power in the Eaton Affair," *Journal of the Early Republic* 17 (1997): 237–275; Allgor, *Parlor Politics.*

12. Michel Foucault, "The Discourse on Language," in *The Archaeology of Knowledge and the Discourse on Language,* trans. A. M. Sheridan Smith (New York: Pantheon Books, 1972), 215–237.

13. Catharine E. Beecher, "Circular Addressed to Benevolent Ladies of the U. States," *Christian Advocate and Journal and Zion's Herald* (New York), 25 Dec. 1829, 65–66. Subsequent references are to page 65 unless noted.

14. Anne M. Boylan, *The Origins of Women's Activism: New York and Boston, 1797–1840* (Chapel Hill: University of North Carolina Press, 2002), 137–145.

15. *Christian Advocate and Journal and Zion's Head*, 19 Mar. 1830, 115.

16. Ibid., 9 Jan. 1829, 74.

17. Ibid., 14 May 1830, 147.
18. Ibid., 25 Mar. 1831, 118.
19. Ibid., 4 Dec. 1829, 53.
20. Ibid., 18 Dec. 1829, 61.
21. I am inspired by a point made by Carroll Smith-Rosenberg in her essay, "Discovering the Subject of the 'Great Constitutional Discussion,' 1786–1789," *Journal of American History* 79 (1992): 847: "The assignment of primary causality to any single factor in this complex chain of actions and reactions, even supposing such an assignment possible, seems far less interesting than the careful mapping of their exquisitely patterned interaction." See also Michael Warner, *Letters of the Republic: Publication and the Public Sphere in Eigthteenth-Century America* (Cambridge, Mass.: Harvard University Press, 1990), xi–xii.
22. On the completion of the postal routes, see Richard R. John, *Spreading the News: The American Postal System from Franklin to Morse* (Cambridge, Mass.: Harvard University Press, 1995).
23. Benedict Anderson, *Imagined Communities: Reflections on the Origin and Spread of Nationalism,* rev. ed. (London: Verso, 1991), 81, 33, 35.
24. Warner, *Letters,* xiii.
25. Ibid., 36.
26. John, *Spreading the News,* 57, 7.
27. Ibid., 7. John says information from Congress "helped to introduce" these ideas to United States Americans. I avoid that construction because I think the ideas emerged simultaneous to, not as a result of, the wide dissemination of information.
28. Ibid., 191.
29. On the significance of petitioning in the United States, see for example Garry Wills, *Inventing America: Jefferson's Declaration of Independence* (Garden City, N.J.: Doubleday, 1978); Raymond C. Bailey, *Popular Influence upon Public Policy: Petitioning in Eighteenth-Century Virginia* (Westport, Conn.: Greenwood Press, 1979); Stephen A. Higginson, "A Short History of the Right to Petition Government for the Redress of Grievances," *Yale Law Journal* 96 (1986): 142–166; David C. Frederick, "John Quincy Adams, Slavery, and the Disappearance of the Right of Petition," *Law and History Review* 9 (1991): 113–155; William Lee Miller, *Arguing about Slavery: The Great Battle in the United States Congress* (New York: A. A. Knopf, 1996); and Susan Zaeske, *Signatures of Citizenship: Petitioning, Antislavery, and Women's Political Identity* (Chapel Hill: University of North Carolina Press, 2003).
30. James W. North, *The History of Augusta, from the Earliest Settlement to the Present Time: with Notices of the Plymouth Company, and Settlements on the Kennebec; Together with Biographical Sketches and Genealogical Register* (1870; repr., with a foreword by Edwin A. Churchill, Somersworth, N.H.: New England

History Press, 1981); Emma Huntington Nason, *Old Hallowell on the Kennebec* (Augusta, Maine: Burleigh and Flynt, 1909); Writer's Program of the Work Projects Administration in the State of Maine, *Augusta-Hallowell on the Kennebec* (Augusta, Maine: Kennebec Journal Print Shop, 1940); Katherine H. Snell and Vincent P. Ledew, *Historic Hallowell* (Augusta, Maine: Kennebec Journal Print Shop, 1962); *American Advocate*, 17 Apr. 1830.

31. Joseph B. Doyle, *20th Century History of Steubenville and Jefferson County, Ohio and Representative Citizens* (Chicago: Richmond-Arnold Pub. Co., 1910).

32. Petition of the Inhabitants of Twinsburgh Portage County Ohio, against a removal of the Indians (endorsed 8 Feb. 1831); Committee on Indian Affairs: Removal of Indians; Petitions and Memorials Referred to Committees (HR21A-G8.2). Petition of the inhabitants of Nelson Portage County Ohio, against a removal of the Indians (endorsed 3 Mar. 1831); Committee on Indian Affairs: Removal of Indians; Petitions and Memorials Referred to Committees (HR21A-G8.2). Memorial of the Inhabitants of the town of Mainfield, in the County of Windham, and the State of Connecticut, against the removal of Indians (endorsed 29 Mar. 1830), Committee of the Whole House: Removal of Indians; Petitions and Memorials Referred to Committees (HR21A-G23.3). Memorial of the Inhabitants of Marlborough, in the State of Connecticut (endorsed 22 Mar. 1830); Referred to the Committee on Bill 287 [Committee of the Whole House: Removal of Indians]; Petitions and Memorials Referred to Committees (HR21A-G23.3). For a detailed description of the antiremoval petitions located at the National Archives, see Alisse Theodore, "'A Right to Speak on the Subject': The U.S. Women's Antiremoval Petition Campaign, 1829–1831," *Rhetoric and Public Affairs* 5 (2002): 601–624.

33. During the antislavery petition campaign in the late 1830s it became general practice for men and women to sign the same petition, though their signatures frequently were separated into "male" and "female" columns. In a study of these petitions, Susan Zaeske concludes that the segregation aimed to distinguish voters from nonvoters, rather than to prevent "improper sexual mixing." But we cannot generalize retrospectively. In 1830 and 1831, segregated petitions marked gender differences, not suffrage qualifications. First, as I detail in this chapter, in their petitions most female antiremovalists used different arguments than male antiremovalists. Second, the antislavery petitions to which Zaeske refers were submitted after Congress passed the gag rule, basically a rule that provided a means by which Congress could refuse to consider or discuss antislavery petitions. Many people read the gag rule as a violation of citizens' First Amendment right to petition, so at the end of the decade it was important for voters to identify themselves as a way to emphasize the violation. That concern had not yet arisen in 1830 and 1831. Susan Zaeske, "Signatures of Citizenship: The Rhetoric of Women's Antislavery Petitions," *Quarterly Journal of Speech* 88 (2002): 152.

34. Petition of Ladies of the Town of Huntsburgh for the Protection of Indian Rights (no endorsement date); Committee of the Whole House: Removal of Indians; Petitions and Memorials Referred to Committees (HR21A-G23.3). Petition of the citizens of the town of Huntsburgh for the protection of Indian rights (endorsed 21 Feb. 1831); Committee of the Whole House: Removal of Indians; Petitions and Memorials Referred to Committees (HR21A-G23.3).

35. Memorial of the subscribers female of the town of Virgil for the protection of Indian rights, 25 Apr. 1830 (no endorsement date); Committee of the Whole House: Removal of Indians; Petitions and Memorials Referred to Committees (HR21A-G23.3). Memorial of the subscribers inhabitants of the town of Virgil for the protection of Indian rights (endorsed 12 Apr. 1830); Committee of the Whole House: Removal of Indians; Petitions and Memorials Referred to Committees (HR21A-G23.3).

36. Petition of Inhabitants of Farmington, Maine (endorsed 22 Feb. 1830); Committee on Indian Affairs: Removal of Indians; Petitions and Memorials Referred to Committees (HR21A-G8.2). Memorial of the inhabitants of Farmington, Maine, protesting Indian Removal (endorsed 26 Mar. 1830); Committee of the Whole House: Removal of Indians; Petitions and Memorials Referred to Committees (HR21A-G23.3). Petition from citizens of Hallowell protesting Indian Removal (endorsed 8 Feb. 1831); Petitions and Memorials Referred to Committees (SEN21A-G8).

37. Memorial of the Ladies of Steubenville, Ohio, against the forceable [sic] removal of the Indians without the limits of the United States (endorsed 15 Feb. 1830); Petitions and Memorials Which Were Tabled: Indian Matters (HR21A-H1).

38. Memorial of the Ladies of Burlington, New Jersey, praying that Congress would protect the Indians in their rights and in the possession of their lands (endorsed 23 Feb. 1830); Petitions and Memorials Referred to Committees (SEN21A-H3).

39. Petition of Inhabitants of Farmington, Maine (endorsed 22 Feb. 1830); Committee on Indian Affairs: Removal of Indians; Petitions and Memorials Referred to Committees (HR21A-G8.2).

40. Philip Gould, *Covenant and Republic: Historical Romance and the Politics of Puritanism* (Cambridge: Cambridge University Press, 1996), 62. Carroll Smith-Rosenberg, "Domesticating 'Virtue': Coquettes and Revolutionaries in Young America," in *Literature and the Body: Essays on Populations and Persons,* ed. Elaine Scarry (Baltimore, Md.: Johns Hopkins University Press, 1988), 165. Catharine E. Beecher, *The Elements of Mental and Moral Philosophy, Founded Upon Experience, Reason, and the Bible* (1831; photocopy repr., Ann Arbor, Mich.: University Microfilms, 1969), 393–394, 392. Beecher used the conventional generic "he" although her textbook was written for girls.

41. James Jasinski, "The Feminization of Liberty, Domesticated Virtue, and the Reconstitution of Power and Authority in Early American Political Discourse,"

Quarterly Journal of Speech 79 (1993): 158. On the feminization of virtue in the early republic, see also Ruth H. Bloch, "The Gendered Meanings of Virtue in Revolutionary America," *Signs: Journal of Women in Culture and Society* 13 (1987): 37–58; Dorinda Outram, "*Le Langage Mâle de la Vertu:* Women and the Discourse of the French Revolution," in *Social History of Language,* ed. Peter Burke and Roy Porter (Cambridge: Cambridge University Press, 1987), 120–135. On women's "deferential politics," see also Boylan, *Origins,* 152.

42. Memorial of Sunday Ladies of Hallowell, Maine; Memorial of the Ladies of Steubenville, Ohio. The use of ambiguous terms in these petitions did more than widen the domain of the removal debates. These examples illustrate "those dynamic moments of social change when disparate groups, battling for hegemony, form and reform language," a process Smith-Rosenberg calls "discursive interchange" in "Domesticating 'Virtue,'" 166–167. See also Jay Fliegelman's description of "serviceable dialectics," in which an ambiguous term can be seen as "a verbal representative of an emerging cultural dialectic," in *Declaring Independence: Jefferson, Natural Language, and the Culture of Performance* (Stanford, Calif.: Stanford University Press, 1993), 150–152. Studying instances of ambiguous wordplay, discursive interchanges, or serviceable dialectics helps us understand not only historical variations of key concepts but also the synchronic importance of dynamic concepts to the movement of groups within and between different discourse communities. On diachronic conceptual change, see for example Michael J. Shapiro, ed., *Language and Politics* (New York: New York University Press, 1984); Terence Ball, James Farr, and Russell L. Hanson, eds., *Political Innovation and Conceptual Change* (Cambridge: Cambridge University Press, 1989); and Jasinski, "Feminization."

43. Petition of the females Inhabitants of the township of Lewis and the State of New York (no endorsement date); Committee on Indian Affairs: Removal of Indians; Petitions and Memorials Referred to Committees (HR21A-G8.2).

44. Petition of Inhabitants of Farmington, Maine; Memorial of the Ladies of Steubenville, Ohio; Memorial of Sundry Ladies of Hallowell, Maine.

45. For examples of women engaging in a similar strategy—"framing [their] efforts in the language of benevolence or emotion" or "denying or disclaiming any interest in or taste for politics, usually immediately before engaging in political discussion or action"—as they helped their husbands establish political careers in Washington, D.C., see Allgor, *Parlor Politics,* 141, 159.

46. Memorial of Sundry Ladies of Hallowell, Maine.

47. Ibid. On religion as an empowering ideology for women in the early nineteenth century, see for example Cott, *Bonds;* Ginzberg, *Women and the Work of Benevolence.*

48. Memorial of the Ladies of Steubenville, Ohio. On sentimentality and masculinity, see Mary Chapman and Glenn Hendler, eds., *Sentimental Men: Masculinity*

and the Politics of Affect in American Culture (Berkeley: University of California Press, 1999).

49. Memorial of the Ladies of Steubenville, Ohio.

50. Catharine E. Beecher, *Suggestions Respecting Improvements in Education, Presented to the Trustees of the Hartford Female Seminary, and Published at their Request* (Hartford, Conn.: Packard and Butler, 1829), 53.

51. Petition of Massachusetts Ladies of [the town of Monson, County of] Hamden— relative to removal of Indians (endorsed 14 Feb. 1831); Committee on Indian Affairs: Removal of Indians; Petitions and Memorials Referred to Committees (HR21A-G8.2). Petition of the females Inhabitants of the township of Lewis and the State of New York (no endorsement date); Committee on Indian Affairs: Removal of Indians; Petitions and Memorials Referred to Committees (HR21A-G8.2). On sympathy and benevolence, see Cott, *Bonds,* 160–168; Elizabeth B. Clark, "'The Sacred Rights of the Weak': Pain, Sympathy, and the Culture of Individual Rights in Antebellum America," *Journal of American History* 82 (1995): 463–493. On republican motherhood, see Linda K. Kerber, *Women of the Republic: Intellect and Ideology in Revolutionary America* (Chapel Hill: University of North Carolina Press, 1980); Kerber, *Toward an Intellectual History of Women* (Chapel Hill: University of North Carolina Press, 1997); Cott, *Bonds;* Ruth H. Bloch, "American Feminine Ideals in Transition: The Rise of the Moral Mother, 1785–1815," *Feminist Studies* 4 (1978): 100–126.

52. Memorial of the Ladies of Steubenville, Ohio. The text of the Steubenville petition also was submitted by women from Pennsylvania as the Memorial of Ladies, Inhabitants of Pennsylvania, Praying That the Indians may be protected in their rights, and in the possession of their lands (endorsed 3 Mar. 1830); Petitions and Memorials Which Were Tabled: Indian Matters (HR21A-H1.1). The men's petition is a recurring petition from men in Pennsylvania. See for example Memorial of Certain Inhabitants of Pennsylvania, Praying that the Indians may be protected in their rights, &c (endorsed 7 Jan. 1830); Committee on Indian Affairs: Removal of Indians; Petitions and Memorials Referred to Committees (HR21A-G8.2). Petition protesting Indian removal from inhabitants of Hadley, Massachusetts (endorsed 15 Feb. 1831); Committee on Indian Affairs: Removal of Indians; Petitions and Memorials Referred to Committees (HR21A-G8.2).

53. Memorial of Certain Inhabitants of Pennsylvania.

54. Petition of Inhabitants of Farmington, Maine [women]. Memorial of the inhabitants of Farmington, Maine, protesting Indian Removal (endorsed 3 Mar. 1830); Committee of the Whole House: Removal of Indians; Petitions and Memorials Referred to Committees (HR21A-G23.3).

55. Ibid.

56. Richard E. Vatz, "The Myth of the Rhetorical Situation," *Philosophy and Rhetoric* 6 (1973): 154–161. Barbara A. Biesecker, "Rethinking the Rhetorical Situation from Within the Thematic of *Différance,*" *Philosophy and Rhetoric* 22 (1989):

110–130. Vatz and Biesecker differ in that Biesecker argues that texts, not rhetors, are the source of interpretations, but both agree that exigencies are not simple reflections or functions of material conditions.

57. Edwin Black, "The Second Persona," *Quarterly Journal of Speech* 56 (1970): 109–119; Wayne C. Booth, *The Rhetoric of Fiction,* 2nd ed. (Chicago: University of Chicago Press, 1983). For studies of audience as a rhetorical construct, see Karlyn Kohrs Campbell, "The Rhetoric of Women's Liberation: An Oxymoron," *Quarterly Journal of Speech* 59 (1973): 74–86; Michael C. McGee, "In Search of 'The People': A Rhetorical Alternative," *Quarterly Journal of Speech* 61 (1975): 235–249; Maurice Charland, "Constitutive Rhetoric: The Case of the *Peuple Québécois,*" *Quarterly Journal of Speech* 73 (1987): 133–150; Biesecker, "Rethinking the Rhetorical Situation"; Cynthia Duquette Smith, "Discipline—It's a 'Good Thing': Rhetorical Constitution and Martha Stewart Living Omnimedia," *Women's Studies in Communication* 23 (2000): 337–366.

58. "Created" connotes a more active process than the one suggested by Booth and Black, who say that personae are "implied" by the text.

59. In rhetorical studies, see for example Kenneth Burke, *A Rhetoric of Motives* (1950; repr., Berkeley: University of California Press, 1969); Kenneth Burke, *Language as Symbolic Action: Essays on Life, Literature, and Method* (Berkeley: University of California Press, 1966); Booth, *The Rhetoric of Fiction;* Charland, "Constitutive Rhetoric": 133–150; Biesecker, "Rethinking"; Sharon Crowley, *A Teacher's Introduction to Deconstruction* (Urbana, Ill.: National Council of Teachers and English, 1989); Ronald Walter Greene, "Another Materialist Rhetoric," *Critical Studies in Mass Communication* 15 (1998): 21–44; James Jasinski, "A Constitutive Framework for Rhetorical Historiography: Toward an Understanding of the Discursive (Re)constitution of 'Constitution' in *The Federalist Papers,*" in *Doing Rhetorical History: Concepts and Cases,* ed. Kathleen J. Turner (Tuscaloosa: Univeristy of Alabama Press, 1988), 72–92, 261–267; Steven Mailloux, *Reception Histories: Rhetoric, Pragmatism, and American Cultural Politics* (Ithaca, N.Y.: Cornell University Press, 1998); Sharon Crowley and Debra Hawhee, *Ancient Rhetorics for Contemporary Students,* 3rd ed. (New York: Longman, 2003); Robert Hariman, ed., *Prudence: Classical Virtue, Postmodern Practice* (University Park: Pennsylvania State University Press, 2003); Edward Schiappa, *Defining Reality: Definitions and the Politics of Meaning* (Carbondale: Southern Illinois University Press, 2003). In other disciplines, see for example Anthony Giddens, *Central Problems in Social Theory: Action, Structure and Contradiciton in Social Analysis* (1979; repr., Berkeley: University of California Press, 1994); Stephen Greenblatt, *Renaissance Self-Fashioning: From More to Shakespeare* (1980; repr., Chicago: University of Chicago Press, 1984); Judith Butler, *Gender Trouble: Feminism and the Subversion of Identity* (1990; repr., New York: Routledge, 1999); Joan W. Scott, review of *Heroes of Their Own Lives: The Politics and History of Family Violence,* by Linda Gordon, *Signs: Journal of*

Women in Culture and Society, 15 (1990): 848–852, 859–860; James Boyd White, *Justice as Translation: An Essay in Cultural and Legal Criticism* (Chicago: University of Chicago Press, 1990); Anne Norton, *Republic of Signs: Liberal Theory and American Popular Culture* (Chicago: University of Chicago Press, 1993); and Priscilla Wald, *Constituting Americans: Cultural Anxiety and Narrative Form* (Durham, N.C.: Duke University Press, 1995).

60. On women's antislavery petitioning, see Zaeske, *Signatures of Citizenship;* Gerda Lerner, "The Political Activities of Antislavery Women," *The Majority Finds Its Past: Placing Women in History* (New York: Oxford University Press, 1979), 112–128; Judith Wellman, "Women and Radical Reform in Antebellum Upstate New York: A Profile of Grassroots Female Abolitionists," *Clio Was a Woman: Studies in the History of American Women,* ed. Mabel E. Deutrich and Virginia C. Purdy (Washington, D.C.: Howard University Press, 1980), 112–127.

61. Memorial of Philadelphia Females against Slavery in District of Columbia (endorsed 29 Dec. 1831); Petitions and Memorials (National Archives Box 6 of Library of Congress Box 58); 22nd Congress; National Archives Building, Washington, D.C.

62. *Register of Debates in Congress,* 24th Cong., 1st sess., 25 May 1836, 4030. On the gag rule, see Miller, *Arguing;* Zaeske, *Signatures.*

63. Angelina Grimké, *Appeal to the Christian Women of the South* (New York: American Anti-Slavery Society, 1836), 26.

64. *Register of Debates in Congress,* 24th Cong., 1st sess., 12 Feb. 1836, 487.

65. *Register of Debates in Congress,* 24th Cong., 2nd sess., 9 Jan. 1837, 1329. Some abolitionist petitions slipped into House petition reports despite the gag by, for instance, being very short or by having particularly descriptive titles.

66. *Register of Debates in Congress,* 24th Cong., 1st sess., 19 Jan. 1836, 186.

67. Charland, "Constitutive Rhetoric," 137. Biesecker, "Rethinking," 121. See also Joan W. Scott, "The Evidence of Experience," *Critical Inquiry* 17 (1991): 792.

68. *Emancipator* (New York), 16 June 1837.

69. *An Appeal to the Women of the Nominally Free States, Issued by an Anti-Slavery Convention of American Women* (1838; repr., Freeport, N.Y.: Books for Libraries Press, 1971), 13.

70. "To the Women of the United States." Accompanies a petition from the women of Oxford, Massachusetts, remonstrating for the abolition of slavery in the District of Columbia and the end of the Slave Trade in the United States (endorsed 18 Feb. 1839); Petitions and Memorials (National Archives Box 38 of Library of Congress Box 133); 25th Congress; National Archives Building, Washington, D.C.

71. Angelina Emily Grimké, *Letters to Cath[a]rine E. Beecher, in Reply to an Essay on Slavery and Abolitionism, Addressed to A. E. Grimké* (1838; repr., Freeport, N.Y.: Books for Libraries Press, 1971), 111–112.

72. "Address of the Boston Female Antislavery Society, to the Women of Massachu-setts," 13 July 1836 (endorsed 25 Sept. 1837); Petitions and Memorials (National Archives Box 17 of Library of Congress Box 84); 25th Congress.

3. "The Difference between Cruelty to the Slave, and Cruelty to the Indian"

1. *National Intelligencer* (Washington, D.C.), 15 Apr. 1829.
2. Ibid., 26 Apr. 1837. Some African Americans owned black slaves as well, but these men were rare exceptions. Furthermore, their property rights (including land as well as slaves) were less secure than the rights of Native Americans de-spite the often cantankerous debates over Native American property rights in the 1820s and 1830s. For example, in 1830 Louis Sheridan, a free African Amer-ican who lived in North Carolina, owned sixteen slaves. But "if he remained away from North Carolina for more than ninety days, his entire estate would be subject to confiscation." Willard B. Gatewood Jr., "'To Be Truly Free': Louis Sheridan and the Colonization of Liberia," *Civil War History* 29 (1983): 335.
3. Thomas Jefferson, *Notes on the State of Virginia*, ed. William Peden (Chapel Hill: University of North Carolina Press, 1982), for example, 139–140.
4. Henry Clay to Gentlemen of the Colonization Society of Kentucky, 17 Dec. 1829, *Papers of Henry Clay*, vol. 8, *Candidate, Compromiser, Whig*, ed. Robert Seager II and Melba Porter Hay (Lexington: University Press of Kentucky, 1984), 138–139. Also printed in full in the *National Intelligencer* (Washington, D.C.), 12 Jan. 1830.
5. See for example Andrew Jackson's address to the Creek Indians, reprinted in the *National Intelligencer*, 9 June 1829: "[I] now speak to you as your Father and friend . . . You know I love my white and red children."
6. When I use "people of color" in this chapter, my usage imitates that of the people featured in this study.
7. James Madison, quoted in Jane Tompkins, *Sensational Designs: The Cultural Work of American Fiction, 1790–1860* (New York: Oxford University Press, 1985), 109.
8. *National Intelligencer*, 9 Mar. 1830.
9. Ibid., 9 Feb. 1831.
10. Memorial of Philadelphia Females against Slavery in District of Columbia (endorsed 29 Dec. 1831); Petitions and Memorials (National Archives Box 6 of Library of Congress Box 58); 22nd Congress; National Archives Building, Wash-ington, D.C.
11. *National Intelligencer*, 9 Oct. 1833.
12. William Lloyd Garrison, *Thoughts on African Colonization: Or An Impartial Exhibition of the Doctrines, Principles and Purposes of the American Colonization Society. Together with the Resolutions, Addresses and Remonstrances of the Free People of Color* (1832; repr. New York: Arno Press, 1968), 1:155.

13. Social Circle of the Female Seminary in Charlestown, Massachusetts, quoted in Mary Kelley, "'A More Glorious Revolution': Women's Antebellum Reading Circles and the Pursuit of Public Influence," *New England Quarterly* 76 (2003): 174.

14. Hugh Davis, "Northern Colonizationists and Free Blacks, 1823–1837: A Case Study of Leonard Bacon," *Journal of the Early Republic* 17 (1997): 652. See also Lawrence J. Friedman, "Purifying the White Man's Country: The American Colonization Society Reconsidered, 1816–40," *Societas* 6 (1976): 1.

15. On the participation of Madison, Webster, and Douglas, see Friedman, "Purifying," 5.

16. *National Intelligencer*, 18 June 1831.

17. On state advocacy, see for example Garrison, *Thoughts on African Colonization*, app., 20–22; P. J. Staudenraus, *The African Colonization Movement, 1816–1865* (New York: Columbia University Press, 1961).

18. Bruce Dorsey, *Reforming Men and Women: Gender in the Antebellum City* (Ithaca, N.Y.: Cornell University Press, 2002), 139.

19. We are used to thinking of Garrisonians, immediate emancipationists, and immediate abolitionists as "abolitionists," but colonizationists frequently argued that their plans would lead to a gradual abolition of slavery. Lyman Beecher saw no contradiction between abolition and colonization, for example, but resisted the idea of immediate abolition. Between 1820 and 1833, most of the colonists were slaves manumitted on the condition that they emigrate to Liberia, so the ACS argued it was their program that actually emancipated slaves. Thus it could be argued that to use "abolitionist" to refer to immediate abolitionists but not colonizationists is misleading. Because "immediate abolitionist" is cumbersome, however, where the referent can be clearly deduced I will follow convention and use "abolitionist" to refer to immediate abolitionists of the Weld-Garrison persuasion.

20. There were some prominent Native American and African American leaders who protested removal and colonization, including William Coodey and James Forten. We need to increase dramatically the recovery and study of their contributions, and the contributions of other Native and African Americans, to these debates. Newspapers including the *Cherokee Phoenix* and the *Freedom's Journal* are treasure troves for this line of inquiry. Because this study focuses on the ways a dominant group advocated on behalf of people they perceived to be oppressed, though, it features primarily European American voices (exceptions include the rare news report reprinted in the *National Intelligencer*, reprints in Garrison's *Thoughts on African Colonization*, and excerpts from abolitionists James and Sarah Forten). My point is not that Native Americans and African Americans played no role in their own advocacy—absolutely they did, and we should be recovering more of their advocacy as well as their resistance. But it also is important to study the ways others advocated on their behalf in terms of understanding intersections of language and power, which is why I focus on

European American voices in this project. For a study of Native American imaginings of their own nations, for example, see Cheryl Walker, *Indian Nation: Native American Literature and Nineteenth-Century Nationalisms* (Durham, N.C.: Duke University Press, 1997).

21. For further discussion, see Joan Wallach Scott, "The Evidence of Experience" *Critical Inquiry* 17 (1991): 773–797; Robert Asen, *Visions of Poverty: Welfare Policy and Political Imagination* (East Lansing: Michigan State University Press, 2002); Edward Said, *Orientalism* (1978; repr., New York: Vintage, 1994); Scarry, "The Difficulty of Imagining Other People," *For Love of Country: Debating the Limits of Patriotism,* ed. Joshua Cohen (Boston: Beacon Press, 1996): 98–110.

22. The disciplinary range of "imagining" as a theoretical construct (Scarry works in literary studies, Asen in communication studies, and Anderson in government) illustrates its interdisciplinary utility. Scarry, "Difficulty of Imagining Other People," 98, Robert Asen, "Imagining the Public Sphere," *Philosophy and Rhetoric* 35 (2002): 347; Benedict R. Anderson, *Imagined Communities: Reflections on the Origin and Spread of Nationalism,* rev. ed. (London: Verso, 1991), 6. See also Etienne Balibar, "The Nation Form: History and Ideology," in *Race, Nation, Class: Ambiguous Identities,* by Etienne Balibar and Immanuel Wallerstein, trans. by Chris Turner (London: Verso, 1991): 86–106; Elaine Scarry, "The Difficulty of Imagining Other Persons," *The Handbook of Interethnic Coexistence,* ed. Eugene Weiner (New York: Continuum, 1998), 40–62.

23. Nancy Cott makes a similar argument about citizenship when she calls citizenship "a political fiction." Cott explains, "Being a fiction does not mean that citizenship is false but that it is purposefully constructed, all the more reason that its meanings and the rewards and obligations it conveys may vary over time and among citizens." Nancy Cott, "Marriage and Women's Citizenship in the United States, 1830–1934," *American Historical Review* 103 (1998): 1440.

24. William Lee Miller, *Arguing about Slavery: The Great Battle in the United States Congress* (New York: A. A. Knopf, 1996), 16; Kwando M. Kinshasa, *Emigration vs. Assimilation: The Debate in the African American Press, 1827–1861* (Jefferson, N.C.: McFarland, 1988), 13.

25. For additional media (for example drama, art, dance, and minstrelsy), see Susan Scheckel, *The Insistence of the Indian: Race and Nationalism in Nineteenth-Century American Culture* (Princeton, N.J.: Princeton University Press, 1998); Dale Cockrell, *Demons of Disorder: Early Blackface Minstrels and Their World* (Cambridge: Cambridge University Press, 1997); W. T. Lhamon Jr., *Raising Cain: Blackface Performance from Jim Crow to Hip Hop* (Cambridge, Mass.: Harvard University Press, 1998).

26. On Africans being "recaptured," see for example *National Intelligencer,* 18 June 1831, 30 July 1832, 4 Feb. 1835.

27. Staudenraus, *African Colonization Movement,* 57–58. My brief history of colonization relies on a collection of sources: daily issues of the *National Intelligencer,*

1827–1838; Staudenraus, *African Colonization Movement;* Friedman, "Purifying"; Davis, "Northern Colonizationists"; Winthrop D. Jordan, *White Over Black: American Attitudes Toward the Negro, 1550–1812* (Chapel Hill: University of North Carolina Press, 1968), especially 546–569; Bruce Rosen, "Abolition and Colonization, the Years of Conflict, 1829–1834," *Phylon* 33 (1972): 177–192; Gatewood "'To Be Truly Free'"; Frankie Hutton, "Economic Considerations in the American Colonization Society's Early Effort to Emigrate Free Blacks to Liberia, 1816–36," *Journal of Negro History* 68 (1983): 376–389; Thomas D. Matijasic, "Whig Support for African Colonization: *Ohio As A Test Case,*" *Mid-America* 66 (1984): 79–91; Douglas R. Egerton, "'Its Origin Is Not a Little Curious': A New Look at the American Colonization Society," *Journal of the Early Republic* 5 (1985): 463–480; Marie Tyler McGraw, "Richmond Free Blacks and African Colonization, 1816–1832," *Journal of American Studies* 21 (1987): 207–224; Kinshasa, *Emigration vs. Assimilation;* Amos J. Beyan, *The American Colonization Society and the Creation of the Liberian State: A Historical Perspective, 1822–1900* (Lanham, Md.: University Press of America, 1991); Douglas R. Egerton, "Averting a Crisis: The Proslavery Critique of the American Colonization Society," *Civil War History* 43 (1997): 142–156; Hugh Davis, *Leonard Bacon: New England Reformer and Antislavery Moderate* (Baton Rouge: Louisiana State University Press, 1998); Bruce Dorsey, "A Gendered History of African Colonization in the Antebellum United States," *Journal of Social History* 34 (2000): 77–103.

28. Quoted in Friedman, "Purifying," 2.

29. Dickson D. Bruce Jr., "National Identity and African-American Colonization, 1773–1817," *Historian* 58 (1995): 17–20. See also Julie Winch, *Philadelphia's Black Elite: Activism, Accommodation, and the Struggle for Autonomy, 1787–1848* (Philadelphia: Temple University Press, 1988).

30. Egerton, "'Its Origin Is Not,'" 465–467; Staudenraus, *African Colonization Movement,* 4. Jefferson also considered establishing colonies for African Americans in Canada and Latin America. Jefferson, *Notes,* 137–138.

31. Staudenraus, *African Colonization Movement,* 9–11. See also Philip S. Foner, *History of Black Americans* (Westport, Conn.: Greenwood Press, 1975), 1: especially 581–584.

32. Egerton, "'It's Origin Is Not,'" 465–470.

33. Staudenraus, *African Colonization Movement,* 19–30.

34. For example, *National Intelligencer,* 19 June 1832, 11 Apr. 1833, 1 Nov. 1834, 4 Feb. 1837. On state donations, see *National Intelligencer,* 29 Aug. 1835, 30 Jan. 1837.

35. *National Intelligencer,* 18 June 1831.

36. Ibid.

37. Rosen, "Abolition and Colonization," 179–180.

38. *National Intelligencer*, 31 July 1830, reprinted from the *Commercial Advertiser* (New York) and on the same page as an advertisement for someone wanting to buy 150 slaves. This idea recurs frequently, for example 22 Oct. 1831.

39. *National Intelligencer*, 11 Aug. 1829.

40. Lyman Beecher, "Dr. Beecher's Address," *African Repository and Colonial Journal* 10 (1834): 282; James Madison quoted in Jordan, *White Over Black*, 553. Senator Felix Grundy (Tennessee) used black codes and other restrictions on free people of color in northern states, including Ohio and Illinois, to argue that "free people cannot live amongst us," as reported in the *National Intelligencer*, 14 Apr. 1830. For more on early nineteenth-century disfranchisement and legislated segregation, see Jordan, *White Over Black*.

41. David Walker, *Appeal, in Four Articles, Together with a Preamble, to the Coloured Citizens of the World, But in Particular, and Very Expressly, to Those of the United States of America*, ed. Peter P. Hinks (1830; repr., University Park: Pennsylvania State University Press, 2000), 58. On black opposition to colonization and occasional endorsements from black northerners, see Philip S. Foner, *History of Black Americans* (Westport, Conn.: Greenwood Press, 1983), 2:290–303; Winch, *Philadelphia's Black Elite*.

42. The *Boston Gazette* reported that "a young sailor, steward of a vessel from Boston, was formally indicted by the grand jury, tried, convicted, and this day sentenced to twelve months imprisonment and a fine of 2,000 dollars, for circulating some four or five copies of these pamphlets among negroes" in South Carolina. Reprinted in the *National Intelligencer*, 8 June 1830.

43. "While many thinkers and forces influenced Garrison's transformation, the role of Walker was unquestionably paramount," explains Peter P. Hinks in his introduction to Walker's *Appeal*, xliii. The *Appeal* and the *Liberator* were linked in southerners' minds as well. An article warning people about Garrison's newspaper began by reminding readers of the trouble "the notorious 'Walker pamphlet'" caused at the height of its circulation. *National Intelligencer*, 15 Sept. 1831.

44. *National Intelligencer*, 20 Aug. 1830.

45. For example, Gilbert Hobbs Barnes, *The Antislavery Impulse, 1830–1844* (1933; repr., New York: Harcourt, Brace, and World, 1964); Aileen S. Kraditor, *Means and Ends in American Abolitionism: Garrison and His Critics on Strategy and Tactics, 1834–1850* (New York: Pantheon Books, 1969); Gerda Lerner, *The Grimké Sisters from South Carolina: Pioneers for Woman's Rights and Abolition* (1967; repr., New York: Schocken Books, 1971); Nancy A. Hewitt, *Women's Activism and Social Change: Rochester, New York, 1822–1872* (Ithaca, N.Y.: Cornell University Press, 1984); Jean Fagan Yellin and John C. Van Horne, eds., *The Abolitionist Sisterhood: Women's Political Culture in Antebellum America* (Ithaca, N.Y.: Cornell University Press, 1994); Miller, *Arguing*; Richard S.

Newman, *The Transformation of American Abolitionism: Fighting Slavery in the Early Republic* (Chapel Hill: University of North Carolina Press, 2002).

46. *National Intelligencer,* 26 May 1835.

47. For colonizationist attacks against abolitionists, see for example the *National Intelligencer,* 20 June 1833, 12 June 1833, 28 Oct. 1834, 16 Sept. 1835, 1 Sept. 1836. For attacks written by free blacks, see 16 Sept. 1835.

48. Davis, *Leonard Bacon,* 56.

49. James Fenimore Cooper, *The Pioneers, or the Sources of the Susquehanna; A Descriptive Tale,* in *The Leatherstocking Tales,* ed. Blake Nevius (New York: Library of America, 1985), 1:352, 180. Subsequent references are noted parenthetically.

50. On this topic and also cataloging of Indian "types" in this literature (for instance the good Indian, the bad Indian, the noble Indian, the savage Indian) see for example Robert F. Berkhofer Jr., *The White Man's Indian: Images of the American Indian from Columbus to the Present* (New York: Knopf, 1978); Brian W. Dippie, *The Vanishing American: White Attitudes and U.S. Indian Policy* (Middletown, Conn.: Wesleyan University Press, 1982); Amy Kaplan, *The Social Construction of American Realism* (Chicago: University of Chicago Press, 1988); Roy Harvey Pearce, *Savagism and Civilization: A Study of the Indian and the American Mind* (1953; rev., Berkeley: University of California Press, 1988); Lucy Maddox, *Removals: Nineteenth-Century American Literature and the Politics of Indian Affairs* (New York: Oxford University Press, 1991); Arnold Krupat, *Ethnocriticism: Ethnography, History, Literature* (Berkeley: University of California Press, 1992); Amy Kaplan and Donald E. Pease, eds., *Cultures of United States Imperialism* (Durham, N.C.: Duke University Press, 1993); and Scheckel, *The Insistence of the Indian.* See also collections of primary texts, including Nancy B. Black and Bette S. Weidman, eds., *White on Red: Images of the American Indian* (Port Washington, N.Y.: Kennikat Press, 1976); William M. Clements, ed., *Native American Folklore in Nineteenth-Century Periodicals* (Athens: Swallow Press/Ohio University Press, 1986).

51. On the popularity of *Hobomok,* see Carolyn L. Karcher, "Introduction," *Hobomok and Other Writings on Indians* by Lydia Maria Child, ed. Carolyn L. Karcher (1824; repr., New Brunswick, N.J.: Rutgers University Press, 1986), ix–xxxviii. On *Hope Leslie,* see Mary Kelley, "Introduction," *Hope Leslie; Or, Early Times in the Massachusetts* by Catharine Maria Sedgwick, ed. Mary Kelley (1827; repr., New Brunswick, N.J.: Rutgers University Press, 1987), ix–xxxvii; Suzanne Gossett and Barbara Ann Bardes, "Women and Political Power in the Republic: Two Early American Novels," *Legacy: A Journal of American Women Writers* 2 (1985): 13–30. For the popularity of Seaver's *Narrative,* including its role in reinvigorating the genre, see June Namias, "Introduction," *A Narrative of the Life of Mrs. Mary Jemison,* by James E. Seaver, ed. June Namias (Norman: University of Oklahoma Press, 1992), 3–45; Pearce, *Savagism.* For these texts in combination,

see Carol J. Singley, "Catharine Maria Sedgwick's *Hope Leslie:* Radical Frontier Romance," in *Desert, Garden, Margin, Range: Literature on the American Frontier,* ed. Eric Heyne (New York: Twayne Publishers, 1992), 110–122; Tompkins, *Sensational Designs;* Maddox, *Removals.*

52. Seaver, *A Narrative of the Life of Mrs. Mary Jemison,* 55, 51. Subsequent references are noted parenthetically.

53. Kelley, notes, *Hope Leslie,* 358. Sedgwick, *Hope Leslie,* 56. Subsequent references are noted parenthetically.

54. Karcher, notes, *Hobomok and Other Writings,* 305; Child, *Hobomok and Other Writings,* 62. Subsequent references are noted parenthetically.

55. Cooper often is criticized for unrealistic plots and Indians. But Jane Tompkins argues that his characters are "kinds" or "stereotypes" easily recognizable by readers. If Cooper had nuanced his characters or reined in his plot, Tompkins implies, he would have been unable to get to the heart of his project: social criticism. *Sensational Designs,* 102–114.

56. James Fenimore Cooper, *The Prairie, A Tale,* in *The Leatherstocking Tales,* ed. Blake Nevius (New York: Library of America, 1985), 1:887. Subsequent references are noted parenthetically.

57. Scarry, "Persons," 46.

58. For a broad discussion of race in early United States literature, see Dana Nelson, *The Word in Black and White: Reading "Race" in American Literature, 1683–1867* (New York: Oxford University Press, 1992).

59. James Fenimore Cooper, *The Last of the Mohicans; A Narrative of 1757,* in *The Leatherstocking Tales,* ed. Blake Nevius (New York: Library of America, 1985), 1:601, 532, 717, 862, 602. Subsequent references are noted parenthetically.

60. Toni Morrison, *Playing in the Dark: Whiteness and the Literary Imagination* (1992; repr., New York: Vintage, 1993), 46.

61. Morrison, *Playing.*

4. "Merely Public Opinion in Legal Forms"

1. *National Intelligencer* (Washington, D.C.), 4 Jan. 1830. Subsequent newspaper citations are for the *National Intelligencer* unless noted.

2. 23–27 June 1836. This chapter discusses the significance of terms including "people of color," "negro," and "Africans and their descendants." Clarity often necessitates my use of conventional nineteenth-century terms in my analyses. Among most European Americans in the early nineteenth century, "people of color" meant African Americans, not Native Americans or other nonwhite peoples. When I use "people of color" I use it to reflect conventional early nineteenth-century usage, which therefore reflects this limited scope.

3. Blackface minstrelsy grew popular during this period, but as Dale Cockrell explains, "Blacks almost never appeared on the legitimate American stage during

this period." Dale Cockrell, *Demons of Disorder: Early Blackface Minstrels and Their World* (Cambridge: Cambridge University Press, 1997), 26. "Black dancing" (rather than blackface minstrelsy) occurred in places such as New York's Catherine Market in the early nineteenth century, but in domains very distinct from Washington, D.C., or even New York, theaters. On black dance, including its relationship to blackface performance, see W. T. Lhamon Jr., *Raising Cain: Blackface Performance from Jim Crow to Hip Hop* (Cambridge, Mass.: Harvard University Press, 1998).

4. 5 Oct. 1831.

5. This history relies on Frank Luther Mott, who calls the *National Intelligencer* "a leading American newspaper . . . in some respects [the] greatest of the long line of Washington papers." Frank Luther Mott, *American Journalism: A History of Newspapers in the United States Through 250 Years, 1690 to 1940* (New York: Macmillan, 1941), 176, 178.

6. A quick glance through several months of the *National Intelligencer* reveals news from more than seventy newspapers based in states including Alabama, Connecticut, Georgia, Kentucky, Maine, Maryland, Massachusetts, Michigan, Mississippi, Missouri, New York, North Carolina, Ohio, Pennsylvania, South Carolina, Tennessee, Vermont, and Virginia, as well as countries including England, France, and Liberia.

7. 2 Feb. 1838.

8. Gales and Seaton enjoyed full access to both houses of Congress until the mid-1830s. In addition to recording select debates in the pages of their newspaper, the extensive information they gathered composed the *Register of Debates,* our only history of the business of Congress from 1824 to 1834. In 1834 editors of the Jacksonian-leaning *Globe* began a competing record of that business, the *Congressional Globe.* The party in power favored the *Congressional Globe* and made it difficult for Gales and Seaton to compile the *Register,* which became defunct in 1837. See Mott, *American Journalism,* 177. The *National Intelligencer* remained a strong competitor of the *Globe,* though, for decades, justifying Lumpkin's appeal to its editors.

9. Native Americans were enslaved in this period, but in small enough numbers that they did not register in the national imagination as enslaved.

10. Michael A. Gomez, *Exchanging Our Country Marks: The Transformation of African Identities in the Colonial and Antebellum South* (Chapel Hill: University of North Carolina Press, 1998).

11. In states including Georgia, Native Americans' individual rights to speak against European Americans was severely restricted, but as a community they could appeal to and treat with federal and state governments.

12. Winthrop D. Jordan, *White Over Black: American Attitudes Toward the Negro, 1550–1812* (Chapel Hill: University of North Carolina Press, 1968).

13. 1 July 1829.
14. 21 July 1829; 28 Aug. 1829.
15. For consistencies over time, see for example the ad five years later for "my negro slave Davy" (7 Mar. 1834) and the ad another four years later for "a negro boy named HARRY" (19 June 1838).
16. 4 Sept. 1829.
17. 31 Mar. 1836. For consistencies over time, see for example 12 Mar. 1831.
18. 1 Jan. 1836.
19. 22 Apr. 1836.
20. 23 Sept. 1830.
21. 26 Nov. 1829.
22. 1 Aug. 1828.
23. 23 Nov. 1833. See also 12 Nov. 1831.
24. 23 Dec. 1831, 5 Nov. 1831.
25. 15 Nov. 1828.
26. 27 June 1829, reprinted from the *Episcopal Watchman*.
27. 18 June 1830.
28. 13 Aug. 1834, reprinted from the Kentucky *Commonwealth*.
29. 3 Feb. 1835.
30. 5 Aug. 1835.
31. For a discussion, see Priscilla Wald, *Constituting Americans: Cultural Anxiety and Narrative Form* (Durham, N.C.: Duke University Press, 1995).
32. 5 Aug. 1829; 8 Aug. 1829.
33. 9 Sept. 1829.
34. 27 Aug. 1829; 31 Aug. 1829; 4 Sept. 1829; 10 Sept. 1829; 15 Sept. 1829.
35. 24 Jan. 1831.
36. 2 Feb. 1832; 1 Mar. 1832.
37. On wars, see for example 3 Aug. 1832; 8 Feb. 1836. On culture exchanges, see for example 26 June 1837. On appropriations, see for example 21 May 1836; 2 Mar. 1837.
38. 28 June 1834.
39. 18 Mar. 1831.
40. 29 Apr. 1837.
41. 16 Oct. 1832.
42. 16 Oct. 1832.
43. 7 Aug. 1833.
44. 4 May 1831.
45. 10 May 1833. See also for example 11 Mar. 1836.
46. 21 June 1833.
47. Henry Clay to Gentlemen of the Colonization Society of Kentucky, 17 Dec. 1829, *Papers of Henry Clay*, vol. 8, *Candidate, Compromiser, Whig*, ed. Robert

Seager II and Melba Porter Hay (Lexington: University Press of Kentucky, 1984), 138. Reprinted in the *National Intelligencer,* 12 Jan. 1830.

48. 28 June 1834.

49. 3 July 1836.

50. 3 Feb. 1835.

51. *Register of Debates in Congress,* 24th Cong., 2nd sess., 6 Feb. 1837, 1586–1587.

52. 9 Feb. 1837.

53. 17 Feb. 1837.

54. 22 Jan. 1835.

55. 27 Feb. 1837.

56. Leon F. Litwack, *North of Slavery: The Negro in the Free States, 1790–1860* (Chicago: University of Chicago Press, 1961); Hugh Davis, "Northern Colonizationists and Free Blacks, 1823–1837: A Case Study of Leonard Bacon," *Journal of the Early Republic* 17 (1997): 651–675.

57. 22 Feb. 1837.

58. 18 Aug. 1828.

59. 2 July 1829.

60. 2 June 1830; 28 Sept. 1830.

61. 14 July 1830.

62. 26 Mar. 1830.

63. 14 July 1830.

64. 17 Aug. 1830.

65. 20 June 1831.

66. 8 June 1833.

67. 18 Sept. 1834.

68. 1 Sept. 1836.

69. 22 Nov. 1836.

70. 29 June 1830; 21 July 1834. See also 16 Apr. 1833; 6 Oct. 1835.

71. 4 May 1831.

72. Lydia Maria Child, *An Appeal in Favor of That Class of Americans Called Africans* (1833; repr., Amherst: University of Massachusetts Press, 1996), 161–162; Catharine Maria Sedgwick, *Hope Leslie; Or, Early Times in the Massachusetts,* ed. Mary Kelley (1827; repr., New Brunswick, N.J.: Rutgers University Press, 1987), 6.

73. Child, *Appeal*; William Lloyd Garrison, *Thoughts on African Colonization: Or An Impartial Exhibition of the Doctrines, Principles and Purposes of the American Colonization Society. Together with the Resolutions, Addresses and Remonstrances of the Free People of Color,* ed. William Loren Katz (1832; repr., New York: Arno Press, 1968); Theodore Dwight Weld, *American Slavery As It Is: Testimony of a Thousand Witnesses* (New York: American Anti-Slavery Society, 1839), http:// docsouth.unc.edu (accessed 20 Apr. 2005). Subsequent references are noted parenthetically.

5. "On the Very Eve of Coming Out"

1. Angelina Grimké, *Walking by Faith: The Diary of Angelina Grimké, 1828–1835,* ed. Charles Wilbanks (Columbia: University of South Carolina Press, 2003), 158.
2. Ibid., 154, 163.
3. Sarah Forten to Angelina Grimké, 15 Apr. 1837, *Letters of Theodore Dwight Weld, Angelina Grimké Weld, and Sarah Grimké, 1822–1844,* ed. Gilbert H. Barnes and Dwight L. Dumond (New York: D. Appleton-Century, 1934), 1:37; *An Appeal to the Women of the Nominally Free States, Issued by an Anti-Slavery Convention of American Women,* 2nd ed. (1838; repr., Freeport, N.Y.: Books for Libraries Press, 1971), 1. The second edition replicates the first edition, so the pagination is the same. I use the second edition since the 1971 reprint readily is available as a book. Subsequent references are noted parenthetically. Angelina Gimké, *Letters to Cath[a]rine E. Beecher, in Reply to An Essay on Salvery and Abolitionism, Addressed to A. E. Grimké,* rev. ed. (1838; repr., Freeport, N.Y.: Books for Libraries Press, 1971), 38.
4. Sarah and Angelina Grimké to Theodore Weld, 18 May 1837, *Letters of Weld,* 1:387.
5. Sarah Forten to Angelina Grimké, 15 Apr. 1837, *Letters of Weld,* 1:379–380.
6. Lyman Beecher, *The Autobiography of Lyman Beecher,* ed. Barbara M. Cross (Cambridge, Mass.: Harvard University Press, 1961), 2:242, 244; Lyman Beecher, "Dr. Beecher's Address," *African Repository and Colonial Journal* 10 (1834): 282.
7. Lyman Beecher, "Address," 281.
8. James Forten quoted in William Loren Katz, "Introduction," *Thoughts on African Colonization: Or An Impartial Exhibition of the Doctrines, Principles and Purposes of the American Colonization Society. Together with the Resolutions, Addresses and Remonstrances of the Free People of Color,* by William Lloyd Garrison (1832; repr., New York: Arno Press, 1968), ix; Garrison, *Thoughts on African Colonization,* 2:10, 11; Sarah Forten to Angelina Grimké, 15 Apr. 1837, *Letters of Weld,* 1:380.
9. *Liberator* announcement in *National Intelligencer* (Washington, D.C.), 20 Aug. 1830; Henry Clay to Jeremiah Evarts, 23 Aug. 1830, *The Papers of Henry Clay,* vol. 8, *Candidate, Compromiser, Whig,* ed. Robert Seager II and Melba Porter Hay (Lexington: University Press of Kentucky, 1984), 255; Garrison against women's antiremoval petitions, *Genius of Universal Emancipation* (Baltimore, Md.), 12 Feb. 1830. On Garrison's regret for denouncing women's antiremoval petitions, see Wendell Phillips Garrison and Francis Jackson Garrison, *William Lloyd Garrison, 1805–1879: The Story of His Life Told by His Children* (1885; repr., New York: Negro Universities Press, 1969), 1:157.

10. On the Sabbatarian movement and Evarts's transformation of petitions, see Richard R. John, *Spreading the News: The American Postal System from Franklin to Morse* (Cambridge, Mass.: Harvard University Press, 1995).

11. Ibid., 181.

12. Bertram Wyatt-Brown, "Prelude to Abolitionism: Sabbatarian Politics and the Rise of the Second Party System," *Journal of American History* 58 (1971): 330, 331, 337.

13. *Genius,* 2 Sept. 1829, quoted in Garrison and Garrison, *William Lloyd Garrison,* 1:142, 144.

14. Ibid., 144. On the "Black List" and the story of Garrison's arrest, see Garrison and Garrison, *William Lloyd Garrison,* 1:163, 165, 171.

15. *Genius,* July 1830, 55.

16. Lyman Beecher to Catharine Beecher, 21 Nov. 1829, Schlesinger Library, Radcliffe Institute, Harvard University, A-102, Beecher-Stowe Collection of Family Papers, 1798–1956, folder 4.

17. Theodore Weld to James Birney, 28 May 1834, *Letters of James Gillespie Birney, 1831–1857,* ed. Dwight L. Dumond (New York: D. Appleton-Century, 1938), 1:113; James Birney to Lewis Tappan, 28 Nov. 1835, Dumond, *Letters of Birney,* 1:275–276.

18. Theodore Weld to James Birney, 20 Oct. 1834, *Letters of Birney,* 1:146–147; James Birney to Gerrit Smith, 14 Nov. 1834, *Letters of Birney,* 1:147–151.

19. James Birney to Gerrit Smith, 14 Nov. 1834, *Letters of Birney,* 1:150–151.

20. James Birney to Gerrit Smith, 11 Nov. 1835, *Letters of Birney,* 1:258.

21. Smith's complete denouncement of colonization received national and even international attention. See for example *National Intelligencer,* 29 Apr. 1837.

22. *Letters of Birney,* 16 Sept. 1834, 1:135; *National Intelligencer,* 20 Dec. 1837; Theodore Weld to Sarah and Angelina Grimké, 15 Aug. 1837, *Letters of Weld,* 1:426.

23. James G. Birney, *Letter on Colonization, Addressed to the Rev. Thornton J. Mills, Corresponding Secretary of the Kentucky Colonization Society* (1834; repr., New York: American Anti-Slavery Society, 1838), 8, 9.

24. See for example *National Intelligencer,* 8 June 1830.

25. Carolyn L. Karcher, "Introduction," *An Appeal in Favor of That Class of Americans Called Africans,* by Lydia Maria Child, ed. Carolyn L. Karcher (1833; repr., Amherst: University of Massachusetts Press, 1996), xx–xxvi.

26. Theodore Weld to James Birney, 19 June 1834, *Letters of Birney,* 1:121.

27. Ibid., 27 Sept. 1832, 1:27.

28. See for example *National Intelligencer,* 17 Nov. 1832; 10 Jan. 1832; 18 Jan. 1832; 28 June 1832; 17 Nov. 1832. These examples are from the same year as Weld's declaration of allegiance, but there are many others throughout the decade.

29. See for example a reprint of a Maryland law that charged the state with removing all manumitted slaves from the state, preferably to Liberia. If slaves refused to go, they were forced back into slavery. If there were no means by which to

transport the slaves, the state had the authority to hire out their services to pay their relocation costs. *National Intelligencer,* 29 Mar. 1832.

30. James Birney to Ralph R. Gurley, 27 Dec. 1832, *Letters of Birney,* 1:50.

31. James Birney to Ralph R. Gurley, 13 Apr. 1833, *Letters of Birney,* 1:71.

32. Ralph R. Gurley to James Birney, 21 Aug. 1833, *Letters of Birney,* 1:84–85; Ralph R. Gurley to James Birney, 17 Dec. 1833, 1:110–111.

33. John P. Cushman to Theodore Weld, 8 Feb. 1830, *Letters of Weld,* 1:34; T. Parmele to Theodore Weld, 12 May 1831, *Letters of Weld* 1:46–47; Lewis Tappan to Theodore Weld, 25 Oct. 1831, *Letters of Weld,* 1:50; F. Y. Vail to Theodore Weld, Nov. 1831, *Letters of Weld,* 1:59; H. B. Stanton, E. Weed, S. W. Streeter, and C. Waterbury to Theodore Weld, 2 Aug. 1832, *Letters of Weld,* 1:82.

34. Theodore Weld to James Birney, 27 Sept. 1832, *Letters of Birney,* 1:27.

35. Lyman Beecher, *Autobiography,* 2:241.

36. The Reverend Asa Mahan explained, "No important city in any free State had so direct and immediate connection with, and dependence for its prosperity upon, the Southern States as Cincinnati. No such city, consequently, was so deeply imbued with the Southern sentiment." Asa Mahan, *Autobiography: Intellectual, Moral, and Spiritual* (London: T. Woolmer, 1882), 172.

37. Theodore Weld to William Lloyd Garrison, 2 Jan. 1833, *Letters of Weld,* 1:98. It took another month for word to get out widely that Weld no longer was a colonizationist. Elizur Wright Jr. and Beriah Green to Theodore Weld, 1 Feb. 1833, *Letters of Weld,* 1:101.

38. James Birney to Ralph R. Gurley, 24 Jan. 1833, *Letters of Birney,* 1:51–52.

39. Theodore Weld to Lewis Tappan, 18 Mar. 1834, *Letters of Weld,* 1:132; James Birney to Ralph R. Gurley, 3 Dec. 1833, *Letters of Birney,* 1:97; James Birney to Ralph R. Gurley 11 Dec. 1833, *Letters of Birney,* 1:98–99; Kentucky Constitution, *Letters of Birney,* 1:99–100; address on the constitution, *Letters of Birney,* 1:100–109; Theodore Weld to Arthur Tappan, Joshua Leavitt, and Elizur Wright Jr., 22 Nov. 1833, *Letters of Weld,* 1:120.

40. Theodore Weld to Lewis Tappan, 18 Mar. 1834, *Letters of Weld,* 1:132–135. On the Lane debates, see Lawrence Thomas Lesick, *The Lane Rebels: Evangelicalism and Antislavery in Antebellum America* (Metuchen, N.J.: Scarecrow Press, 1980); Barnes and Dumond, *Letters of Weld;* Dumond, *Letters of Birney;* Lyman Beecher, *Autobiography;* Vincent Harding, *A Certain Magnificence: Lyman Beecher and the Transformation of American Protestantism, 1775–1863* (Brooklyn, N.Y.: Carlson Publishing, 1991); Mahan, *Autobiography,* 172–196.

41. Lesick, *Lane Rebels,* 79.

42. On the riots, see Leonard L. Richards, *"Gentlemen of Property and Standing":
Anti-Abolition Mobs in Jacksonian America* (New York: Oxford University Press, 1970), 34–35; Lesick, *Lane Rebels,* 75.

43. Lyman Beecher, *Autobiography,* 2:244.

44. Ibid., 2:244.

45. Ibid., 2:242–243.

46. Elizur Wright to Theodore Weld, 5 Sept. 1833, *Letters of Weld,* 1:114.

47. Theodore Weld to James Birney, 28 May 1834, *Letters of Birney,* 1:114.

48. Lyman Beecher quoted in Mahan, *Autobiography,* 175–176.

49. Lyman Beecher, "Address," 281, 282, 283.

50. James Birney to Lewis Tappan, 29 Apr. 1836, *Letters of Birney,* 1:321; James Birney to Lewis Tappan, 29 July 1837, *Letters of Birney,* 1:399; Elizur Wright to James Birney, 14 Aug. 1837, *Letters of Birney,* 1:414.

51. Theodore Weld to James Birney, 28 May 1834, *Letters of Birney,* 1:112.

52. Theodore Weld to James Birney, 17 June 1834, *Letters of Birney,* 1:115–118; Theodore Weld to James Birney, 19 June 1834, *Letters of Birney,* 1:119–122; Theodore Weld to James Birney, 8 July 1834, *Letters of Birney,* 1:122–125; Huntingdon Lyman to James Birney, 11 July 1834, 1:125–126.

53. Elizur Wright to Theodore Weld, 14 Aug. 1834, *Letters of Weld,* 1:166.

54. Review of *Letter on Colonization* by James Birney, *African Repository and Colonial Journal* 10 (1834): 257, 279.

55. Richards, *Gentlemen;* Lesick, *Lane Rebels.*

56. The authoritative biography on Catharine Beecher, from which this account is drawn, remains Kathryn Kish Sklar's *Catharine Beecher: A Study in American Domesticity* (New York: W. W. Norton and Company, 1976).

57. Catharine E. Beecher, *An Essay on the Education of Female Teachers. Written at the Request of the American Lyceum, and Communicated at their Annual Meeting* (New York: Van Nostrand and Dwight, 1835). Subsequent references are noted parenthetically.

58. Sklar, *Catharine Beecher,* 130.

59. Catharine Beecher, *Letters on the Difficulties of Religion* (Hartford, Conn.: Belknap and Hamersley, 1836). Subsequent references are noted parenthetically.

60. Angelina Grimké, *Appeal to Christian Women of the South* (New York: American Anti-Slavery Society, 1836). Subsequent references are noted parenthetically. Gerda Lerner, *The Grimké Sisters from South Carolina: Pioneers for Woman's Rights and Abolition* (1967; repr., New York: Schocken Books, 1971), 86. For a basic biography of Angelina Grimké, see Lerner, *Grimké Sisters,* especially 24–38, 66–86. Much of the history here comes from this groundbreaking book.

61. Lerner, *Grimké Sisters,* 109.

62. Ibid., 144.

63. Angelina Grimké, *Walking,* Sept. 1835 (undated entry), 211–212.

64. *Liberator* (Boston), 19 Sept. 1835.

65. Lerner, *Grimké Sisters,* 127, 130–131.

66. Ibid., 136–138.

67. *Liberator,* 22 Aug. 1835.

68. *Liberator,* 19 Sept. 1835.

69. Lerner, *Grimké Sisters,* 147, 153; Sklar, *Catharine Beecher,* 132; "Pastoral Letter," reprinted in *American Rhetorical Discourse,* ed. Ronald F. Reid, 2nd ed. (Prospect Heights, Ill.: Waveland Press, 1995), 367.

6. "Coming from One Who Has a Right to Speak"

1. Catharine E. Beecher, *Educational Reminiscences and Suggestions* (New York: J. B. Ford, 1874), 62.

2. Catharine E. Beecher, "Circular Addressed to Benevolent Ladies of the U. States," *Christian Advocate and Journal and Zion's Herald* (New York), 25 Dec. 1829, 65–66. The newspaper hereafter is referred to as *CAJZH.*

3. Angelina Grimké, *Appeal to the Christian Women of the South* (New York: American Anti-Slavery Society, 1836), 25. Subsequent references are made parenthetically.

4. Catharine E. Beecher, *An Essay on Slavery and Abolitionism, with Reference to the Duty of American Females* (Philadelphia: Perkins and Marvin, 1837), 103–104. Subsequent references are made parenthetically.

5. Angelina Grimké, *Letters to Cath[a]rine E. Beecher, in Reply to An Essay on Slavery and Abolitionism, Addressed to A. E. Grimké,* rev. ed. (1838; repr., Freeport, N.Y.: Books for Libraries Press, 1971), 127. Subsequent references are made parenthetically.

6. Mary Hershberger, "Mobilizing Women, Anticipating Abolition: The Struggle Against Indian Removal in the 1830s," *Journal of American History* 86 (1999): 34; Kathryn Kish Sklar, *Catharine Beecher: A Study in American Domesticity* (New York: W. W. Norton and Company, 1976), 132.

7. Gerda Lerner, *The Grimké Sisters from South Carolina: Pioneers for Woman's Rights and Abolition* (1967; repr., New York: Schocken Books, 1971), 183, 184, 186; Lorman Ratner, *Powder Keg: Northern Opposition to the Antislavery Movement, 1831–1840* (New York: Basic Books, 1968), 99, 100.

8. Aileen S. Kraditor, ed., *Up From the Pedestal: Selected Writings in the History of American Feminism* (Chicago: Quadrangle Book, 1968), 58; Sklar, *Catharine Beecher,* 132; Hershberger, "Mobilizing," 34; Mark Perry, *Lift Up Thy Voice: The Grimké Family's Journey from Slaveholders to Civil Rights Leaders* (New York: Viking, 2001), 152, 156.

9. Browne acknowledges that "Garrison and his acolytes had savaged the ACS," but that is the extent of Browne's commentary on that organization. Stephen Howard Browne, *Angelina Grimké: Rhetoric, Identity, and the Radical Imagination* (East Lansing: Michigan State University Press, 1999), 92.

10. Ibid., 84, 90, 93, 94, 104.

11. Beecher had published other texts designed as conversations with men. In her *Essay on the Education of Female Teachers. Written at the Request of the American Lyceum, and Communicated at their Annual Meeting* (New York: Van Nostrand

and Dwight, 1835), she argued for increased support for female education and clearly targeted men (who financially could support those endeavors) as well as women. Beecher used the conceit of writing to male interlocutors in her 1836 manifesto, *Letters on the Difficulties of Religion* (Hartford, Conn.: Belknap and Hamersley).

12. Theodore Weld to Sarah and Angelina Grimké, 22 May 1837, *Letters of Theodore Dwight Weld, Angelina Grimké Weld, and Sarah Grimké, 1822–1844,* ed. Gilbert H. Barnes and Dwight L. Dumond (New York: D. Appleton-Century, 1934), 1:391; Theodore Weld to Sarah and Angelina Grimké, 22 July 1837, *Letters of Weld,* 1:413–414; Theodore Weld to Sarah and Angelina Grimké, 28 Dec. 1837, *Letters of Weld,* 1:505; James Birney to Lewis Tappan, 29 July 1837, *Letters of James Gillespie Birney, 1831–1857,* ed. Dwight L. Dumond (New York: D. Appleton-Century, 1938), 1:400; James Birney to Lewis Tappan, 8 Aug. 1837, *Letters of Birney,* 1:412. *Philanthropist* (Cincinnati), 4 Aug. 1837. Grimké's letters first were published in the *Emancipator,* then Garrison's *Liberator* (Boston) and Birney's *Philanthropist.* Garrison was the only editor to relegate her letters to the "Ladies' Department," which appears to have been a way for Garrison to emphasize the immorality of antiabolitionists: they would not even let women "[plead] for the dumb" (23 June 1837). This placement probably influenced contemporary evaluations of the Beecher-Grimké debate as marginal; since the *Liberator* currently is available more easily than the other two abolitionist papers, many historians refer to the *Liberator* when researching Grimké's *Letters.*

13. Sarah and Angelina Grimké to Theodore Weld, 20 Sept. 1837, *Letters of Weld,* 1:451.

14. *An Appeal to the Women of the Nominally Free States, Issued by an Anti-Slavery Convention of American Women,* 2nd ed. (1838; repr., Freeport, N.Y.: Books for Libraries Press, 1971), 3.

15. *National Intelligencer* (Washington, D.C.), 4 May 1833; 20 June 1833; 21 June 1833.

16. *CAJZH,* 10 May 1833; 23 May 1834; 2 Aug. 1833; 23 May 1834; 15 Aug. 1834; 5 June 1835.

17. *National Intelligencer,* 10 May, 1833; 2 Oct. 1833; 3 Oct. 1833; 28 Oct. 1834; 5 Aug. 1834; 7 Aug. 1835; 3 Oct. 1835. Supreme Court Chief Justice John Marshall spoke of the "malignant effects of the insane fanaticism of those who defeat all practicable good, by the pursuit of an unattainable object" in *CAJZH,* 19 June 1835.

18. *National Intelligencer,* 26 May 1835; 7 June 1836; *CAJZH,* 10 May 1833.

19. *CAJZH,* 9 Oct. 1835; 11 Nov. 1836; 7 Aug. 1835; *National Intelligencer,* 26 May 1835, reprinted from the *Commercial Advertiser* (New York).

20. *National Intelligencer,* 12 Aug. 1833; 14 July 1834; 10 Sept. 1835; 21 July 1834.

21. *National Intelligencer,* 28 Sept. 1835; on treason, 6 Nov. 1833 and 3 Oct. 1835; 9 Aug. 1836, reprinted from the *Whig* (Cincinnati); 21 July 1834; 14 July 1834.

22. *National Intelligencer,* 17 Dec. 1835; *CAJZH,* 2 Aug. 1833; *National Intelligencer,* 19 Sept. 1835; 6 Nov. 1833.

23. *National Intelligencer,* 8 Aug. 1835, reprinted from the *Atlas* (Boston), 6 Nov. 1833.

24. *CAJZH,* 2 Aug. 1833; *National Intelligencer,* 4 May 1833; *CAJZH,* 14 July 1837; *National Intelligencer,* 26 May 1835, reprinted from the *Commercial Advertiser;* 23 Sept. 1835, reprinted from the *Commercial Advertiser.*

25. Beecher, "Circular," 65; Hershberger, "Mobilizing," 34. For debates about Indian removal petitions that make no mention of petitioners' sex, see for example *Register of Debates in Congress,* 21st Cong., 1st sess., 11 Jan. 1830, 506–511; 24 Feb. 1830, 580–583; 1 Mar. 1830, 590–594; 17 May 1830, 1019–1037, especially 1019, 1020, 1022, and 1031; 24 May 1830, 1122–1123. For reports that neutrally mention petitioners' sex, see for example *Register of Debates in Congress,* 21st Cong., 1st sess., 6 Mar. 1830, 596–597, 19 May 1830, 1080. For the sole disparaging senator, see Senator Thomas H. Benton, *Register of Debates in Congress,* 21st Cong., 1st sess., 2 Feb. 1830, 109. The other critical congressmen to whom Hershberger refers are Jackson sympathizers who attack all antiremovalists, regardless of their sex.

26. For scholars who argue that Beecher was constrained by gender, see for example Jacqueline Bacon, *The Humblest May Stand Forth: Rhetoric, Empowerment, and Abolition* (Columbia: University of South Carolina Press, 2002); Hershberger, "Mobilizing."

27. Pastoral letter, reprinted in *American Rhetorical Discourse,* ed. Ronald F. Reid, 2nd ed. (Prospect Heights, Ill.: Waveland Press, 1995), 366.

28. Grimké went so far as to declare women suitable for the role of United States president: "*If* Ecclesiastical and Civil governments are ordained of God, *then* I contend that woman has just as much right to sit in solemn counsel in Conventions, Conferences, Associations and General Assemblies, as man—just as much right to [s]it upon the throne of England, or in the Presidential chair of the United States" (*Letters,* 119).

29. Francis Paul Prucha, introduction to *Cherokee Removal: The "William Penn" Essays and Other Writings,* by Jeremiah Evarts (Knoxville: University of Tennessee Press, 1981), 34.

Index